REFLECTIONS ON

GROUPS AND

ORGANIZATIONS

ON THE COUCH WITH MANFRED KETS DE VRIES

On the Couch with Manfred Kets de Vries offers an overview of the author's work spanning four decades, a period in which Manfred F. R. Kets de Vries has established himself as the leading figure in the clinical study of organizational leadership.

The three books in this series contain a representative selection of Kets de Vries' writings about leadership from a wide variety of published sources. They cover three major themes: character and leadership in a global context; career development; and leadership in organizations. The original essays were all written or published between 1976 and 2008. Updated where appropriate and revised by the author, they present a digest of the work of one of today's most influential management thinkers.

Published Titles
Reflections on Character and Leadership
Reflections on Leadership and Career Development
Reflections on Groups and Organizations

REFLECTIONS ON GROUPS AND ORGANIZATIONS

Manfred F. R. Kets de Vries

JOSSEY-BASS
A Wiley Imprint
www.josseybass.com

To Henriette, my mother, whom I miss and mirror every day.

CONTENTS

INTRODUCTION

In individuals, insanity is rare; but in groups, parties, nations, and epochs, it is the rule.

—Friedrich Nietzsche

Leaders must encourage their organizations to dance to forms of music yet to be heard.

—Warren G. Bennis

A CLINICAL APPROACH TO LEADERSHIP

This is the final book in a three-part series that has anthologized a selection of my writing on leadership, associated with some key themes: character, career development, groups, and organizations. In the collection here, I apply the clinical approach to issues of leadership within groups and organizations, moving steadily from studies of the dysfunctional to descriptions of the ideal. I begin with the notion of *folie à deux*, looking at ways in which people can transmit and broadcast various forms of organizational madness; and I end with a vision of the authentizotic organization, the kind of organization where people are invigorated by their work, feel a sense of balance and completeness, a sense of effectiveness and competency, a sense of autonomy, initiative, belonging, and creativity.

I am often asked to define the clinical approach and justify its application. In essence, it condenses two principal approaches. The first is psychodynamic and has to do with the way people think, feel, and act. For example, the more recent financial meltdown in the West is a good indication that the people in charge of some of the largest and seemingly most successful organizations are far from being the rational decision-makers we might expect them to be—there are lots of other things at work in their decision-making processes that should be taken into consideration. There is often a great discrepancy between what people say they do, and what they really do.

The other approach is systemic, meaning that we have to see things in context. We have to view people in the context of their family, their culture, and their work environment. I believe organizations also need to be looked at in this way. A systemic view gives us a more realistic perspective on difficult situations. The clinical approach refers to the psychodynamic-systemic way of looking at people in organizations.

This approach deals with the fact that most of our behavior is not really rational. What's more, much of it is outside conscious awareness, something many find hard to accept. To have an inkling of what is going on outside of conscious awareness, we need to pay attention to emotions. This probably explains why there is resistance to the clinical approach within many organizations, where what lies beneath, including emotions, is given short shrift in the normal course of events.

Yet nothing is more central to who we are than the way we express and regulate our emotions. In addition, we have many defensive mechanisms—some quite primitive, others very sophisticated. And these resistances should be seen in the context of avoiding the pain of realizing what really may be going on in organizational life. We all have a shadow side and a tendency to avoid troubling aspects of our experiences. There are many distressing thoughts and feelings we are reluctant to deal with.

Furthermore, we are all a product of our past—many things that we learned in childhood will determine the way we behave in adulthood. The past is the lens through which we can understand the present and shape the future. Scratch an adult, and we find a child. So if we want to understand people, we have to get a better sense of the context from which they come. And I have discovered that everyone is normal—until you get to know them better.

The first organization we know is our family of origin. The nature of its relationships will have an enormous influence on us. I come from a divorced family, which led to very complex dynamics between my mother and father. The complexity was increased by my brother, and a half-sister and -brother from my father's second marriage. This *dramatis personae* provided me with much raw material to better understand the human condition. For children (I am not excluding parents), divorce is extremely hard to deal with—and I am no exception. My parents' divorce very much colored my life. The situation to which my brother and I were exposed required a solid dose of emotional intelligence and many of the lessons we learned during that time have a sour-sweet taste. Although I may not have realized it at the time, whatever my parents did, in their (at times) convoluted ways, they were trying to do the best they could. Unconsciously or consciously, they also helped me to be effective in the path I took. Thanks to the two of them, human nature and its vicissitudes were going to be the subject of my life's work.

As I recount in the introduction to Part 2 of this book, I began to study human behavior particularly when I looked at toxic organizations with dysfunctional organizational environments. I became interested in how leaders can create 'neurotic' organizational cultures. In one of my earliest books, *The Neurotic Organization*, I tried to establish an interrelationship between personality, leadership style, corporate culture, and patterns of decision-making (Kets de Vries and Miller, 1984).

The world has been dominated by economists. I used to be an economist myself but always felt that the rational economic model didn't work. It has recently been demonstrated in a fairly dramatic way that this model is not realistic. The dismal science has become even more dismal. Economists, from being econometrically oriented, are suddenly all becoming behavioral economists. They have begun to realize that there are many other factors that they need to insert into their economic models. This kind of turnaround is probably not enough, but at least is a step in the right direction.

I have described in an earlier book in this series the events that took me from economics, to management education, to psychoanalysis and, ultimately, to a field of expertise in which I could practice all three: management, with a particular focus on strategy and organizational behavior; economics, particularly business economics; and psychoanalysis in its widest sense, encompassing family-systems theory, cognition, neuropsychiatry, evolutionary psychology, and so on (Kets de Vries, 2009b). But whatever hat I have found myself wearing, I am essentially a pragmatist and eclectic in my outlook and interventions. My major motivation is to make things happen—and make things work for the better. More than anything, I want to help people create great places to work, because too many organizations are like gulags—unpleasant places to be. I like to try to make a contribution—minuscule as it may be—to changing this situation.

BRINGING THE PERSON BACK INTO THE ORGANIZATION

When I started to study organizational behavior, the focus was on structures and systems and how to make them work. But I have always been more interested in the role of people in the organization. I have always wondered why people do what they do—how to make sense out of their behavior. For example, I have devised and for many years run two major, year-long, executive development programs. One is a program for top executives—CEOs and those aspiring to be CEOs. I created this program with the fantasy that if I could influence the minds of those 20 people in my seminar, who together were responsible for a few hundred thousand people, it might affect their organizations in a positive way. In the second program, 'Consulting and Coaching for Change,' of which I am one of the designers, I try to help HR directors, people in consulting and coaching firms, and line managers to become better at people management.[1]

I am interested in programs that help people change for the better. Most leadership programs are only Band-Aids; they don't do much more than soothe the superficial symptoms. After people go through this kind of program they may get a temporary high: they feel good, particularly if they have had good teachers, and then, unfortunately, they revert to their previous behavior. I like to go beyond the quick-fix and create programs that have a true impact, that help people change, that push people to take important steps in their personal and organizational lives. As a result, at INSEAD, I and my associates have developed the second-largest coaching center in the world, the Global Leadership Center. We also have become the largest center in group coaching, because group leadership coaching is a very effective way to help people change. I have learned to take advantage of the powers of self-revelation and catharsis, of realizing the universality of problems, of guidance, of interpersonal and vicarious learning, of the corrective recapitulation of the primary family group, and of altruism.

THE INNER THEATER

In this book, I refer frequently to the 'inner theater,' which relates to questions like: What are the things that motivate you? What are the things that are important to you? What do you feel deeply passionate about? How well do you understand how you affect other people? And what drives you crazy? All these things have to do with our inner theater, in which we play out the scripts that define our character and our life. When it comes down to it, all my work is centered on helping people to understand themselves better. If we don't know what we are doing, it is hard to be effective, so if we want to be effective leaders, it is important that

---

[1] See Chapter 10 for an exclusive view of the first of these programs.

we have a sense of what we are all about; what we do well, and what we are not so good at. As far as the latter is concerned, there may be something we can do about it; or a better strategy might be to find people who can complement us, drawing from our strengths while compensating for our weaknesses. We have to give up the messianic ideal: the image of the leader as superhero has mercifully retreated into the realms of fiction. Real change is driven by teams of people.

Of course, when we get anxious, we all look for somebody to help us, just as we did when we were children and looked to our parents to get us out of difficult situations. But in the modern organization—with highly complex, matrix-like structures and very diverse, virtual teams— the trick is how to have the different parts working together, how to work in teams, how to build good lateral relationships, how to trust each other. In my programs, I do a lot of interventions with top executive teams, working on precisely these things, because most do not function very well.

To do this, I have developed numerous survey instruments[2] that jump-start the process of understanding the inner theater. Helped with the information from these instruments, executives can have courageous conversations with the people they work with, something that does not usually happen. The insights provided by these instruments help people see what they usually do not see—and find ways to do something about it.

THE DARKER SIDE OF LEADERSHIP

I first became well known as an organizational pathologist, meaning that people came to me when things had got really bad. It was a niche that I occupied only reluctantly. In management now we find the emergence of positive psychology and positive organizational behavior. This is fine, but we have to be realistic—total optimism can only get us so far. But being overly-optimistic can lead to disaster. Convinced that the *Titanic* was unsinkable, its captain ignored three warnings, a mindset that had catastrophic results. We all have a darker side. We have seen the terrible things people do to each other in times of war and on other occasions.

[2]The Global Executive Leadership Inventory; the Leadership Archetype Questionnaire; the Personality Audit; the Internal Theater Inventory; the Organizational Culture Audit.

Frequently, this darker side is induced by past experiences. To quote the philosopher Kierkegaard, 'Life can only be understood backward; but it must be lived forward.'

We have to deal with the past; we have to see things in perspective, otherwise we will not learn anything. What was effective when we were young may no longer be very effective when we are adults. We need to obtain that insight to be able to change.

If we look at what has happened in the financial sector since the most recent crisis, I sometimes have the sense they have learned nothing, and forgotten everything. The power of negation—of not wanting to see—is formidable. The financial community have apparently reverted to normal, retaining their feeling of entitlement. Once again, they are awarding themselves outrageous bonuses, while their organizations have been bailed out with public money. Obviously, it is far too easy to come to terms with the dark side.

Yet focusing only on the dark side is not good for morale. After many years studying the darker side of leaders and organizations, and becoming a leader in that field, I began to think about what I could do to make things better. This is not to say that I have lost sight of the dark side. We have to be realistic about these things—it's well and truly there.

LEADERS—BORN OR MADE?

Not everyone has leadership potential but, on the other hand, I don't believe in the concept of the 'born leader.' Undoubtedly, some people have a head start but I strongly believe that leadership potential can be developed.

Leadership potential is a delicate interplay between nature and nurture. People who grow up in a family where their parents encourage them, push them to do something with their life, and perhaps give them some solid values about doing something for the greater good, are more likely to become leaders than people coming from very dysfunctional families. But nothing is really that black and white: some people, in spite of having had a very difficult upbringing, have become highly effective leaders, demonstrating the complexity of these interrelationships.

I have seen examples of both. For example, in the early 1990s I wrote a number of case studies about Richard Branson, the founder and owner of the Virgin conglomerate. Branson had a textbook family background: two parents who loved their son, were very supportive, and encouraged him in his various entrepreneurial ventures. But I've also seen situations where people come from very miserable circumstances, having experienced many hardships—deaths in the family, separation, divorce and so on—but have never given up hope. They felt they could make a difference. They would say, 'I'll give it a try. I'm going to show these people, show the world that I can do certain things.' There are many different combinations and variations on the themes of leadership potential and success.

Becoming successful is dependent on the highly complex interface between leaders, followers, and the contexts they operate in. Being the managing director of McKinsey requires a very different leadership style than running a steel mill—many factors have to be taken into account. In Chapter 12, I develop my concept of an effective leader, someone who, as I see it, is a little like a Zen riddle, or kōan—a paradox who is comfortable dealing with paradoxes. Because a leader has to be active and reflective, an introvert and an extrovert, engaged in both divergent and convergent thinking. A leader needs IQ, but also EQ. A leader has to think atomistically, but also holistically, for the short term and the long term. Anyone who can balance these contradictions effectively will do well.

There have been many attempts at a definition of leadership but for me, a true leader is someone who gets extraordinary things out of ordinary people. As the saying goes, people will work for money but die for a cause. The crucial thing is how to get people to deliver that extra effort. There are several basic things that any leader has to do: provide focus, understand what makes their people tick, set an example, and make things happen. However, the distinguishing factor between mediocre and great leadership is always the same: the creation of meaning. The most effective leaders I have encountered are good storytellers; they know how to tell the stories that provide meaning in their organizations. This may not be so easy if they are running a cigarette or armaments company. But when it comes down to it, people are searching for meaning. I hear it all the time.

PRESCRIPTIONS FOR EFFECTIVE LEADERSHIP

In my book *The Leadership Mystique* (Kets de Vries, 2001), I suggested four 'Hs' for effective leadership: hope, humanity, humility, and humor. Acronyms are neat organizing devices and easy to remember. Real life is more complex and we have constantly to refine our ideas in response to it—however, if I were to summarize the essence of leadership now, I would still start with hope. In Chapters 6 and 7 of this book, I look at the importance of generating hope as leaders steer their organizations through turbulent times. Leaders have to be merchants of hope; they have to speak to the collective imagination of their people to create a group identity, focus, and a vision of the future.

Leaders also need integrity. An organization that has no trust in its leadership will not do well in the long run. If leaders say 'We need to downsize,' while giving themselves a raise and having a new Jaguar delivered to their personal parking space, they will lose credibility. If they talk about the importance of developing people but fail to develop their own people, they will not be believable. They have to walk the talk.

The third thing leaders need is courage—the courage to make tough decisions, in crisis situations, and not sit on their hands—and the fourth is emotional intelligence. They have to figure out the important things that motivate people and be very good at emotional sense-making. Some people are entrepreneurial; they will need to be left to do their own thing. Other people are dependent, and will need things to be spelled out for them. Others are counter-dependent: if they are told they can't do something, they'll go all out to prove they can. Leaders have to be sensitized to the different needs of the individuals they lead.

Finally, self-awareness is critical for leaders. They need to know their limitations and shortcomings, as well as their strengths. If they don't have all the qualities needed for the environment they are operating in, they must find people who can complement them. I have seen leaders who are terrible at certain things, but know it, and find others to help them.

THE FUTURE OF LEADERSHIP

Management, as a discipline, has very much been a product of the US. But many of the American paradigms are being questioned and overruled by developments in the East, especially in China and India. Management theory, though, is still dominated by American business schools. Take a look at the faculty list of any international business school: most have done their doctorate in America even though their first degree might have been from China, India, Russia, Indonesia, Holland or elsewhere—although I recently read a list of 'the world's top 50 management thinkers' and discovered that there are some non-Americans on it (including me). So facetiously, I can say that perhaps there is some hope for non-American management thinking.

It is interesting to speculate about the influence Southeast Asian management, or Islamic management, will have in the future. There are distinct Chinese and Japanese leadership styles, and we cannot even talk about a 'European' style, because Europe is a very complex entity. For example, in Europe, we have the Anglo-Saxon way, the Scandinavian way, the Germanic way, and the Southern European, and Russian ways, all of which are characterized by major differences.

Some convergence may be taking place in Europe—and even the world—but it is not easy. I doubt if my generation will see it. Perhaps the next generation will. With increasing travel, and exchanges of people, there is going to be an increasing amount of convergence. I believe that time will show that alone we can do very little, while together, we can do a lot. As Benjamin Franklin, one of the founding fathers of the US, once said, 'We must, indeed, all hang together or, most assuredly, we shall all hang separately.'

ABOUT THIS BOOK

In the final book in this series, I look at leadership issues in the context of groups and organizations, starting with examples of the effects of dysfunctional leadership and ending on an optimistic note with a description of the organizations of the future, the kinds of 'best places to work' to which we would all like to belong.

Part 1 Interpersonal and Group Processes begins with an explanation of *folie à deux*, and examines various ways in which neurotic individuals create neurotic organizations. From a clinical perspective, I offer an overview of how group dynamics work and describe how high-performance teams function, using the time I spent with the Baka pygmies of Cameroon as a case example.

Part 2 The People Dimension in Organizations is all about bringing the person back into the organization and takes organizational culture as its theme. In these chapters, I discuss the importance of corporate culture, culture creation, and attempt a definition of this largely intangible yet critical element of organizational life. I examine how a strong culture can help an organization withstand the pain of downsizing, restructuring, merger, and acquisition; create the right environment for change; and sustain a vision for the future. This section ends with a look at the very particular people dimension of family firms.

Part 3 Changing People and Organizations is about the ways in which organizations and the people within them can best prepare for change. I advocate the building of an organization-wide coaching culture and describe how this can be introduced and implemented through individual, group, and organizational coaching. In this Part, I also look at how organizational leaders can identify and develop star performers.

In the **Conclusion**, I discuss the need to build 'best places' to work and introduce my concept of the authentizotic organization, one where the organizational culture is congruent with our basic motivational needs, and in which people can be, and perform, their best.

Manfred Kets de Vries
Paris 2010

ACKNOWLEDGEMENTS

This is the final book in the series *On the Couch with Manfred Kets de Vries*, which brings together a representative selection of my writing on leadership and organizational behavior. Many of the earlier chapters in this book have appeared as articles in various journals, now revised and brought up to date, while the last section contains previously unpublished material. I would like to take this opportunity to acknowledge my co-authors in the original iterations of some of these articles, Danny Miller and Katharina Balasz.

I would also like to thank my editor, Sally Simmons, who first suggested the idea of these 'collected works.' Our brief conversation translated into a disproportionate amount of work and I am grateful for her support throughout the project. I also want to express my gratitude to Elizabeth Florent, who has shared my journey of discovery.

As always, I must thank Sheila Loxham, my assistant and personal strategic defense system. Not only does she shield me from others, she is also very skilled at defusing harmlessly the occasional harsh missiles I launch before they fall to earth.

INTERPERSONAL AND GROUP PROCESSES

INTRODUCTION

In her book *Albert Speer: His Battle with Truth* (1995) the writer and journalist Gitta Sereny retells Albert Speer's account of his father's visit to his office to see the maquette his son had made of Hitler's new Berlin—the world capital that would be the seat of government for the Thousand Year Reich. Speer's father, also an architect, had previously been dismissive about his son's skills but since his son had become the Fuehrer's architect, had become proud of his success. However, his reaction to the maquette was unexpected: 'He stood and looked at the model for a long moment. Then he said, "You've all gone completely insane," and walked out ... But it didn't end there. The next evening he came to the theater with me. Hitler sat in the box across from ours and sent his aide to say that if the old gentleman with me was my father, he would like to meet him. As soon as my father stood facing Hitler, I saw him pale and tremble—his whole body shuddered as if he had the ague ... Stupidly, I thought he was just unbearably moved' (Sereny, 1995, p. 158). Speer reflected later that he believed his father had 'somehow felt that night that other "id" in Hitler ... and from then on he identified me with that madness too' (Sereny, 1995, pp. 158–9).

Speer senior was right, of course, but by the time of this encounter things had gone too far. Hitler's preference had Speer happily in thrall: 'Hitler became my life ... I just accepted ... that I was going to have a wonderful life, wonderful beyond any dreams' (Sereny, 1995, p. 106). The man who had worked himself and others 24 hours a day for nine months to deliver the new Chancellery building two days ahead of schedule (a project a fellow architect said should have taken nine years) would turn his awesome capacity for work and his logistical brilliance to Hitler's war effort—with the result that, despite intense Allied bombing in the final year of the war, German armaments production actually increased.

Albert Speer, like the others in Hitler's immediate coterie, was caught up in an extreme expression of *folie à deux*—a blanket term that describes far more than its literal 'madness shared by two': it can signify a wide range of delusional beliefs and actions. Although its clinical classification is dependency psychotic disorder, or induced delusional disorder, *folie à deux* is still more generally used in psychiatric literature.

Folie à deux can lend itself to farce, as well as tragedy. The 2008 film *Be Kind Rewind* is the story of a luckless video store employee who inadvertently erases the entire stock of the store. Desperate to keep the disaster from his absent employer, and keep his customers happy, he enlists the help of friends to remake the movies. The new versions swiftly develop a cult following and when the store owner returns and discovers that the ersatz movies do better business than the originals, he collaborates with the deception. Justice finally arrives with a prosecution for copyright violation but not before the culprits prove that you can fool some of the people all of the time.

In the first chapter of this book, I describe how *folie à deux* can work in an organizational context, examining how individuals' activity or passivity and tendency toward conformism can contribute to the process. I look at the checks and balances organizations can use to forestall and manage dysfunctional leader–follower relationships, as well as the self-monitoring we can all use to assess our susceptibilities.

Chapter 2 brings together my reflections on a key element of my work and is an attempt to explain why I believe it is essential to understand the way human dynamics work within organizations. I am bound to regret, after a career built on advocating the clinical psychodynamic approach, that there is still resistance to its implementation. I believe that the refusal to acknowledge the value of a psychoanalytical approach to organizational behavior is a serious handicap to modern management scholarship and practice. In this chapter, I make a defense of psychoanalytic principles and argue that unconscious dynamics have a significant impact on life in organizations, urging organizational leaders to recognize and plan for them.

I begin by addressing some key issues: Why do organizations attempt to function on the basis that executives are logical, rational, dependable human beings? And why does the belief persist that management is a rational task performed by rational people according to rational organizational objectives? Isn't it time we confronted and dismissed these myths once and for all? In this context, I take a close look at the psychology of groups and apply this to the organizational setting. People in organizations operate on the assumption of rationality and normal functioning but this assumption is deeply untrue: we all bring our personal quirks, idiosyncrasies, dysfunctions, and neuroses with us into the workplace. We have our own conscious behaviors and we observe and respond to those of others—but our outer performance is governed by our responses to our inner unconscious processes. Below the surface, something quite different may be going on.

There is a Sufi tale about a man who noticed a disturbing bump under a rug. He tried everything to flatten the rug, smoothing, rubbing and squashing the bump, but it kept reappearing. Finally, frustrated and furious, the man lifted up the rug, and to his great surprise, out slid a very angry snake. In an organizational context, this story can be viewed as a metaphor for the occasions when interventions fail because they deal only with the symptoms and do not recognize the real underlying problem. Inevitably, attempts to smooth things over will leave the snake underneath the rug, working its mischief. As coaches, consultants, and change agents we should be pulling the snake out from under the rug and dealing with it. If we don't, it will confound our best efforts to improve organizational efficiency. I present the case for clinically informed organizational interventions by people trained in applying the psychodynamic approach to group situations, illustrating my arguments with a case history drawn from my own practice.

Readers of the previous book in this series[1] will know that I have always been drawn to physical challenges, especially exploration in extreme conditions. A few years ago I had the opportunity to spend some time with the pygmies in the rain forest of Cameroon. The pygmy peoples of central Africa are hunter-gatherers whose way of life is increasingly threatened by discrimination, deforestation, and intermarriage with other African ethnic groups. I stayed with the Baka pygmy, followed them in their hunting, shared their accommodation, and observed their interaction over several days. Their survival is dependent on a highly evolved group system that is characterized by trust and respect, protection and support, open communication, rapid resolution of conflict, common goals, shared values and beliefs, putting the needs of the group before the needs of the individual, and distributed leadership. I gained some fascinating insights about the functioning of high-performance groups from this experience, which I later formulated as some key lessons for organizational teams. In Chapter 3, I show how those key values are demonstrated among the pygmies and how they can be applied to the composition and functioning of high-performance teams within organizations.

The chapters in this first part of the book draw on some wide-ranging examples to illustrate group dynamics, from devastatingly dysfunctional to high-functioning. In the next section, I will look at how organizations accommodate their people, how they look after them—or fail to do so— during difficult times, and how organizational life is both enhanced and complicated within family firms.

[1] Kets de Vries, M. F. R. (2009) *Reflections on Leadership and Career Development*. Chichester: John Wiley & Sons Ltd.

CHAPTER 1

FOLIE À DEUX: ACTING OUT YOUR SUPERIOR'S FANTASIES[1]

... We shouldn't overlook the argument that folly finds favor in heaven because she alone is granted forgiveness of sins, whereas the wise man receives no pardon. So when men pray for forgiveness, though they may have sinned in full awareness, they make folly their excuse and defense.

—*Erasmus*, In Praise of Folly

Experience—the wisdom that enables us to recognize in an undesirable old acquaintance the folly that we have already embraced.

—Ambrose Bierce

You're only given a little spark of madness. You mustn't lose it.

—Robin Williams

Folly enlarges men's desires while it lessens their capacities.

—Robert South

POWER IN THE LEADER–SUBORDINATE RELATIONSHIP

In psychiatric literature, the idea of mental contagion is a recurring theme (Christakis and Fowler, 2009). *Folie à deux* originally referred to a seriously

---

[1] The material in this chapter has been compiled from the following previously printed sources:
Kets de Vries, M.F.R. (1978) '*Folie à deux*: Acting out your superior's fantasies', *Human Relations*, 31(10), 1978, pp. 905–24.
Kets de Vries, M.F.R. (1979) 'Managers can drive their subordinates mad', *Harvard Business Review*, July–August, No. 79404, pp. 125–34.

disturbed relationship between two people that involved spreading mental processes from one person to another (and was viewed as being limited to the behavior of individuals within families). However, as we will see from examples in this chapter, it can also be a collective phenomenon whereby groups of individuals are influenced by the delusions of one affected person.

Senior executives should never underestimate the degree of influence they wield in organizations. Given the fact that dependency—the need for direction—is one of man's most universal characteristics, managers need to be aware that their subordinates might in certain circumstances go so far as to sacrifice reality for its sake. To preserve such a dependency, both subordinates and superiors can create closed communities, losing touch with the immediate reality of the organization's environment. Subordinates will, on occasion, willingly participate in even irrational decisions without challenging what is happening.

It is my hypothesis that *folie à deux* is a regularly occurring phenomenon in organizations and, indeed, can be considered one of the hazards of leadership. I would argue that it has received less attention than it deserves because within relatively isolated organizational environments there is often a high degree of tolerance for unusual or eccentric behavior. However, I believe that by studying emotionally charged superior–subordinate relationships characterized by some kind of impaired ability to see things realistically, one can often gain insight into what is frequently excused as just an 'eccentric' leadership style.

In fact, notable examples of such behavior can be found throughout history, and two clear illustrations are the FBI under the leadership of J. Edgar Hoover, and what happened between Hitler and his close followers in the last days of World War II. I will explore both of these in a little more detail.

HOOVER AND THE FBI

As an administrator, J. Edgar Hoover struck many as an erratic autocrat, banishing agents to Siberian posts for the most whimsical reasons and terrorizing them with so many rules and regulations that adherence to all of them was impossible (Schott, 1975; Cox and Theoharis, 1988). Hoover viewed his directorship as infallible; subordinates soon learned that dissent equaled disloyalty. No one could risk ignoring his slightest whim. For example, non-participation in an anti-obesity program was likely to incur his wrath, and rumor had it that chauffeurs had to avoid making left turns while driving him. It was said that his car had once got struck by another car when he was making a left turn but, according to others, 'left' reminded Hoover of communists.

Any trivial, unimportant, or unclear order originating from Hoover had to be acted upon and subordinates could expect trouble if they did not take directives seriously. These directives often assumed a life of their own. Only slavish obedience to the rules, and statistics—level of fines, number of convictions, fugitives apprehended—counted. Problems arose if these figures did not increase year on year.

Naturally, those agents who embraced the concept of the director's omnipotence were more likely to succeed. To ensure compliance, inspectors would be sent out to field offices in search of violations (the breaking of some obscure rule or instruction). If a contract was out on a special agent in charge of the office, a violation would inevitably be found. The future of the inspectors themselves would be at stake if no violations were discovered because a contract might be issued in turn on *them*. Participation in these absurdities was unavoidable if people wanted to survive within the organization. However, many of these bizarre activities seem to have been treated as quite normal aspects of organizational life and were carried out with great conviction.

HITLER AND THE FALL OF BERLIN

The *folie à deux* displayed by Hitler and his followers was particularly clear during the last months of the war. Isolated in his bunker in Berlin at this time, Hitler withdrew into his fantasies, now more than ever inhabited by delusions. Encouraged by an intimate clique of old party members (particularly Bormann, Goebbels, and Ley),[2] he increasingly denied the reality of the approaching end (Speer, 1971). Even six weeks before Germany's total unconditional surrender, Speer tells how Hitler participated in an armaments conference during which nonexistent crude steel production, quotas for anti-tank guns, and the employment of imaginary new super-weapons were discussed. At such conferences, the dismal record of the previous war years was attributed to treason and sabotage by army officers. But, it was argued, since these traitors had now been exposed, the situation would be turned around. Victory was near.

[2] In Hitler's Germany, Bormann was *Reichsleiter,* secretary to the Fuehrer, and eventually party minister; Goebbels was Minister of Propaganda while Ley was *Reichsleiter* and head of the German Labor Front. Both Goebbels and Ley committed suicide (Goebbels together with his family in the bunker). Bormann's fate has been contested.

Speer recalls how in these twilight days of the Thousand Year Reich, innumerable fantasies blossomed between Hitler and his close companions. Roosevelt's death was hailed as a sign of providence, a turning point in the war that was compared with the way in which history had once given a last-minute victory to a hopelessly beaten Frederick the Great. Another example was the delusion that a new 'death ray' was about to be invented, a weapon that would change the outcome of the war. All this occurred one month before the final assault on Berlin, a time when Germany was in a complete shambles.

A particularly striking part of Speer's reminiscences is his description of the delusional interplay of fantasies among Hitler and his inner circle—to whom the reality of the approaching end was totally unacceptable. While most fantasies originated with Hitler, his close entourage not only participated but also enhanced these irrational thoughts. In this small, increasingly isolated community the belief persisted that everything was not lost. Miraculous developments were just around the corner. Setbacks were only temporary. The deteriorating situation was the result of betrayal and sabotage. This delusional spell over the inner circle was broken only by advancing Russian troops, after which communal suicide and imprisonment followed.

In Speer's recollections, one can identify the transferring of delusional ideas and unusual behavior patterns from one person to others in close association with the person primarily affected. These partners not only participated in the delusional ideas, but frequently developed them even further—a major characteristic of *folie à deux*.

I will now consider the origins of this idea within psychodynamic theory.

PSYCHODYNAMIC ASPECTS

The term *folie à deux* was first coined in 1877 by two French psychiatrists, Ernest-Charles Lasègue and Jean-Pierre Falret, to describe *folie imposée* (imposed psychosis), a clinical variety of this disorder (Rioux, 1963). From then on, an extensive number of articles were published to describe and analyze this phenomenon (Deutsch, 1938; Gralnick, 1942; Pulver and Brunt, 1961; Rioux, 1963). *Folie à deux* also has been called double insanity, collective insanity, or psychosis of association. (The reason for the latter term is that in true *folie à deux* the symptoms described are usually of a psychotic nature, e.g., illusions of grandeur and delusions of persecution.)

In a number of instances, religious, grandiose, and depressive delusions have also been identified (Gralnick, 1942; McNiel *et al.*, 1972). Whatever its specific content, *folie à deux* essentially involves the sharing of a delusional system by two or more individuals. Among the psychodynamic factors we observe in *folie à deux* are:

- extreme (mutual) dependency;
- separation anxiety (about the feared loss of the dominant partner, an attitude not without ambivalence);
- identification with the aggressor (the dominant partner);
- close association (frequently implying a condition of relative isolation);
- deflection of hostility (usually through the mechanism of projection).

Etiology

For an explanation of this phenomenon we have to look to early childhood because at its core lies the degree of success a child experiences in developing basic trust reactions, particularly with parents. Lack of basic trust and the arousal of anxiety because of frustrating, humiliating, and disappointing experiences can lead a child to develop an unsatisfactory interpersonal equilibrium, a sense of betrayal, and a perception of the environment as hostile. The individual's personality will develop accordingly. Such a person, in his dealings with the outside world, will take precautions to be ready for any confirmation of his expectations (Polatin, 1975).

Apart from such emerging paranoia, the person's lack of trust frequently leads to an absence of closeness and, consequently, to frustrated dependency needs (Bowlby, 1969, 1973). The world becomes a dangerous place, in which only a very few individuals can be trusted. Contingent on the degree of deprivation, if an opportunity arises for people to satisfy their dependency needs, their attachment to another person can become extremely intense—totally overpowering the individual's other forms of behavior to the detriment of rational thought and reality testing.

Individuals who engage in *folie à deux*, accept, support, and share each other's delusional ideas, creating a symbiotic type of relationship. This usually occurs under conditions of prolonged and close association. Dewhurst and Todd (1956) mention the need for a high degree of similarity in general motif and delusional content of the two partners' system of ideas.

Not only dependency but also identification seem to be important aspects of *folie à deux*. Hartman and Stengel (1931) argued that because of the extreme dependency of the participants on each other, total identification with the partner becomes a way of avoiding the intolerable thought of separation. A feeling of closeness is preserved through identification, which eventually will imply the acceptance of the delusional ideas of one party (which develop for reasons described later) by the other. Fliess (1953) suggested that this is a mutual, not a unilateral process. Both parties will depend upon and identify with each other—it is a process of identification and counter-identification.

Identification with the aggressor Bonnard (1954) mentioned that this identification process is of a special nature and suggests that it belongs to the defense mechanism 'identification with the aggressor'—an unconscious process by which a person incorporates within himself a mental image of a person who represents a source of frustration (Freud, 1946). This is a role played very often by the dominant partner in *folie à deux*. Through identification with the aggressor (discussed in Volume 1 of this series), individuals defend themselves against their own hostile and destructive wishes (a reaction to feelings of helplessness and dependency on the dominant party and fear of retaliation about these wishes) (Kets de Vries, 2009b). Strength will be gained through the alliance with the aggressor, rather than allowing themselves to be the victim.

Identification with the aggressor usually implies participating in the delusion of the existence of a common outside enemy. These persecutory fantasies also become the rationalization for the lack of fulfillment brought by the dominant individual's elaborately constructed grandiose schemes. As we saw in the example of Hitler and his inner circle, lack of success will be blamed on sabotage and opposition of this common enemy. The shared delusions are usually kept within the limits of possibility and are based on actual past events or certain common expectations.

HOW *FOLIE A DEUX* DEVELOPS

Pulver and Brunt (1961), who probably formulated the most exhaustive description of *folie à deux*, identified the critical aspects of it as:

- the need for a dominant partner;
- mutual dependency between participants;
- hostility over these dependency needs.

During the period preceding *folie à deux* one of the participants is strongly dependent on the other and has few outside sources of gratification. Eventually the dominant partner becomes preoccupied (not necessarily consciously) by the feeling that the less dominant partner is increasingly taking advantage of his or her dependency needs. This causes the dominant partner to become more and more hostile while at the same time feeling guilty about this rising hostility. Because he or she is afraid of giving up the relationship with the other party, a defense is formed against this hostility, usually of a projective nature. Hostility is externalized and attributed to others and in most instances takes the form of a paranoid delusion. The dominant partner needs the support of the more submissive individual and wants him to share the delusion. He or she is afraid to lose the close contact with the other party if the delusion is rejected and therefore has no choice but to induce the more submissive person to participate in the delusion.

If the submissive partner resists participating in this, the dominant partner will become more overtly hostile toward him or her (while excluding the submissive partner from the accusation process). This will raise the submissive partner's level of anxiety and guilt. The actions of the dominant individual will cause the submissive one to be placed in a double bind. He or she will be threatened with either the loss of gratification of his or her dependency relationship, or the loss of reality. In some instances, he or she will see (again, not necessarily consciously) no alternative but to give in to this ultimatum—i.e. to identify with the aggressor, thus satisfying dependency needs, and also deflecting the hostility of the dominant party. The reason for this choice is probably that separation from the person who started the process is a much more direct and conceivable loss than the loss of reality.

Through participation in similar fantasies, submissive partners can maintain their source of gratification, lower their level of anxiety and guilt, and express anger at the projected form of the dominant partner. The process resembles a mirror effect; the actions of the initiator become reflected in those of the more submissive partner and vice versa. *Folie à deux* becomes the means to save the alliance of mutual dependency from breaking up.

EXAMPLES FROM LITERATURE

The interplay of these variables and how they create the interactions of *folie à deux* has been noted by playwrights and other creative artists. In his 1919 play *Where the Cross is Made* (1972), Eugene O'Neill describes an incidence of *folie à deux*. The play tells the story of a retired sea captain who is waiting for his ship, the *Mary Allen* (which was sent out many years before on a treasure hunt), although it is known that the ship sank three years ago. This catastrophe, causing total financial disaster, became emotionally unacceptable to the captain, who created the delusion that the ship would return.

The captain's son, embittered because of increasing emotional and financial pressures, is making preparations to have his father sent to a mental hospital. Not only is the mortgage on the house going to be foreclosed if his father continues to stay in the house, but the son is becoming more and more afraid of being drawn into his father's delusions. At the end of the play, when the moment of separation is drawing near, the father declares that the ship has arrived, pointing at the blackness of the night and cursing his son for turning traitor. The son cannot stand this pressure any longer, accepts the delusion and participates, agreeing that there is a ship out there. When the doctor comes to take the father away, the emotion causes the father's death from heart failure, but despite this his son continues the delusionary fantasy.

In Thomas Mann's Story *The Blood of the Walsungs* (1921), a twin brother and sister named Sieglinde and Siegmund are acting out Wagner's opera *Die Walküre* in real life. Brought up without economic worries in an emotionally impoverished environment, the siblings' contact with others has become disturbing and minimized. Eventually, the impending marriage of Sieglinde becomes the catalyst for total identification with their namesakes in the opera and leaves us at the end of the story with unanswered questions about incest and adultery.

In Ingmar Bergman's film *Hour of the Wolf* we find yet another example of *folie à deux* in the story of the painter Johan Borg who believes that he is tormented by demons during his stay with his wife on an isolated island. It is only at the end of the film that we discover that his wife, who originally appears to be a very earthy, sane, submissive individual, is in fact a partner to his delusions.

In a clinical context the psychoanalyst Robert Lindner describes in one of his case histories, 'The Jet-Propelled Couch' (1956), how he gradually got drawn into the delusions of one of his patients, a scientist, who found escape from reality by constructing an extremely elaborate science-fiction world. Only with great effort was the psychoanalyst Lindner able to wrest himself away from this world of galactic fantasy.

These four examples (and many others) indicate the key features in *folie à deux*:

- the relative isolation of the characters;
- their closeness (family or otherwise);

- the existence of a dominant partner;
- the emergence of a delusion.

In many ways the process by which *folie à deux* evolves is similar to that of brainwashing.

COMPARING *FOLIE A DEUX* WITH OTHER PROCESSES

Three phases can be distinguished in both *folie à deux* and brainwashing: unfreezing, changing, and refreezing (Lewin, 1947; Schein, 1961). Initially there is a disorganizing or regressive phase during which the defensive structure of the submissive party is gradually broken down. A strong demand is made to fulfill heightened dependency needs. During this period, motivation to change is induced. (In brainwashing, this process is usually facilitated through social isolation and sensory deprivation.) Subsequently, change occurs through identification with the beliefs and attitudes of the aggressor. New responses are created based on new information. Finally, refreezing takes place, whereby the new responses are stabilized and integrated.

We can also compare the process of change in belief systems in *folie à deux* with the general effects of group processes on an individual. The experimental work of Asch (1951, 1956) and Schachter (1951), indicates the impact of group pressures and social comparison on the behavior of an individual subjected to this form of influence, and the role of sanctions in the case of nonconformity. The basic premise is that individuals like to be correct in their perceptions and want to live up to others' expectations. This is particularly true for individuals with a weak sense of self-esteem, often indicated by strong dependency needs. But there are differences in the degree of conformity. If private choices become similar to public ones, then because of these group pressures, the individual appears to be completely persuaded. If this is not the case, and individuals are only acting this way in public and are going against their own judgment to mollify the group, then their actions are more superficial and ritualistic.

The avoidance of punishment (such as rejection or ridicule by others), fear of separation, and obtaining rewards (such as gratification of dependency needs) seem to be the main motives for such behavior. In his famous experiment, Milgram (1963, 1965) found that a large proportion of the population will cause pain to others in order to pander to authority. We seem to be dependent on others to validate our conceptions of reality. In cases of difference our sense of stability and security is easily threatened and we try to conform.

Conformity can also result through others' behavior being the only guide to appropriate action and determination of reality. Festinger's studies (1954) on cognitive dissonance point in that direction. Individuals will make great efforts to reduce the dissonance between two or more cognitions that are experienced as inconsistent with each other. When reality is unclear and uncertain, other people become the source of information about how to behave, and in this way social bonds are maintained.

Contagious participation: a collective phenomenon

Given people's dependence on others for guidance, as described above, we can see why delusion formation can spread and eventually infect an entire society. In this context the term *'folie à beaucoup'* or *'folie collective'* is occasionally used. Helene Deutsch noted the resemblance of group phenomena with *folie à deux* and once remarked:

> We also find the process as a mass phenomenon, where entire groups of physically healthy people are carried away by psychically diseased members of the group: world reformers and paranoids, for example. Indeed, great national and religious movements of history and social revolutions have had, in addition to their reality motives, psychological determinants which come very close to the psychological processes of *folie à deux*. (1938, p. 307)

Prejudice and some political attitudes or religious views can be considered variations of *folie à deux*, since these attitudes are sometimes created by situations of fear and terror during which individuals seem more susceptible to mental contagion. This is especially true during the quieter periods of anticipation of such situations when the 'work of worrying' occurs and the level of anxiety tends to rise (Janis, 1958). Religious beliefs, in particular those promising alleviation of experienced suffering, become very communicable, particularly in periods of greater upheaval and change. Lycanthropy fears, witch mania, lynching and looting mobs, and some of the more popular Eastern mystical cults such as the Sun Moon and Hare Krishna movements are examples of variations of *folie à deux* on a larger scale. Senator Joe McCarthy's investigations and hearings and the Stalin purge trials are other illustrations. Frequently, we find a central image of a vast, mysterious, and frightening conspiracy. This has been a common notion throughout history, whether represented by the Elders of Zion, Jesuits, Freemasons, communists, or by collusion among large oil companies. It is a world in which absolute good is fighting absolute evil, and where there is a lack of compromise and, consequently, unrealistic goal setting—which only heightens participants' sense of frustration.

DEGREES OF PERMANENCE

Having read this far you may now be wondering about the permanence of the behavior patterns and belief systems instigated by *folie à deux*. Some guidance in this matter is offered by Kelman (1961) who suggests dividing the relative permanence of conforming behavior or, generally, responses to social influence, into three types: compliance, identification, and internalization.

○ **Compliance**—a mode of behavior triggered by a desire to gain reward or to avoid punishment.
○ **Identification**—a response to social influence based on the individual's desire to be like the influencer. Individuals come to believe the values and opinions they adopt, but since the basis of the relationship is the attractiveness of the other person, this implies the maintenance of an active relationship between the two parties. The continuation of the relationship is satisfying since the other person becomes the model for self-definition. But the belief in the values and opinions of the other person is not necessarily very strong and will disappear in the absence of close interaction. We find here a parallel with charismatic authority.
○ **Internalization**—the most deeply rooted response to social influence using Kelman's classification. Here the beliefs or values are intrinsically rewarding and become part of the system of values. The basis of the influencer's power becomes expertise and credibility. Internalized beliefs are independent of the other party's continued presence and therefore extremely resistant to change. Naturally, the influencer does not necessarily have to be a superior; peers, subordinates, and even complete outsiders can set this process in motion. But given the effect of authority on most people's behavior, and the usual prevalence of a relationship of dominance–submission in *folie à deux*, this disorder will be most common in superior–subordinate relationships.

It is often difficult, from the observer's point of view, to distinguish between compliance, identification, and internalization. Subordinates may seem to be engaged in a *folie à deux* but the intensity and seriousness of their reactions will remain open to question. Only an understanding of subordinates' private motivations and the nature of their behavior after the two parties have been separated will yield insight into the type of social influence process that has been occurring. And only in the case of identification and internalization can we speak of true *folie à deux*, where the psychodynamic processes I described earlier are applicable.

FOLIE A DEUX IN ORGANIZATIONS

In reviewing the literature I have found only one recorded business example of *folie à deux* that has been diagnosed under this particular name (Lang, 1936). This situation concerned a partnership between two barbers. One of the partners suddenly became preoccupied with the idea of starting a barber college. According to him, the financing would come from a number of mysterious millionaire friends and the proceeds from this college would be phenomenal. This rather unrealistic plan soon resulted in business losses, which were explained as the result of a group of unknown people operating against both partners. The more submissive partner believed completely in these grandiose plans and delusions. The delusions eventually became so serious that both partners had to be hospitalized.

Despite the lack of recorded examples, I believe *folie à deux* is a far more common phenomenon in work organizations than has been recognized, probably because the power, attractiveness, or expertise of the individual in a position of authority easily leads to conformity, identification, or internalization of behavior patterns by managers in subordinate positions. Not all managers have a sense of personal identity strong enough to withstand the pressures placed on them. Giving in, even if this is only compliance, is usually much easier.

Senior executives' need for a mirror image

Despite often declaring a desire for independent-mindedness in their subordinates, many senior executives find this hard to deal with in practice. Such executives frequently possess relatively closed belief systems (Rokeach, 1960) and in fact like to see their subordinates as mirror images of themselves, compliant with their wishes.

This tendency in senior executives can have serious consequences in terms of subordinates' career advancement in organizations. Senior executives with these attitudes will select subordinates who have compatible behavior patterns and belief systems. Many managers who are perceived as likely to react in an active nonconforming manner—unwilling to participate in possibly irrational behavior patterns—are automatically excluded. Others will be dismissed or resign soon after joining the organization. This process of organizational socialization is the phase in which new recruits' compatibility with existing organizational norms and values is tested. Difficulty in adjustment will make for exclusion.

The same can be said about career advancement. Reward systems will be based on participation. To the subordinate, the alternative to compliance, identification, or internalization of the norms and values predominating in the organization is far from attractive since it frequently implies dismissal, demotion, or other forms of career stagnation. Because of this selection and reward system (which doesn't necessarily exist in a formal sense) currently operating delusional patterns in the organization will be enhanced, creating a fertile territory for *folie à deux*.

Organizational subgroups will foster and maintain organizational myths and fantasies often only remotely related to the reality of the situation. In these instances, for some cliques, the organization's overall objectives and strategies become of lesser interest than tactical considerations. Members of these groups appear to live in a polarized world that no longer includes compromise or the acceptance of differences. Everyone is pressured to choose sides. It is also a world in which one continuously has to be on one's guard against being singled out as a target for unfriendly actions. In such an organization, scapegoating is directed not only toward individuals within the organization but also toward such groups as government, labor unions, competitors, suppliers, customers, or consumer organizations. What may have been a well-thought out program can become distorted. For instance, alertness to the environment, which at one time may have been an organizational strength, can turn into a watch for imminent attack—a caricature of its original purpose.

Because of structural arrangements, subgroups frequently overlap with departments or other units. When this happens, people jealously guard areas of responsibility and the determination of boundaries between departments can lead to disputes. Seeking or accepting help from other groups may be considered a weakness or even a betrayal.

For example, in one large electronics company, a vice president of product development began to imagine that two of his colleagues, a vice president of R&D and a vice president of manufacturing, wanted to get rid of him. He perceived that his two colleagues were trying to reorganize his department and incorporate it into their own functional areas. At every available opportunity, he communicated this concern to his subordinates and expected them to confirm his own suspicions. Disagreement was not tolerated; resistance resulted in either dismissal or transfer to another department. Gradually, many of his executives began to believe in his statements and to develop a siege mentality, which led to a strong sense of group cohesion.

Relationships between this group and members of other departments became strained. What were once minor interdepartmental skirmishes deteriorated into open warfare. Committee meetings with members of other departments became public accusation sessions about the withholding of information, inaccurate data, and intrusion into each other's territory. In addition, because of his recurring complaints about poor quality of delivered material and late deliveries, the vice president's contacts with some of his suppliers deteriorated. (A subsequent examination by a new vice president found that most of these accusations were unwarranted.)

Eventually, managers of other departments began to avoid contact with product development staff, thereby confirming their suspicions. Over time, the rest of the company built up a number of separate, fairly informal information systems to avoid any dealings with the product development group. Finally, after the product development group made a number of budgetary mistakes because of distorted information, the company president transferred the vice president and reorganized the department.

Despite all that has been said so far, *folie à deux* is not always dysfunctional from an organizational point of view. Initially, it can be a source of great strength by making for group cohesiveness, goal directedness, and effective scanning of the environment (a side effect of hyper-alertness). However, unfortunately, in the long run the tendency for this to become organizational pathology will be substantial.

MODES OF OPERATION OF *FOLIE A DEUX* IN ORGANIZATIONS

Clearly superior-subordinate relationships occur most frequently in organizational situations, and for this reason I have created a matrix that conceptualizes the various ways in which *folie à deux* can operate in organizations—see Table 1.1. In this section I describe in more detail employees' responses to influence from superiors.

Nonconformers

Both active and passive nonconformers refuse to participate in the irrational behavior patterns of their superiors. The group that has a more passive orientation usually withdraws into routine, nonessential activities.

Table 1.1 Subordinates' behavior patterns in *folie à deux*

Level of activity		
Responses to influence	**Passive**	**Active**
Nonconformance and opportunism		
Nonconformers	Withdrawal into routine low-key activities. Participation in delusions avoided. Retreatist behavior.	Leaves organization (resignation or dismissal). Occasionally plays the role of change agent.
Compliers	Participation in delusions without private conviction. Ritualistic behavior.	Participation and enhancement of delusions without private conviction.
Folie à deux		
Identifiers	Participation in delusions with private conviction. Relationship relatively unstable.	Participation and enhancement of delusions with private conviction. Relationship relatively unstable.
Internalizers	Participation in delusions with private conviction. Stable relationship.	Participation and enhancement of delusions with private conviction. Stable relationship.

Immersion in the technological aspects of the job (as long as these are not an emotionally important part of the delusions of the superior) will be their solution for avoiding participation in the behavior patterns of the superior. Their basic strategy is to avoid activities considered essential to the organization. Because of its low profile (given the pressures for conformity and participation inside the organization) there are usually no rewards for this behavior regardless of its importance to the organization. Career stagnation or demotion is often the logical consequence.

In contrast, more active nonconformers will refuse to participate in the delusions or other irrational behavior patterns of senior executives. Taking a more active stand may provoke the wrath of senior management. Eventually, their choices will be limited—either they leave the organization voluntarily, or the organization will force their resignation.

In some instances active nonconformers will play the role of change agent. Because of their active stand the delusionary spell may be broken and organizational participants brought back to reality. However, this is a relatively rare occurrence. The power and authority of active nonconformers are usually limited and so too is their effectiveness in instigating change.

Compliers

Active and passive compliers are those who participate as irrational behavior patterns emerge in the organization but do so without private conviction. The only reason for their participation is opportunism: the organization's reward system encourages conformity to the wishes of the superior. The behavior of passive compliers is more ritualistic, characterized by an attitude of 'I'm not sticking my neck out' or 'I'm playing it safe.'

Identifiers

Identifiers participate in delusions and other irrational behavior patterns with private conviction. The only difference between the active and passive group is that the active group will elaborate upon the delusions. Managers who use the response of the active identifiers probably create the most true and common variety of *folie à deux*. Continuous association between the parties is needed for the delusions to hold. The alliance remains relatively unstable since subordinates usually stop behaving in this way when the relationship breaks up.

Internalizers

The final group, the internalizers, will not only participate in the delusions and other irrational behavior patterns with private conviction but continue in these beliefs even after the relationship is broken. Change is more complete and definitive. This is the most deeply rooted variety of *folie à deux*. The difference between active and passive identifiers depends, again, on the willingness to elaborate on these delusions. But, according to clinical evidence, this variety is comparatively rare (Gralnick, 1942).

This conceptual scheme demonstrates that each category of response can evolve into another. This implies a progression of intensity and degree of participation with the activities of the senior executive. Mere compliance may eventually transform into internalization, making for a sense of commitment and permanence.

ENTREPRENEURIAL AND FAMILY FIRMS

Because of the great intensity and closeness that develops in small isolated groups, entrepreneurial ventures tend to be particularly susceptible to *folie à deux* behavior patterns. In many instances the venture begins because the entrepreneur tries to overcome his or her feelings of dependency, helplessness, and rejection by adopting an opposite posture—one of financial and psychological risk-taking style. In addition, the entrepreneur may have a strong need for achievement, control, and power, as well as an intense concern for autonomy.

The relationship between entrepreneur and enterprise is usually an involved and conflict-ridden one in which the company has great emotional significance for the individual. Frequently, this type of attachment may lead to growth and succession crises, episodes aggravated by developments of a *folie à deux* nature, as the following example shows.

The president and founder of one medium-sized electronics company often expressed concern about the need for more professional management in his company. He liked to state that the entrepreneurial phase had been passed and that the time had come to make organizational changes, prepare to go public, and plan for succession. To that end, he became personally involved in the recruitment of MBAs at various business schools. His charismatic appeal and his strong advocacy of professional management attracted a great number of MBAs. The MBA influx was balanced, however, by a steady exodus of many of the same MBAs who soon realized the difficulties in conforming to the president's demands.

Under the guise of being a happy family, the founder felt he could intrude into the private family affairs of his subordinates. He promised to delegate a great deal of responsibility to the newcomers but these responsibilities turned out to be poorly defined assignments without much authority, which frequently ended in failure. People's career advancement depended on their closeness to the president, compliance with his wishes, and willingness to participate in often irrational behavior patterns. Exile to various obscure sales offices was the price of resistance. Eventually, the company had to pay a price for this leadership. However, the president simply blamed the steady drop in sales and profits on government intervention, union activities, and sabotage by a number of singled-out employees.

MANAGEMENT OF *FOLIE A DEUX*

The first steps in the containment of *folie à deux* in an organizational situation are recognizing the individual and organizational symptoms and taking action.

Check out your managers

Managers likely to initiate this type of behavior usually show specific personality characteristics, such as a great deal of personal charm and seductiveness—qualities that may originally have been responsible for their personal attractiveness. A closer look, however, will reveal that this behavior is often a cover-up for attitudes of arrogance and self-righteousness. Individuals prone to *folie à deux* find it extremely difficult to alter their concepts and ideas, and their actions often contain a rigid quality.

Because of their need to dominate and control other people, executives of this type will deeply resent any form or use of authority by others. They are frequently preoccupied with people's hidden motives and look for confirmation of their suspicions. They evince a great concern about details, often amplifying and elaborating on them. Such executives will feel easily slighted, and their lack of trust and confidence in others can make them extremely self-conscious, reserved, and moody, prone to dramatic mood swings. If an attitude of friendliness and companionship temporarily prevails, such behavior will be quickly shattered by the slightest provocation, after which the full force of hate, mistrust, and rage may break loose. Such individuals seem to lack a sense of playfulness and humor.

When *folie à deux* behavior starts to spread, the people influenced may show similar behavioral patterns, but not usually so intensively.

Look at their operating structures

The danger signals of *folie à deux* in an organization as a whole can also be detected by looking at possible peculiarities in the organization's culture and ways of operation. One symptom is unusual selection and promotion procedures that largely reflect a senior executive's idiosyncrasies rather than a concern for a candidate's overall managerial capabilities.

Other indications may be a department's preoccupation with details at the cost of overall company effectiveness, and manifestations of excessive stress in the organization, such as a high rate of executive turnover and high absenteeism. Frequent changes in organizational goals, and the existence of unrealistic plans, as well as an insistence on supposed conspiracies (or the actual creation of the latter) are other signs.

Establish a trusting relationship

When *folie à deux* is in full swing the people involved are actually beyond self-help. For the individual executive who started the process, the route back to reality is particularly difficult. A disposition toward delusional thinking can be difficult to overcome. Appealing to executives' logic and reality does not help; on the contrary, it can evoke uncompromising and hostile reactions. Rather, in these instances, one has to establish some degree of trust and closeness with the affected individuals to make them willing to entertain the possibility that their assumptions about the organizational environment are invalid.

Although this change in attitude is not going to be arrived at easily, without such a change it won't be possible for affected executives to make a realistic self-appraisal of their own inner strengths and weaknesses. Substituting reality for fantasies is likely to be a slow and difficult process involving reintegration and adjustment of many deeply ingrained behavior patterns. Because of the intensity of the delusions, in many instances these people may need professional guidance.

The outlook for the affected followers is more positive and usually less dramatic. Frequently, disrupting their closeness to the affected senior executive will be sufficient to break the spell. Some form of disorientation may occur at the beginning, but proper guidance by other non-affected executives will soon help to bring their affected colleagues back into more normal, reality-oriented behavior patterns.

Monitor your own susceptibilities

In order to prevent yourself from entering into a *folie à deux* pattern you should also periodically appraise your own values, actions, and interpersonal relationships. Because it is hard to recognize one's own blind spots and irrational behavior patterns, you might (if particularly concerned) consider getting help in this appraisal process from outside the organization.

It is also important to recognize that a certain amount of courage will be needed to face these confrontations with yourself. Nonetheless, those executives with the willingness to test and reevaluate reality will be the ones who in the end possess real freedom of choice, acting out of a sense of inner security. A capacity for self-examination enhances a person's identity, fosters adaptation to change, and limits susceptibility to controlling influences.

Solicit the help of interested parties

You might by now find yourself thinking that being able to recognize *folie à deux* is of limited use when the instigator is a powerful senior executive who happens to be a major shareholder. Occasionally, however, support can be found in dealing with such an individual from a countervailing power such as the government or a union, which can help guide the organization away from self-destructive adventures. Other possible interested parties who could also blow the whistle are customers, suppliers, and bankers.

The situation is somewhat less problematic when the CEO is not a major shareholder, since the board of directors and shareholders can play a more active monitoring role. One of their responsibilities will be to watch for possible danger signs. Of course, it is also possible that board members will be drawn into the delusionary activities of a senior executive. Such an event is less likely to happen with a board of outside directors. However, because boards traditionally follow the directives of the CEO, this indicates just how important the careful selection of board members is.

Reorient the work climate and structure

Organizational solutions to *folie à deux* are obviously more feasible when the instigator is not a senior executive officer. Then confrontation, transfer, or, in serious cases, dismissal will be sufficient to stop the process. Also important, however, are organizational systems and procedures. For instance, reward systems that promote irrational behavior also give it implicit approval. It is therefore crucial to foster a healthy climate where irrational processes cannot take root.

Supporting individual responsibility and independence of mind in the organization, as well as selecting and promoting managers who behave accordingly, can be a buffer against *folie à deux*. An organizational culture of mutual collaboration, delegation, open conflict-resolution, and respect for individuality will expose a process of mental contagion before it can spread. Such organizational patterns will also lessen dependency needs and force conflict into the open, counteracting the vicious circles of interpersonal behavior.

Objective information systems can also assist managers to focus on reality, as can the use of many different sources for information gathering and processing. Interdepartmental committees and formal control systems can fulfil a similar function.

Contemporary pressures for more participative management, or work democratization, are other ways of preventing, or at least limiting, the emergence or proliferation of *folie à deux*. These structural changes can reduce the power of senior executives and restrict their ability to take advantage of their subordinates' dependency needs.

CHAPTER 2

GROUP DYNAMICS

There are more things in heaven and earth, Horatio,
Than are dreamt of in your philosophy.
—*William Shakespeare*, Hamlet, I, v. 166

What could an entirely rational being speak of with another entirely rational
being?
—*Emmanuel Levinas,* Totality and Infinity

I have yet to meet the famous Rational Economic Man theorists describe.
Real people have always done inexplicable things from time to time, and
they show no sign of stopping.
—*Charles Sanford, Jr*, US business executive

The Greek writer Aesop tells the tale of a hungry, thirsty fox who
saw some clusters of ripe black grapes hanging from a vine. She tried all
the tricks she knew to get at them, but she could not reach them and
exhausted herself in vain. At last she gave up and turned away, hiding her
disappointment and saying, 'The grapes are sour, and not ripe as I thought.'
Aesop's fable illustrates how skilled we are at rationalization, distorting
our images of self or others in order to regulate self-esteem. We reduce
cognitive dissonance by altering our belief or desire states, even if doing
so leads to irrational behavior. Of course, it can often be difficult to tell
where an objective consideration of realities leaves off and rationalization
begins. But trying to justify our behavior or beliefs while failing to recognize the inconsistencies or contradictory evidence is a good illustration
that human beings can engage in what appears as extremely irrational
behavior.

Too many management scholars, in studying organizational effectiveness, restrict themselves to a very mechanical view of life in the workplace.

They look at surface phenomena, not at deep structure. The collective unconscious of business practitioners and scholars alike subscribes to the myth that it is only what we see and know (in other words, that which is conscious) that matters. That myth is grounded in organizational behavior concepts of an extremely rational nature—concepts based on assumptions about human beings made by economists (at worst) or behavioral psychologists (at best). The social sciences, ever desperate to gain more prestige, cannot stop pretending to be natural sciences; they cannot relinquish their obsession with the directly measurable. For far too many people, the spirit of the economic machine seems to be alive and well and living in organizations. Though the existing repertoire of 'rational' concepts has proven time and again to be insufficient to untangle the really knotty problems that trouble organizations, the myth of rationality persists.

Consequently, organizational behavior concepts used to describe processes such as individual motivation, leadership, interpersonal relationships, group and inter-group processes, corporate culture, organizational structure, change, and development are based on behaviorist models, with an occasional dose of humanistic psychology thrown into the equation for good measure. Such an approach (over which the irrepressible ghost of scientific management advocate Frederick Taylor still hovers) has set the stage for a rather two-dimensional way of looking at the world of work. Many executives believe that behavior in organizations concerns only conscious, mechanistic, predictable, easy-to-understand phenomena. The more elusive processes that take place in organizations—phenomena that deserve rich description—are conveniently ignored.

That the organizational man or woman is not just a conscious, highly focused, maximizing machine of pleasures and pains, but also a person subject to many (often contradictory) wishes, fantasies, conflicts, defensive behavior, and anxieties—some conscious, others beyond consciousness— is not a popular perspective. Neither is the idea that concepts taken from such fields as psychoanalysis, psychodynamic psychotherapy, and dynamic psychiatry might have a place in the world of work. Such concepts are generally rejected out-of-hand on the grounds that they are too individually based, too focused on abnormal behavior, and (in the case of the psychoanalytic method of investigation) too reliant on self-reported case studies (creating problems of verification).

Valid as some of these criticisms may be, the fact remains that any meaningful explanation of humanity requires different means of verification. In spite of what philosophers of science like to say about this subject, no causal claim in clinical psychology (or history and economics, for that matter) can be verified in the same way as can be done in empirical sciences such as experimental physics or astronomy. When we enter the realm of someone's inner world—seeking to understand that individual's desires, hopes, and fears—efforts at falsification (in an attempt to discover an observed exception to science's postulated rules) become a rather moot point (Popper, 2002).

Though the notion that there is more to organizational behavior than meets the eye is anathema to many management scholars, practitioners who deny the reality of unconscious phenomena—who refuse to bring them to consciousness and take them into consideration—increase the gap between rhetoric and reality. Rejecting a psychoanalytically informed approach to studying human issues is a mistake, plain and simple. After all, it is individuals that make up organizations and create the units that contribute to social processes. Even en masse, people are subject to different laws than can be tested in experimental physics. Moreover, like it or not, abnormal behavior is more 'normal' than most people are prepared to admit. All of us have a neurotic side. Mental health and illness are not dichotomous phenomena but opposing positions on a continuum. Moreover, whether a person is labeled normal or abnormal, exactly the same dynamics apply.

Given these observations, business scholars and leaders need to revisit the following questions: Is the typical executive really a logical, dependable human being? Is management really a rational task performed by rational people according to sensible organizational objectives? Given the plethora of highly destructive actions taken by business and political leaders, we shouldn't even have to ask. It should be clear that many of these 'incomprehensible' activities (incomprehensible from a rational point of view, that is) signal that what really goes on in organizations takes place in the intrapsychic and interpersonal world of the key players, below the surface of day-to-day behaviors. That underlying mental activity and behavior needs to be understood in terms of conflicts, defensive behaviors, tensions, and anxieties.

It is something of a paradox that, while at a conscious level we might deny the presence of unconscious processes, at the level of behavior and action we live out such processes every day all over the world. Though we base business strategies on theoretical models derived from the 'rational economic man,' we count on real people (with all their conscious and unconscious quirks) to make and implement decisions. Even the most successful organizational leaders are prone to highly irrational behavior, a reality that we ignore at our peril.

When the illusions created by the concept of *homo economicus* prevail over the reality of *homo sapiens,* people interested in what truly happens in organizations are left with a vague awareness that strange things are occurring, things they cannot make sense of. When faced with organizational situations such as dysfunctional leadership, interpersonal conflicts, collusive relationships, ineffective team processes, and similar disturbing organizational phenomena, they feel ineffective and helpless.

In the case of many knotty organizational situations, a psychodynamic/ systemic orientation can go a long way toward bringing clarity and providing solutions. No body of knowledge has made a more sustained and successful attempt to deal with the meaning of human events than psychoanalysis. The psychoanalytic method of investigation, which observes people longitudinally, offers an important window into the operation of the mind, identifying meaning in the most minute personal, emotional experiences. Its method of drawing inferences about meaning out of otherwise incomprehensible phenomena is more effective than what competing theories have to offer. By making sense out of executives' deeper wishes and fantasies, and showing how these affect their behavior in the world of work, the psychodynamic orientation offers a practical way of discovering how organizations *really* function. Far too many well-intentioned and well-thought-out plans derail daily in workplaces around the world because of out-of-awareness forces that influence behavior. Only by accepting that executives (like the rest of us) are not paragons of rationality can we understand how such plans derail and put them back on track again—or better yet, keep them from derailing in the first place.

Though a growing group of management scholars is coming to realize that they need to pay attention to weaker, below-the-surface signals in organizational systems, that trend is belied by frequent articles in popular journals asking whether Freud is dead. People who pose that question are typically unaware of recent developments in the theory and the practice of psychoanalysis. They usually attack Freudian views of the early twentieth century, forgetting that psychoanalytic theory and therapy have continued to evolve since that time. Psychoanalytic theory and technique have become increasingly sophisticated, incorporating the findings from domains such as dynamic psychiatry, developmental psychology, ethology, anthropology, neurophysiology, cognitive theory, family systems theory, and individual and group psychotherapy. To condemn present-day psychoanalytic theory as outdated is like attacking modern physics because Newton did not understand Einstein's relativity theory. Although various aspects of Freud's theories are no longer valid in the light of new information about the workings of the mind, fundamental components of psychoanalytic theory and technique have been scientifically and empirically tested and verified, specifically as they relate to cognitive and emotional processes (Barron, Eagle *et al.*, 1992; Westen, 1998). As disappointing as this fact may be to some of his present-day attackers, many of Freud's ideas have retained their relevance.

A broad integrative, clinically oriented, psychodynamic perspective that draws on psychoanalytic concepts and techniques has much to contribute to our understanding of organizations and the practice of management. A psychoanalytically informed perspective can help us understand the hidden dynamics associated with individual motivation, leadership, interpersonal relationships, collusive situations, social defenses, corporate culture, 'neurotic' organizations (that is, organizations dominated by the particular neurosis of the top executive), and the extent to which individuals and organizations can be prisoners of their past (Zaleznik, 1966; Levinson, 1972; DeBoard, 1978; Kets de Vries, 1984; Kets de Vries and Miller, 1984; Kets de Vries, 1991; Czander, 1993; Kets de Vries, 1994; Gabriel, 1999; Levinson, 2002). Advocates of the clinical psychodynamic approach recognize the limits of rationality and reject a purely economist, behaviorist view of the world of work. Behavioral and statistical data-gathering experiments can make only a partial contribution to the understanding of complex organizational phenomena, though advocates of management as a natural science would like to believe differently. An additional dimension of analysis is needed to comprehend organizational behavior and the people working in the system. We have to factor in the directly observable.

Scholars of management need to recognize that organizations as systems have their own life—a life that is not only conscious but also unconscious, not only rational but also irrational. The application of the clinical paradigm[1] is helpful in providing insight into that life, into the underlying reasons for executive (and employee) behavior and actions. To understand the whole picture, we need to pay attention to the presenting internal and social dynamics, to the intricate playing field between leaders and followers, and to the various unconscious and invisible psychodynamic processes and structures that influence the behavior of individuals, dyads, and groups in organizations. People who dismiss the complex clinical dimension in organizational analysis cannot hope to go beyond a relatively impoverished, shallow understanding of life in organizations. In business as in individual life, psychological awareness is the first step toward psychological health. Organizations cannot perform successfully if the quirks and irrational processes that are part and parcel of the organizational participants' inner theater are not taken into consideration by top management.

[1] See Chapter 9 for an explanation of the clinical paradigm.

THE GROUP CONUNDRUM

A study of organizations necessarily addresses the psychology of groups. The psychiatrist Wilfred Bion identified three basic assumptions to be studied in group situations, a trio that has become a cornerstone of the study of organizational dynamics (Bion, 1959). These basic assumptions— which take place at an unconscious level—create a group dynamic that makes it much harder for people to work together productively. They deflect people from the principal tasks that have to be performed in the organization, because they result in pathological regressive processes that lead to more archaic (that is, primitive) patterns of functioning. Freed from the constraints of conventional thinking, groups subject to such regressive processes retreat into a world of their own. The result is often delusional ideation—in other words, ideas completely detached from reality—which is fertile soil for the proliferation of rigid ideological patterns of decision-making.

Basic group assumptions

Let's look at each of Bion's three assumptions: dependency, fight–flight, and pairing.

Dependency   People often assume, at an unconscious level, that the leader or organization can and should offer protection and guidance similar to that offered in earlier years by parents. Groups subject to the *dependency assumption* are looking for a strong, charismatic leader to lead the way. The members of such groups are united by common feelings of helplessness, inadequacy, neediness, and fear of the outside world. They perceive the leader as omnipotent and readily give up their autonomy when they perceive help at hand. Remarks typical of groups subject to this process include, 'What do you want me/us to do?' and 'I can't take this kind of decision; you'll have to talk to my boss.' Such comments reflect the employees' anxiety, insecurity, and professional and emotional immaturity. While unquestioning faith in a leader contributes to goal-directedness and cohesiveness, it also impairs followers' critical judgment and leaves them unwilling to take initiative. Although they are willing to carry out their leader's directives, they require the leader to take all the initiative, do all the thinking, and be the major catalyst. And once a leader on whom followers leaned heavily is gone, bureaucratic inertia may take hold. People may be frozen in the past, wondering what their leader would have done, if still around.

Fight–flight   Another common unconscious assumption is that the organizational world is a dangerous place and organizational participants must use fight or flight as defense mechanisms. In groups subject to the fight–flight assumption, an outlook of avoidance or attack predominates. When the fight–flight mechanism takes hold, there is a tendency to split the world into camps of friends and enemies. Fight reactions manifest themselves in aggression against the self, peers (in the form of envy, jealousy, competition, elimination, boycotting, sibling rivalry, fighting for a position in the group, and privileged relationships with authority figures), or authority itself. Flight reactions include avoidance of others, absenteeism, and resignation in the sense of giving up. Remarks typical of people in a fight–flight situation include, 'Let's not give those updated figures to the contracts department; they'll just try to take all the credit,' and 'This company would be in good shape if it weren't for the so-and-sos who run the place.' Us-versus-them language is common. Taking personal responsibility for problems is unheard of; instead, blame is routinely (and vindictively) assigned elsewhere. Subscribing to a rigid, bipolar view of the world, these groups possess a strong desire for protection from and conquest of 'the enemy,' in all its varied manifestations.

Because conspiracies and enemies already populate their inner world, leaders who fall victim to the fight–flight assumption encourage the group tendency toward splitting. Externalizing their internal problems, they inflame their followers against real and/or imagined enemies, using the in-group/out-group division to motivate people and to channel emerging anxiety outward. The shared search for and fight against enemies results in a strong (but rigid) conviction among participants of the correctness and righteousness of their cause, and it energizes them to pursue that cause. It also enforces the group's identity (Lasswell, 1960; Volcan, 1988). Leaders who encourage fight–flight mechanisms by radiating certainty and conviction create meaning for followers who feel lost. The resulting sense of unity is highly reassuring. As followers eliminate doubters and applaud converts, they become increasingly dependent on their leader.

Pairing   Bion's third unconscious assumption is that pairing up with a person or group perceived as powerful will help an individual cope with anxiety, alienation, and loneliness. Wanting to feel secure but also to be creative, people experiencing the pairing assumption fantasize that the most effective creation will take place in groups or pairs. Unfortunately, pairing also implies splitting up. The inevitable diversity within groups may result in intra- and inter-group conflict, which in turn may prompt individuals or groups to split up the group and build a smaller system— one in which an individual can belong and feel secure. This assumption also manifests itself in ganging up against the perceived aggressor or authority figure. In the pairing mode, often seen in high-tech companies, grandiose, unrealistic ideas about innovation may become more important than practicality and profitability. Remarks typical within an organization subject to the pairing assumption include, 'Leave it to the two of us, we can solve this problem,' and 'If only the CEO and COO had a better relationship our company would be in really good shape.'

Group development

We can often see a sequential movement in the development of groups. Frequently, groups move from a dependency stage, where the members of the group look for the leader to give them guidance, to fight–flight, where the group members start to resist the leader's direction in various ways; to pairing, a stage where there will be a substantial increase in group cohesiveness. If these basic assumptions have been dealt with in one way or another, there will be a greater possibility that the group will engage in real work.

Basic social defenses

The basic assumptions discussed above all reveal underlying anxiety about the world and one's place in it. When these assumptions prevail in the workplace, they offer strong proof that the organization's leadership is not dealing adequately with the emerging anxiety of working in a social setting (Menzies, 1960; Jaques, 1974). When the level of anxiety rises in an organization, executives typically rely on existing structures (rules, regulations, procedures, organization charts, job descriptions, and organization-specific ways of solving problems) to contain that anxiety. When those structures offer insufficient containment—that is, when there are no opportunities to discuss and work through emerging concerns—people in organizations engage in regressive defenses, such as splitting, projection, displacement, denial, and other defensive routines.

When such defenses are adopted organization-wide, we call them social defenses. They can be viewed as new structures, new systems of relationships within the social structure, constructed to help people deal with anxiety. The purpose of social defenses is to transform and neutralize strong tensions and affects such as anxiety, shame, guilt, envy, jealousy, rage, sexual frustration, and low self-esteem. They function like individual defenses but are woven into the fabric of an organization in an effort to assure organizational participants that the workplace is really safe and accepting. When these ways of dealing with the angst and unpredictability of life in organizations become the dominant mode of operation (rather than an occasional stopgap measure), they become dysfunctional for the organization as a whole. They may still serve a purpose (albeit not necessarily a constructive one), but they have become bureaucratic obstacles. These bureaucratic routines and pseudo-rational activities gradually obscure personal and organizational realities, allowing people to detach themselves from their inner experience. Task forces, administrative procedures, rationalization, intellectualization, and other structures and processes are used to keep people emotionally uninvolved and to help them feel safe and in control. While these processes do in fact reduce anxiety—the original goal—they also replace compassion, empathy, awareness, and meaning with control and impersonality.

Neurotic organizations

Like every person, every organization has a history. The repetition of certain phenomena in a given workplace suggests the existence of specific motivational configurations. Just as symptoms and dreams can be viewed as signs with meaning, so can specific organizational statements and decisions. Organizations, as embodied in those statements and decisions, tend to reflect the personalities of their leaders, particularly when power is highly concentrated (Kets de Vries and Miller, 1984; Kets de Vries and Miller, 1988). Thus exemplary leaders help their companies become highly effective organizations, while dysfunctional leaders contribute to organizational neurosis. Whether healthy or neurotic, they externalize and act out their inner theater on the public stage of the organization, their inner dramas developing into corporate cultures, structures, and patterns of decision-making. I deal with these neurotic cultures in Chapter 4.

In an organization that is struggling, an analysis of the prevailing neurotic organizational culture may help executives figure out why the organization continues to perpetuate various behaviors and why personnel continue to demonstrate resistance or acceptance patterns. Identifying the prevailing neurotic culture can also help executives understand otherwise incomprehensible behavior and actions on the part of their colleagues.

An understanding of the prevailing organizational neurotic culture may help to shape expectations of what needs to be done, and what can be done. It may also help answer bothersome questions such as 'Why does X keep happening?' and 'Why does something that works someplace else not work here?' The recognition of neurotic organizational cultures—rooted as they are in history and personality—also helps executives realize that change will be slow and difficult.

ORGANIZATIONAL INTERVENTION: BEYOND BRAINS ON A STICK

Organizational intervention to foster individual and system-wide change is part and parcel of life in organizations. Unfortunately, many people dedicated to change—change agents and consultants, for example—are inclined to focus on the symptoms and not on the underlying causes. More often than not, they deal only with surface behavior. Such consultants are very talented at number-crunching—they are like brains on a stick when it comes to cold facts—but not very good at paying attention to the elusive signals that reveal the heartbeat of an organization. Too often, their slogan is, 'What cannot be directly seen doesn't really exist.' Thus they resort to oversimplified quick fixes in trying to institute change (Levinson, 2002).

When change agents want to change particular behaviors in an individual (or cluster of individuals), their usual impulse is to put a simplistic behavioral modification program into place. Such a program may have a positive effect, to be sure—but that effect will not last long. Making that sort of an intervention is like trying to change the weather by turning up the heating system inside your house. It may keep the inhabitants warmer for a time, but it will not change the temperature outside.

That is not to say that traditional management change agents and consultants cannot be helpful. In many specific areas their specialized expertise is invaluable. However, when it comes to more general problem solving in people-intensive situations, it is clinically informed consultants who are needed. A clinically informed intervention is designed to address the complexity of human behavior that exists in organizations, and goes beyond the more simplistic, reductionistic formulae that characterize traditional consulting methods.

Focal areas of intervention

As any executive knows, the cost of poor leadership, ineffectual management teams, mistaken hiring decisions, corporate culture clashes, and inadequate succession planning is steep (though not precisely calculable). Likewise, the cost of a large-scale traditional management consultancy effort is high—and that cost is wasted when such an effort is directed at problems that are in essence psychological. When organizational problems are centered on interpersonal communication, group processes, social defenses, uneven leadership, and organization-wide neurosis, money is better spent on the three-dimensional approach to organizational assessment and intervention that clinically informed consultants or change agents employ. Consultants well versed in the clinical paradigm understand the levers that drive individual and organizational change, and they know just how complex the change process is. Furthermore, they know how to help bring about the necessary relinquishing of defenses, encourage the expression of emotions in a situation-appropriate manner, and cultivate a perception of self and others that is in accord with reality (McCullough Vaillant, 1997; Kets de Vries, 2002). They also recognize that if system-wide change is going to happen, they need to highlight the 'pain' in the system, link past to present through a new vision, help the key players buy into the change effort, and reconfigure systems, structures, cultural elements, and behavior patterns. They know how to help an organization's leadership create a shared mindset, build attitudes that contribute to changed behavior, train for a new set of competencies, create small wins leading to improved performance, and set up appropriate reward systems for people who support the intended changes.

Typical areas where the clinically informed consultant can make a contribution include:

- identifying and changing dysfunctional leadership styles;
- resolving interpersonal conflict, intergroup conflict, and various forms of collusive relationship (folie à deux);
- disentangling social defenses;
- bringing neurotic organizations back to health;
- planning for more orderly leadership succession;
- untangling knotty family business problems;
- helping create a better work–life balance for leaders and subordinates.

Clinically informed consultants use the ways members of the organization interact with them as a crucial source of data. What differentiates these consultants from their more traditional counterparts is their skill at using transferential and countertransferential manifestations as a basic experiential and diagnostic tool. The ever-present 'triangle of relationships'— comprised in this case of the person being interviewed, some significant past 'other' from that person's life, and the change agent/consultant— provides a conceptual structure for assessing patterns of response and then pointing out the similarity of past relationships to what is going on in the present. Anyone hoping to make sense of interpersonal encounters at anything but an intuitive level needs to understand these transferential processes, which are a major part of the consultant's change toolbox (Kets de Vries, 2002).

Clinically informed consultants also recognize the importance of projective identification. A psychological defense against unwanted feelings or fantasies, projective identification is a mode of communication as well as a type of human relationship (Ogden, 1982). We can see this process in action when covert dynamics among individuals or groups of individuals get played out in parallel form by other individuals or groups with which they interact. For example, if executives in a department deny or reject (and thus alter) an uncomfortable experience by imagining that it belongs to another group of executives, that latter group—the recipients of the projection—are inducted into the situation by subtle pressure from the first group to think, feel, and act in congruence with the received projection.

Paying attention to transference, countertransference, projection, and projective identification, clinically informed consultants process their observations, looking for thematic unity (Kets de Vries and Miller, 1987). They then employ pattern matching, looking for structural parallels within multi-layered relationships and between current events and earlier incidents (knowing that any aspect of the organizational 'text' can have more than one meaning and can be viewed from a number of different perspectives). Creating meaning at multiple levels helps the consultants determine the individual and organizational roots and consequences of actions and decisions. When the link between present relationships and the distant past is made meaningful to people at all levels of the organization, the process of large-scale change is more likely to be successful.

Given their orientation, clinically informed consultants and change agents also recognize the presence of complex resistances (ranging from denial, to lack of access, to firing the messenger). Since the aim of a clinical intervention is not just symptom suppression—not merely a 'flight into health'—but durable, sustainable change, clinical consultants must always be attentive to hidden agendas. They appreciate that manifest, stated problems often cover up issues that are far more complex. They know that there is usually a very good reason why their particular expertise was asked for (even though that reason may not have been, and perhaps cannot be, articulated by the client), and they attempt, for the sake of a successful intervention, to identify that reason quickly. In addition to identifying and addressing the organization's core psychological concerns, clinically informed consultants strive to instill in the organization's leadership an interest in and understanding of their own behavior. Ideally, those leaders can internalize the ability to learn and work in the psychological realm, allowing them to address future issues without the help of a consultant.

A case example

One type of intervention in which a clinically informed consultant can add value is illustrated in the following case study of a telecommunications company. Although the request for consultation came directly from the CEO, a man in his fifties named John, it later turned out that he had been strongly encouraged to visit the consultant by the non-executive chairman of his board. After the initial interview, conducted in the CEO's office, the consultant suggested doing a leadership audit of the top executive team, to be followed (eventually) by a top executive team development workshop to improve the performance of the organization.

From the discussions that the consultant had with executives at various layers in the organization, as well as with non-executive members of the board, it appeared that although the majority of the interviewees appreciated John's talent at foreseeing developments in the marketplace, his behavior had aroused a great deal of irritation. A number of executives accused him of having a short fuse and expressed concern over his outbursts of irritation; they felt that he was far too prepared for a fight, even when circumstances called for conciliation. Furthermore, some of the interviewees who had worked closely with him noted that he often resorted to 'mushroom treatment,' springing surprises on them—projects that he had been nurturing in the dark. Very few of his senior people felt that they were kept adequately informed of his decisions, and they did not feel that they themselves were given the information and resources to make informed decisions. Some noted that the CEO's uncommunicative style now permeated the organization, with information-hoarding a preferred mode of operation. There were objections, too, that the company seemed to be operating in fight-or-flight mode. Furthermore, a certain amount of fiefdom formation was noticeable, and trust was becoming an increasingly scarce commodity. Some executives observed that the company's competitive position was deteriorating. Moreover, several of their more capable colleagues had left for greener pastures, leaving the company with no obvious successor. One of the non-executive directors insinuated to the consultant that he and a number of the other directors were thinking of contacting a headhunter to explore the possibility of replacing John.

At a relaxed moment over dinner one night, as the consultant probed the CEO about his background, John explained that he came from a divorced family. But, departing from his usual reserve, he didn't end the conversation there. (The consultant attributed the executive's unusual openness to the latter's awareness of the urgency of the situation.) John reported that after the divorce, his mother had quickly remarried, and from that marriage had come one much younger half-brother and half-sister. Encouraged by the consultant, John explained that he'd had a terrible relationship with his stepfather, who sometimes resorted to physical violence to discipline the youngster. John still, decades later, resented the fact that his mother, apparently insecure in her relationship with her new husband, had always taken her husband's side in any dispute between the man and the boy. That strained parental relationship seemed to have left a legacy of humiliation and anger.

It became clear from the conversation that John's lack of trust and prickly temper originated in a family constellation that had been unpredictable and hostile. From the time he was a young child, his circumstances had been harsh and lonely, engendering mistrust and necessitating constant vigilance. Having learned early the need to be on guard, he retained his constant state of alertness into adulthood. He felt he needed to be ready for a fight at any time. That core conflictual relationship theme shaped the script of his inner theater and dictated his interactions with the world. But while vigilance and aggression may have been effective ways of coping with difficult circumstances as a child, they were dysfunctional in John's role as CEO. Now that the real threat—the threat of the unpredictable stepfather that he carried with him from childhood—could no longer be addressed, John substituted various external threats instead, taking preemptive action whenever he could in order to gain a modicum of control. Given that inner script, it is not surprising that John was secretive with colleagues and was constantly waging war against perceived enemies (his latest fight being with two of his non-executive directors). It was clear from the various discussions the consultant had with colleagues that John's position as CEO was threatened. If he continued on the same path, he had a good chance of being fired.

With the information gleaned from his many interviews, the consultant was now in a position to explore with John some of the connections between his past and present behavior. The consultant heeded the counsel given by many therapists to 'strike when the iron is cold'—in other words, to intervene when the person is prepared to hear unpleasant information without engaging in defensive maneuvers. After a number of discussions with the consultant, John began to recognize his own responsibility for the mess he had created and no longer blamed all his problems on others. That realization made him take the initiative to reach out to the people he had previously considered his enemies. He made a valiant effort to be a better communicator as well, though he recognized, especially after the revelations of the consultation, that his personality was never going to allow him to be the 'welcome wagon' of the world. He now saw the wisdom of building on his strengths and finding others to compensate for his weaknesses. Realizing that there were too many people in the organization who (by design or indoctrination) were likewise poor communicators, John hired a new vice president of human resources. That single step went a long way toward making the company more transparent. John's efforts to change, with the support and encouragement of the consultant, created a significant improvement as well, allowing him to mend his relationship with various members of the board. Able to appreciate his talent as a strategist and turnaround artist once he had become less prickly and more open, the board discontinued its search for a replacement CEO. With greater emotional stability in the organization, the consultant decided that a top executive team development workshop would be next on the agenda, helping the executives to build trust, commitment, and accountability, and to become more effective in constructive conflict resolution.

What the example of John shows us is how a person can harm both himself and his organization, not through conscious malice or lack of talent but through ignorance of his own inner theater and slavery to psychological patterns of which he is unaware. By addressing these issues— by making conscious what had been unconscious and then working to address leadership behavior patterns that were determined to be dysfunctional—the consultant and CEO together were able to disable prevailing social defenses and heal organizational neurosis.

CREATING HEALTHY ORGANIZATIONS

The challenge for twenty-first-century leadership is to create healthy organizations. The first major step toward this is for management to acknowledge and find ways to accommodate the complexities of human behavior. It is highly unlikely that they can do this spontaneously or alone. In this chapter, I have argued that the dynamics of group psychology and the interplay of personal neuroses call for recognition and clinical appraisal. Interventions using the psychodynamic approach will help organizations get to the root of dysfunctionalities; iterate relationships and interactions; identify problem areas; and forestall the development of organizational pathologies.

The best organizations create environments that offer an antidote to stress, provide a healthier existence, expand the imagination, and contribute to a more fulfilling life. These organizations can be easily recognized:

employees maintain a healthy balance between personal and organizational life; employees are offered—and gladly take—time for self-examination; and employees aren't merely 'running,' but want to know what they are running for and where they are running to—in other words, they constantly question themselves and others about individual and corporate actions and decisions. Recognizing that minds are like parachutes—they function only when they are open—these organizations equip their people to think, and then encourage that revolutionary action. With these impressive characteristics, these organizations will be the winners in tomorrow's marketplace, able to deal with the continuous and discontinuous change that the new global economy demands. I call these authentizotic organizations—and I will be saying a lot more about them in the Conclusion of this book.

CHAPTER 3

HIGH PERFORMANCE TEAMS: LESSONS FROM THE PYGMIES[1]

What is not good for the beehive cannot be good for the bees.
—Marcus Aurelius, *Meditations*

Tell me the company you keep, and I'll tell you who you are.
—Miguel de Cervantes, *Don Quixote*

You don't lead people by hitting them over the head; that's assault, that's not leadership.

—Dwight Eisenhower

What is a committee? A group of the unwilling, picked from the unfit, to do the unnecessary.

—Richard Harkness

Most readers are probably familiar with the label 'pygmy,' an anthropological term referring to various populations inhabiting central Africa, whose adult males average less than 1.5 meters in height. The Greek word *'pygme'* represents the length between a person's elbow and knuckles, a measurement applied descriptively to this group of unusually small people. The pygmies are thought to be among the earliest inhabitants of the African continent and are probably the oldest human dwellers of the rain forest. The pygmy culture has existed since prehistoric times, and there is a great deal we can learn from it. It is a window on our past, a primary model of human behavior, giving us a glimpse of the way people behaved before the rise of agriculture some 10 000 years ago. Already in ancient Egyptian history, some 2300 years BCE, the existence of the pygmies was noted in the record of an expedition looking for the source of the Nile.

[1] Much of the material in this chapter is based on the article: Kets de Vries, M.F.R. (1999) 'High Performance Teams: Lessons from the Pygmies', *Organizational Dynamics*, 27(3) pp. 66–77.

A message sent to Pharaoh Phiops II of the 6th Dynasty by Prince Herkhuf of Elephantine, the expedition commander, described the discovery of 'dancing dwarfs from the land of the spirits' (Siy, 1993, p. 16). Reference to the existence of the pygmies can also be found in Homer's description of a battle between Greek and Trojan forces in the *Iliad*. According to a description in his *Historia Animalium*, Aristotle was also aware of the existence of pygmies living in the land where the Nile rises.

Unfortunately, humankind's knowledge of the pygmies advanced only slowly from these early reports. Over the centuries, increasingly fictitious depictions turned the pygmies into a mythical tribe. Early Arab traders, for example, told stories about dwarfs who jumped at them from underground, killing the unfortunate with poisoned arrows. Tall tales about the pygmies continued well into the nineteenth century. Most of these stories, however, recent as well as ancient, were clearly figments of the imagination, fanciful, extravagant descriptions far removed from reality. (Consider, for example, stories in which pygmies were depicted as subhuman monsters who, like monkeys, flew about in treetops using their tails.) In short, the pygmies remained a people of mystery.

Starting with the explorers of the Congo at the end of the nineteenth century, a more realistic picture of the pygmies emerged. In 1870 the German explorer George Schweinfurth rediscovered the pygmies about 4000 years after Prince Herkhuf's first encounter. Shortly afterward, the British journalist Henry Morton Stanley, reporting for the *New York Herald* about his adventures in central Africa, mentioned the existence of the forest pygmies. Gradually, through the writings of various explorers, more was learned about the pygmies' semi-nomadic hunter-gatherer existence. Those who observed the pygmies reported accurately about their ability to survive in a harsh forest environment by hunting game and gathering honey, fruits, nuts, roots, plants, and certain insects, and trading with nearby villagers for vegetables, tobacco, metal, tools, and cloth (Hallet, 1973; Bailey, 1989; Bahuchet, 1991).

Pygmies are now defined as a number of tribes scattered among the rain forests of central Africa in small, temporary settlements. Although the basic unit is the nuclear family (that is, mother, father, and their children), several extended families generally make up a camp numbering from 10 to 35 people. Each nuclear family builds its own dome-shaped hut; these are then placed in a circle around a common area (Duffy, 1984).

Life in a pygmy camp is lived mostly outside. There is very little privacy in the camp; pygmies are rarely alone. Eating, drinking, bathing, and sexual intercourse take place in close proximity, necessitating considerable sharing and tolerance. Empathy and cooperation are therefore important qualities of pygmy society.

Pygmies have no written language. Their history and knowledge are preserved in an oral tradition. Their detailed knowledge of the rain forest ecosystem is kept alive in the minds of the people and passed on verbally from generation to generation. Pygmies also possess a rather enlightened moral code, one that was in place long before missionaries tried to impose their world view on them. Included in that code are injunctions against killing, adultery, lying, theft, blasphemy, devil worship and sorcery, lack of love for children, disrespect for elders, and other forms of misbehavior. It is not surprising, then, that the pygmies, in contrast to many other tribes in their region, have never indulged in cannibalism, human sacrifice, mutilation, sorcery, ritual murder, intertribal war, debilitating initiation ordeals, and other cruel customs (Hallet, 1973).

The twentieth century was not good to the pygmies. Encroaching civilization has taken its toll as other population groups have pushed them out of an ever-shrinking habitat. A low birth rate, high infant mortality rate, and extensive intertribal breeding with invading non-pygmy peoples have added to their decline. Furthermore, missionaries and government officials have been settling the pygmies in permanent villages, forcing them to abandon the life that their people have lived for thousands of years. Because the pygmies' entire upbringing and culture are geared toward a nomadic forest existence, becoming sedentary has often led to moral and physical disintegration. There are very few pygmies left who still live in their original state, and at the pace things are going, their world will soon be gone forever.

I have spent some time among the Baka pygmies in the rain forest of Cameroon. As my guides in the jungle, they taught me some of the basics of jungle lore. It was with considerable awe that I observed their knowledge of the forest, their ability to read the signs made by different animals, and their expertise with respect to edible mushrooms, fruits, tobacco, and vegetables. What to the untrained eye would have no significance was full of meaning for the pygmies.

From the first day of my stay, it was clear that to the pygmies the forest is the main source of well-being; it is the center of their existence. For an outsider, however, the forest can be frightening, particularly when thunder and lightning conspire with rain to turn small streams into raging torrents and topple heavy branches or even whole trees. Drama of that sort makes you feel small and insignificant; it is a very intimidating experience. But for the pygmies, the forest remains a source of beauty and goodness despite its potential for harm; the forest is the great provider.

I was intrigued by the relationships I observed among the pygmies in a variety of contexts. I saw them operating as a hunting team, I watched their dances, I listened to their songs. I was struck, in all their interactions, by the degree of mutual respect and trust they showed toward each other. I also noted that they seemed to be a generally happy group of people. Their outlook toward the world appeared to be very positive, perhaps because trust is a core characteristic.

THE IMPORTANCE OF BASIC TRUST

As we attempt to understand this positive outlook toward the world, we need to remember that the anchor point for basic trust is the primal relationship with our initial caregivers (Erikson, 1963). Because of the influence child development has on later behavior, adult attitudes are a giveaway of the kind of early relationships people experienced. As child development studies have shown, primary interaction patterns color all later experiences; our original ways of dealing with caregivers remain the model for all future relationships. Thus the earliest social experimentation of children toward the people close to them leads to a lasting ratio of trust versus mistrust and creates a sense of mutuality (a reciprocity that, as we depend on each other in the development of our respective strengths, determines our later *Weltanschauung*). In consequence, children brought up in a caring environment can be expected to feel safe and secure as adults.

Trustworthy parental figures who respond to the needs of children with warm and calming envelopment make for a positive world image. Pygmy society seems to be full of this kind of adult. As an example of their caring environment, everyone in the same age group as their parents is called 'mother' or 'father,' while the older adults are called 'grandparents.' As far as pygmy children are concerned, all adults are their parents and grandparents. Given the nature of pygmy society, there is always someone around to take care of children's needs; children are rarely without physical contact. Fathers are actively involved in the direct care of their infants. In fact, they engage in more infant care–giving than fathers in any other known society. They spend almost 50% of their day holding or within arm's reach of their children (Hewlett, 1991). Child neglect and abuse are almost unknown in pygmy society; cruelty to children is the most serious violation covered by pygmy laws and commandments. No wonder pygmies have such a positive, trusting way of relating to each other. We can also hypothesize that the pygmies' deeply anchored sense of independence and autonomy is a consequence of their early exposure to their parents' egalitarian role in the family model.

This positive attitude toward the world, these feelings of independence, and this sense of basic trust are reflected in the pygmies' attitude toward the forest. Their strong faith in the goodness of the forest is probably best expressed through their great *molimo* songs. When pygmies have something to celebrate, or are upset about something, they sing. They simply cannot do without dancing, singing, and making music. They believe that this form of emotional expression awakens the forest, and in time makes everything right again.

Molimo is a song-based ritual performed nightly by the men. In the *molimo*, also called 'the animal of the forest,' participants make believe that the sounds they produce are made by an animal dancing around the camp. The same word, *molimo*, is used for the long, trumpet-like instrument that plays an important part in the ritual. The *molimo* is called for whenever things seem to be going wrong, especially in times of crisis: the hunting is bad, somebody is ill, or someone has died. By calling out the *molimo,* the pygmies initiate the process of making things good again.

PYGMY SOCIETY AS A METAPHOR FOR EFFECTIVE TEAMWORK

Although the pygmies are not necessarily better than more 'civilized' people, there is something fascinating about the relationships among these relatively simple people, and the relationship they enjoy with the forest. The intensity with which they live and the joy they feel despite their hardships, problems, and tragedies are worth studying in greater depth. Could it be that their simple wisdom and the good nature reflected in their human relationships hold a lesson for humankind in our postindustrial society? When I first read of the pygmy way of life, I became curious to learn more about their ancient, primordial culture, their ways of doing things. I also wondered whether their effectiveness in operating as a team—an effectiveness that I later experienced in my personal dealings with them—could teach us something about operating in small groups in the workplace.

This issue is very topical, since most work in organizations is done in small groups or teams. The capability for effective teamwork is essential to success in the global village, with its rapid changes in product and market conditions, and to success in the postindustrial organization, with its focus on networking and its need for a cross-functional process orientation. Organizations that know how to use teams effectively can get extraordinary performances from their people, while companies that lack that knowledge encourage mediocrity. Thus it will not come as a surprise that effective teamwork has been identified as one of the core values in high-performance organizations. Companies that continue to perform successfully have cultures where teamwork occupies a central position.

Referring to teamwork, the terms quality, respect for the individual, and customer orientation can be heard in most organizations, but too often this is merely lip-service or quickly turns into cliché. What does teamwork mean? It is easy and popular to claim to want to be a team-oriented company; actually implementing that intention, however, is extremely difficult. Many of the companies I have studied have a long way to go before they reach a genuine team orientation. The pygmies, however, as described in the seminal work of Colin Turnbull and other anthropologists (and as I observed myself), seem to make teamwork happen (Turnbull, 1961, 1965). Their approach to teamwork makes them less susceptible than most corporate teams to the processes that corrode group efforts. Many of their practices are models for effective human behavior.

WHAT DESTROYS TEAMWORK?

Many factors can hamper successful teamwork. If we identify those factors, perhaps we can find ways to counter them in the workplace. In the following cry for help, a senior executive in a new biotechnology company talks about the situation in his organization. In his description, we can identify many of the factors that hamper successful teamwork—factors that in his case have led to a climate of mistrust and a dangerous decline in innovation and production.

> In this company we lack an overarching, solid framework. The signals given from the top executive team are very confusing. There just isn't enough clear direction coming from these people. Looking at it from my perspective, it seems as if our top team doesn't share any common values or goals. This has a terrible effect on the rest of the organization.
>
> Because we get no clear signals from the top group, we end up with distracting political battles. Turf fights are the norm. Since there's no clear mandate from the top, a few people want to control everything. This obviously discourages frank, open communication and sharing of information. I don't think people trust or respect each other. Everybody seems to be looking out for themselves, making sure they look good at their colleagues' expense. It makes you feel quite alone. That's been my experience anyway. I know I can't expect much support from others. I have to make things happen on my own.
>
> The rot in the top team has trickled down; there are many other work teams that are going nowhere. It makes life in this place very chaotic. Look

at the lack of discipline: there's no accountability, so people do what they want. And the results are very disturbing. We're hemorrhaging money. We miss deadline after deadline. In the meantime, our competitors aren't sitting on their hands waiting for us to solve our problems. We're in an industry where innovation is essential. If we don't keep ahead of the competition, we could very quickly lose our market share. Our competitors are probably delighted with our situation. I don't know how long we can go on like this.

In my opinion, it all has to do with leadership. Our new CEO means well, but in his desire to create a participatory ambiance, he abdicates responsibility. He seems unable to set clear boundaries and to communicate priorities. Decisions that need to be made aren't made. And even when decisions are made, they aren't adhered to. As I said, there's a lack of accountability. I know what I'm talking about. I've been present at some of the meetings of the top team. And I can tell you, being there takes a lot of energy. As these meetings drag on, some of these people can't do anything but argue. Their personal agendas often overshadow very exciting business ideas. In the end, it takes too much effort to contradict them; a lot of us end up just going along with what they say. We want the meeting to end; we want to have it over with. I'm sure some of our institutional investors will start screaming for changes before long.

This senior executive raises issues that occur frequently in organizations that have trouble developing effective work teams: conflict, power hoarding, status differences, self-censorship, and groupthink.

Conflict

One of the most obvious team destroyers is conflict, whether covert or overt and unresolved. Although occasional tension is inevitable in teams, by virtue of their nature as collective phenomena, conflict has to be brought out and addressed. When conflict is left unresolved, hidden agendas take over, detracting from the real work at hand. Even a discussion that seems to be centered on substantial issues may, at a deeper level, concern issues of power, prestige, and other personal needs. The fact that lack of trust between team members is often the catalyst for conflict-concealing dysfunctional behavior makes the problem especially insidious, because the cure is all but out of reach: in the absence of at least a minimal level of trust, constructive conflict resolution is a daunting task. In the meantime, crucial decisions are tabled and deadlines are missed; meetings flounder, sometimes degenerating into rituals whereby everyone assumes a fixed position and plays a stereotyped role. When team members are merely going through the motions, constructive and creative ideas are stifled.

Power hoarding

Another common weakness of teams is their susceptibility to control at the hands of specific individuals or small coalitions. Power hoarding has two primary negative consequences: to those in power, winning may become more important than constructive problem solving; while to those lacking power, participation may seem futile. Those in the latter category, who are generally the majority, take on the role of silent bystanders, keeping their real opinions to themselves and limiting their involvement. Convinced that they are not being heard, they stop putting their opinions forward and simply give up. As a consequence of this dysfunctional behavior, agreements may be realized prematurely, mediocre compromises may be reached, and courses of action contrary to what each team member envisioned may be chosen. Any team members who do not feel committed to the resulting action plan may resort to tacit subversion, insubordination, and even outright sabotage. This is a group that probably includes all members who did not contribute or whose contributions were ignored.

Status differences

This kind of self-limiting behavior may be exacerbated if one or more team members are perceived as having special expertise, as being especially qualified to take decisions about the issues on the table. In addition to this respect-conferred status, status differences due to position may confound teamwork: lower-status members may doubt their ability to contribute. Hidden agendas may also play a role. As an example, lower-status team members may be more concerned with making a favorable impression on senior team members than with solving problems.

Self-censorship

Members of the team who believe that they are the odd one out may opt to keep their opinions to themselves. They may keep quiet in group deliberations and avoid issues that are likely to upset the group, a lack of action they may come to regret later on. Because people assume that those who remain silent are in agreement, self-censorship often leads to an illusion of unanimity among the members of the group—a sort of pseudo-consensus. Sometimes self-censorship also turns into censorship of others: those who feel the need to protect the team leader and/or other key members of the team from information that might shake the complacency of the group put 'mind guards' in place.

Groupthink

In this context, the phenomenon of groupthink, the pressure to conform without taking seriously the consequences of one's actions, should be mentioned (Janis, 1972). Team members suffering from groupthink may intimidate members who express opinions contrary to the consensus, creating enormous pressure to conform, to submit to the party line, and avoid rocking the boat. People who verbalize their disagreement may be labeled obstructionists. If team members succumb to this overwhelming drive for consensus and compromise, dysfunctional group dynamics sway the decision-making process and inhibit the potential for healthy dissension and criticism. This is dangerous not only because of the bad decisions that may result. Groupthink also leads to an absence of individual responsibility: those who wanted to dissent but felt pressured to keep quiet feel no responsibility for team decisions and consequently behave less carefully than they would otherwise do.

In situations of groupthink, team members may also develop the illusion of invulnerability, the perception that there is safety in numbers. The consequence may be excessive risk taking, manifested in the failure to regard the obvious dangers of any chosen course of action. Team members may collectively construct rationalizations that discount warnings or other sources of information that run contrary to their thinking; they may discount sources of negative information in their group deliberations. Stereotyped perceptions of other people or groups may come to the fore, clouding the group's judgment and blocking possible relationships with the colleagues in question.

All these factors can and do stifle the efficacy of successful teamwork; they turn teamwork into a waste of time and energy, and they dissipate synergy. Whatever the objectives of a team ruled by these factors, the outcome will be disappointing.

INTO THE HEART OF AFRICA: EFFECTIVE TEAMWORK

In light of all the things that can go wrong in teamwork, we must ask ourselves how we can avoid the pitfalls. What are some of the qualities of successful teams? What makes for effective teamwork? More specifically, in this case, what do the pygmies do to make teamwork happen? Are there lessons to be learned from pygmy society that are relevant for organizations in our postindustrial age?

Lesson 1: members respect and trust each other

Among the pygmies, given the potential hardships of the forest, there is a great dependence on one another. Merely staying alive can be a challenge; simple things that we take for granted can be major burdens. Food is not always plentiful, for example, and hunting can be dangerous. After all, the forest is inhabited by vicious red buffaloes, short-tempered forest elephants, swift-footed leopards, deadly snakes, and frightening army ants. These dangers have to be dealt with on an almost daily basis. Trust and mutual dependency play an important role in overcoming such threats, because without trust the hazard of these existing dangers would be magnified. Trust is an essential factor for survival in the pygmy community. Each person needs to be able to count on every other team member. This mutuality and trust anchor the pygmies' hunter-gatherer society and allow it to function. Whatever the context—rain forest or western workplace— when there is trust many other things fall into place. Trust is an antidote to a proliferation of rules and regulations.

Pygmy society is a good example of how trust can simplify and expedite decision-making processes. Although to outsiders life in a pygmy community may be striking in its simplicity and apparent lack of organization, it is underpinned by a complex trust-based system; the informal rules that make up this system help the community function effectively. While an excess of rules and regulations (and massive paperwork) is a good indicator of trust disorder and paranoid thinking, a high degree of trust allows the informal organization to dominate the formal one. In other words, implicit rules become more important than explicit rules.

Trust also implies respect for the other members of the group. In a trust-based community, differences are appreciated. And as students of high-performance teams understand, diversity can be a competitive advantage. Pygmies know how to harness the energy from the different parts of the small group into a well-functioning whole. They also exhibit great fluency in relationships and roles; rigidity in behavior is absent.

The mutual respect so essential to good teamwork also characterizes male–female relationships among the pygmies. Unlike in other populations of Africa, the woman is not discriminated against in pygmy society. Male–female relationships are extremely egalitarian. Sex-role flexibility is the norm. One telling indication of this is the fact that pygmy language is genderless. Husbands and wives cooperate in a wide range of activities, while respecting each other's feelings and peculiarities. They never force each other to do something against their will.

Apart from spear and bow-and-arrow hunting, there is very little specialization according to gender. Women are essential members of the work team. They contribute substantially to the diet and are actively involved in the distribution and exchange of food. Both men and women net-hunt, usually together. A man collects mushrooms and nuts when he comes across them, gathers firewood, fetches water, cooks, washes up, and cleans a baby when needed. A woman participates in discussions and does heavy work when required.

The moral in all of this is that if we want teams to work, we need to build interpersonal trust and mutual respect among team members. If such feelings are not present, other factors conducive to effective team behavior become irrelevant. When there is no sense of mutuality among the members of a team, the group soon becomes dysfunctional and suffers from many of the problems listed earlier.

Trust does not occur instantaneously, however. It is like a delicate flower that takes time to blossom. Trust grows best if the basics were met for each team member in childhood—if individuals developed a trusting attitude as one of the anchors of their personality (as is the case in pygmy society). In such instances, the trust equation falls more easily into place. When there is a solid foundation, however, trust can be learned, just as we can cultivate honesty, integrity, consistency, credibility, fairness, competence, and the ability to listen. Leaders who 'walk the talk' and do not kill the bearer of bad news exhibit behavior patterns conducive to a culture of trust.

Lesson 2: members protect and support each other

One corollary of trust and respect is a system of a mutual support and protection among the members of a team. Members of any work team should share the conviction that they can rely on each other. An important component of that mutual support equation is the maintenance of each individual's self-esteem.

Let's take behavior in pygmy society as a point of departure. In spite of the mutually supportive nature of male–female relationships, marital conflicts do occur. Physical violence against women is almost nonexistent, however. Quarrels are usually resolved through dialogue, mediation, jokes, physical separation, or the reframing of the conflict. In general, however, women are more outspoken than men in showing their displeasure. One common way in which a woman shows anger with her husband is by tearing down the house. (Because women tend to be better house builders, the huts in which the pygmies live are considered to be the woman's property.)

Turnbull gives an example of a domestic quarrel that got out of hand and led to a surprising sequence of events, a sequence that, as I understand from my discussions with the pygmies, is not uncommon. In Turnbull's example, the matrimonial argument had come to an impasse. The wife, to express her displeasure, began methodically to pull all the leaves off the hut. Usually in such a case the woman would be stopped halfway by the husband. In this case, however, the husband was a rather stubborn fellow and did not budge. Consequently, his wife saw no alternative but to keep going. Eventually, the hut was stripped of all its leaves. At that point, the husband commented that it was going to be awfully cold during the night. Because the woman felt that her husband still had not reacted in an appropriate way that would settle the dispute she saw no choice but to continue. Hesitantly, she began to pull out the sticks that formed the frame of the hut.

By this time the whole camp, party to the quarrel since the beginning, was upset. Clearly things were going too far; the boundaries of mutual care were being transgressed. The woman was in tears, and the husband was equally miserable, because the last thing he wanted was to lose his wife. (If the hut were completely demolished, the woman would have no choice but to pack her belongings and return to her parents' home.) The question became how to reverse the situation, how to stop the conflict while preserving each person's self-esteem and allowing each to save face.

In this instance, the husband had a flash of insight into how he might solve his predicament. He 'reframed' the whole conflict. He mentioned to his wife that there was no need to pull out the sticks, as it was only the leaves that were dirty. Initially puzzled, she quickly understood what he was trying to do, and asked him to help her carry the leaves down to the stream. There they both pretended to make an effort to wash the leaves; then they brought them back. She cheerfully started putting the leaves back on the frame, while he went off with his bow and arrows to see if he could bring back some game for a special dinner. He had defused the argument by pretending that the leaves were taken off not because she was angry but because they were dirty. Everybody knew what had really been the matter, but people were happy that the quarrel was over. In fact, to show solidarity and support some of the other women took a few leaves from their own huts to wash in the stream, as if this were a common procedure.

This incident illustrates an important factor in effective work teams. Conflict is inevitable; indeed, it is part of the human condition. But while that may be the case, when push comes to shove in an organization, each team member must be willing to support, protect, and defend the others. In effective teams, members go to great lengths to sort out differences between themselves while maintaining individual self-respect. Whenever possible, what can be interpreted as conflictual is reframed as collaborative. It is part of the mindset of team members that they all have a stake in a constructive outcome. Such an attitude of mutual support and protectiveness provides the glue that makes for teamwork and helps a team survive when times are tough.

Lesson 3: members engage in open dialogue and communication

In pygmy society, participation is an essential part of the group culture. Everyone can expect it; everyone can demand it; everyone is supposed to give it. Obedience to authority figures is minimal among the pygmies. Nobody has the right to force others to do something against their will. Because there is not much of a power gulf between the various members of the group, people are unafraid to speak their mind. All members of the group interact and demonstrate involvement, and everyone has a say in decisions that affect the group. Disputes are settled informally. Constructive conflict resolution is the norm. Although individuals have the personal responsibility to attempt dispute settlement, they also have the right, if this effort fails, to get others involved in the matter until it is resolved.

For example, if a pygmy male has an argument with his wife that disturbs him so that he cannot sleep, he simply has to raise his voice—all the huts in a particular community are in close proximity—and ask his friends and relatives to help him. His wife will do the same, getting the whole camp involved until the dispute is settled. Conflicts are dealt with as they occur, to minimize bad feelings; problems are faced, not pushed underground.

Various techniques used to defuse disputes among the pygmies also work well with workplace teams. Jokes and laughter are common methods of resolving problems between team members. Humor helps people overcome the stresses and strains that are an inevitable part of group togetherness. Diversions are also useful; they help people forget what the conflict was all about.

Emotional management also plays an important role in conflict resolution. Pygmies are completely unselfconscious about showing emotions.

They love to laugh; they love to sing. Their willingness to express emotions makes conflict resolution much easier. In fact, a silent pygmy camp is a camp that has problems. As pygmy interaction patterns illustrate, it is better to err in the direction of noise. Furthermore, a willingness to show emotions by all members of the team helps reduce defensiveness and leads to more honest communication. The ability to drop one's defenses and bare one's soul is not for everyone, however; it requires considerable self-confidence. But people's efforts at self-revelation are generally well rewarded.

When there are pressing issues on the table, it helps to talk about them. Thus open dialogue and communication are important ingredients in making teams work. As can be observed in the pygmy community, effective teams share their ideas freely and enthusiastically; team members feel comfortable expressing opinions both for and against any position. Teams that meet these criteria are the ideal vehicles for creative problem solving.

Frankness and candor are also key to team effectiveness. In well-functioning teams, shared open, honest, and accurate information is the norm. In addition, members are prepared to provide feedback about the quality of each other's work when appropriate. Critical reviews are seen as opportunities to learn and do not result in defensive reactions. Moreover, team participants learn to defuse narcissistic injuries and to minimize damage to other members' sense of self-esteem by letting critical comments center around ideas, not people. Substantive issues are separated from those based on personality. Furthermore, members of high-performance teams avoid disruptive behavior, such as peripheral conversations or insider jokes, as much as possible.

Lesson 4: members share a strong common goal

Cooperation is the key to pygmy society. One of their overriding common goals is survival in an extremely difficult environment and hunting for meat is one of the major survival tasks. A pygmy can take his bow and arrows and try to shoot a bird or a monkey by himself, of course, and this is done regularly. The most effective way of obtaining meat, however, is through communal hunting, driving animals into nets. Net-hunting cannot be done alone; it would be impossible for a single hunter to cover sufficient territory to drive an antelope, for example, into a net. A necessarily cooperative affair, net-hunting therefore implies shared interests and a common purpose among the men, women, and children of participating families. This shared purpose encourages teamwork. At the time of a hunt, the nets owned by each family in the group are joined together in a long semi-circle. Usually, the women and children drive the animals into the nets while the men stand behind the nets and kill animals that become entangled. But it does not have to be this way. It can be the other way around, the men playing the role of beaters while the women do the killing. Afterward, the meat is shared among the various participants according to a set of very specific rules.

In organizations, as in pygmy society, teamwork is ineffective without mutually agreed upon goals. To give team members a sense of purpose and focus, what needs to be accomplished and how to go about it has to be articulated clearly. If a goal is ambiguous or ill-defined, the group will lack motivation and commitment. Although goals have to lie within realistic boundaries, offering a vivid description of what the organization expects of its members, they should also encourage team members to stretch. When met, stretch goals give a sense of pride; their execution creates a sense of achievement among the members of the team.

In conjunction with a clear sense of purpose, certain mutually agreed qualitative and quantitative targets need to be expressed. Such targets help team members determine the degree of their success in pursuing their given tasks. These targets serve as a roadmap, creating order out of chaos and generating excitement about future direction.

Lesson 5: members have strong shared values and beliefs

Closely related to a sense of purpose is the group's culture—its shared values and beliefs. Because these values and beliefs define the attitudes and norms that guide behavior, they play the role of a social control mechanism. They also provide another form of glue, binding the members of a work team. Hence the internalization of shared values and beliefs by team members is extremely important in the realization of the organization's goals.

Although to the uninitiated observer forest life among the pygmies may seem to be happy-go-lucky, that appearance is deceptive. Beneath the apparent disorder of the community lies considerable order. As I mentioned earlier, the importance of informal systems should never be underestimated. All pygmies in the camp, from early childhood onward, internalize rules of behavior that are transferred orally from generation to generation. Cultural values and beliefs are at the base of these rules and make this small society work.

To understand the making of culture we have to start at the beginning. In other words, we have to take a closer look at early socialization

patterns. As I have already indicated , in pygmy society all adults participate in the upbringing of children, contributing to their training and
helping them understand the rules. They also help the children internalize
strongly held social expectations about appropriate attitudes and behavior.
What pygmy elders attempt is to make effective hunter-gatherers of their
younger generation, teaching children the art of survival in the rain forest.
They train them early to become autonomous and acquire subsistence
skills. They provide them with the collective wisdom that has accumulated
over thousands of years, instilling in the children the lore of pygmy
society.

Pygmy elders want their youngsters to share a common heritage. To
reinforce the behaviors deemed appropriate by that heritage, rewards and
punishments are handed out when needed. To make sure that the rules
are adhered to, pygmy society imposes a number of deterrents. For
the most terrible offenses, no action is taken by the other members of the
group; indeed, none is needed, because it is expected that some form of
supernatural retribution will follow. While in the case of minor infractions
the accused are given the opportunity to argue their case with the other
members of the group, serious incidents are referred to the *molimo,* which
acts on behalf of the community. The *molimo* players may show their
public disapproval of a violation of social standards by attacking the transgressor's hut , for example, or by attacking the transgressor during an early
morning rampage. The *molimo* is an important part of pygmy tradition,
and in this kind of situation represents the collective conscience of the
group.

Sharing, cooperation, independence, and autonomy are among the
basic values of pygmy society. Another strongly shared value is maintaining peace among group members. This desire for peace sometimes even
transcends the rights and wrongs of a particular case. Turnbull describes
an incident in which one of the younger pygmies had gone on an amorous
expedition to the hut of his neighbor, who had an attractive daughter
(Turnbull, 1961). Shortly after entering the hut, he was thrown out by a
furious father, who was screaming and yelling and throwing sticks and
stones at the intruder. Because of all the noise, the whole camp woke up.
The father yelled that he was upset not because the young man had tried
to sleep with his daughter but because he had had the nerve to crawl right
over him and wake him in the process. He felt this was unacceptable.
Any decent person would have made a date with the girl to meet her
elsewhere.

In this particular incident, the argument was not resolved quickly; the
commotion kept going, keeping everyone awake. Finally, one of the
elders told the father, in a no-nonsense way, that he was making too much

noise; the elder was getting a headache, he said, and wanted to sleep. When the father continued shouting, the elder commented that he was 'killing the forest and he was killing the hunt.' Although the father was right—the behavior of the young man was inappropriate—he was causing a greater wrong by disturbing the whole camp, making so much noise that he was frightening the animals away and spoiling the hunt for the next day.

Although this may seem a rather far-fetched example, it does illustrate the application of norms of social behavior. In this instance, we can see how one norm supersedes the other; how everyone buys into what is viewed as suitable behavior. The lesson that can be learned from this relatively primitive society is that any organization or smaller work team needs to articulate its core values and beliefs and define appropriate attitudes and behavior for its members. The dos and don'ts of social behavior need first to be clarified and then reinforced through stories and traditions. The latter in turn reinforce the group's identity. A specialized language may further add to the bonding of the group. To strengthen this bonding process, successful organizations make a great effort to recruit people who are likely to subscribe to the core values of the organization. Furthermore, these organizations go to great lengths to socialize their new members, helping them internalize the group's core values and beliefs. Finally, these organizations clearly articulate sanctions for transgressions of shared values and beliefs.

Lesson 6: members subordinate their own objectives to those of the team

One of the stories I heard while among the pygmies concerned the breaking of a major rule. Apparently, one of the hunters had committed one of the greatest sins possible in the forest. During a hunt, frustrated by his poor luck—he had not trapped a single animal all day—he had slipped away and placed his own net in front of the others, catching the first of the animals fleeing from the noise of the beaters. Unfortunately, he was not able to retreat in time and was caught committing the serious crime of placing his own needs before those of the community.

In a small hunting band, as I have noted, survival can be achieved only by close collaboration and a system of reciprocal obligation that ensures that everyone gets a share of the daily catch. This particular man had clearly broken this unwritten rule. He had been selfish. Humiliation and ridicule were the punishment meted out by the group for his unacceptable behavior. He was laughed at by the women and children, and nobody would speak to him; he was ostracized. (This may not sound like much in the way of punishment, but what disturbs pygmies most is contempt and ridicule. Ostracism in pygmy society can be compared to solitary confinement in ours.) The ostracism was only temporary, however. Pygmies do not carry hard feelings for a long period of time. In a very small community, hunters cannot afford to ignore a fellow hunter.

This example illustrates that good team members operate within the boundaries of team rules. They understand personal and team roles. They do not let their own needs take precedence over those of the team. They control their narcissistic tendencies and subordinate their personal agenda to the agenda of the group.

Teamwork is an interesting balancing act. A form of participation that can flourish only in an atmosphere that encourages individual freedom and creative opportunity under the umbrella of the overall organizational goals, teamwork represents an interdependent balance between the needs of the individual and the needs of the organization. To make such a balance work, however, all members of the team need to recognize the limitations on their freedom; and this requires considerable self-discipline.

Lesson 7: members subscribe to distributed leadership

Pygmies are strong believers in the concept of distributed leadership. As I have shown, pygmy society is characterized by a disarming informality. Among the pygmies, it is difficult to talk about a single leader. Unlike other African societies, pygmy groups have no 'big men' among them; leadership is not the monopoly of one glorious leader. There is no person with ultimate authority and no real chiefs or formal councils; pygmy society is probably as egalitarian and participatory as human societies can get. Among the pygmies it is considered bad taste to draw attention to your activities. Many subtle means are used to prevent this from happening. Bragging about your abilities is an invitation to become the butt of rough jokes, a very effective leveling device.

Pygmies are not intimidated by rank, seniority, or status. All members of the group are empowered to make decisions. Respect may be given to elders, but it is based not on wealth or status but on their knowledge and expertise. Likewise, if certain people are listened to more than others during decision-making, it is because of their special ability or skill, whether this is bow making, hunting, or playing an instrument. Although some members' opinions may be more valued than others—those members having become somewhat more equal than their peers—all members of the pygmy community are prepared to challenge authority whenever they believe that the team effort is jeopardized. As a result, each team member is likely to accept ownership for the team's decisions.

The pygmies seem to have figured out that the best form of leadership is a configuration where leaders are distributed throughout the community and everyone can be involved in decision-making. However, individuals who are accorded exceptional respect are expected to subscribe to a number of leadership practices that foster effective teamwork. If they fail to do so, they are reminded of their obligation by the group.

Look behind the scenes at a high-performance organization, and you will find a similar attitude toward leadership. Among the practices that successful team leaders use to encourage full participation is a willingness to share goals with the other members of the team. Effective team leaders avoid secrecy of any kind at all costs. They treat members of the team with respect, listen to feedback and ask questions, address problems, and display tolerance and flexibility. They offer guidance and structure, facilitating task accomplishment, and they provide a focus for action. They encourage dialogue and interaction among participants, balancing appropriate levels of participation to ensure that all points of view are explored (and withholding their own point of view initially to prevent the possible swaying of opinion). They capitalize on the differences among group members when those differences can further the common good of the group. They give praise and recognition for individual and group efforts, and they celebrate successes. They accept ownership for the decisions of the team and keep their focus sharp through follow-up. By acting in these ways, they create an atmosphere of growth and learning. In the process, they encourage group members to evaluate their own progress and development.

AUTHORITATIVE (NOT AUTHORITARIAN) LEADERSHIP

In discussing these lessons from the pygmies, I have emphasized the important role of team leaders in making successful teamwork happen. Team leaders, and their own leaders in the corporate hierarchy, have to set up the matrix within which teamwork can be most effective. They have to create the right ambiance and lead by example. The old paradigm of command, control, and compartmentalize has to be discarded. In fact, rules and regulations should be minimized.

The need for transitional space

In the context of team leadership in the workplace, a few more caveats are needed. First, however participatory one likes to be, there is a need for direction from the top, with clear communication about the organization's priorities. Second, executives and team leaders must create an atmosphere that encourages people's natural exploratory capabilities. People need room to play—and they need to see top management's commitment to that endeavor—because with play come creativity and innovation. Without innovation, an organization stagnates and dies. Thus senior executives must not only encourage people to take risks but also accept occasional failure, protecting those who stick their necks out in a good cause.

While strong, committed leadership is necessary to foster innovation, such leadership need not, indeed should not, be authoritarian. On the contrary, authoritative leadership is a prerequisite of the supportive climate. What organizations need is leaders who are respected because of what they can contribute; who 'walk the talk'; who get pleasure out of developing their people; who are willing to play the role of mentor, coach, and cheerleader; who know how to stretch others. Authoritative leaders accept contrarian thinking and encourage people to speak their mind; they want people to have a healthy disrespect for authority. They also know how to celebrate a job well done, how to recognize achievements, and how to put appropriate reward systems into place to align behavior with desired outcomes.

In our time of transformation and change, conflict in organizations is a fact of life. The ability to solve conflict is therefore an important competency for people in team leadership positions. Effective leaders in the years to come will be masters of clarity and candor, skills that are important enablers in diffusing conflict. They will communicate what has to be done in clear, unambiguous terms that leave little room for misinterpretation. They will transform conflict from an obstacle into an instrument for creative problem solving and increased performance.

Teamwork remains, above all else, a balancing act. On the one hand, individual members of the team deserve to have their place in the sun, to have their achievements recognized. On the other hand, team members need to recognize the value of collaboration, subordinating their own needs to those of the group. Yet collaboration is rarely easy. An atmosphere of constructive give-and-take goes a long way toward making it happen.

A community like the pygmies, operating in a harsh environment like the rain forest, is acutely aware of this need for collaboration. All the problems associated with teams notwithstanding, the pygmies realize that it is harder to operate without teams than with them. Indeed, without teamwork they have little chance of survival, given the challenges of their environment. Members of business organizations would do well to heed these lessons from the pygmies, the product of knowledge accumulated over thousands of years.

Open versus closed systems

Perhaps the most telling lesson from the pygmies is a negative one that I have not yet addressed. As I said at the beginning of this chapter, recent times have not been good to the pygmies. Their way of life is now threatened, because the epicenter toward which their whole being has been directed, the rain forest, is in danger. Their focus on a hunter-gatherer existence has determined their socialization and training practices over the centuries; it created their unique culture and continues to color their outlook on life. As long as there is a rain forest, their world will be aligned; everything will fall into place, and their life will have real meaning. Unfortunately, the building of new roads—allowing large-scale plantation farming to gain a foothold—and the migration of people from other parts of Africa to the rain forest in search of farmland, have led to massive deforestation. The world of the pygmies is disappearing at an alarming rate, creating a sense of dislocation in these wanderers. Of those who have been forced to leave the rain forest, many have been unable to find a new focus. In the agricultural and industrial society that surrounds their old world, their particular expertise has become less relevant. Very few pygmies have been able to adjust to the dramatic societal discontinuities that have taken place around them; very few have been able to make the transition into 'our' world. The consequences for their various communities have been dire.

Thus, as a final lesson from the pygmies, we learn that survival requires not only an inward but also an outward focus; changes in the external environment have to be accounted for. Boundary management is important; building bridges with key outside stakeholders is an essential task. Members of effective teams recognize the need for external relations. In the case of the pygmies, making this external adjustment may simply not be possible. Conforming to the larger society would require a complete reinvention of themselves, a draconian transformation of their culture that would mean the end of the world as they know it.

The world of business organizations is not as closed a system as that of the pygmies, of course. And there are many other differences as well, but the parallels are still striking. Like the pygmies, business organizations have no choice but to look beyond their boundaries; they have to look out for emerging discontinuities to ensure at least a chance at survival and success. If they do not look beyond their borders in this fast-moving, competitive, globally interdependent world, they too will face dire consequences: an inexorable winding down of their life cycle, culminating in death.

As I have described here, one way of managing for continuity, creating companies that last, is through teamwork. Companies that acquire the tools of effective teamwork have a distinct competitive advantage, a leg up toward organizational success. To master those tools takes considerable psychological work, however. The French statesman and novelist François-René Chateaubriand once said, 'One does not learn how to die by killing others.' The pygmies have taken this statement to heart. They know the importance of taking care of each other. Members of teams in our postindustrial society would do well to gain that same knowledge.

PART 2

THE PEOPLE DIMENSION
IN ORGANIZATIONS

INTRODUCTION

Nobody who, like me, had spent some time among the pygmies of central Africa could deny the effects of a strong organizational culture. In the rainforests of Cameroon, there is no philosophy of transformative leadership spearheaded by a charismatic individual. Personal security is ensured only by the effectiveness and survival of the group, and these people operate within an environment where group survival depends on every individual achieving his or her full potential. As the pygmies show, a strong, supportive organizational culture can produce greater results than a strong individual leader—a body of people with the right motivation and clear shared goals can move mountains.

Happily, the importance of organizational culture is rarely disputed nowadays. Indeed, many organizations make explicit public statements about their culture, frequently allied with their organizational values. Microsoft, for example, makes it clear that they look for employees who are aligned with company values: 'As a company, and as individuals, we value integrity, honesty, openness, personal excellence, constructive self-criticism, continual self-improvement, and mutual respect. ... We hold ourselves accountable to our customers, shareholders, partners, and employees by honoring our commitments, providing results, and striving for the highest quality.'[1] Similarly, W. L. Gore takes the time not only to describe its culture in some detail but also to explain how it works in terms of organizational structure and their expectations of their 'associates (not employees)': 'Leaders may be appointed, but are defined by "followership." More often, leaders emerge naturally by demonstrating special knowledge, skill, or experience that advances a business objective.'[2] Here, too, culture is firmly linked to company values, the guiding principles of the company's founder, which include fairness to all, helping

[1] http://www.microsoft.com/about/en/us/default.aspx
[2] http://www.gore.com/en_xx/aboutus/culture/index.html

and encouraging fellow associates, making and keeping commitments, and consultative processes that ensure that individual actions are aligned with the company's reputation.

However, despite this recognition of the importance of organizational culture, and many companies' attempts at iteration, it still remains elusive. Culture has to do with values, beliefs, norms, behavior, policy, structure, language, and symbolism. It is largely intangible, an invisible contract between you and the organization. In Chapter 4, I look at how culture emerges within an organization, and examine issues of 'fit'—with people's outlook, especially in the case of mergers and acquisitions, and strategy. Like all other aspects of today's organizational world, culture is challenged by the issues of change. The last part of this chapter deals with these and I offer a diagnostic tool for tackling them—an organizational culture audit that provides a comprehensive assessment and evaluation of existing culture and a detailed understanding of the culture that should be aimed for.

For the most part, organizational participants take organizational culture for granted—and it is probably most visible when it is obviously violated. This can have a serious negative aspect: dysfunctions in organizational culture can be as intangible as the positives and just as hard to pin down. In the early 1980s, I was working at McGill University, Montreal, and it was a very stressful, but also an extremely stimulating period: I was teaching, trying to write, training to become a psychoanalyst, and raising a young family. Like many psychoanalysts, my time was parcelled out in 50-minute sessions. Then suddenly my clinical training was over, school was out, and I had a burst of creativity. I was writing and writing because all the learning I'd had scrunched up over the years when I'd very little time to produce suddenly had an outlet. The transitions I had been making in my professional life—between economics, business education, and psychoanalysis—had been joining up in my mind and forming the kernel of the ideas on which my teaching and writing over the next three decades would be built. My observations as a psychoanalyst inevitably informed my observations as a management professor. I began to see how the dysfunctional personalities of those at the top of an organization were reflected in the culture of the organization itself. Put simply, sick people can create sick organizations. I joined forces with a fellow academic, Danny Miller, who had been my very brilliant doctoral student, and we began work on a book: Danny's biorhythm meant that he wrote at night; I wrote during the day. When I was finished I left my draft on his doorstep (remember, this was before email). Danny would continue and in the morning I picked up what he'd written from his step, carried on writing till around three or four o'clock in the afternoon, then dropped the next draft at his doorstep again. Once a week, we had meetings to discuss our progress. We finished the book in four weeks. That book was *The Neurotic Organization*, which turned out to be a seminal contribution and is still in print. In Chapter 5 I look at five types of neurotic organization—paranoid, schizoid, depressive, compulsive, and histrionic—and describe a framework that allows us to draw parallels between these neurotic styles of behavior and organizational failure. I also advocate the use of external analysts to map dysfunctional organizations and organizational types.

Chapters 6 and 7 are related. The first looks at downsizing, the business practice that characterized the 1990s as a quick-fix solution to the problems caused by, among other things, increasing globalization. The second looks at how organizational transformation can be managed by paying attention to parallels with the psychodynamics of personal change.

The negative effects on morale and performance stimulated by downsizing cannot be overestimated: stress levels soar and people experience a wide variety of psychological and emotional reactions, including anxiety, anger, guilt, envy, relief, and denial. Downsizing has drawn parallels with the processes of grief and bereavement, and has been linked to increased rates of depression, suicide, and violent aggression. There are three groups of people intimately involved in a downsizing process. We think instinctively of the victims and the survivors, but what about those making the layoffs? What are the psychological effects on them? In Chapter 6, I draw on interviews with people in all three groups to analyze different ways of coping with the fallout from downsizing. The insights from these observations will not eliminate the hurt—but preparation for psychological reactions can help us address the pain in the organization and limit potential disaster. I end with some ideas about the best way to handle downsizing and, like Pandora, discover that one of the most powerful is hope. Leaders who know how to channel hope can create the vision of a future that will drive the change effort forward and go some way toward reconciling people to the hurt.

Hope is a key theme of Chapter 7, as well, but I begin by explaining how pain within the individual and organization is a necessary prerequisite of the desire to make much-needed change efforts. This chapter is an exposition of how the dynamics of personal transformation can be applied to the organizational setting, and why taking this clinical perspective is valid, rewarding, and potentially a powerfully creative way of managing change initiatives. Taking a case-study approach, I show how the staging of key focal events gives organizational members the opportunity to mourn the past, become excited about the future, and adjust to a new reality.

Part 2 ends with an exploration of a very particular kind of group: the family business. When they are good, family firms are very, very good—in fact, some of the best companies to work for: but when they go bad, they can be very horrid indeed. The challenge for anyone dealing with a family firm—but particularly the coach or consultant—is the clash of two systems, the family and the business. Those of us involved in interventions in family firms are likely to be more inured than the average viewer to the absurdities of soap operas like *Dallas*, *Dynasty*, or *Brothers and Sisters*. Likely we have had to deal with people who would rather see the company collapse than see a much-resented sibling prosper from it; or an aging founder whose Oedipal fear of being usurped and inability to accept his personal mortality translate into a death grip on the company, hindering its development and any effective succession planning.

The playwright George Bernard Shaw once said, 'If you cannot get rid of the family skeleton, you may as well make it dance.' And given the rise and fall of family businesses, we may as well make them dance. Family firms are playing a significant role in terms of generation of new employment and GDP growth. In Chapter 8, I point out that interpersonal family dynamics—spousal, parental, father–son, father–daughter, sibling, and in-law—can be a major factor in the family firm's failure to thrive. Succession is a particularly difficult issue in family firms. The inability to deal with such transitions becomes a death sentence for many. Conversely, in successful transitions, heirs are reasonably well-prepared, family relationships tend to be positive, and succession planning and related control activities are taken seriously.

As I say at the end of this chapter, you are unlikely to be bored when working with family firms—but you must also be prepared for a whole gamut of emotions, from frustration and bewilderment to satisfaction and, in the very best of worlds, triumph. Success can be outstanding but failure can be correspondingly dire.

CHAPTER 4

THE QUESTION OF ORGANIZATIONAL CULTURE

Culture is the collective programming of the mind which distinguishes the members of one group from another.

—Geert Hofstede

Culture hides more than it reveals and strangely enough what it hides, it hides most effectively from its own participants. Years of study have convinced me that the real job is not to understand foreign culture but to understand our own.

—Edward T. Hall

If you have ever seen the movie 'Night of the Living Dead', you have a rough idea how modern corporations and organizations operate, with projects and proposals that everybody thought were killed constantly rising from their graves to stagger back into meetings and eat the brains of the living.

—Dave Barry

The average person learns, under proper conditioning, not only to accept but to seek responsibility. The capacity to exercise a relatively high degree of imagination, ingenuity, and creativity in the solution of organizational problems is widely, not narrowly, distributed in the population.

—Douglas McGregor

DEFINING ORGANIZATIONAL CULTURE

Few topics have generated more interest and led to more concerns than the topic of organizational culture. Organizational culture makes up the uniqueness and identity of the organization. It contains all the values, beliefs, attitudes, norms, and behaviors of individuals in a company. It is the organization's *modus operandi*—understanding an organization's culture helps us to understand why organizations do what they do and achieve what they achieve.

The idea that corporate culture was a phenomenon worth studying took off in the 1980s, influenced by the Japanese threat to the US car manufacturing industry, as presented in Richard Pascale and Anthony Athos' bestseller, *The Art of Japanese Management* (1981). According to Pascale and Athos, organizational culture was the major factor for Japanese success. This was corroborated by other bestsellers, such as Peters and Waterman's *In Search of Excellence* (1982), and Collins and Porras' *Built to Last* (1994). All these books maintained that organizational culture plays a major role in determining the difference between average or excellent performance.

A seminal study that added to the literature was carried out by an organizational behavior specialist from MIT, Edgar Schein, whose earlier work concerned the brainwashing of American prisoners during the Korean War. In his study of organizations, Schein was struck by the similarities between coercive persuasion and the ways corporations were indoctrinating their employees. In his book *Organizational Culture and Leadership*, he presented organizational culture as 'a pattern of shared basic assumptions that the group learned as it solved its problems of external adaptation and internal integration, that has worked well enough to be considered valid and, therefore, to be taught to new members as the correct way to perceive, think, and feel in relation to those problems' (Schein, 1985, p. 19).

Schein's writings had the effect of placing organizational culture in the mainstream, at a time when other scholars in the field were also exploring the topic. For example, Charles Handy, in his book, *Understanding Organizations* (1993), presented a typology of different types of organizations, an orientation that has had many followers. However, these rather simplistic models of different types of organizational culture have often contributed to a very mechanical view of culture change.

Many organizational scholars were interested in the relationship between organizational culture and performance. John Kotter and James Heskett presented an important study on this topic in their book *Corporate Culture and Performance* (1992). Using empirical evidence canvassed in more than 200 blue-chip enterprises in 22 industries, and covering an 11-year span, they found that corporate culture can have a significant impact on a firm's long-term economic performance. According to Kotter and Heskett, companies with cultural values that paid equal attention to customers, stockholders, and employees improved their net incomes significantly as opposed to companies that did not. Strong and adaptive cultures seem to create an unusual level of motivation in an organization's employees. The authors caution, however, that cultures that function adequately in one economic context may prove disastrous in another.

Over the years, hundreds of researchers have worked on the applications of organizational culture, particularly academics in organizational design and development, and the concept has now become embedded in management vocabulary and thought. Today, an increasing number of successful organizations have attributed their success at least in part to effective culture management (Dennison, 1900; Harrison and Stokes,1992). Indeed, most executives now accept that all organizations have cultures or sets of values and beliefs that influence people's behavior in their working life. And virtually all the top strategy consulting and human resource management firms have added cultural management to their lists of capabilities under the rubric of change management or organizational transformation.

Although the term organizational culture has become ingrained in general management vocabulary, the concept nevertheless remains something of a mystery. Not only is it hard to describe, it is still harder to manage and to change, and changing it takes time.

According to Schein (1985), there are three levels of organizational culture: artifacts, espoused values, and basic underlying assumptions. Deconstructing organizational culture is like peeling the layers off an onion. At the core are the invisible basic assumptions that drive the members of the organization and are reflected in their actions. These underlying assumptions are about people, the company, and the world. They structure the way they do things, how they behave and why they value such behavior. These assumptions in turn shape the values adopted by members of an organization, and are reflected in strategy, goals, operation methodology, decision-making methods, and management styles. The outermost layer consists of artifacts, which are the explicit and visible signs of organizational culture in practice, such as organizational structures, policies, and employee behavior. Thus, organizational culture can be viewed as a series of invisible contracts with the organization's employees that shape the way that work is done (established through goals, plans, evaluation measures, and rewards) and how the infrastructure (systems, processes, and structures) is used. Culture, in many ways, lays the tracks for strategy development. Conversely, aligning the organizational culture with a suitable strategy provides a powerful means for gaining competitive advantage.

Another way of explaining organizational culture is as the mental framework shared by members of the organization. It contains the basic assumptions and values held in the organization, which are transmitted to new members as a way to perceive, think, feel, and behave within the organization, and which they can expect others in the organization to adhere to in the same way. Organizational norms, guidelines or expectations develop from these organizational values and beliefs. They prescribe the kinds of behavior that are appropriate in particular situations and influence the behavior of organizational members toward one another. Organizational culture thus encompasses the ways in which people behave, how they are held accountable, and how they are rewarded.

Organizational culture also includes many elusive phenomena. It operates through symbolism, such as language and behavior, and encompasses cultural taboos like sharing information on salary ranges, proprietary, strategic, competitive, or sensitive internal data, and financial records. Organizational culture can also be reflected in the dos and the don'ts in the organization: 'Don't make mistakes,' 'Work long hours,' 'Cover your back,' 'Don't make waves,' and so on. These overt and covert symbols develop in the mind of organizational members over time. Employees who share a significant number of important experiences in the organization will tend to develop a shared view of the world around them and their place of work.

I define organizational culture as a mosaic of basic assumptions expressed as the beliefs, values, and characteristic patterns of behavior that are shared in the organization and adopted by the organization's members in an effort to cope with internal and external pressures. Organizational culture is the water in which fish swim. Unaware of the environment in which they exist, fish take the water for granted until the moment they are taken out of it. Similarly, many of the elements of organizational culture operate at an unconscious level, without organizational members paying too much attention to it.

Organizational culture is created in an organic way, stemming from the actions of the company's founder and others who have been with the organization for some time and who have contributed to its success. Behavior that has been successful in the past is likely to be reinforced by current employees and sought out in new employees who are brought into the organization. (See Figure 4.1 for an overview of how organizational culture emerges.)

In this manner, culture spreads, permeates, and is embedded into every aspect of organizational life. It becomes the glue that holds the organization together. At the same time, it may also be the glue that keeps things stuck when there is mounting pressure for change. This is partially due to its complexity and embeddedness as well as the difficulty of defining and measuring it. Thus in managing organizational culture, we have

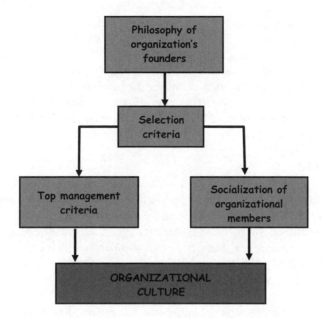

Figure 4.1 How organizational culture emerges

to be prepared to manage paradoxes: on one hand, organizational participants must become aware of and adopt the peculiarities of their culture—if
organizations are going to maintain continuity, employees need to be
socialized to the culture; on the other hand, too strong a socialization may
have a negative effect on the organization's ability to adapt and change.

WHY ORGANIZATIONAL CULTURE IS SO IMPORTANT

Building and maintaining the right culture can make or break an organization. An organization's culture determines its ability to deal successfully
with increased competition, globalization, mergers, acquisitions, strategic
alliances, the introduction of new technologies, talent management, and
diversity issues. If executives do not understand the role that organizational
culture plays in these processes, many of their efforts at corporate change
will fail.

I have already described organizational culture as the glue, or coalesc-
ing agent, for creating a high performance workforce for executing an
organization's strategy. It sets the ground rules for integration into the

organization and provides a template for treating external stakeholders (shareholders, customers, and suppliers) and its own people (talent management) with optimal success. It influences the organization's selection and socialization methods and sets the criteria for successful performance and career advancement. It determines the appropriate style of interpersonal relationships, characterizing the climate in the workplace, and it influences what is considered to be an appropriate style of leadership.

Cultural fit

People fit Organizations have traditionally focused on recruiting people on the basis of their skills and experience. With a better understanding of the importance of organizational culture, the notion of cultural fit has taken precedence. Indeed, in top companies such as Google, listed as Fortune's 2008 Best Place to Work (Fortune 2008), finding the right Googlers, that is, people with the Google mentality and way of working, is an essential part of the recruitment process.

When executives hire an employee these days they frequently consider whether the candidate will be a good cultural fit. This involves finding out whether a potential new employee endorses their organizational values and fits into their organizational culture. Usually, individuals selected on the basis of cultural fit will contribute faster, perform better, and stay in the organization longer. In contrast, a poor cultural fit may contribute to low morale, decreased productivity, conflict, dissatisfied customers, and costly employee turnover.

It is not always easy to know if a person will fit a specific organizational culture. However, a well planned communication and recruiting process can greatly improve the chances of finding a good fit. The best way to start is by having a clear description of what the organization stands for, the working environment and the types of people who work there, and communicating this information to the marketplace (including search consultants). To do this, executives need to have a deep understanding of their own current or desired organizational culture. A clear description of an organization's values and aims will allow potential candidates to self-select and increase the chances of attracting appropriate candidates. Executives also have to make it clear why their organization is an attractive place to work and to assess whether the potential candidate's values, beliefs, and attitudes are aligned with those of the organization. But this is not enough. There are many other questions to take into consideration. What does the organization offer that no other can? Is the potential new hire a team player or a loner? What is his leadership style? How well will she fit into the organization? Does he have an autocratic or a coaching style? Will she be a good corporate citizen? Moreover, human resources needs to have a comprehensive description of the position to be filled (competencies as well as personality), and to make sure everyone is aware of the importance of cultural fit throughout the hiring process.

But even the best-intentioned recruitment processes—those that focus on competencies and relevant behaviors as well as education and experience—may fail to assess the issue of cultural fit accurately. This is because a candidate's actual behavior may turn out to be contrary to expectations: in practice, they fail to walk the talk and do not live up to the organization's cultural values.

Indeed, any organization that wants to make its culture work for it has to guard against such disingenuous behaviors. The chances of organizational culture decline are increased if the executives who fail to live up to the organizational values—sometimes called the SOBs—are retained. Because such members hold socially sanctioned and hence influential roles within the organization, their actions and behaviors may frequently go unchallenged and even be protected within the organization. If senior executives in the organization tolerate such behavior, cultural deterioration will occur and the values that once made the organization a great place to work will start to disappear.

Hence, the management of cultural fits and misfits is an important part of preserving and perpetuating desired organizational cultural values. Those who are genuine and trustworthy in their behavior should be rewarded and those whose actions are contradictory, nonbeneficial and even detrimental to the organization should receive help, and failing to change their behavior, be asked to leave. The alignment between the needs of the organization (living the values and getting the results) and those of the individual will be essential. (See Figure 4.2 for a simple matrix describing the various management options.)

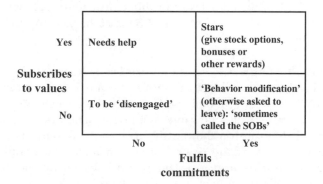

Figure 4.2 Managing cultural fit

Not knowing how new people will fit into the culture of the organization leaves their future productivity to chance. At best, there may be problems of employee attrition; at worst, the organization may end up with a dysfunctional and unproductive workforce. Hence, finding the best fit of people and culture is critical to maximizing individual productivity and creativity as well as an organization's overall success.

Mergers and acquisitions fit   Another common example of cultural fit or misfit is found in mergers and acquisitions. Nowadays companies are merging with and acquiring each other in unprecedented and growing numbers. While it is generally agreed that cultural compatibility is the greatest barrier to successful integration in partnerships, cultural factors are the least likely to be investigated during the critical due diligence phase of a merger or acquisition. Not surprisingly, corporate mergers are like a substantial percentage of modern marriages: they end on the rocks. According to numerous studies, most completed M&As fail to meet the strategic and fiscal objectives that initially justified the deal and more than half result in later divestiture or shutdown as a result of a culture clash and unresolved conflict in the merged organization.

Because of this, deal makers need to recognize that financial and strategic fit on their own do not guarantee a viable entity. Integration should be driven by a combination of strategic, financial, and operational factors, as well as the psychological dynamics of pre-existing organizational cultures. Understanding the merging organizations' cultures is critical for weaving them and their employees together quickly and successfully, and to ensure that work flow continues as seamlessly as possible. Companies must make cultural assessment part of their due diligence process so that they are fully aware and prepare for potential difficulties before the merger takes place. Successful mergers and acquisitions require a compatible marriage of organizational cultures, a situation that can become intensely complicated when the complexity of different national cultures is added to the integration process. (See Figure 4.3 for a schema comparing organizational cultures.)

Strategic fit   Organizational culture has been viewed as a key strategic building block of successful organizations. It can have a significant impact on a firm's long-term economic performance, influencing business strategy and goal attainment. Companies with strong cultures are more likely to achieve their goals than those with relatively weak ones. Their higher degree of organizational success (measured in market value or other financial measures of performance) is largely attributed to the fact that their employees are aligned in their way of thinking, are clear about the goals

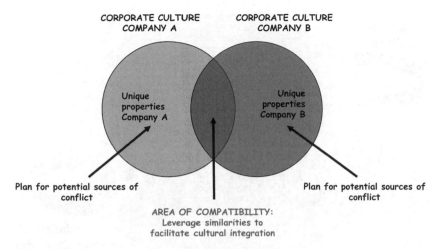

CORPORATE CULTURE
COMPANY A

CORPORATE CULTURE
COMPANY B

Unique
properties
Company A

Unique
properties
Company B

Plan for potential sources of
conflict

Plan for potential sources of
conflict

AREA OF COMPATIBILITY:
Leverage similarities to
facilitate cultural integration

Figure 4.3   Assessing cultural compatibility and potential conflict

of the organization, and are better motivated to achieve these goals. If all employees in an organization are familiar with the key elements of their organizational culture, and practice them, this cohesiveness becomes a strategic business asset.

To enhance the company's success, its corporate culture should be aligned with its articulated business priorities and its business objectives must be reached in a manner consistent with its values. Furthermore, a successful business strategy can close the gap between an existing and desired culture. By contrast, business strategies can fail if the culture does not support the actions necessary to achieve corporate goals.

ASSESSING ORGANIZATIONAL CULTURE

Earlier, I likened organizational culture to an onion: to get to its core, the layers have to be peeled away one by one. One layer might be national culture—French companies are managed quite differently from German or Chinese companies. Another layer is industry characteristics—working for a strategic consulting firm will be quite different from working in a steel company or a bank. This is followed by the specific culture of an organization, with its own language of myths, stories, rituals, sagas, and ceremonies. Yet another, more profound, layer would be the organization's values, beliefs, attitudes, and norms. The deepest layers of all have archaic origins, related to the ideas of the original founder of the company and the current major powerholders. The deeper layers of the culture—

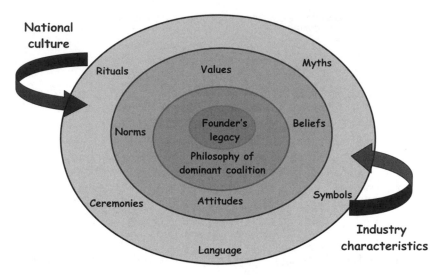

Figure 4.4   Culture: from surface to deep structure

like those of the onion—determine the shape and character of successive layers (see Figure 4.4 for an overview of the levels of organizational culture, from surface to deep structure).

Culture profiling

The goal of culture profiling is to identify and map out the different layers of culture within an organization. In putting together an organization's culture profile, one of the first and most accessible things to do is to look at a company's physical premises—the architecture, office layout, and furnishings—all of which reveal something about an organization. Layout and furnishings can be significant indicators of organizational culture. Consider what reasons lie behind the ease (or difficulty) of entry and exit. Inside the building the organizational language, messages on bulletin-boards, the dress code, and other organizational policies provide further clues as to the working life of organizational members.

Going deeper, questions about employees, their relationships to one another, meeting protocols, customs, and routines can provide a fairly clear picture of the organization's culture. What are the employees like? Are they a homogeneous group or are they very different from each other? What are the criteria for inclusion and exclusion in specific circumstances? Is there a high turnover among employees? How do people in the organization interact with each other? Who comes to meetings? Where do they sit? Who sits next to whom?

A look at the executives and what they do will reveal another dimension to the organizational portrait. Does conversation with executives reveal consensus about the primary task of the organization? Can an outsider easily discern what the organization is trying to accomplish? Are executives clear about the criteria that determine where power and status will be allocated? What sort of people do they identify as high potentials? And how do employees perceive key powerholders and the CEO?

When interpreting these descriptions, it is important to go beyond the official narratives (which might just be slogans) and to listen carefully to what employees say, as these often reveal a number of implicit cultural values: 'Look busy even when you're not,' 'Don't take risks. It will cost you dearly,' 'If it ain't broken, don't fix it,' 'Before you make a decision, check with the boss,' and so on. All these statements reveal what it is really like to work in a particular organizational environment.

Owing to the fish bowl effect, long-tenured executives may have become too used to their environment to recognize the specificities of their organizational culture. To obtain an even broader perspective of one's organization, it is rewarding to look outside and talk to former employees (what was their experience like? what were the reasons for leaving?), suppliers, consumers, competitors, and third parties who have observed the organization over time. Their stories will add another dimension to the organization's profile. Newcomers are a particularly interesting group to talk to, as they can make comparisons with their previous organization and highlight the features that set their new organization apart (see Figure 4.5 for culture profiling sources).

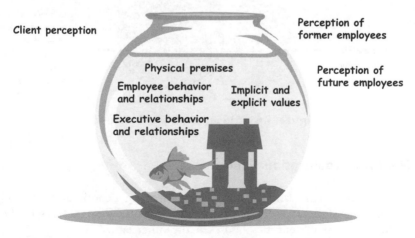

Figure 4.5   Different sources of feedback for cultural profiling

The impact of subcultures

Through these questions and reflections, a representation of the organization's culture will begin to emerge. Do not assume, however, that there will be just one homogenous culture. Large, complex organizations are likely to have a number of subcultures that shape the perceptions, attitudes, and beliefs of individuals in specific departments, specialized groups, and professional disciplines. For example, the culture in the marketing department of a specific organization may be quite different from the culture in finance or R&D.

While some subcultures are strongly congruent with the dominant culture, the core values of others can actually run counter to it. In yet other subcultures, the core values of the dominant culture are accepted together with a separate, nonconflicting set of values.

Subcultures can facilitate or thwart attempts to implement change at the organizational level. Hence, one of the challenges for an organization's leadership is to reconcile and accommodate subcultural differences within an organization, or to accelerate the process of mutual adjustment between them (see Figure 4.6 for an overview of different subcultures). While cultural change cannot be forced, an organization's natural capacity to change can, however, be released, shaped, and cultivated.

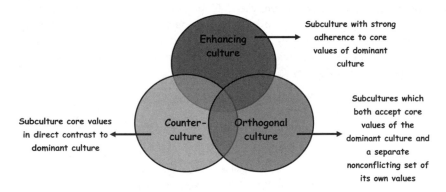

Figure 4.6   Organizational subcultures

Neurotic organizational cultures

If we imagine organizational cultures as lying along a continuum, we find healthy, well-functioning cultures at one end, mediocre cultures in the middle, and toxic, neurotic cultures at the other end.

Like individuals, each organization has its own personality. And organizations—as embodied in their culture—tend to reflect the personalities of their leaders, particularly when power is highly concentrated. Senior executives strongly influence the culture of the organization through their own behaviors because it is they who determine how work gets done. They externalize and act out their inner theater on the public stage of the organization, and these inner dramas develop into corporate cultures, structures, and patterns of communication and decision-making.

If the leader of an organization has a dysfunctional personality, the chances are high that conflicts due to this dysfunction will be reflected in the culture of the organization. For every neurotic organization, there is a dysfunctional leader, who, by virtue of his or her own handicaps, creates an environment characterized by high levels of distress, dissatisfaction, and stress that surpass normal work conditions.

In my book, *The Neurotic Organization* (Kets de Vries, 1984), I explore five types of toxic organizational cultures induced by the personality and behaviors of their leaders. I try to show how the leaders' conflicts become embedded in the corporate culture. While exemplary leaders help their companies to become highly effective, dysfunctional leaders do just the opposite: they create organizational neurosis.

In neurotic organizational cultures, employees are not treated as assets, no matter what rhetoric or slogans are espoused by its leadership. Employees' ideas, skills, and talents are not valued. They are often burdened with unreasonable workloads and deadlines, and unclear expectations. They suffer intellectually, emotionally, spiritually, and even physically. If they approach their leaders with these issues, no attempts at reform are made. Hence, this intensifies feelings of hopelessness and helplessness. Not surprisingly, many people do not stay in neurotic organizations for long. Those that do stay may act out by engaging in forms of organizational sabotage such as absenteeism and low productivity. They may also react by demonstrating extremely aggressive behavior such as theft or even violence.

Hence, executives who govern with a dysfunctional leadership style may find themselves paying a huge price in terms of personal health and career development. Employees on the receiving end of this style, obliged to operate in an unhealthy workplace, have a limited number of choices: they can take stress management classes, hope for a leadership change, or—the most usual choice—get out.

Understanding an organization's neurotic style can help determine what needs to be and can be done. Recognizing that neurotic organizational cultures exist and are rooted in the organization's history and the leader's personality also helps organizational members to realize that change, while possible, will also be slow and difficult.

CHANGING ORGANIZATIONAL CULTURE

In an age of increasing global and local competition, one of the more important factors for sustainable success is an organization's ability to develop a corporate culture that attracts and retains talented people. Focusing on cultural values is an essential building block for high performance and strategic effectiveness.

Organizational culture will be the foundation upon which an organization's vision, strategy, brand, and identity are based. As the dynamics and demands of the market change, an organization must be able to adapt its culture to meet them. If it refuses to change, the company will start to lose its focus and drift; the environment will influence and change its culture, and senior executives will lose control over what is happening in their organization. Sometimes a cultural change process is set into motion by the arrival of a new CEO (particularly someone coming from outside who is not restrained in the way an insider would be); sometimes a new technology can be the impetus for a change effort (the increasingly important strategic influence of the Internet, for example). Mergers and acquisitions can have implications for cultural change—and so can scandal, which can lead to reorganization or even bankruptcy, as the striking example of Enron demonstrates.

Planned change

Instead of external pressures forcing a sudden change, an organization will be much better off taking a proactive stand to change. The senior executive team should start by asking themselves whether change is needed and if they are really ready to change. If so, this is where an organizational culture audit can play an important role.

The organizational culture audit can be invaluable as a source of data to start the change process, especially if it is combined with qualitative data gathered from interviews and group sessions (which I will describe later). Once the features of the organizational culture are mapped out and made visible through a culture audit, the senior executive team can compare existing employee values with the behavior they feel is needed to effectively implement the organization's strategy. Concurrently, attention needs to be paid to the kind of new culture that is desired and how this can be achieved in the context of the existing organizational culture.

(As a caveat it should be noted that organizations may also have transitional values that may take on an interim function in the change effort to close the gap between what people desire—their aspired values, and what they practice—their present values.)

When there is a serious gap between the real and desired state of an organization, steps can be taken to develop a shared set of values carefully aligned to the direction the senior executive group wants to take. To start the change process and create an action plan, the senior executive team has to reach agreement on the areas that need attention. They need to tackle the cultural gaps that have the greatest effect on the enterprise's ability to implement its strategic success model.

Closing the culture gap

One way of closing the organizational culture gap is to bring together a diverse team of high potential employees to give momentum to the cultural change process. At this stage, it is often recommended to ask an outside facilitator (leadership group coach or consultant) to help guide this process. This person can start by interviewing the senior management team to obtain a sense of the organizational dynamics—including their major concerns. This information (combined with the data from the culture audit) will then be shared with this group of executives. Later, it may be worthwhile to take them through a number of exercises to complement the audit's findings. (I often engage the senior leadership team in a culture exercise to highlight discrepancies between desired and actual behavior.) It is useful for this team to discuss the current culture and explain what parts of it are already highly effective and need to be supported, as well what practices hold the organization back. A vision of a more effective organizational culture, and what the organization should look like in the future, can then be created, based on the audit's snapshot of the entire organization, using audit data and the outcomes of the qualitative analysis. Whatever the nature of these interventions, this process needs to be cascaded down through the organization to arrive at buy-in from all employees.

Culture change is complex work. The organizational culture audit will identify the kinds of changes necessary for an organization to achieve its strategic objectives. This usually involves identifying and removing dysfunctional behaviors and practices and introducing new, more productive ones. In addition, the information gathered during this group intervention can be used for a series of interventions cascading down the organization to create awareness of the cultural change process in the organization as a whole.

Not everyone in the organization is immediately going to think that these efforts are worthwhile. Change is not easy. Resistance will come when long-standing cultural assumptions are challenged and threatened. Employees may have to discard well-established and deeply held values and norms about the nature and importance of their work. They may have to get rid of the familiar, comfortable ways of doing things. They may have to learn and adopt new values, beliefs, and behavior that will serve the organization more effectively, and they may have to acquire new skills and knowledge. Culture change may be more difficult in older organizations where people are more set in their ways.

The best way to engage in a major organizational change effort is to do several things simultaneously. Senior management has a number of levers it can operate. To start with, the top executive team must have a clear focus on what they want to accomplish and agree on their vision of the future. Second, they need to inspire people's collective imagination to create a group identity. Third, the Internet and other forms of IT can play a major role in influencing the culture by tapping into the needs of both clients and employees. Fourth, structural rearrangements (including reward systems) give out the right signals about the direction the organization wants to take. Most importantly, programs will be needed to help people change their mindset. The organizational culture audit can play a major role in providing information on what needs to be done. (See Figure 4.7 for an overview of the organizational culture change process.)

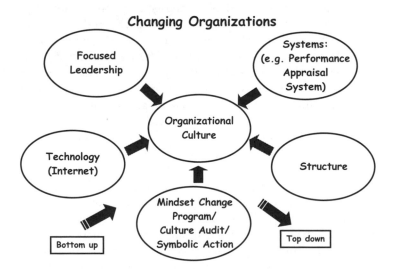

Figure 4.7 Levers for changing organizational culture

Culture change is like any other form of change. It requires champions: people who are committed to the idea of creating the new culture and will be able to create the momentum needed to get the change process off the ground. Employee buy-in is critical. As mentioned earlier, change should not be a top-down process in which a new culture is imposed by senior management; other levels in the organization must be fully implicated.

WHY A CULTURE AUDIT?

To remain competitive, an organization should constantly evaluate its values and practices to ensure they are aligned with its corporate strategy. A culture audit allows an organization to map and assess its organizational values and current practices. It can also be used to measure how near or far from the mark the organization's actual behavior is compared to its desired values, that is, whether executives and employees really practice what they preach. This knowledge of both the actual and desired state of one's organization can then be used to determine the strategic maneuvers, competitive actions, investments, new developments, organizational changes, and many other actions needed to reorient the enterprise in the proper direction. In particular, a cultural assessment plays an important role in aligning behavior and performance indicators with the future vision for the organization.

Conducting an organizational culture audit

What we strive to be as an organization and what we think we endorse may be different than the beliefs and values that are actually being played out. It is therefore critical that we find out what we really are before we can decide what we want to be.

The most effective way to map out a company's shared critical values and assumptions is to conduct a culture audit. Such an assessment can help an organization's executives to better understand their culture so they can change, enhance, and benefit from it. To do so, I have developed an *Organizational Culture Audit* (OCA) to assess 12 key (commonly identified) dimensions of organizational culture (Kets de Vries, 2010b, 2010c). It consists of a simple, easy to use, psychometrically valid tool to measure perceived importance of a number of key cultural values in one's organization and current practice.

The 12 organizational culture dimensions used are:

- competitiveness;
- social responsibility;
- client/stakeholder orientation;
- change orientation;
- teamwork;
- fun;
- responsibility and accountability;
- trust;
- learning environment;
- results orientation;
- respect for the individual;
- entrepreneurship.

The OCA feedback pages provide a picture of how an organization operates and the values that characterize it. The audit gives the organization's executives a comprehensive diagnostic of their current culture as well as a detailed understanding of the culture they are aiming for, by examining employees' perceptions of the organization's current practices and the values they consider desirable. Individual surveys are collectively tabulated into a graphical profile that compares the organization's culture to a normative global database.

But the OCA is not an end in itself. Usually, I use it as a starting point to address cultural strengths and weaknesses within an organization and to begin the discussion on what needs to be done to facilitate organizational change; to explore an organization's culture and assess whether the gaps between desired and actual practices can be dealt with.

TO CHANGE OR NOT TO CHANGE?

It has been said that when you are through changing, you are through. The wheels of change will go on turning. Moreover, change is not necessarily comfortable. As the social scientist Kurt Lewin used to say, 'If you want to truly understand something, try to change it.' Our only hope is that we have the ability to change. Like it or not, things will not stay the way they are.

Most organizational change comes about as a result of a stream of interaction between the various stakeholders in the system, each of which is complex in its own way. I emphasize this complexity, as most change agents seem to have a rather mechanical view of organizational change processes—asking what needs to be done to be an effective consultant; how it is possible to re-engineer or fix an organization; and what tools are most useful in doing so.

In the twenty-first century the major challenge faced by leaders of the future will be to manage their organizational culture to prevent increasing occurrences of corporate malfeasance. They need to meet market requirements by ensuring that the company's internal environment keeps pace with external forces. This implies that the leaders of the future should be bold enough to give equal attention to both hard issues (structure, systems, and technology) and soft ones (people and culture). They should continually be on the alert that everything is not well in the organization. They should avoid becoming a victim of the 'boiled frog' syndrome.

If we put a frog into boiling water, it will feel the heat and try to escape. Or, more probably, it will die. However, if we plop a frog into lukewarm water and gradually raise the temperature, the frog happily becomes poached alive. Without an acute change in temperature the frog has no stimulus to make a change and jump out of the water. This is the boiled frog syndrome and is an important metaphor that we can all learn from in our business lives. It stands as a warning to executives not to ignore the signs of organizational dysfunctioning that portend eventual failure. For an improved work environment; it's better to steer clear of the boiled frog syndrome. It is important to recognize the signs of hot water early enough to turn down the heat.

Unfortunately, too many change agents try to offer rational approaches to change, a method of intervention that may satisfy the need for certainty and assurance. However, many patterns are unconscious in nature, and to be effective change agents need to have a deep understanding of unconscious behavior (Kets de Vries, 2001, 2006). Cultural change agents must combine rationality and irrationality, hard and soft ways of problem-solving. And while they engage in this process, in instances of organizational culture change, they should always strive for the best, and know why they are doing so.

CHAPTER 5

PERSONALITY, CULTURE AND ORGANIZATIONS[1]

A tyrant is always stirring up some war or other, in order that the people may require a leader.

—Plato

In every tyrant's heart there springs in the end this poison, that he cannot trust a friend.

—Aeschylus

It is a paradox that every dictator has climbed to power on the ladder of free speech. Immediately on attaining power each dictator has suppressed all free speech except his own.

—Herbert Hoover

Dictators ride to and fro upon tigers which they dare not dismount. And the tigers are getting hungry.

—Winston Churchill

THE ROT STARTS AT THE TOP

As an organizational researcher, I am interested in finding out why certain decisions are made in organizations and why particular strategies are

---

[1] Material in this chapter has appeared elsewhere in print in the following publications:

Kets de Vries, M.F.R. and Miller, D. (1984) 'Neurotic style and organizational pathology', *Strategic Management Journal* 5, 35–55.

Kets de Vries, M.F.R. and Miller, D. (1984) 'Unstable at the top,' *Psychology Today*, October 1984.

Kets de Vries, M.F.R. and Miller, D. (1986) 'Personality, culture and organization,' *Academy of Management Review* II(2), 266–79.

chosen. Why does an organization end up with a particular kind of structure? Why is a certain individual selected for a particular job? I have come to believe that the problems of many troubled companies are deeply ingrained, based as they are on the deep-seated neurotic styles and fantasies of their top executives.

In dealing with life's problems all of us have specific styles 'ways of thinking and perceiving, ways of experiencing emotion, modes of subjective experience in general and modes of activity that are associated with certain pathologies' (Shapiro, 1965, p.1). Our patterns of dealing with the environment are deeply embedded in our personalities. Human functioning is generally characterized by a mixture of these often neurotic styles. The same person can possess elements of several different styles, each of which is triggered in different circumstances. However, in many individuals one specific neurotic style or other will dominate and come consistently to characterize many aspects of their behavior. Extreme manifestations of any one style can signal significant psychopathology that seriously impairs functioning.

My interest in this particular field began because as a practicing psychoanalyst, management professor, organizational consultant, and coach I kept noticing similarities between findings in my psychoanalytic practice and my consulting and coaching work. Organizational problems and orientations seemed very much to mirror my clinical findings about the personalities of the top echelon of executives. For example, organizations run by those with a paranoid disposition manifest many elements of paranoia in strategy, structure, and organizational climate.

I and my colleague at the time, Danny Miller, were trying to identify recurrent organizational *Gestalts* (or common configurations)—those that highlight the integral interdependencies among elements of organizational strategy, structure, and environment. The original idea behind this framework was that parallels could be drawn between common neurotic styles of behavior and common modes of organizational failure. Pathological organizational types seemed to mirror the types of dysfunctions common to the most widely discussed neurotic styles among individuals (APA, 2000; Shapiro, 1965; Miller and Friesen, 1978, 1984).

Scope

In my research I focused upon relatively dysfunctional top executives—that is, those with significant neurotic tendencies that influenced their managerial behavior. Most executives in healthy firms do not let whatever neurotic tendencies they have influence their performance. I tried to relate the most common neurotic styles to the problems of some very common pathological types of organizations. For this reason, my model is more useful for understanding dysfunctional rather than healthy organizations.

The model is most applicable to firms in which decision-making power is centralized in the hands of a more neurotic top executive or a small, homogeneous, dominant coalition. Where power is broadly distributed throughout a firm, its strategies will be determined by many managers, each of whom may have quite a different personality—and this would make it difficult to draw inferences between human and organizational behavior.

In this chapter, I am mainly concerned with the highest levels of management. Senior executives usually have the greatest impact on their organizations, so it seemed wise, as a first step, to focus attention on them, although neurotic styles can have an impact at all levels of the organization, of course.

Approach

Interdisciplinary research is fraught with hazards. It is all too easy to take a conceptual framework from one field and to apply it blindly to another very different field. For example the organismic analogy in organizational theory has been exceedingly popular and perhaps of considerable value, but has resulted in obscuring key differences between organisms and organizations (Keeley, 1980). What is needed is a plausible rationale for making the link between intra-psychic, interpersonal, and group phenomena as manifested by neurotic style, and organizational adaptive characteristics.

I will identify a number of very common, well-established intrapsychic 'fantasies' and neurotic styles, found in the psychoanalytic and psychiatric literature (Fenichel, 1945; Millon, 1981; Nicholi, 1978; Shapiro, 1965), together with various personality disorders found in the *Diagnostic and Statistical Manual of Mental Disorders* (DSM-IV-TR) published by the American Psychiatric Association (2000). I develop conjectures about the relationship between each style, its predominant motivating fantasy, the emerging organizational culture, and the strategy and structure of the overall organization.

My discussion is speculative, and based on my experience with many sick organizations and their top executives. It should therefore be treated as a series of complex hypotheses, not as a final word or rigid framework (see Text Box 5.1). I should also point out that the types identified are

---

Text Box 5.1   General hypotheses

1. The more centralized the organization, the more powerful the CEO; the greater the impact of his/her personality (that is, fantasy and neurotic style) on culture, strategy, and structure.
2. The more similar the personalities of the top executives, the purer the cultural and organizational types—that is, the more closely they will adhere to the five types I discuss here.
3. The purer and more pronounced the personality type of the CEO, as measured by the DSM IV-TR (APA, 2000) or Millon Inventory (1980), the more it will be reflected in the culture, structure, and strategy of the firm. This is especially true in smaller, centralized organizations.
4. Healthy firms will have a mixture of personality types that are not as dysfunctional. These hypotheses will not be borne out in such samples.

---

by no means the only dysfunctional types of organizations, and that mixed types are quite common.

Much formal, empirical, and anecdotal evidence has already been gathered to support the link between the personalities of top executives and their influence on organizational climate (Kernberg, 1979; Jaques, 1951, 1970; Maccoby, 1976; Payne and Pugh, 1976). However, the tendency has been to look at one simple aspect of personality, such as locus of control (Phares, 1976; Lefcourt, 1976), need for achievement (McClelland, 1961), and need for power (McClelland, 1975), and to relate it to one or two organizational variables such as the degree of participative decision-making (Vroom, 1960; Tosi, 1970), formalization, or bureaucratization (Merton, 1968). However, research built on single traits or attitudes can be quite misleading. Complex situations are reduced to one dimension as though that dimension alone could explain many of the phenomena under study or could exist independently of the broader aspects of personality.

I believe that the psychoanalytic, psychiatric, and psychotherapeutic literature[2] might be more useful than the more standard psychological

---

[2] Especially as represented by the works of Fenichel (1945), LaPlanche and Pontalis (1973), Shapiro (1965), Freedman, Kaplan and Sadock (1975) and Nicholi (1978).

literature because they provide a more complete and integrated view of intra-psychic functioning and behavior. Instead of focusing on one narrow trait or attitude, they consider personality styles—those patterns of behavior by which individuals relate to external reality and their own internal disposition. Personality styles can explain a multiplicity of behaviors, because they focus on clusters of behavior patterns that remain relatively stable over the years, as opposed to simple dimensions of behavior. I believe that personality styles enable us to make a more explicable link between executives' intra-psychic world and their behavior in organizations.

I start by considering the origins of personality styles in early life.

THE EMERGENCE OF NEUROTIC BEHAVIOR PATTERNS

A major stream in psychoanalysis emphasizes that interpersonal interactions as well as intra-psychic fantasies are central to the development of personality (Klein, 1948; Fairbairn, 1952; Balint, 1965; Guntrip, 1969; Jacobson, 1964).Child observation studies have revealed that behavior is determined by an individual's representational psychic world, populated by enduring images of self and others. These images (or mental constructs) develop through the process of maturation and are encoded in the brain, becoming organizing units that enable individuals to perceive, interpret, and react to sensations in a meaningful way.

Typically, instinctual needs become linked to these mental representations and are transformed into various kinds of wishes that are articulated through fantasies. Fantasies are our original rudimentary schemata for viewing the world. They evolve in complexity and can be taken as 'scripts (scenarios) of organized scenes which are capable of dramatization' (LaPlanche and Pontalis, 1973, p. 318). I am not talking about fantasies in the whimsical sense of daydreaming, but about complex and stable psychological structures (Breuer and Freud, 1893–5, p. 22), which are the building blocks for specific personality styles—some will be well-adjusted to the environment, others can become dysfunctional, i.e. toxic or neurotic.

Let me give a brief illustration here that should help to clarify my argument at this point. In an organization in which power is highly centralized in a leader with paranoid tendencies, the prevailing fantasy will be something like 'Everybody is out to get me.' This will lead to the development of many control and information systems, a CIA-like fascination with gathering intelligence from inside and outside the firm.

Paranoia will also result in centralization of power: the top executive responds to his distrust by wanting to control things himself. His strategy is likely to emphasize 'protection' and reduce dependency on particular markets or customers.

Another reason for examining the link between neurotic styles and organizational functioning is that the use of a rich set of dysfunctional neurotic styles allows us to predict aspects of each dysfunctional organization. For example, once we have decided that a paranoid climate prevails at the shared fantasy level in an organization, we can more easily identify indications of paranoia in strategy, structure, and organizational culture— even in the environment—that feed on or result from paranoia.

FIVE COMMON NEUROTIC STYLES

Five neurotic styles are well established in the psychoanalytic and psychiatric literature. They are paranoid, compulsive, histrionic (or dramatic), depressive, and schizoid (or detached). These are discussed in the *Diagnostic and Statistical Manual of Mental Disorders* by the American Psychiatric Association (DSM IV-TR 2000). Each style has its specific characteristics, predominant motivating fantasy, and associated dangers. Table 5.1 shows an overview of the salient characteristics for each style.

Five essential polarities are used to characterize the five common neurotic styles as well as the five common organizational configurations to which they give rise. I have derived these dimensions from various studies concerning individual differences in styles of functioning as follows:

- internal–external (Jung, 1920);
- active–passive (Fries and Woolf, 1953);
- high control–low control (White, 1972);
- impulsion–deliberation (Murray, 1938); and
- broad–narrow (Shapiro, 1965).

These polarities, defined below, guide my description of various organizational neurotic styles.

○ **Internal–external** This polarity is concerned with the way in which a person's interests are directed, that is either focused on subjective experiences, internal needs and goals, or focused toward external events.

○ **Active–passive** At one extreme we can find patterns such as initiative, assertion and exploration of surroundings. At the other extreme there is a reliance on others to initiate action.

Table 5.1 Summary of the five neurotic styles

Neurotic styles

Key factors	Paranoid	Compulsive	Histrionic (or dramatic)	Depressive	Schizoid (or detached)
Characteristics	Suspicion and mistrust of others; hypersensitivity and hyperalertness; readiness to counter perceived threats; over-concern with hidden motives and special meanings; intense attention span; cold, rational, unemotional	Perfectionistic; preoccupation with trivial details; insistence that others submit to own way of doing things; relationships seen in terms of dominance and submission; lack of spontaneity; inability to relax; meticulousness, dogmatism, obstinacy	Self-dramatization; excessive expression of emotions; incessant drawing of attention to self; a craving for activity and excitement; incapacity for concentration or sharply focused attention	Feelings of guilt, worthlessness, self-reproach, inadequacy. Sense of helplessness and hopelessness—of being at the mercy of events; diminished ability to think clearly, loss of interest and motivation; inability to experience pleasure	Detachment, non-involvement, withdrawal; sense of estrangement; lack of excitement or enthusiasm; indifference to praise or criticism; lack of interest in present or future; appearance cold, unemotional

(*Continued*)

Table 5.1 (*Continued*)

Neurotic styles

Key factors	Paranoid	Compulsive	Histrionic (or dramatic)	Depressive	Schizoid (or detached)
Fantasy	I cannot really trust anybody. A menacing superior force exists which is out to get me. I had better be on my guard	I don't want to be at the mercy of events. I have to master and control all the things affecting me	I want to get attention from and impress the people who count in my life	It is hopeless to change the course of events in my life. I am just not good enough	The world of reality does not offer any satisfaction to me. All my interactions with others will eventually fail and cause harm so it is safer to remain distant
Dangers	Distortion of reality due to a preoccupation with confirmation of suspicions. Loss of capacity for spontaneous action because of defensive attitudes	Inward orientation. Indecisiveness and postponement; avoidance due to fear of making mistakes. Inability to deviate from planned activity. Excessive reliance on rules and regulations. Difficulties in seeing 'the big picture'	Superficiality; suggestibility. The risk of operating in a nonfactual world—action based on 'hunches.' Over-reaction to minor events	Overly pessimistic outlook. Difficulties in concentration and performance. Inhibition of action, indecisiveness	Emotional isolation results in frustration of dependency needs of others. Bewilderment and aggressiveness may be the consequence.

○ **High control–low control** At one extreme there is a preoccupation with dominating action by making and enforcing rules, curbing behavior, and controlling others. At the other end of the spectrum we can find a more *laissez-faire*, relaxed attitude toward control.

○ **Impulsion–deliberation** Here we find, on the one hand, the tendency to respond quickly without reflection or forethought. On the other, we observe hesitation, caution. and reflection before initiating action; there is a predilection to pre-planning and organizing.

○ **Broad–narrow** The distinction to be made along this dimension is between organizations that are open to many factors, and those that are preoccupied with a narrow range of details.

The five organizational types are summarized in Table 5.2.

A few riders

In describing the five dysfunctional types, I have, for purposes of simplification, focused on the characteristics of 'pure' constellations. In reality, the clinical picture is usually much more complicated, with combinations or mixes among types often occurring. The pages of *Fortune, Forbes, Business Week*, or the *Wall Street Journal* regularly portray hybrids such as the paranoid-compulsive, depressive-compulsive or schizoid-depressive type. I have also not elaborated on other possible constellations such as the narcissistic and passive-aggressive, including additional hybrids.To make matters still more complex, movement across organizational types is often found, depending on who is in power and the stage of the organization's life cycle. In addition, the style of the leader or the dominant coalition may change through interactions with the evolving organization.

It must be stressed that although the personality of senior executives can vitally influence their organizations, a reverse relationship can also exist. A failing organization, rife with disappointment, can cause leaders to become depressed. A series of vicious threats from the competition can awaken dormant paranoia. Clearly, then, the influence between organizational orientations and managerial disposition is reciprocal. Mutual causation is the rule.

WHY USE THIS TYPOLOGY?

Bearing the opening sections of this chapter in mind, I want to begin by explaining the various advantages or strengths of the typology I use here.

Table 5.2 The five types along the five dimensions

Organizational type

Orientation	Paranoid firm	Compulsive firm	Histrionic (or Dramatic) firm	Depressive firm	Schizoid (or Detached) firm
Internal–external	External	Internal	External	Internal	Internal
Active–passive	Active	Active/passive	Very active	Very passive	Passive
High control–low control	High	High	Low	Medium	Low
Impulsive–deliberative	Deliberative	Deliberative	Impulsive	Not applicable	Impulsive
Broad–narrow	Broad	Narrow	Broad	Narrow	Narrow

1. As I mentioned earlier, it is holistic and avoids the complexity of the 'one variable at a time' approach by searching for common types and the psychological and cultural factors that underlie them.
2. It treats personality in a global way, looking for major adaptive styles that motivate and characterize much behavior, while eschewing narrow dimensions of affect or cognition.
3. The framework gets at the roots of some strategic, structural, and cultural problems in organizations.
4. The assignment of firms to a particular type can alert the organizational analyst to a range of unobserved but frequently related manifestations (helping the selection of the appropriate intervention strategy). Instead of dwelling on specific symptoms about the distribution of authority or the design of information systems, we can search for the underlying cause of the conjunction of various symptoms. In doing so, we should become more effective as organizational diagnosticians (or at least more attuned to the limits of change).

THE PARANOID (OR SUSPICIOUS) ORGANIZATION

In this type of organization, executives' suspicions translate into a primary emphasis on organizational intelligence and controls. Managers develop sophisticated information systems to identify threats from the government, competitors, and customers, and they develop budgets, cost centers, profit centers, cost-accounting procedures, and similar methods to control internal business. The elaborate information-processing apparatus reflects their desire for perpetual vigilance and preparedness for emergencies.

This paranoia also influences decision-making. Frequently, key executives decide that it may be safer to direct their distrust externally rather than withhold information from one another. In these situations they share information, and make concerted efforts to discover organizational problems and to select alternative solutions for dealing with them. Unfortunately, this type of decision-making can become overly consultative, with different people being asked for similar information. This 'institutionalization of suspicion' ensures that accurate information gets to the top of the firm; but it may also lower morale and trust as well as waste valuable time and energy.

Paranoid firms tend to react rather than anticipate. If competitors lower prices, the firm may study the challenge and, eventually, react to it. If other firms introduce a successful product, the paranoid firm will probably imitate them. But strategic paranoia carries with it a sizeable element of conservatism. Fear often entails being afraid to innovate, over-extend resources or take risks. This reactive orientation impedes development of a concerted and consistent strategy. The paranoid firm's direction has too much to do with external forces and not enough with consistent goals, plans, or unifying themes and traditions. Paranoid firms frequently try product diversification to reduce the risk of reliance on any one product—but because diversification requires more elaborate control and information-processing mechanisms, this actually reinforces the firm's paranoia.

Corporate paranoia often stems from a period of traumatic challenge. A strong market dries up, a powerful new competitor enters the market, or damaging legislation is passed. The harm done by these forces may cause executives to become very distrustful and fearful, to lose their nerve, or to recognize the need for better intelligence.

A case history in paranoid behavior

Paratech, Inc., a semiconductor manufacturer, illustrates how a paranoid organization can develop under those conditions.[3] The organization was run by its two founders, who had earlier worked for a much larger electronics firm that did a good deal of top-secret defense contracting. Three factors contributed to the founders' paranoia. The first was an episode at the large electronic firm in which Chinese spies had stolen valuable designs. Second, a competitor regularly beat Paratech to the marketplace with products that Paratech had conceived. Finally, there was a high rate of bankruptcy in the semiconductor field.

The two founders took all kinds of precautions to prevent their ideas from being stolen. They fragmented jobs and processes so that only a few key people in the company really understood the products. They rarely subcontracted work. And they paid employees very high salaries to give them an incentive to stay with the firm. However, these three precautions combined to make Paratech's costs among the highest in the industry.

The founders also found other ways to create problems for themselves. First, they were financially conservative in an industry known for rewarding risk-takers. Paratech spent much less on R&D than the competition and thus was slow to develop products, making its profit margins among the lowest in the industry. Secondly, although the founders carefully scanned the environment to see what the competition was up to,

[3] All names in case study examples are fictitious, but the situations are real and drawn from my consulting experience.

they waited too long for the market's reaction before deciding what to imitate. The delay was costly, as markets for high-technology products become saturated very quickly.

Finally, since Paratech did not want to be left out of any segment of the market or be overly dependent on any one sector, it diversified. But the spread was too thin, and the firm was therefore unable to develop any distinctive competence. All these tendencies squeezed Paratech's profit margins and made it one of the least successful firms in a booming industry.

Relationships in a paranoid firm

In the paranoid organization, the interpersonal relationships between leader and subordinates are often characterized by a persecution theme. The boss may feel hostile to those who report to him or her—he or she may want to harm or attack others as a defensive reaction to his own feelings of persecution and mistrust. Leaders see their subordinates either as malingerers and incompetents, or as people who are deliberately out to provoke their ire. As a consequence, they are likely to gravitate toward two extremes:

- Trying to exert a tremendous amount of control through intensive personal supervision, formal controls and rules, and harsh punishments. This takes away all initiative from executives, lowers their self-esteem, and causes them to engage in a battle of wills with the boss. The absence of opportunity for growth or development may induce the most promising executives to leave.
- Less commonly, overt aggression such as being reluctant to provide emotional or material rewards and striving always to come out on the winning side of any 'trades.' Morale can suffer a good deal under these conditions, as subordinates hold back their contributions and concentrate mostly on protecting themselves from exploitation.

Suspicious top executives generate group cultures pervaded by distrust, suspicion, and the identification of enemies. As described in Chapter 2, Bion (1959) has called these 'fight/flight cultures,' in which members come to fear the same things as the top executives. An atmosphere of fear of attack prevails and an enemy on whom one blames everything is usually identified. Group members deny responsibility for their own actions, and lack insight into their weaknesses.

It is important to note that Bion (1959) believed that all groups have these fight/flight and other phases as part of their normal evolution. But in paranoid cultures people become stuck at this level, so that the fight/flight fantasy endures and comes to dominate perceptions.

The five dimensions and the paranoid organization

We can now summarize the paranoid organization along our five dimensions in Table 5.2.

- The focus is clearly *external*, as the threats brought about by the environment to a large extent determine the nature of strategy. It is not internal objectives that given the firm direction so much as the jolts given the firm by the environment.
- The firm has an *active* orientation—there is diligent effort devoted to adaptation, and changes in strategy do take place, but changes are incremental and conservatism prevails, so the firm is only moderately active.
- The firm tends to be very *high* on the *control* scale, constantly monitoring what is happening in the environment. These types of organization are very preoccupied with information gathering.
- The firm is much more *deliberative* than impulsive. All action tends to be purposeful, and is usually directed toward a defensive end. Scanning, analysis, and interpreting the information gathered by information systems are the order of the day. Fear causes careful deliberation rather than impulsive action.
- The orientation is *broad* not narrow. Firms try to adapt and react to all kinds of threats. Since there is no concerted strategic emphasis, efforts are made to compete upon a wide variety of fronts. Experts from many different areas are brought into the decision-making process, and they all have some influence upon the course of action being decided.

THE COMPULSIVE ORGANIZATION

Like the paranoid firm, the compulsive firm emphasizes formal controls and information systems. There is a crucial difference, however: in compulsive organizations, controls are really designed to monitor internal operations, production efficiency, costs, and the scheduling and performance of projects, while the paranoid firm is interested chiefly in external conditions.

The compulsive firm is wed to ritual. Every detail of every operation is planned carefully in advance and carried out in routinized fashion. Thoroughness, completeness, and conformity to established procedures are emphasized. Operations are standardized as much as possible, and an elaborate set of formal policies and procedures evolves. These include not only production and marketing procedures but also dress codes, frequent sales meetings, and even suggested employee attitudes.

The compulsive organization is exceedingly hierarchical, a reflection of the leader's strong concern with control. Compulsive individuals are always worried about the next move and how they are going to make it. Such preoccupation has often been reinforced by periods when the firm was at the mercy of other organizations or circumstances. To prevent this from recurring, compulsive executives try to reduce uncertainty and attain a clearly specified objective in a carefully planned manner. Surprises must be avoided at all costs.

Compulsive firms show the same preoccupation with detail and established procedures in all their business strategies. They generally create a large number of action plans, budgets, and capital expenditure plans. Each project is designed with many checkpoints, exhaustive performance evaluations, and detailed schedules.

Unlike the paranoid company, the compulsive firm has a specific orientation and distinctive competence, and its plans reflect this orientation. It is this (rather than what is going on in the world) that serves as a major guide for the firm's strategy. For example, some organizations take pride in being the leading innovator in the marketplace; they try to be the first out with new products, whether or not these are called for by customers. Innovation may be inappropriate in the light of new market conditions, but the firm's strong inward focus prevents any realization of this fact. Change is difficult.

The compulsive firm: a case study

The Minutiae Corporation was a classically compulsive firm. It was dominated by David Richardson, its founder and CEO for the last 20 years. The firm manufactured roller bearings for railroad cars, costlier than the competitors' but easily the best available. They had been designed by Richardson himself, a mechanical engineer of great ability who made sure that the bearings were manufactured to extremely precise specifications. Minutiae's quality-control procedures were the tightest and most sophisticated in the industry. The machines were always kept in excellent repair. The firm's strategy strongly emphasized selling a very durable, high-quality product, and for many years this strategy paid off, making Minutiae the largest firm in the industry.

In the previous five years, however, smaller firms in the industry had begun to pioneer the use of new materials. Able to produce good-quality bearings for a fraction of the cost of the old products, they lowered their prices. Richardson steadfastly refused to adopt the new material and technology because these produced inferior wearing qualities. But Minutiae's product was now twice as expensive as the competition's, and lost much of its market. Richardson's obsessive attention to product quality focused Minutiae's strategy too narrowly to allow it to survive in a changing environment.

Relationships in a compulsive firm

In the compulsive firm, there is a fair degree of mistrust between leader and subordinates. The leader would rather rely on formal controls and direct supervision to effect coordination, than on the good will, shared objectives, or talent of the executive team. There is a constant preoccupation with loss of control. Controls, however, can rob subordinates of their sense of discretion, involvement, and personal responsibility and the atmosphere of suspicion will sap their enthusiasm.

Above all, the bureaucratic group culture is depersonalized and rigid, permeated by top management's preoccupation with control over people, operations, and the external environment. The rules may be legacies of the past, codifying the notion of the original founder(s) about how to run a successful company.

Formal policies, standard operating procedures, and detailed specifications for the accomplishment of tasks and the management of employees prevail. All are vehicles that top executives use to control the firm, managing by rules rather than through personal guidance or directives. The only executives who can survive happily in this setting are bureaucrats who love to follow rules and fear taking initiatives. Independent managers will find that they do not have enough latitude to act on their own, and leave.

The controlling top executive is not willing to relinquish sufficient control over operations to allow for a deliberative, participative mode of decision-making. Policies are not subject to discussion. As a caveat, I do not use the term 'bureaucracy' here in a strictly Weberian way. The notions discussed here do not so much conform to a sociological construct describing an ideal form of formal organization, as to a mode of operating that is highly ritualistic and inwardly focused.

The five dimensions in relation to compulsive firms

To summarize the compulsive firm along the five dimensions identified in Table 5.2:

- The orientation is *internal*, not external. The firm tries to buffer itself from its environment, to do things in a planned, programmed, and ritualized way. This deprives it of the adaptive responsiveness of its paranoid counterparts.
- The firm is both *active* and *passive*. It is active to the extent that its strategic theme requires innovation or to the extent that controlling internal operations requires more administrative procedures and controls. It is passive in its reluctance to deviate from established policies and methods.
- The firm scores *high* on the *control* scale, preoccupied as it is with the need to monitor even minute technical details, living with the notion that any relaxation of programmed activity is dangerous.
- The firm is somewhat *deliberative* although not to the same degree as the paranoid firm. Since the firm acts according to long-established guidelines rather than any recent deliberation on newly discovered facts, we might say that it is deliberative about means, but not about basic goals or strategic themes. The latter are deeply engrained.

It is clear that a *narrow* rather than a broad focus prevails. Strategies are unified by a dominant element and are highly integrated. The organization is designed with particular purposes in mind and these are carefully circumscribed and explicitly articulated. Dominant firms such as Xerox, IBM and Microsoft have many compulsive aspects (Rodgers, 1969; Miller, 1976).

THE HISTRIONIC (OR DRAMATIC) FIRM

In contrast to compulsive firms, dramatic firms are hyperactive, impulsive, dramatically venturesome and dangerously uninhibited. Their decision makers live in a world of hunches and impressions rather than facts as they haphazardly address an array of disparate markets. Instead of reacting to the business environment, the top decision-makers (who often also possess strong narcissistic tendencics) attempt to create their own environment. They enter some markets and leave others; they are constantly switching to new products while abandoning older ones, placing a sizable proportion of the firm's capital at risk.

Unbridled growth is the goal, reflecting the top executives' considerable narcissistic needs, their desire for attention and visibility. They want to be at center stage, showing what great executives they really are.

The structure of the dramatic organization is usually far too primitive for its broad markets. First, too much power is concentrated in chief executives, who meddle even in routine operating matters because they want to put their personal stamp on (and take credit for) everything. A second problem follows from this overcentralization—namely, the absence of an effective information system. The top executives do too little scanning of the business environment because they have too little time and prefer to act on intuition rather than facts. Finally, the leader's dominance obstructs effective internal communication, which is mostly from the top down.

A case study of the histrionic and depressive firm

The Stevens Corporation and Pyrax International exemplify two contrasting neurotic styles—the histrionic and the depressive (which I will consider in detail later). Pyrax was a rapidly expanding conglomerate making incursions into various industries. The company was run by Alex Herzog, a vain, ambitious, and domineering entrepreneur who was the founder, prime mover, and (many thought) tyrant-in-chief. He drove his employees ruthlessly, seized the lion's share of the decision-making power, and was noted for his boldness in acquiring firms, some larger than Pyrax itself. A self-made man, Herzog wanted desperately to run a powerful and gigantic enterprise. Through aggressive acquisition, he had gone a long way toward achieving his dream, incurring massive amounts of long-term debt in the process. Mounting interest rates and sinking profits were already starting to threaten Pyrax when it acquired Stevens.

Before the acquisition, Stevens was almost as large as Pyrax. A parts manufacturer in the heavy equipment field, Stevens was a lively firm whose product innovations had produced a respectable growth rate and whose manufacturing economies had given it the highest rate of return on equity in the industry. The president, David Morse, was devoted to balancing innovation with efficiency and growth with financial strength. Stevens' products were known for their high quality.

Things began to change soon after the acquisition. Herzog disliked having strong managers in charge of his companies and insisted on making all the major decisions at Stevens, even though he knew nothing about the industry. He kept Stevens' top executives busy supplying him with trivial information, and he questioned—even scolded—them when they failed to consult him on decisions. David Morse rapidly became disenchanted and finally quit after Herzog insisted on several misplaced cost-cutting measures. It became more and more apparent that Herzog saw Stevens as merely a source of cash to finance his grandiose expansion plans.

The departure of Morse allowed Herzog to install Byron Gorsuch as chief executive at Stevens. Gorsuch, a shy and insecure bureaucrat, knew little about Stevens' markets. His expertise lay in his ability to follow Herzog's directives to the letter. Stevens' managers were forced to play a purely advisory role, and as Herzog and Gorsuch generally failed to heed their advice, the most competent managers left. The remaining executives were passive and fearful; anxious about job security, they slavishly adhered to the rituals laid down by Herzog. Strategic issues were ignored, and as the firm began to stagnate, profitability and sales declined.

The situation at Stevens was not helped by what was happening at Pyrax. The stubborn, grandiose Herzog and his staff had become enmeshed in still more ambitious, and ultimately disastrous, acquisitions. They were too busy to recognize the danger signs at Stevens, and the depressed, passive managers at Stevens were too insecure to do anything themselves.

In terms of organizational neurosis, Pyrax was a dramatic firm, a company whose bold, grandiose leader caused the firm to overextend its resources. Stevens was a depressive firm; its decline was due to strategic stagnation. In both firms the personalities of the top managers, Herzog and Gorsuch, were strongly reflected in the companies' problematic strategies, structures, and managerial climates.

Relationships in a histrionic (dramatic) firm

Subordinates in these firms tend to *idealize* the dramatic or 'charismatic' leader—to ignore his faults and accentuate his strengths. They become highly dependent on the idealized person, feeling a need to appeal to, support, and ingratiate themselves with him. They are prone to be very flattered by a few words of praise, and are devastated by the mildest of reprimands. They thus become extremely dependent on the leader and very easy to control and manipulate. This is generally the exact situation that the dramatic leader wants to encourage, needing, as he does, others to nourish him with their confirming and admiring responses. Such superiors in fact seek out idealizing subordinates—they demand not only conformity but also praise and adulation (Kohut, 1971).

In this charismatic culture, the hopes and ambitions of the other executives and managers center around this idealized person. Charismatic leaders are people of action who strive aggressively and single-mindedly to implement a central goal that becomes a focal concern for the followers.

A tremendous uniformity derives from the leader's charisma—there is only one leader and many followers. There is thus an unquestioning, trustful climate of subordination among group members. Zealous followers help create an atmosphere in which the leader is seen as infallible. There is too little reflection or analysis as executives rely on the inspired judgment of the boss. Typically, the leader does not permit any resistance or dissent from subordinates and this, as elsewhere, means that independent-minded executives cannot last very long in this culture.

The five dimensions and the histrionic (dramatic) firm

The histrionic organization along the five dimensions from Table 5.2 looks like this:

- The orientation is *external* more than internal. There is an effort to control the environment, dominate it, expand, and become visible. The focus is on areas of opportunity in different markets and industries. Many internal problems are ignored.
- Histrionic firms fall at the extremely *active* polarity of the active–passive scale. There is a dramatically venturesome and decisive strategy, and a strong proclivity to embrace risk.
- Histrionic firms are very *low* on the *control* scale. The top executive's lack of interest in systems and preference for quick impressions thwart the implementation or use of well-developed control and information systems.
- An *impulsive* rather than a deliberative orientation prevails. Decisions are made quickly and little effort is devoted to ensuring complementarity among different decisions, or to analyzing their implications carefully.
- There is a *broad* rather than narrow focus, at least when it comes to product-market strategy. The firm is broadly diversified and caters to a great variety of markets.

THE DEPRESSIVE ORGANIZATION

As I have shown in the example of Stevens, depressive firms are characterized by inactivity, lack of confidence, extreme conservatism and insularity. What gets done is what has been programmed and routinized and requires no special initiative.

Most depressive firms are found in stable environments—the only setting in which they can survive for any length of time. Typically, depressive firms are well established and serve a mature market, one that has had the same technology and competitive patterns for many years. Trade agreements, restrictive trade practices, and substantial tariffs are the rule. Many of these companies can also be found in government-controlled industries.The low level of change and the absence of serious competition, simplify the administrative task.

Formal authority is centralized and based on position rather than expertise. The organization is not guided by any real leader and does not show clear evidence of making decisions. Control is really exercised by bureaucratic programs and policies rather than by managerial initiatives. Suggestions for change are resisted and action is inhibited. It is almost as if the executives just don't feel they can control events or that they have what it takes to revitalize the firm.

Content with the status quo, these organizations do little to discover the key threats and weaknesses in markets. It is difficult to say whether stagnation causes inattention to information gathering or vice versa. In either event, the two aspects go hand-in-hand in the depressive firm. In such firms there is a *leadership vacuum*. The firm drifts aimlessly without any sense of direction. The top executives have become caretakers who have given up trying to direct the enterprise. They merely serve as passive functionaries, operating at low levels of performance and maintaining the status quo.

Strategy is never explicitly considered, so no meaningful change occurs. Yesterday's products and markets become today's, not because of any policy of conservatism, but because of lethargy. Executives spend most of their time working out routine details while procrastinating on major decisions. Where there should be effort to adapt, to grow, and to become more effective, there is only inactivity and passivity.

Some of these organizations ended up where they are due to a take-over. After the departure of the previous top decision-maker—often an entrepreneur or an executive with entrepreneurial inclinations—many of these firms were subjected to a new style of management. Detailed new control procedures were introduced by the parent company, many of which were irrelevant for the specific type of business. This lack of understanding on the part of the parent eventually stifled initiative and induced apathy among the key executive group, who felt that they had very little control over the firm.

Depressive leaders and managers

Depressive-style executives lack self-confidence and initiative. According to DSM-IV-TR, depressive-style managers often have dependent-avoidant mixed personalities, with a strong need for affection and nurturance and possessing very little self-esteem (Jacobson, 1971; Nicholi, 1978; APA, 2000).

In this depressive style, individuals downgrade themselves; they are self-deprecating, feel inferior to others, and claim a lack of ability and talent. They abdicate responsibility. External sources for sustenance are needed to combat insecurity. Depressives submerge their individuality and look for protectors. They try to be ingratiating, adapting their behavior to please those on whom they depend, and allowing others to assume responsibility for major areas of life.

Depressive-style leaders are often subject to such feelings of powerlessness as a result of unpleasant past relationships. Anger about their powerlessness may give rise to wariness toward others and guilt, while at the same time they seem to be looking for a messiah to protect them from the dangers around them (Bion, 1959). They experience a need to idealize others, whether they are consultants, members of their constituency such as bankers or directors, or other figures with whom they are in regular contact.

Relationships in the depressive organization

The culture of these firms can be characterized as 'avoidant.' The executives view the organization as a machine that simply has to be fed with routine input, thus reducing their contributions to the minimum that is required of them. The CEO sets a climate of negativity and lethargy and the second-tier executives take their cues from this.

In some cases the boss's personality alone causes the depressive atmosphere. In others, an external force, such as the loss of the founder or a takeover by a conglomerate, causes healthy executives to lose their sense of control, their authority and, consequently, their initiative. In either event, an avoidant culture is permeated by unmotivated, absentee executives; buck-passing; delays; and an absence of meaningful interaction and communication among executives. There is distinct 'decidophobia.' Things continue along the same path, even when the firm begins to run into trouble.

The five dimensions and the depressive firm

We can now situate the depressive firm along our five dimensions:

* There is clearly an *internal* rather than an external focus. The firm concentrates on trivial details of operations rather than key threats or opportunities in the environment.
* Depressive firms are extraordinarily *passive*. They are unsurpassed in this respect by the other four types.
* Although well developed control systems are in existence, they are all form without substance. The system has become rather meaningless. The depressive firm is somewhere in the *middle* of the *control* scale.
* The firm is *neither deliberative* nor *impulsive* as these terms can only take on meaning when they describe strategic decision-making—an activity too rare to study in the depressive context.
* The strategic focus is *narrow*—typically the firm addresses itself to a homogeneous and well-established niche of the market and almost never strays from that niche. We can recapitulate all this by saying that the depressive organization is apathetic, somnolent, andmechanical.

THE SCHIZOID (OR DETACHED) ORGANIZATION

This kind of company, like the depressive type, suffers from a leadership vacuum. Its chief executive, often because of past disappointments, believes most contacts will end painfully and is inclined to daydream to compensate for lack of fulfillment. In some of these organizations, second-tier executives are able to make up for the leader's deficiencies with their own warmth and extroversion. Too often, however, the executives see the withdrawn (or seemingly uninterested) nature of the person at the top as an opportunity to pursue their own needs.

The second tier thus becomes a political battlefield for gamesmen who vie to win favor from an unresponsive leader. The combination of leadership vacuum and political infighting produces interesting strategic and structural results. No integrated market strategy develops. The leader figure, withdrawn and noncommittal, vacillates between the proposals of one favored subordinate and those of another.

Strategy-making resides in a shifting coalition of careerist second-tier executives who try to influence the indecisive leader and simultaneously advance their pet projects and minor empires. The firm muddles through and drifts, making incremental changes in one area and then reversing them whenever a new group of managers wins favor. The initiatives of one group of managers are often neutralized or severely blunted by those of an opposing group.

The divided nature of the organization thwarts effective coordination and communication. Information is used more as a power resource than as a vehicle for effective adaptation; in fact, managers erect barriers to prevent the free flow of information. But this is not the only shortcoming of the information system. Another is the absence of information on the outside business environment. The company's focus is internal—on personal ambitions and catering to the top manager's desires. Second-tier executives find it more useful to ignore real-world events that might reflect poorly on their own behavior or conflict with the wishes of the detached leader.

Case study of a schizoid (detached) organization

The Cornish Corporation, a women's clothing manufacturer run by Selma Gitnick, was a political battlefield for two of these second-tier managers. Gitnick had once been a very successful executive, but the suicide of her daughter and her recent divorce had turned an already shy woman into a recluse. She rarely left her office or had other managers visit her there. Instead, everything was done through written memos. In a firm that required rapid adaptation to a dynamic and uncertain fashion market, this slowdown in communication caused serious difficulties.

Gitnick reserved the right to make all-important final decisions herself, but she was very difficult to reach, and very imprecise in allocating responsibilities and authority to the second-tier executives. Executives were thus required to make most decisions, but because they were unclear about their own and everyone else's authority and responsibilities, each decision inevitably involved a power struggle between them.

The design people believed they could make the final choice of designs. Their boss began to clash frequently with the head of the marketing department, who accused the design people of incompetence and tried to veto their decisions. Both department heads wrote to Gitnick, complaining about the other and asking for a final decision. Gitnick was ambiguous in her reply, instructing the managers to give each other full cooperation. The bickering continued, and the consequent delays allowed competitors to purchase the best designs. Moreover, Cornish was two months late with its new line, which proved disastrous for sales.

The schizoid (detached) leader

.Generally, someone suffering from a schizoid personality disorder finds little enjoyment in close relationships. (Note that there is quite a difference between being schizoid and schizophrenic, while there are similarities between being an introvert and being schizoid, the latter being a more extreme case of introversion.) To make matters even more complicated, psychiatrists have identified both avoidant and schizoid personalities.

People with avoidant and schizoid personalities may fear that their interactions with others will eventually fail and cause harm; this produces in them a pattern of social detachment. Avoidant personalities have experienced interpersonal rejections that have caused them to be mistrustful; however, they also long for closer attachments and greater social acceptance. In contrast, schizoid personalities often have cognitive and emotional deficits that render them unconcerned about their social isolation (Kernberg, 1975; Kets de Vries, 1980, 2009). Given the similarity in the behavioral manifestations of the two types, in practice it is difficult to differentiate between them, since both tend to be socially hesitant and unresponsive (APA, 2000).

A pattern of non-involvement and withdrawal characterizes this detached style. Detached individuals are reluctant to enter into emotional relationships. They prefer to be by themselves and feel no need to communicate. They distance themselves from close personal attachments and pursue non-involvement. Although, on the surface, there may be great indifference to praise, criticism, or the feelings of others, this behavior is often a defense against being hurt. Whatever the underlying reasons, these individuals appear cold and aloof. They display emotional blandness and an inability to express enthusiasm or pleasure. Detached executives are unable to engage in the give-and-take of reciprocal relationships, appearing to possess minimal human interest.

The five dimensions and the schizoid (detached) firm

The schizoid organization can now be characterized along our five dimensions:

- The orientation is *internal* rather than external. Very little attention is paid to the external environment. The emphasis is on internal gamesmanship.
- The firm is much more *passive* than active. Their leaders are insecure, taking few decisive actions. Their subordinates often neutralize each

other's initiatives so that the net result is drifting or muddling through, rather than an integrated or bold strategy. There is a lack of control over organizational actions.

- Although there might be well-developed control systems, they are poorly used, making for a low rating on the *control* scale.
- There is little reflection or analysis—decisions or proposals are based on the *impulsive* pursuit of personal goals. Although such Machiavellianism requires a certain degree of calculation, it does not induce considered analysis of key elements of strategy.
- The orientation is a *narrow* political one. While the different subunits of the organization may collectively represent a diversity of viewpoints, factionalism prevents these from being integrated into a multifaceted action plan. Thus one narrow viewpoint eventually falls out of favor and is replaced by another, equally narrow. The schizoid firm is therefore an insular, isolated, political, and fragmented organization with an inconsistent strategy.

COMPARING ORGANIZATIONAL STYLES

Table 5.2 provided a summary of how the paranoid, compulsive, histrionic, depressive, and schizoid firms ranked on the five personality dimensions. Table 5.3 allows us to compare the five types of organizations and gain an overview of the strengths and weaknesses of each organizational neurotic style.

It is important to recognize that neurotic executives contribute strengths as well as weaknesses to their firms; some neurotic tendencics can be somewhat functional in particular environments. For example, paranoid executives may be helpful in setting up sophisticated scanning and control systems and diversification strategies useful in a competitive and hostile environment. Compulsives whose emphasis is on quality products may be useful in some engineering or high technology industries. Histrionics may be of use in establishing companies and in reviving somnolent firms. In general, however, such dysfunctional behavior patterns are harmful in the long run because of the grave strictures they place upon adaptive capacity.

OPERATIONALIZING THE FRAMEWORK

The top decision-makers in firms closely resembling our five types would be strongly advised to reach a better understanding of the consequences of their behavior. As I have described, if power is highly centralized in

Table 5.3 Strengths and weaknesses of the five organizational styles

Potential strengths	Potential weaknesses
Paranoid style	
Good knowledge of threats and opportunities inside and outside the firm	Lack of a concerted and consistent strategy—few distinctive competences
Benefits of reduced market risk from diversification	Insecurity and disenchantment among second-tier managers and their subordinates because of the atmosphere of distrust
Compulsive style	
Fine internal controls and efficient operation	Traditions embraced so firmly that strategy and structure become anachronistic
Well-integrated and focused product-market strategy	Things so programmed that bureaucratic dysfunctions, inflexibility, and inappropriate responses become common
	Managers discontented due to their lack of influence and discretion; stifling of initiative
Histrionic (dramatic) style	
Creating the momentum for passing through the start-up phase	Inconsistent strategies that have a very high element of risk and that cause resources to be squandered
Some good ideas for revitalizing tired firms	Problems in controlling widespread operations and restoring their profitability
	Rash and dangerous expansion policies
	Inadequate role played by second-tier executives
Depressive style	
Efficiency of internal processes	Anachronistic strategies and organizational stagnation
Focused strategy	Confinement to dying markets
	Weak competitive posture due to poor product lines
	Apathetic and inactive managers
Schizoid (detached) style	
Second-tier managers share in strategy formulation; a variety of points of view may be brought to bear	Inconsistent or vacillating strategy
	Issues decided by political negotiation rather than facts
	Lack of leadership
	Climate of suspicion and distrust that prevents collaboration

the organization, their leadership styles will have a serious impact on how their companies are run. Having classified the firm and its executives, it is then a relatively simple matter to compare the results to determine whether the nature of organizational dysfunction bears any relationship to the severity and nature of the neurotic styles of the top executives. Cross-tabulation and analysis of variance procedures could be used for this purpose.

ACHIEVING CHANGE IN ORGANIZATIONS

Unfortunately, neurotic styles of behavior are deeply rooted: CEOs are very hard to change, especially when they hold all the power. In many cases, meaningful turnarounds in the organization would be expected to occur only after dramatic failure erodes the power base of the CEO, or after a new CEO takes over.

The authors of much of the normative literature on policy, structure, and culture might do well to recognize that many managerial prescriptions will run counter to the personalities of the CEO and be resisted, or, where implemented, would not fit into the overall configuration of the organization and thus lack appropriateness and impact. Organizational change agents will be effective only if they get at the roots of dysfunctions—but this might be very difficult. Piecemeal changes will not do much good, while revolutionary changes are expensive, hard to implement, and politically inexpedient.

Since these five common pathologies seem to be so multifaceted and thematically unified, it is unlikely that they will be adequately addressed by management consultants using their standard bag of tools. The implementation of information systems, the use of strategic business units, committees and matrix structures, or the creation of organizational development and quality of working life programs will be of little help as long as an organization's executives cling to their dysfunctional, sometimes toxic behavior patterns. The new programs will have little effect unless they are complemented by more realistic views of the business and its environment or, failing that, by more adaptive executives.

My framework also implies that executives must themselves be on the lookout for these pathological styles operating among their number. However, since it is hard to recognize these in our own attitudes, it might be easier to examine the organization to see if its concrete structure, strategy, or climate conforms across the board to one of our pathological types. If so, it might be time for an open discussion of shared fantasies—to the extent that they can be articulated—in order to scrutinize them. The stimulus for such dialogue usually has to come from a knowledgeable outsider and needs a considerable investment in time and effort.

During such a process it would also be useful to examine the degree of similarity of fantasies among top executives. The more uniform they are, the greater the dangers of being out of touch with reality and falling into the trap of insularity. It may then be recognized that perhaps the time has come to open up the organization to those with different personalities and fantasies in order to create a climate of healthy diversity.

Recruitment and promotion policies might need to be changed in order to ensure substantial differences in the personalities of key executives. The tendency among executives to select and promote in their own image should not be underestimated. There are also socialization processes that occur in very subtle ways in organizations and that tend to have a molding effect on character. Since organizations easily become gathering stations for managers with similar styles, there will always be a danger that the lack of diversity may give way to organizational pathology.

CHAPTER 6

THE DOWNSIDE
OF DOWNSIZING[1]

I have striven not to laugh at human actions, not to weep at them, nor to hate them, but to understand them.

—Spinoza

I think re-engineering or restructuring or downsizing or rightsizing or whatever you want to call it, it's basically firing, has gone way too far. Employees, as I've talked to them across the country, feel that they are not respected, they are not valued, they are worried about their jobs. They simply feel that the company is no longer loyal to them. Why should they be loyal to the company, they ask me. Why should I go the extra mile? Why should I care?

—Robert Reich

You cannot shrink your way to greatness.

—Tom Peters

HIGH PRICE TO PAY

Downsizing—the planned elimination of positions or jobs—is a relatively recent phenomenon that has become a favorite business practice for a large number of troubled corporations. Starting with factory closures in sunset industries during the recession of the early 1980s and continuing

---

[1]This chapter is based on an article published under the same title: Kets de Vries, Manfred F.R., and Balazs, Katharina (1997) 'The Downside of Downsizing,' *Human Relations*, 50(1), 11–50.

as an after-effect of merger and acquisition mania, downsizing has become one of the inevitable outcomes of living in a global world where continual adjustments to products, services, and the price of labor are needed to remain competitive.

Since the late 1980s, nearly all of the *Fortune 1000* firms have engaged in downsizing, and this trend seems to be continuing. Various developments in management indicate that the end of downsizing is nowhere in sight. One major contributing factor is the increasing popularity of global benchmarking. Finding one's overhead costs wanting compared not only to domestic but also to global competitors is now seen as a convincing argument for taking large numbers of employees off the payroll. Another reason for the continued use of downsizing is the administrative impact of the revolution in information and communication technologies. Changes in these technologies have led to a growing redundancy of the traditional, go-between role of middle management—a group of people previously preoccupied with collecting, analyzing, and transmitting information up and down the hierarchy. Last, but certainly not least, downsizing is sometimes the price paid for strategic errors made by top management—the erroneous interpretation of market trends, for example.

Among the expected benefits of downsizing are such factors as lower overheads, decreased bureaucracy, faster decision-making, smoother communication, greater 'intrapreneurial' behavior, increased productivity, and better earnings. Its major *raison d'être,* however, is to make a company more efficient compared to its competitors. But whether these benefits materialize is another question. The effectiveness of downsizing as a way to bring a company back to organizational health and increased competitiveness has been seriously challenged. The actual gains may be much less than originally thought—for the majority of the restructured firms surveyed reported that productivity either remained stagnant or deteriorated after downsizing (Henkoff, 1990). Most downsized companies would experience problems with morale, trust, and productivity. Layoffs and restructuring have a severe adverse impact on the morale of the survivors. Research results have indicated that many organizations enjoy an initial upsurge in productivity immediately after downsizing but then become depressed and lethargic (Appelbaum, Simpson, and Shapiro, 1987; Custer, 1994). The stock price of these firms is similarly negatively affected.

Dictated by tough economic principles, following the call of the stock market, downsizing was seen as solely positive in its early days, though it was unclear to what extent its effects would alter the rules of the corporate world. It was expected that, once a company had gone through downsizing, everything would 'return to normal.'

While nobody was willing or able to anticipate the detrimental social consequences this new practice might have, those consequences soon appeared on the horizon. The most prevalent one can be seen in the situation of white-collar workers. In the past (in cases of cyclical downturns, for example) it was blue-collar workers who had to bear the brunt of reductions in personnel. Now—downsizing having brought 'cutback democracy' to the workplace—people in all job positions are included. Lower level employees have always been used to, and have sometimes even anticipated, fluctuations in the job market, but an increasing number of executives are now on the receiving end of cost-cutting programs and have been taken by surprise by downsizing's initial impact on job security. Over the past two decades, the protected middle class has had to learn to live with the shattered illusion of prosperity. They can no longer take it for granted that their children will have a better life than they did, for example; instead, downward mobility has become more common. And these are just some of the first, rippling effects of the new downsizing way of life—frightening indicators for the future.

The illusion of the quick fix

Some management scholars have argued that one of the reasons for the failure of many downsizing efforts is an overly simplistic approach. Too many executives implement downsizing through an across-the-board headcount reduction. This is generally an excessively short-sighted business strategy. Executives who take this approach, focusing on perceived internal efficiency rather than challenging the overall way the company does business, limit themselves to the implementation of superficial changes. Paradoxically, in situations of attrition, hiring freezes, or forced early retirement, the star performers are often the first to leave the company. Consequently, crucial skills in human capital disappear, and organizational memory is disrupted or completely lost. Furthermore, those who remain are often stuck with an increased workload. The result is a group of unhappy, overworked employees, some of whom have to do tasks for which they have not been trained. To ease the disruption, patch-up solutions have to be found, sometimes with the help of costly consultants (an irony, given the initial drive to cut expenses and save money). Furthermore, due to the prevailing malaise in the company, downsizing may eventually beget more downsizing, causing 'change fatigue' in executives and employees. It is because of consequences such as these that the effectiveness of downsizing has been called into question.

Granted, slashing people from the payroll generally has a temporary beneficial effect in the form of reduced overhead (as would holding back on capital investments and R&D), but mere cost-cutting is inadequate to prepare a corporation for the global business Olympics. More is needed to ensure increased market share and profitability. Companies that take the downsizing route seem to be preoccupied with their past rather than focused on their future. As a consequence, they delay long-term investments for short-term gains, in part to elicit a positive reaction (often temporary) from the stock market.

The fact that future success depends on such employee-centered factors as constant innovation, exceptional customer satisfaction, and good corporate citizenship (i.e. teamwork rather than turf defending) implies that substantial investments have to be made in employees. Therefore, merely cutting people from the payroll is not the way to go. Wholesale cuts create resentment and resistance and thus affect employee loyalty and commitment. In fact, firms that engage repeatedly in downsizing have difficulty attracting the best and the brightest due to bad publicity (regardless of whether that publicity is issued officially or by word of mouth). As one wit very appropriately noted: 'downsizing, rightsizing, dumbsizing … capsizing.' Symptomatic of downsizing's darker side is the fact that most firms do not succeed in their original effort and end up downsizing again a year later (Pearlstein, 1994).

From downsizing to reinventing

It is clear from this discussion that downsizing can take many forms, all of which attempt to improve organizational effectiveness, efficiency, productivity, and competitiveness. Despite this commonality, there is a progressive differentiation in people's perceptions of the downsizing phenomenon: from merely restructuring (getting smaller), to reengineering (getting better), to reinventing the corporation (getting smarter). In its broadest sense, downsizing is part of a continuous corporate renewal process.

A number of students of organizations have argued that this broader approach to downsizing—as opposed to across-the-board reductions—leads to a more positive long-term impact. These theorists see downsizing as affecting all the work processes in the organization. With the enlarged definition offered by this viewpoint, the goal of a downsizing effort becomes to reassess and alter the company's fundamental business practices. Thus the company's organizational design, work processes, corporate culture, and mission may face an overhaul. Not only functions but also hierarchical levels and even complete business units may need to be eliminated. In its widest sense, then, the term *downsizing* describes a complete strategic transformation effort that changes the values and attitudes of the company's corporate culture. In this definition, downsizing is not a stand-alone shortcut; rather, it is part of a company's continuous improvement scheme. As such, it takes on a long-term perspective, its objective being to look for ways to improve productivity, cut costs, and increase earnings.

Its mixed press notwithstanding, corporate downsizing is likely to remain an attractive option for many organizations. Even if the long-term benefits are questionable, downsizing shows that decisions are being made and actions taken. In addition, many consulting firms, recognizing a new and profitable niche, have thrown themselves into the downsizing arena. Yet, as mentioned before, there is a high social cost attached to this newest rage in management. Indeed, it appears that continuous downsizing and a motivated workforce are mutually exclusive.

DOWNSIZING: SALIENT ISSUES

In spite of being a relatively new phenomenon in organizational life, corporate downsizing has inspired a great deal of research concentrating on different issues pertaining to the subject—research that has resulted in a number of important findings. One of the most extensive and systematic surveys of corporate downsizing is a four-year study done by Kim Cameron, Sarah Freeman, and Aneil Mishra (Cameron, Freeman, and Mishra, 1991; 1993; Freeman and Cameron, 1993; Cameron, 1994). This study offers a theoretical framework of the process, focusing on possible implementation strategies, the organizational effects of downsizing, and best practices. A significant negative correlation between organizational effectiveness and downsizing through layoffs is one of the major findings of this research project. Although the study points to the effective management of the human resource system as one of the most critical factors in successful downsizing, it does not examine the downsizing process from the perspective of the individual.

Unfortunately, much of the subsequent literature follows this line of investigation. All too often employees, in the typical approach to downsizing—whether in corporate offices or in the research arena—are still treated in an abstract fashion. In the human-engineering approach to downsizing, people are seen more as liabilities than as assets, the emotional experience of the individual getting short shrift. It is exactly this changing nature of the relationship between individual and organization, however, that warrants further attention. It is difficult to be successful as an organization with a group of demotivated employees. Fortunately, some students of the downsizing phenomenon have taken on this problem from a more individual perspective.

The breaking of the psychological contract

The major issue for those on the receiving end of downsizing—the survivors and the victims—concerns the 'psychological contract.' This term was coined by Harry Levinson to describe the unspoken agreement that exists between every organization and its employees—an agreement in which the organization promises lifetime employment in return for hard work and loyalty, a supportive response to employees' psychological needs and defenses in return for employees' meeting the organization's unstated needs (Levinson, 1962).

Downsizing breaks this implicit psychological contract between employer and employee. As a result, the feeling of employee dependency that, over many years with an organization, may have evolved into a sense of entitlement is twisted into a sense of betrayal.

The concept of employability

It is becoming increasingly clear that lasting, beneficial changes in the corporate world require the painful adaptation of those concerned to a radically different way of life—one without job security in the traditional meaning of the term. In response to that reality, many vanguard organizations are espousing the notion that fostering an intrapreneurial environment—one that allows employees to approach their jobs as individual entrepreneurs, moving in and out of the organization as their and the organization's needs dictate—requires a new relationship between the employee and the organization.

Career self-management—that is, taking control of one's job and career as opposed to letting the company take care of them (as in the old employment contract)—is viewed as one possible solution to the problem of diminished job security. Toward that end, the term *employability* is replacing the concept of *job tenure*. The organization of the future is described as taking on a guiding role to help employees toward a self-employed attitude. To provide at least a modicum of security, organizations encourage employees to keep their work experience as up-to-date as possible so that they are better able to get a new job if laid off. A new, shorter-term employment contract is proposed as part of this solution—a contract that gives limited security for a defined period of time.

Helpful as these new ideas may sound on paper, this way of operating goes against the basic need for connectedness and affiliation and necessitates a great shift in thinking and expertise on the part of both employees and executives. For many people—particularly those having trouble dealing with ambiguity—employability comes with a considerable amount of stress.

Stress reactions in the workplace

Researchers sharing this perspective on the individual consider stress to be the crucial theoretical construct underlying the psychological dynamics pertaining to job loss. In Joel Brockner's study of the effects of work layoffs on survivors, for example, he shows clearly that organizational downsizing is a significant stress-inducing factor that has a profound influence on the work behaviors and attitudes of the remaining workforce (Brockner, 1988). The continued threat of job loss—stimulating feelings of loss of control over one's environment and threatening one's internalized concept of self—is regarded as the primary cause of deteriorating psychological well-being in the workplace and accounts for many stress-related illnesses, such as heart disease and ulcers. These findings underline the importance of managing interpersonal relations to help employees deal with the stress caused by the downsizing process.

Researchers assessing how employees differ in their reactions to downsizing have identified financial distress and previous attachment to the job as the major factors contributing to employees' sense of despair (Leana and Feldman, 1990). In those employees who are devastated by downsizing, losing the job often evokes reactions comparable to those experienced at the death of someone close (Greenhalgh and Rosenblatt, 1984). Feelings of desperation over job loss may even culminate in violence or self-destruction, as illustrated by statistics that denote murder in the workplace as the fastest-growing form of homicide in the United States, with about 40 % of those homicides followed by suicide (Thornburg, 1992).

Some researchers have explored possible defensive reactions aroused by the downsizing process. One common reaction seems to be denial, a coping mechanism common to both management and employees in the downsizing process, though the higher the organizational level, the stronger the denial tends to be (Noer, 1993). Other researchers have identified various cognitive coping strategies leading to one of two different reactions to downsizing: denial–detachment (through which people distance themselves psychologically from the perceived threat) and hypersensitivity (through which they closely monitor for danger signs) (Greenhalgh and Jick, 1989).

The view from the top

In most of these studies, little attention has been paid to the role of those in charge of the downsizing process. Yet a 1991 survey of 1005 companies conducted by the Wyatt Company indicates that the behavior of top executives—especially their treatment of surviving employees—is one of the main determinants of the success or failure of the downsizing process (Bennett, 1991; Lalli, 1992). The way top executives handle layoffs has been shown to have a significant impact on the degree of dysfunctionality in survivors' work behavior and attitudes (Brockner, 1988). The competence, knowledge, dynamism, and accessibility of leaders, along with their ability to clearly articulate a vision that provides motivation for the future, are crucial to a positive outcome (Cameron, Freeman, and Mishra, 1991). What makes downsizing so difficult for the executives involved is that they often have to discard the values that furthered their own advancement up the organizational career ladder. Many executives, to escape dealing with that conflict, become psychologically detached, focusing not on their employees but on projected organizational outcomes. This way of coping proves ineffective, however, as they attempt to deal with hostility, depression, absenteeism, and substance abuse among the workforce (Leana and Feldman, 1988; Noer, 1993; Smith, 1994).

Adding to the stress of the process for executives is the likely scapegoating of leaders and the loss of leader credibility (Cameron, Kim, and Whetten, 1987). This scapegoating (and the politicized environment that fosters it) causes many top executives to distance themselves from their employees to avoid criticism and antagonism (Cameron, Freeman, and Mishra, 1993). They frequently react to layoffs by withdrawing from the remaining workforce. Already lonely top executives thus become even more isolated during downsizing and layoffs. Moreover, many of these executives are not prepared for the strong reactions of the survivors.

Many senior executives do not recognize the extent to which the productivity of the remaining employees depends on apparently trivial details of the implementation of the downsizing process. These implementation details—such as spelling out what milestones have to be achieved to arrive at the desired end-state and involving the remaining executives in the process—have a positive effect. By ignoring these details and the surviving subordinates' emotional state, however, executives become prone to grave mistakes—mistakes that may lead to self-destructive behavior in survivors. Executives should expect their surviving subordinates to experience a wide variety of psychological emotional reactions, including anxiety, anger, guilt, envy, relief, and denial (Cameron, Freeman, and Mishra, 1993; Brockner, 1988; Henkoff, 1994), and they should help employees work through those reactions. In addition, they should work to avoid another common executive mistake: telling the survivors (in hopes that guilt will make them work harder) to be grateful that they still have jobs, a response that creates resentment and results in oppositional behavior (Noer, 1993).

Downsizing from a different perspective

Most authors in the existing literature on downsizing focus on the emotional and professional costs to those individuals at the receiving end of the process: the victims and the survivors. They deal—usually in a very descriptive way (listing various stress symptoms, for example)—with the question of how the people whose jobs have been terminated cope with sudden unemployment. They also address the consequences for the survivors.

To get a better grasp of the psychology of the downsizing process, we have to go beyond what happens with victims and survivors. While the consequences to those individuals are important, we also need to address how the people who actually do the downsizing are psychologically affected. Interviews with executives involved in the process show quite clearly that this unpleasant task can have considerable emotional impact. For many executives, as was noted earlier, downsizing contradicts long-held attitudes toward business life. Those leaders, then, have to cope with the double burden of their own emotional reactions and those of the other survivors. They have to deal with major change while experiencing it themselves. These are very important considerations, especially given that the executives' psychological state is likely to have a serious effect on corporate culture, strategy, and structure.

In the discussion that follows, I will first focus on the victims and survivors, reviewing their reaction patterns. Then I will address the reactions of the 'executioners.'

WAYS OF COPING

Doing open-ended interviews with 60 'victims,' 60 'survivors,' and 80 'executioners' (the population mainly drawn from my INSEAD leadership seminars), I asked questions based on psychiatric, clinical psychological, and organizational diagnostic interviewing techniques. The questions elicited biographical and attitudinal information on employment, job situation, job loss, the downsizing process, and physical and mental health.

As a result of the interviews, victims were assigned to one of four reaction classifications (adaptable, depressed, Gauguin-emulating, or antagonistic) and 'executioners' to one of six reaction classifications (adjusted, compulsive/ritualistic, depressed, alexithymic/anhedonic, abrasive, and dissociative). I made no attempt to classify survivors, limiting myself to a general description of how downsizing was experienced by that group of people.

Among the victims, the largest group turned out to be the adaptable (43.3%), followed by the depressed (30%), those 'doing a Gauguin'[2] (16.7%), and finally the antagonistic (10%). For the 'executioners,' the largest group was the one without any obvious symptoms (37.5%), followed by the compulsive/ritualistic (17.5%), the depressed (17.5%), the alexithymic/anhedonic (11.25%), the abrasive (8.75%), and the dissociative (7.5%).

The victims

Coping can be seen as a person's cognitive, emotional, and behavioral efforts to manage specific external and internal demands that are experienced as taxing. All of us have our own characteristic ways of dealing with stressful situations. Some people respond by taking a proactive stand, trying to take firm control over their lives, while others cope more reactively, attempting to escape or avoid stress. From my discussions with downsized individuals, I was able to distinguish a number of recurrent patterns. Bear in mind, however, that these descriptions are not exhaustive; rather, they are attempts at categorization in order to clarify how the process of downsizing affects the individual. Many different permutations and combinations are possible.

The adaptable victim   For some individuals in the study, the downsizing process engendered comparatively little drama. These people, who

---

[2]After the painter who gave up a banking career to become a painter on a Polynesian island.

generally had a high skill level, succeeded in finding another job with relative ease, usually in a field similar to the one they had been working in. They tended to join smaller companies so as to feel less like a cog in a wheel. Although the experience of downsizing gave some of these people a rather cynical outlook toward their new organization—after all, in spite of all the rational arguments given for their termination, their belief in the psychological contract had been shaken—being in a new workplace generally had a positive effect. When the transition between jobs was over, these adaptable individuals often discovered that in the new, smaller company, the daily challenges (and rewards) were greater and more immediate. Their position often encompassed a wider or some-what different spectrum of responsibilities than in the previous organiza-tion. This gave them the opportunity to learn new things and offered the chance for renewal. As one executive told me, 'My dismissal was the best thing that's ever happened to me. I was literally dying on the job. Being forced to find a new job and prove myself once more has given me a greater feeling of vitality.'

Those who 'did a Gauguin'   One group of executives turned ter-mination into a completely new opportunity. For this group—those who opted to 'do a Gauguin'—the experience of downsizing offered a new lease on life through career change as well as job change. After all too many working years, these executives were like the walking dead before downsizing struck. As one person described it, 'Over the last decade, until just recently, I sleepwalked through life. The only times I felt alive were when I was with friends playing golf or tennis. This has changed tremen-dously since I shifted fields. I thoroughly enjoy coming to work now. I really like what I'm doing.'

Prior to their termination, these people faithfully and competently went through the motions of work, but they no longer got any pleasure out of it. Because their life was too comfortable to contemplate a change, however, they endured the status quo—but without being really produc-tive (and certainly without being creative). Finding themselves suddenly out of work was exactly the stimulus they needed to come back to life. Unemployment opened up the opportunity to pursue something they had always dreamed of doing but had never dared do. Those who were at midlife when faced with downsizing were forced to stop and reconsider their priorities. For the first time, they asked themselves what they wanted to do as opposed to what others expected from them.

Most of the Gauguin emulators were middle-aged or older—old enough to have the sense that time was running out. They felt that if they failed to take action at this moment of opportunity, change would never happen. After years on the job, they had also acquired adequate financial security to provide them with a safety net. These underlying factors, combined with sudden unemployment, pushed them over the edge: they finally dared to take the leap they had always dreamed of.

People in this group often pursued what might be called a Protean career (after the Greek god Proteus, who was able to continually change shape). Many went for a major career (and often life) change—for example, from senior vice president of a bank to real estate developer, from CEO to public school educator, from computer analyst to art gallery manager. Some were even more adventurous, following Gauguin's example quite literally. In many instances, these apparently dramatic changes came as no great surprise to close friends and family. Those who made major career changes had generally already been involved in some capacity in their new field.

The depressed victim   Some victims of downsizing ended up with depressive reactions. These were the people who had the most difficult time adjusting to the new situation in which they found themselves. Generally, they felt betrayed by the organization to which they had devoted a considerable part of their lives. Because their sense of self-esteem was closely tied to organizational identity, the loss of familiar surroundings made them fall apart. Unable to move on, they became stuck in the mourning process. They avoided dealing with the new reality; they seemed to have no energy left to go out and find a new job; they were unable to concentrate on whatever they were doing; they procrastinated and were irritable. They also experienced a host of emotional and physiological problems: they often neglected their appearance; they had a tendency to suffer from insomnia and loss of appetite; and they were preoccupied with negative thoughts. Because of their depressive outlook, their fear of not being able to find another job often became a self-fulfilling prophecy; some of these victims ended up becoming part of the permanently unemployed. Alcoholism and other forms of substance abuse were common consequences. Marital problems, often resulting in divorce, led to a further deterioration of self-esteem and the fighting spirit, and suicidal thoughts were not uncommon.

Among the people with depressive reactions, one group initially took a proactive stand, making an effort to look for another job. When their efforts were stymied by repeated setbacks in the job market, however, they were forced to the realization that their skills were no longer wanted. Some of them eventually found another job, but one well below their former position. Underemployment became a way of life for these individuals, creating serious problems centered around self-esteem and replacing their original proactivity with a depressive outlook on life.

The antagonistic victim   A natural reaction when we have been hurt is anger; we all experience that reaction on occasion. We manage our anger or aggression by turning it either inward or outward, depending on our basic personality. Those victims who experienced depressive reactions to downsizing—the group described above—tended toward inwardly directed aggression. Another group turned their aggression outward, however. In some of these individuals, outwardly expressed aggression was the norm; in others, it was a heretofore-repressed behavior pattern triggered by the trauma of being 'rejected.' For both subsets of this latter group, verbal and physical violence became a behavioral pattern. The most common victims of their aggression were the members of their family. Sometimes, though, the anger extended outside the family circle. Among those who found other employment, some carried the aggression with them in the form of abrasive behavior on the new job—which led again to dismissal. In extreme circumstances, those who directed their aggression outwardly became quite dysfunctional, deciding to 'get even' with those whom they saw as having caused their misery: they directed their violent impulses toward former employers, superiors, or colleagues, sometimes in the form of harassment or sabotage.

The survivors

One finding that many researchers of the downsizing phenomenon agree upon is a cluster of reactions among those remaining in the organization—a cluster that has become known as 'survivor sickness' or 'survivor syndrome' (Noer, 1993; Cascio, 1993). These terms refer to the way survivors react when many of their friends and colleagues are forced to terminate their relationship with the company.

The issue of survivor guilt was originally dealt with in the context of the survival of the Holocaust. In contrast, 'survivor sickness' describes a set of attitudes, feelings, and perceptions that occur in employees who remain in organizational systems following involuntary employee reductions. These include anger, depression, fear, guilt, risk aversion, distrust, vulnerability or powerlessness, and loss of morale and motivation (Brockner, 1988; Cascio, 1993; Noer, 1993; Navran, 1994). The greater the survivors' perception of violation, the greater their susceptibility to survivor sickness seems to be.

The feeling of loss of control over the situation and the uncertainty caused by the possible loss of their own jobs can cause severe stress reactions in the survivors of downsizing. A sharp increase in the size of survivors' workload, longer working hours, and a reduction in vacation days—natural consequences of a smaller workforce—can reinforce this effect, leading to inefficiency and burnout (Brockner, Davy, and Carter, 1985; Brockner et al., 1987; Brockner, 1988, 1992; Mone, 1994).

By breaking up a complex set of interconnections, downsizing creates dramatic changes in the organizational environment. In the worst case— an all-too-typical scenario—the downsizing process tears the organization's whole value system apart. Consequently, the corporate culture that used to serve as the glue that kept the organization together loses its amalgamating function, and feelings of rudderlessness and anxiety emerge.

My downsizing study showed that job insecurity had an enormous impact on organizational effectiveness: many of the surviving executives asked themselves if they would be next in line; the dismissal of long-term employees resulted in the loss of institutional memory; head-office staffers with a strategic overview were dismissed; specialists on whom people could rely for certain types of decision were no longer there; and decision-making had a short-term emphasis (with serious repercussions for R&D, capital investments, and training and development). All these changes contributed to a sense of disorientation that had permanent consequences: the survivors perceived a significant and lasting change in their relationship to the organization. After an initial upsurge in productivity, they often settled into an attitude of fearful expectancy.

The survivors I spoke with reported that in companies that defined downsizing as a simple cutback in personnel, commitment and loyalty to the employer disappeared. The survivors felt that they were getting very little in return for the additional roles they had been asked to take on. After the psychological contract between employee and employer had been broken, distrust toward top management caused survivors to believe that management was guilty until proven innocent. This blaming phenomenon in those who remained was often a defense mechanism, a form of projection that helped individuals confront their own survivor guilt. Fairness on the part of the organization when implementing layoffs was of crucial importance in minimizing this phenomenon.

The study also showed that survivors either (1) distanced themselves from the layoff victims (the response favored when survivors did not substantially identify with the victims), or (2) distanced themselves from the organization (when they *did* identify with the victims). In addition, to reduce feelings of guilt over their co-workers' dismissal, some employees increased their level of output. Because job insecurity fostered a negative attitude among remaining employees, they felt the need to outperform their co-workers. Furthermore, the remaining workers needed to redress the feeling of inequity elicited by their survival by convincing themselves that those who had been laid off deserved it. In some instances, then, a moderate level of job insecurity actually led to temporarily heightened productivity, but it had the opposite effect on morale.

The executioners

From the interviews, it became clear that downsizing left an indelible imprint on executives who had implemented the process. I turn now to some of the factors that influence the behavior and reactions of executives as they experience downsizing.

Most of us assume an unconscious 'equation' in human interaction: the belief that what we do to others will be done to us. This so-called *lex talionis*—the law of retaliation, often expressed as 'an eye for an eye, a tooth for a tooth'—is an ancient rule with a long history. This principle is first recorded in Babylonian law, which states that criminals should receive punishment equaling the injuries they inflicted on their victims. This exacting retaliation has been the law of many societies throughout history. Although modern Western society has found other systems and forms of justice to compensate for injury, the ancient *lex talionis* still operates in the collective and individual unconscious in the form of subliminal fear of reprisal. Feelings of guilt, a general fear of retribution, and stress symptoms are the manifestations of this subconscious belief.

In those responsible for implementation, downsizing brings a fear of the *lex talionis* to the fore. Knowing that they are causing people hurt and grief, the 'executioners' may fantasize about a reversal of the situation. That fear that someone might try to 'get even,' if taken to the extreme, results in paranoid reactions. Some executives, caught up in an escalation of aggression fueled by paranoia, resort to preemptive action, crushing those they perceive as threats.

The belief in the *lex talionis* offers a partial explanation for the fact that most of the executives I spoke with were reluctant to do unpleasant things to others. Even those 'executioners' who had no fear of reprisals suffered considerable distress, however. Having to fire old friends and acquaintances—people with whom they had worked for years—was very painful. It is not surprising, then, that so many of the participants in the study used euphemisms to disguise what they were doing— terms such as *dehiring*, *disengaging*, and *decruiting*, with their Orwellian overtones.

The executives in the study reacted to the stress associated with downsizing in various ways. Some coped comfortably, while others regressed to troubling behavior patterns. Let's look now at some of the variations in response.

The adjusted executive   One group of executives handled the downsizing operation in a relatively well adjusted way. From the interviews, no obvious dysfunctional reaction patterns could be discerned in these individuals; residual scarring was minimal. (I realized in making this classification that the appearance of normality could have been a veneer, the result of a properly executed defensive process. Because of a lack of corroborative evidence, however, I let this reaction pattern stand.)

The compulsive/ritualistic executive   The compulsive personality is characterized by a preoccupation with order, parsimony, obstinacy, and perfection and by a need for mental and interpersonal control. This orientation is motivated by the aim to reduce anxiety and distress by maintaining a strong sense of control over oneself and one's environment and is achieved through self-imposed high standards. The compulsive's need for control is fulfilled by rigid attention to rules, procedures, and schedules.

The people in the study who belonged to this group were detail-oriented, excessively careful, inflexible, and prone to repetition. Characterized by interpersonal aloofness and restrained affectivity, they kept their emotions—'positive' as well as 'negative'—under tight control. They believed in complete deference to authority, bowing to the wishes of those above them. When they were in charge, they demanded deference from subordinates, giving rigid orders and insisting that those orders be followed to the letter.

Their need for control—whether conscious or not—and their self-imposed high standards often caused these people great distress. However, when the excessiveness of these traits was pointed out to them, they did not change their compulsive behavior, because that behavior served to maintain their psychic equilibrium.

The compulsive personalities in executive positions in the study devoted themselves almost exclusively to work and productivity. They hardly ever participated in leisure activities and when they did, they felt uncomfortable about neglecting work. They were not apt to delegate tasks, and they did not easily work with other people. Meticulous and detailed planners, they were unwilling to consider changes even when the situation itself changed. They controlled both spending and employee conduct as tightly as they controlled their day-planner.

One of the main defensive patterns found in this compulsive group of executives was that of isolation—the separation of an idea from the affect that accompanies it (but that remains repressed). While isolation can take on very primitive characteristics, in organizational life it is usually employed in a rather mature way: it generally takes the form of affect separated from cognition and manifests itself in such patterns as rationalization, moralization, compartmentalization, and intellectualization. As an example, by focusing on all the details of an issue, compulsive executives manage to avoid the affect-laden whole.

Given these tendencies, it is no surprise that compulsive executives reported conducting their downsizing operation in a precise and specific manner. They planned the complete downsizing procedure in great detail and then adhered to the plan exactly, without tolerating even the smallest deviation. They reduced uncertainty as far as was humanly possible by meticulous planning, ritualistic follow-up, tight control, and a complete centralization of power.

Because one of the major impetuses of their behavior was an underlying fear of disapproval and punishment, the compulsive executives did everything to make others regard their behavior as 'proper' and 'correct.' Priding themselves on their (perceived) fairness and sense of duty toward others, they followed rigid, mechanical procedures that reinforced their own and others' perception of the adequacy of such procedures. They hired consulting firms to activate certain functions in an effort to depersonalize layoffs, for example, and called outplacement firms into action to provide those 'rightfully' laid off with a 'fair chance' at reemployment through training in the job-search process. At the same time, the downsizing process provided a legitimate outlet for their repressed hostility. By doing their utmost to present downsizing as a perfectly implemented process necessary for the good of everyone involved, they were able simultaneously to cater to the needs of their personality structure and to appease their sense of guilt.

One of the executives—a man typical of the compulsive/ritualistic type—responded to a question about how he felt when deciding to lay off 300 people with a speech about the company's need to attain a certain return on investment, the cost of the newly installed information system, and the dangers of the global situation. When prompted again about his feelings, he resumed his monologue, going into great detail about the criteria used in selecting both a consulting firm to assist in the restructuring process and an outplacement outfit to assist in helping those laid off. Then he launched into a commentary on the termination benefits that were given to the laid-off employees. In all of these comments, he never once referred to his feelings. When pressed yet again to discuss his feelings with respect to downsizing, he finally said that he felt it had been a job well done.

The abrasive executive Research has shown that people with abrasive personalities share certain characteristics with compulsive/ritualistic individuals (Levinson, 1978). They too are driven, above all, by a strong need for perfection. They push themselves to achieve self-set unrealistic expectations, attempting to match their current self-image to the person they would like to be. Despite all their efforts, however, they are unable to live up to those expectations and experience a mounting sense of frustration, which in turn evokes aggressive feelings. The strength of these is determined by the extent of the discrepancy between where they perceive themselves to be and where they would like to be—a discrepancy that endures despite their best efforts. Because abrasive types have such exaggerated standards for themselves—standards that most likely originated with their first caregivers—they are never able to completely close the perceived gap. Eventually, their anger and aggression can no longer be contained. Like water surging over a broken dam, their hostility and aggression spill over, directed toward colleagues and subordinates, family and friends.

The abrasive personality is usually highly intelligent, possesses excellent problem-solving skills, is quick at grasping situations, and is adept at finding workable solutions. Because of these qualities, people with this personality can frequently be found in senior executive positions. Their intelligence and quick wit, however, are often accompanied by impatience, arrogance, and a lack of interpersonal skills. These executives are intensely rivalrous; they know their own abilities and do not trust others to be equally capable. By showing open contempt for their subordinates, abrasive people create in their co-workers feelings of inadequacy that destroy self-confidence and suppress initiative and creativity. Like compulsive executives, they also feel a strong need for control of both self and others, which results in a tendency to dominate.

Abrasive personalities often show signs of 'reactive narcissism'—signs such as emotional coldness, grandiosity, vindictiveness, and a sense of entitlement. Because age-appropriate development did not occur when these individuals were growing up (probably due to a poor holding environment for frustrating experiences), many acquired a defective, poorly integrated sense of identity, leading to an unstable sense of self-esteem. Those early experiences may have left a legacy of bitterness and vindictiveness. Thus, apart from being forever frustrated in what they set out to do, some of them also experience an urge to get even for the wrongs they feel they have experienced.

Abrasive people use aggressive tactics in dealing with others—tactics learned from their parents or other caretakers who used severe disciplinary measures to 'tame' their offspring. They know from experience that coercion is the way to get other people to do what they want. They view others as extensions of themselves, as devices for their own self-aggrandizement, to be freely and legitimately used for their own purposes. Furthermore, they see themselves as special and feel that they deserve to be treated differently than others. Likewise, they believe that the boundaries of proper behavior do not apply to them.

The abrasive executives in the downsizing study, when put in charge of downsizing, generally adopted reaction patterns that corresponded to their personality traits. When laying people off, they resorted to the primitive defense mechanisms of splitting (as noted earlier, the division of people into 'good' and 'bad') and devaluation in order to appease their strong feelings of guilt. Through splitting, they created an us-versus-them mentality in the organization, putting the blame for the problems the company found itself in on the employees who were about to be dismissed. In addition, they tended to rationalize the process by devaluing those subjected to it—that is, by belittling the people they had downsized—calling them 'deadwood' or 'rotten apples.'

For example, one executive I interviewed kept harping on about the people he had laid off. According to him, 'It was those SOBs in my organization who were responsible for the company's decline in sales and profitability. Firing them was the best thing I've done in a long time. Good riddance. Actually, I've probably been too soft all along. I should have done it much sooner and fired more! Unfortunately, I was given free rein only recently, after the retirement of my predecessor.' He also contrasted other corporate cultures with his own—his was a global corporation—making the splitting even more pronounced. It became clear from his conversation that these corporate cultures had been devalued and had carried the brunt of his downsizing effort. This executive's actions are reminiscent of the behavior of 'Chainsaw Al' or 'Rambo in Pinstripes,' alias Albert Dunlap, the infamous US turnaround artist and downsizer (Dunlap and Andelman, 1997) who was later discredited for a series of accounting frauds. Dunlap was notorious for obtaining short-term results (shareholders always did well, as did he) at the cost of the long-term effects his brutal practices had on the people in corporations he ran. In 2009 he was voted 'the sixth worst CEO of all time.'[3]

The dangers of having an abrasive executive in charge of the downsizing process seem obvious. Even in the best case, such leaders are likely to engender a negative, counterproductive attitude among employees. In the worst case, they can trigger a series of destructive processes among members of the organization that result in a disastrous outcome for the company's attempted renewal process.

[3] www.portfolio.com, April 22, 2009.

The dissociative executive   One of the reaction patterns I found among executives who implemented downsizing was dissociation. Allied to the denial defense, dissociation—the separation and exclusion of mental processes that are normally integrated—is a primitive way of dealing with stressful situations, an emergency measure in times of extreme stress. Typically, what sets this defense in motion is a situation charged with painful emotions and psychological conflict. Dissociation—which serves as a shut-off mechanism, an alteration in the perception of reality—is a way of protecting oneself against what are perceived to be unbearable experiences. As mentioned earlier, a person who resorts to this way of coping removes from conscious awareness and control a complex of associated mental elements such as thoughts, images, feelings, sensations, and desires. Dissociation is a distorted experience of the self associated with a sense of unreality (or strangeness) and profound detachment. In the words of one of the top executives who experienced dissociation, 'I wasn't really there when I had to fire a few hundred people. Granted, I was there physically, but certainly not emotionally. I remember distinctly being in a daze, standing in one of the company's meeting halls, trying to explain to the employees why they were going to be laid off. It was as if I were looking at myself from the outside, watching myself in a play. This sensation became even worse when I had to lay off people a second time. It was like I was acting in a dream.'

Many of the executives in the downsizing study described themselves as being completely detached from what they were doing while engaged in downsizing, firing literally hundreds or even thousands of people. They felt like spectators in the process, going through the motions but not really feeling part of them. Although inner mental processes and external events went on exactly as before, these things lacked personal affect or meaning to the individual concerned. This feeling of unreality was experienced, as the above quote illustrates, as detachment from one's own mental processes or body. The person became an outside observer, feeling like an automaton or someone moving through a dream. Associated features were dizziness, anxiety, hypochondriacal concerns, fears of going insane, and disturbances in the sense of time and space.

A loss of the capacity to experience emotions occurred in dissociated executives, even though they sometimes appeared to express them. Some people experiencing dissociation were driven to vigorous activity to induce sensations intense enough to break through the wall of unreality. In the study, as in general, people prone to this disorder had a keen and unfailing awareness of the disturbance in their sense of reality. As a matter of fact, their self-observation capacities were heightened. Although they complained about feelings of estrangement and absence of emotions and often manifested considerable anxiety, they showed no evidence of either a major disturbance of affect or disorganized thought processes. As an occasional isolated experience, dissociation was rather common among the subjects of the downsizing study. In some people, however, it was a recurrent phenomenon, often accompanying depression.

The alexithymic/anhedonic executive   While dissociation does not cause a major disturbance of affect, alexithymic manifestations can. Executives who suffered from alexithymic-like symptoms—especially people who repeatedly engaged in the process of downsizing—began to have problems with a diminishing ability to feel. In some instances, this developed into alexithymic reactions.

In the first volume of this series,[4] I wrote at length about alexithymics— people who are emotionally color-blind and either struggle, or are unable, to understand their emotions or moods. In the case of serious alexithymic reactions, individuals have an extreme reality-based cognitive style, an impoverished fantasy life, a paucity of inner emotional experience, a tendency to engage in stereotypical interpersonal behavior, and a speech pattern characterized by endless, trivial, repetitive details.

Some of the executives I spoke with had entered the workforce with a mildly alexithymic disposition; that is, they had difficulty experiencing and recognizing emotions from the outset. Others developed such tendencies after a specific stressful event or series of events. Those who worked in organizations in which control of emotions was the norm had these tendencies reinforced; and certainly the traumatic experience of being the main actor in a downsizing process exacerbated them. Some of the people I talked with—veterans of downsizing—had become completely numb after repeated downsizing operations. Executives susceptible to this disorder increasingly experienced difficulty feeling, yet they often ignored the distress signals given by their minds and bodies. Frequently, these people were somatizers—that is, they complained about vague medical problems while the real issue was emotional distress. As one executive said, when asked how he felt during the downsizing process, 'I really don't know how I feel; although it may sound strange, my wife often tells me how I feel. To be honest, I'm quite confused about feelings. It's difficult for me to talk about emotional differentiations. I have no strong positive or negative feelings. But the process of having to engage in downsizing gives me a literal pain in the gut.'

After repeated downsizing efforts, some of these people acquired a sense of deadness; their behavior took on a robotlike quality. Because external details brought some life to their inner deadness, they often ended

---

[4] *Reflections on Character and Leadership* (2009) Chapter 3, p.62.

up using work as a kind of drug. They took flight into *doing* to prevent *experiencing*. The unconscious aim behind their detail-focused work orientation was to avoid painful reflection on the effects of downsizing.

Anhedonia—the loss of interest in and withdrawal from all activities that ordinarily provide pleasure—is closely associated with alexithymia. This pattern manifests itself through difficulty in maintaining concentration and interest in the activities that previously occupied attention. A frequent complaint among the anhedonic executives in the downsizing study was boredom. As their original enthusiasm for work faded, these executives became increasingly disinclined to engage in normal workplace activities. (This loss of pleasure was applicable to their private life as well.) A number of the executives interviewed complained about their lack of work enjoyment, noting that their original enthusiasm for the job had dissipated. With both interest and concentration diminished, they tended toward procrastination, postponing decisions and becoming increasingly ineffective. Most felt that the continuous process of downsizing had contributed to their dissatisfaction with organizational life and life in general.

The depressed executive   It is only a small step from anhedonia to depression. I have already commented on the depressive reactions among the victims of the downsizing process. The experiences of the implementers were similar. In fact, depression was a regular occurrence among most of the downsizing interviewees—though it varied from simply a depressed mood and feelings of guilt to serious thoughts of (and even attempts at) suicide.

The depressed executives in the study generally experienced a flattening of affect—that is, an inability to respond to the appropriate mood of the occasion. They were able to see only the darker side of things, preoccupied as they were with gloomy thoughts. Many perceived life as a burden, not worth living. In addition, they occasionally had inappropriate emotional reactions—bursting into tears at the workplace, for example. They also experienced a noticeable loss of energy: their activity level dropped, and they (like depressive victims) sometimes neglected their personal appearance. They tended to suffer from insomnia as well; and even if they slept, they often felt tired (or even exhausted) in the morning. They complained that food had lost its appeal, with weight loss a common result. Sexual interest also diminished: that special feeling of intimate enjoyment was no longer there, and in some instances impotence occurred.

Often executives who became depressed turned to self-accusation. In many, a remarkable switch took place: after directing aggression outward in the process of downsizing, these executives now directed it inward.

Due to this new sense of culpability, they were ready to believe the worst about themselves. And as the main executioners in a downsizing drama, they did not find it difficult to identify sins. Increasingly, they blamed themselves for the harm they had caused others.

WORKING THROUGH LOSS

Victims and survivors of the downsizing process were at opposite ends of the change spectrum. In comparing their situations, however, I noted some similarities in their reactions and in their cognitive and emotional approaches to events. Both groups had to endure extremely stressful events, both had to cope with the loss of colleagues and friends, and both had to start a new life—one that was bereft of the perceived security that had earlier governed their working identities.

The process of mourning

Most people work for more than just money; they have intrinsic motivators as well. One of these motivators is the need for belonging. A sense of belonging to a larger entity is important in the establishment of a person's identity. To be part of an organization, to pursue a lasting career, offers that opportunity. For many people in the study, organizational and career identity were important in the construction of overall identity and thus constituted a major source of self-esteem.

Given the amount of time people spend at work, companies can be regarded as symbolic families. The people we interact with on the job often become part of our inner world and are therefore important for our overall well-being. In the case of the subjects of the study, separation from members of this 'family,' whether through their own layoff or that of colleagues, came with a sense of separation and loss. Such a loss, for most people, created a need to 'mourn' and resulted in a sequence of mourning reactions (Bowlby, 1969; Kets de Vries and Miller, 1984).

In the first stage, people laid off by organizational downsizing generally experience a sense of numbness interrupted by occasional feelings of panic and outbursts of anger. These are understandable reactions to having been hurt. People who have suffered a loss need the opportunity to work through their feelings in order to be able to go on. Any attempt to suppress these feelings will only cause greater problems. A certain amount of anger is to be seen as a positive sign in this initial phase, an indicator that their have retained their fighting spirit.

The first mourning phase after a downsizing effort is usually followed by a period of yearning and searching for what is lost. This period, which may last for several months, is often accompanied by feelings of disbelief and disorientation and by a denial of the new reality. Preoccupied with the past, those involved in downsizing long for the 'good old days.'

In the third stage—disorganization and despair—survivors as well as victims wonder whether and where they will now fit in. Having lost their strong sense of identity as members of an organization, they despair of belonging again and cannot decide how to proceed. Bouts of self-reproach and sadness are typically part of the picture as well. Although the downsizing actions taken by management are generally completely out of their control, victims and survivors tend to blame themselves for what has happened.

As people work through these three initial stages of the mourning process, they begin to discard past patterns of thinking, feeling, and acting. A gradual acceptance of the new situation develops, both personally and organizationally, along with a willingness to go through a process of self-examination. That self-examination results in a redefinition and even reinvention of the self. As the mourner tentatively explores new opportunities and seeks to establish a new equilibrium, he or she feels a growing sense of hope; new choices seem possible. A more proactive attitude and an orientation toward the future emerge. Arrival at this phase indicates that the person has come to grips with the new reality.

The downsizing study indicated that quite a few executives were unable to finish mourning what had happened to them. Incapable of proceeding beyond the early stages of the mourning process, they held on to primitive defense mechanisms, denying reality and clinging to the past. People caught in this situation continued to function as if nothing had happened, trying to maintain their illusions. Some people responded to the perceived withdrawal of status and respect with aggression and destruction. Others used displacement (redirection of anger away from the responsible party toward someone else), cognitive dissociation, and splitting as defense mechanisms.

Burnout

Research has also pinpointed a relationship between the phenomenon of downsizing and the increase in disability claims for mental disorders and the incidence of stress-induced illness (Smith, 1994). For a number of people, downsizing is generally accompanied by emotional, cognitive, and physiological manifestations that can be grouped under the label 'burnout.'

Burnout is an amalgamation of stress reactions. The main symptoms are feelings of emotional exhaustion, lack of energy, and emptiness. Depersonalization and a cynical, dehumanizing, and negative attitude toward people combine in a stress syndrome that often accompanies cases of severe burnout (Cordes and Dougherty, 1993).

Burnout implies a deterioration of mental health symptomized by self-esteem problems, irritability, depression, helplessness, and free-floating anxiety. In addition to the emotional exhaustion, lack of energy, and emptiness mentioned earlier, symptoms include insomnia, headaches, nausea, chest pains, gastrointestinal disturbances (such as ulcers and colitis), and allergic reactions. The consequences of burnout include an increase in substance abuse, employee turnover, and absenteeism, and sometimes even suicide. Downsizing, because of its chronic stress and the disruption it brings to interpersonal contacts, may accelerate and amplify the manifestations of burnout (although there is no one-to-one correlation).

The downsizing study indicated that many of the victims of the downsizing process showed signs of burnout as a reaction to their layoff. Survivors and 'executioners' also showed signs of burnout, especially after repeated layoffs. Coping patterns for all three groups were colored by these burnout symptoms.

Among the 'executioners,' the conflict surrounding role ambiguity was an important factor in the development of burnout. Executives tended to perceive themselves as the 'builders' of the organization and the guardians of their employees' well-being. Downsizing forced them to fire people—thus violating what they saw as their proper role. The guilt that this inner conflict created, coupled with the fact that downsizing layoffs were generally not a one-time occurrence but had to be implemented repeatedly, contributed to their sense of failure. Blaming themselves for lacking the necessary skills to solve the problems of the organization, executives no longer saw themselves as competent; they lost their sense of achievement. The result was a diminished sense of self-esteem. Eventually, these conflicting feelings gave rise to burnout.

THE TACTICS OF DOWNSIZING

We have seen the great variety of reaction patterns typical among individuals affected by the downsizing process. That process, narrowly defined (that is, as stand-alone across-the-board cuts rather than layoffs that are part of a continuous corporate transformation), however carefully it is done, will leave wounds. However humane one tries to be, individuals will be hurt; and in the process, the company itself will be negatively affected. Successfully implementing a narrow downsizing effort is difficult, if not impossible. Indeed, downsizing as a measure of expediency inevitably causes more harm than good. Only if downsizing is applied in its broader sense is the outlook more positive.

Moreover, even if an organization survives a narrowly construed downsizing, such a process is no guarantee of the company's future success. The most important dilemma remains: people need to believe in the new organization to make it work, but to believe in it they need to see that it works.

Many executives first face others' and their own unexpected emotional reactions when they are already deeply involved in downsizing activities. Even executives who have a detailed strategic plan generally stumble when they set out to realize it, because they fail to take into account one of the most significant determinants of the success or failure of their efforts: the behavior of the people involved. However, by acknowledging from the beginning that downsizing is an emotionally fraught process for all concerned, and by actively preparing themselves and their subordinates for the various psychological reactions that are likely to emerge during the process, executives can significantly limit the likelihood of disaster.

To downsize or not to downsize?

As we have seen, downsizing commands a considerable price in human suffering. And as the previous descriptions have shown, no party in the process is excluded from pain. Although downsizing (in its narrowest sense) has proven to be an operation whose costs generally exceed its benefits, the somber statistics that buttress that view do not seem to have deterred many companies from choosing downsizing (sometimes repeatedly). The key questions, then, are these: Taking into consideration the human factor, if an organization decides, in spite of the obvious risks, to go ahead with a narrowly construed downsizing effort, what is the best way to do it? And what can be done to avoid falling into the classic downsizing traps?

First of all, it must be remembered that every effort at downsizing is an attempt to change both individuals and the organization. That fact has ramifications. Some form of pain is always necessary in effecting change. Pain is a primary motivator and a stimulus to seek a new order of things. But students of human behavior also know that pain alone is not enough. Without pleasure somewhere in the equation, pain simply makes people depressed. Thus an additional necessary ingredient in the change process is hope. It is the hope of a new, exciting future that drives the people affected by the change process forward.

One of the common mistakes in early downsizing efforts, as I have noted, was seeking to remedy excessive costs (often the sole perceived reason for organizational ineffectiveness) through sharply reduced head-count only. Selectivity in the process—a selectivity grounded in an excit-ing vision for a new future—was conspicuously absent in these early efforts (and remains frequently elusive today). As I have emphasized repeatedly, however, mere headcount strategies, if not accompanied by adjustments in other components of the organization, are more often than not doomed to fail. Indiscriminate downsizing is reminiscent of surgery with an extremely dull scalpel. As I have indicated, layoffs, if considered necessary, have to be part of a comprehensive change process in the organization. This often includes a complete, systemic change in the company's culture—a change sometimes described as a 'reengineering' process—achieved partly by the departure of employees lacking the necessary skills and flexibility and partly by an influx of new, enthusiastic people with the creativity and energy to reinvent the organization. Making invest-ments in people in the form of training and education, and in new equip-ment and machines, sends a strong signal about management's belief in the organization's future. Such practices therefore lessen survivor guilt and limit dysfunctional coping patterns.

An important consideration in any downsizing effort is work redesign. A frequent complaint of survivors in the downsized organization is that the dismissal of employees results in an increased workload, putting an additional burden on already anxious and disoriented individuals. In order to avoid this unnecessary strain, it is essential for management to clarify each person's new role, responsibility, and workload.

The dynamics of layoffs

One of the most essential pre-implementation tasks of executives involved in a downsizing operation is the development of a coherent strategic rationale for layoffs. In the early days of downsizing, employees were often laid off *en masse* or encouraged to leave through early retirement offers or 'golden handshakes.' Having made no deliberate personnel selection, management was content to see as many people as possible leave the organization. Such across-the-board cuts usually lead to the loss of organizational muscle, in the form of essential knowledge and memory. The departure of key employees may, in the worst case, result in the complete demise of the organization. By first picturing in detail the future organization and carefully choosing the key employees necessary to run it, and then constructing a new organizational chart around these key people (offering them better positions or an augmentation in salary, even if only a small amount), organizations can avoid expensive mistakes that result in the costly retraining of survivors, the rehiring of once-fired employees (at a price), and the need to resort to outside consultants.

An important consideration when layoffs are deemed unavoidable for the company's survival is the speed with which dismissals are implemented. Even though downsizing should be part of a gradual, continuous corporate renewal process—a way of life rather than a one-shot move—management must remember that a relatively stable working environment is crucial to the psychological well-being of both victims and survivors. Human beings generally have a low level of tolerance for much uncertainty. As a matter of fact, the work of worrying about what might happen can be more stressful than the feared event itself. When faced with the threat of uncertainty, people appease their anxiety by acting impulsively and destructively as they attempt to steady their disturbed psychological equilibrium. Keeping the possibility of layoffs dangling above the survivors' heads for weeks or even months results in an atmosphere of fear and paranoia that leads to diminished productivity and can trigger organizational paralysis.

The importance of communication   Communication is one of the most significant aspects of the downsizing process, yet—as mentioned earlier—executives often reduce communication while downsizing. There are numerous reasons for this. Time constraints head the list: executives face increased pressure—too much to do in too little time—when involved in radical corporate transformation. Furthermore, they are reluctant to confront people face to face with bad news, not realizing that giving false hope to employees might have dire consequences. (Employees who try to cope by denying the situation will, if not given clear warning signals, make no serious attempt to look for other work. As a result, they will be caught unprepared when the axe falls.)

As I have noted, downsizing executives often withdraw from the rest of the workforce, concentrating on the technical aspects of the process out of fear for their own and their employees' emotional reactions. These executives see communication as 'idle chatting,' a waste of time, and do not realize that a lack of accessibility results in growing distrust on the part of employees. They fail to see that being open about the dilemma and showing that they are not indifferent to it are likely to trigger sympathy and thus a greater willingness on the part of employees to cooperate and pull the company through.

A further reason for insufficient communication may be executives' reluctance to share disturbing information for fear of causing damage to morale and productivity. Yet, as has been mentioned, it is precisely the lack of realistic information that is apt to cause the greatest damage. Employees usually know more than management is aware of; and what they do not know, they try to piece together from information obtained from various sources. This gives rise to rumors—often wildly exaggerating reality—that distract employees and mortally wound morale. One of the most effective ways for executives to maintain credibility and trust is to communicate everything, constantly, and in detail. By being accessible and interacting frequently with employees, management is in the position to provide reassurance to those in need of it by clarifying the situation and being honest and open about its consequences.

Managing the victims   One of the most crucial factors in the success of a downsizing process is the executives' behavior toward the victims. Careful handling of those who are laid off benefits the organization as well as the victims. As we have seen, survivors react strongly to what they perceive as unfair treatment of those who have been laid off. Clearly, survivors' behavior, morale, and productivity are directly affected by the way layoffs are managed. By providing the victims with tangible caretaking services (such as outplacement consulting and psychological and career counseling), actively trying to help them find new jobs, and assisting them in bridging the transition, management can make the best of a precarious situation.

CONCLUSION

While I hope that this chapter will contribute to a better understanding of the impact of downsizing on the individual, this exploratory study makes it clear that much more work has to be done before the key parameters of downsizing are fully understood. As I have tried to demonstrate, downsizing is a process that brings out a myriad of poorly understood emotional reactions. We have seen that downsizing, when not done properly (particularly if interpreted in its narrowest sense), can be a very blunt instrument—one that wounds people's deepest value and belief systems and causes a great deal of stress. Monitoring the stress level of the different parties in the process is therefore essential, as is the facilitation of constructive coping strategies.

At the center of the downsizing process is the way people deal with change. Only those who are knowledgeable about the process of individual change and corporate transformation can get a solid handle on downsizing. Indeed, we would do well to abandon the word downsizing altogether and replace it with the term 'corporate transformation'—the process of continuously aligning the organization with its environment and shaping an organizational culture in which the enduring encouragement of new challenges stands central. Reframing the term in this wider sense offers a much more constructive way of looking at the process. Those who are ready to join in this process of continuous challenge and learning can take encouragement from the words of the French philosopher Montaigne: 'It is the journey, not the arrival, that matters.'

BEYOND THE QUICK FIX: THE PSYCHODYNAMICS OF ORGANIZATIONAL TRANSFORMATION AND CHANGE[1]

There is nothing in this world constant but inconstancy.

—Jonathan Swift

Everything has changed except our way of thinking.

—Albert Einstein

Like all weak men, he had an exaggerated stress on not changing his mind.

—W. Somerset Maugham

A story was once told of an enormous pike placed in a large aquarium that was divided into two parts. In one part was the pike, in the other were numerous minnows. When the pike was put in the aquarium, the carnivore made a frantic effort to get at the minnows. Every time it tried, however, it would hit the glass. Eventually, the pike gave up as it realized that getting at the minnows seemed to be impossible. When the glass partition was removed, the pike continued to ignore the minnows. The

[1]Material in this chapter has appeared elsewhere in print in the following:

Kets de Vries, M.F.R. and Balazs, K. (1998) 'Beyond the quick fix: The psychodynamics of organisational transformation and change,' *European Management Journal* 16(8), pp. 611–22.

Kets de Vries, M.F.R. and Balazs, K. (1999b) 'Transforming the mindset of the organisation: A Clinical Perspective,' *Administration & Society*, 31(2), pp. 101–111.

pike had become caught up in a specific behavior pattern that, apparently, it could not unlearn.

Change is not easy. People have a tendency to hold on to dysfunctional patterns, illogical as these may appear to others, and cannot seem to alter their perspective on life without expending a great deal of effort. There are many obstacles, both conscious and unconscious on the path toward personal change.

The same problem prevails in organizations. While the world around them changes daily—advances in technology competing with improvements in communication—many organizations prefer to hunker down in the status quo. Yet, in this age of discontinuity, the companies that last through the coming decades will be those that can respond effectively to the changing demands of their environment. How, then, can corporate leaders proactively drive the process of organizational change? Are there ways in which one can apply what is known about the dynamics of personal transformation to the organizational setting? These questions have become critical now that change has become the rule rather than the exception for those seeking corporate survival and success.

Basing their theories on the findings of developmental and clinical psychologists, some organizational psychologists argue that because organizations are made up of collections of people, successful implantation of organizational change is dependent on understanding individual reactions to the change process. They even go as far as suggesting that a lack of attention to the inner experience of the individual in relation to change will abort the process.

While developmental and clinical psychologists have cast their net widely, looking at individuals in all their diversity, many organizational psychologists have taken a narrower viewpoint, assuming that people are rational, logical beings. Using this simplistic approach to human behavior, the recommendations of such organizational transformation specialists tend to be quick-fix and, being only skin deep, are devoid of enduring influence. Change agents, however, who attend to the rich underlying dynamics of individual change can go beyond the hype and turn the process of organizational transformation into a more realistic endeavor.

Developmental psychologists and clinical psychotherapists hold varying views as to the degree of change possible. Most researchers of personality development agree on the fact that while adulthood may not bring about the kind of dramatic, revolutionary change that people experience in early childhood, some change is possible.

My aim in this chapter is to show that it is possible to draw parallels between individual and organizational change processes by observing the different stages by which individual change takes place from a clinical perspective. I suggest that by applying the insights derived from individual change processes to organizational transformation, it is possible to induce otherwise lengthy organizational intervention and change processes more easily.

Method

The clinical orientation of this chapter is derived from data collected during a large number of interventions in organizations, augmented by a series of in-depth interviews with the executives involved in transformation processes.

WHY CHANGE IS CHALLENGING

The main obstacles to individual (and thus organizational) change are the strong forces prevalent in each individual that actively oppose it. For example, anxiety associated with the uncertainty of engaging in something new (or once again being exposed to old dangers and risks) often prompts people to resist change. In an effort to reduce such anxiety, people allow avoidance-behavior patterns—by which they keep themselves sheltered from frightening situations—to become deeply ingrained. Repeating past behavior, in spite of the suffering it may cause, is an all-too-human attempt to master traumatic situations. In addition, fear of having to acknowledge that the present state of affairs is not good enough can contribute to a frozen stance. Ironically, in many instances we seem to prefer what is painful but familiar to the promising unknown. Thus, people are often willing to put up with extremely unsatisfactory situations rather than take steps to improve things. Furthermore, often people resist change partly because of the 'secondary gain'—the psychological benefits such as sympathy and attention—that may result from continuing one's dysfunctional ways.

PREREQUISITES OF PERSONAL CHANGE

There is a certain sequence to the process of personal change, consisting of negative emotion, a focal event, and a public declaration of intent. Each of these plays an important role in facilitating the process of transformation, and each is a preliminary step in the inner journey that contributes to the internalization of change.

Step 1: Negative emotion

If the human tendency is to resist change, how does the process of change ever get under way? Why does this resistance start to weaken? Given the relative stability of personality, getting the process of change into motion requires a very strong inducement indeed—in the form of pain or distress. In short, discomfort outweighing the pleasure of 'secondary gains' is usually the catalyst for change.

This discomfort can be manifested in several ways:

- Studies of personal change indicate that a high level of stress is a major inducement to individual change. Stress can be caused by family tensions, health problems, negative social sanctions, accidents, feelings of isolation leading to a sense of helplessness and insecurity, problem behavior, distressing incidents happening to someone close, and general daily hassles and frustrations.
- Among those of my interviewees who reported that they had changed, most also mentioned feeling a high level of unpleasant emotion—anxiety, anger, sadness, or frustration, for example—in the period just before change, generally precipitated by a stressor like one of those listed above. This negative emotion brought to awareness the serious negative consequences of dysfunctional behavior patterns continuing.
- Individuals who reported a major change said that they had found the status quo increasingly difficult to maintain. They found themselves deadlocked in situations that unsettled their psychological well-being. Their negative emotions—and the consequences they anticipated if those emotions continued—led to a weighing of the pros and cons (not necessarily a conscious process) of the existing problem in an effort to find a solution. They recalled feeling that something had to be done to break the stalemate.

When the interviewees described above realized that their bad days had turned into a bad year—in other words, that the isolated occurrence of occasional discontent had changed into a steady pattern of unhappiness—they were no longer able to deny that something had to be done. From this point on, every new disturbance was recognized as part of the general pattern of dissatisfaction. A certain crystallization occurred, turning complaints into a coherent entity. Gradually, all the undesirable features of life's circumstances compounded to create a clear picture of the situation. Many people then reported having a kind of 'Aha!' experience—a moment when they were finally able to interpret correctly what was happening to them. They saw clearly that neither the passage of time nor minor changes in behavior would improve the situation—indeed, the situation was likely to become even worse if nothing drastic was done about it.

However, this insight—that drastic measures were required to improve the situation—did not always automatically compel these people to take action. It did, however, usually set into motion some kind of mental process whereby they were willing to consider alternatives to the adverse situation. When people finally made the transition from denying to admitting that all was not well, they found themselves at the beginning of a reappraisal process that was likely to be accompanied by strong feelings of confusion and (at first) even protest. Every alternative to the troubling situation was likely to appear more frightening than the status quo. Gradually, however, a preferable alternative to the stalemate began to crystallize, although the hurdles still seemed insurmountable.

Step 2: The focal event

For the executives I interviewed, accepting the need for change was usually not enough for them to take the final step toward changing their situation. They needed a push, in the form of something that can be described as a 'focal event.' While the expression 'focal event' suggests a significant happening that triggers change, the reality is frequently somewhat different. Focal events are often comparatively minor, yet often prove to be the catalyst in the change process simply because the individual is ripe for initiating change.

Among my interviewees, the focal event was often something that happened to someone else—someone important to the interviewee. For one woman, the focal event was the sudden death of her boss and mentor; she saw in that death a judgment of her own over-dedication to the workplace. This focal event symbolized and called attention to her existing problem, and provided the impetus for change.

It is at this point in the process that the individual becomes ready to take action. Where before there was only a sense of helplessness and hopelessness, new possibilities are now seen. Emotional energy has been transferred from past 'concerns' (such as dysfunctional behaviors) to aspects of the present and future. The individual feels freed from a heavy burden and is now mentally ready to tackle a more constructive future.

Step 3: The public declaration of intent

A good indicator of a high degree of commitment to change is making a public expression of *intent* to change. Even though the individual may be unclear about how to change, and what form this change may take, communicating publicly what one plans to do indicates acceptance that there is a problem, and signifies willingness to defend a new way of looking at things.

Public commitment is important since it creates a doubly potent momentum: it influences both the environment and the individual. In the very act of making other people aware of a desire for change, people in the throes of change become aware that the old conditions are no longer valid, and that they need to adapt their attitude to new conditions. At the same time, by pronouncing their wish (and intention) to change they give themselves an ultimatum: go through with it or lose face. Take excessive drinking, for example. If someone states the wish and intent to give up alcohol, acquaintances who approve of the decision are less likely to offer him alcoholic drinks and will probably make a comment if he takes one. Going public with one's intentions, therefore, enhances one's own determination and enlists the support of the environment, becoming a strong reinforcement of the change process.

Step 4: The inner journey

Such personal resolutions set the stage for an inner journey characterized by a crystallization of discontent, new insights and increased self-knowledge. The end result of these psychological processes may be summed up in Step 5: The internalization of change. The mindset of the person has changed, and this new way of looking at things has been internalized (Figure 7.1).

NAVIGATING ORGANIZATIONAL TRANSFORMATION

As I stated earlier, I believe we can draw a number of parallels between the way individuals and organizations change. Like individual transformation, organizational change tends to be sequential, and the process begins with discomfort in the organizational system. Stress in the system is the

1. **Negative emotion**
- Daily frustration

2. **Focal event**
- External threat to well-being (life balance, job)
- Observation of negative consequences to others

3. **Public declaration of change**
- Reappraisal of goals
- Envisioning new alternatives
- Change of environment

4. **Inner journey**
- Crystallization of discontent
- Sudden insight
- Increased self-knowledge

5. **Internalization of change**

Figure 7.1   The individual change process

main lever that sets the change process in motion. However, pushing that lever is easier said than done because, just as in individual change, there are a lot of resistance factors to deal with.

Organizational resistance to change

For many people in an organization, change implies a loss of the security that goes with a specific job. This insecurity causes anxiety and reinforces the impulse to hang on to old patterns of behavior. Others—those who expect that change will require them to learn a new job or to work harder—may fear that they lack the skills and stamina needed for change. Still others may be afraid that good working conditions or an existing sense of freedom will be taken away. Some employees may fear that change implies a loss of responsibility and authority, with concomitant loss of status, rights, or privileges. Others may interpret change as an indictment of earlier actions, see a proposed change as an attack on their previous performance, and react defensively. Furthermore, change threatens alliances, implying the loss of important friends and contacts. The fear of having to leave friends and familiar surroundings can arouse intense resistance. For workers who deal with budgets, there is also the question of sunk costs: they may be reluctant to accept a change that entails scrapping expensive investment. Finally, change may be resisted because of feared reduction in income.

Unless those directing the change effort manage employee resistance, it will not be successful. People have to realize the implications of not doing anything. Not acting is also a form of action. They have to be made aware of the costs to themselves of not changing—that hanging on to the status quo will create more problems than diving into the unknown.

Creating dissatisfaction

Just as discomfort with current conditions is the engine that drives an individual to change, so stress drives organizational change. Studying organizations undergoing a change process, we can observe pressures on the organizational system indicating that some kind of adaptation is needed. However, many necessary organizational change processes are stalled because of defensive routines.

If such routines continue to be manifested throughout the organization despite bringing extreme discomfort, we can assume that the resistances of the key power holders are still intact and that the fact of the necessity for change still escapes the awareness of these organizational leaders. Locked in behavior patterns that have previously proved effective, these leaders have not yet realized that circumstances have changed. But changing the mindset of key players in the organization is never easy, and generally requires a strong jolt of some kind. Those favoring changes may have to pressure the skeptics into recognizing that the present state is no longer viable and that the alignment of organization and environment is off-center.

Pressures leading to change   Awareness of the need for change is usually achieved when there are pressures coming from both inside and outside the organization. Some of the external factors that can cause discomfort in organizations are:

- threats from competitors
- declining profits
- decreasing market share
- scarcity of resources
- deregulation
- the impact of technology
- problems with suppliers and consumer groups.

Examples of internal pressures are:

- ineffective leadership
- morale problems
- high turnover of capable people
- absenteeism
- labor problems (e.g. strikes)
- increased political behavior in the company
- turf fights.

All these factors have a negative effect on the mindset of the people in the organization. The resulting malaise corrodes corporate culture and impacts on decision-making. Eventually, because they cause increasing day-to-day frustration, these stresses can no longer be ignored; an overwhelming feeling of dissatisfaction with the status quo arises in many individuals. Gradually, the majority realizes that something needs to be done, or the future of the organization will be endangered; this is the organizational equivalent of crystallization of discontent. Those in favor of change need to create a shared mindset characterized by collective ambition, commitment and motivation, a sense of urgency that some form of action is needed, and an external focus.

Engendering hope

In this phase of the change process, hope (in the form of a new vision and mission, and offered through the role of a change agent) is essential in breaking the vicious circle of despair. In the best of all worlds, the change agent who makes the case for change will hold a key power position within the organization—ideally, the CEO or some equivalent. Although people at other levels of the organization can (and sometimes must) take the initiative, given the reality of power dynamics, it is members of the dominant coalition (particularly the CEO) who are most effective at getting the change process started. Their authority, resource control, and the way their dependency relationships are constructed within the organization will all strongly influence their power to effect change.

   Leaders are best placed to identify the challenges faced by the organization, point out the source of the distress, and present the negative consequences of failing to act. Benchmarking with other organizations is a good way to illustrate performance gaps and their consequences. By articulating the reality of the situation, leaders define the existing state of discomfort. However, they must be careful to keep the discomfort at a tolerable level, otherwise people may tune the problems out through fear. To buffer against excessive stress, leaders must present a viable alternative to the existing situation. A collective ambition needs to be created, with a view to drawing up an action plan. At this point it is crucial that followers perceive the change program as something realistic and not as pie in the sky.

When developing the outlines of a change process, change leaders need to reframe the cultural guidelines that people in the organization have become used to and show the positive aspects of the change effort. They need to create pride in the organization's history but also point out how this pride can anchor the organization to the past. By referring to the organization's past accomplishments, while at the same time presenting a new way of doing things, leaders create a sense of hope—a dual approach that makes for a sense of new beginning.

An important factor that must also be addressed is people's fears for their career prospects. To appease the inevitable worries, leaders must first emphasize the personal implication of continuing as before and of ignoring environmental threats. At the same time, they should emphasize the opportunities that would be created by dealing with these threats. A new psychological contract, implying mutual obligations and commitments between the employees and the organization, has to be established. The new values required to make the transformation effort a success must be clearly spelled out to win people's consent and support of the change process. Repetition of the change message is important, with every opportunity taken to transmit the message verbally and visually.

To provide a focus, present the issues in an understandable way, and gain the support of followers, leaders must create symbols that represent the new organization and yet show continuity between the old and the new. Getting people on board demands a certain amount of 'theater'—that is, symbolic action—to clarify goals and draw people into the process.

The impact that symbolic action can have is illustrated by one consumer products company CEO who began making regular store visits and talking to customers. This was his way of emphasizing that the newly espoused value of customer focus was not just another empty slogan. His obsession with customer satisfaction quickly caught on, reverberating throughout the company. Another CEO driving a corporate transformation effort asked all his executives to write a letter of resignation from the 'old' company and a letter of application to the 'new' one. This activity, which made people think about what was wrong with the company and reflect on how to make it a high-performance organization, had a powerful impact. The effectiveness of symbolic gestures in getting employees behind the change initiative should not be underestimated.

In any communication of the change message, leaders must focus on clear, compelling reasons for change. Employees must perceive the entire change process as inspired by vision and driven by solid corporate values. They must be able to see that it not only aims at building and maintaining a competitive advantage but also addresses the individual needs of the people who will be affected. Finally, they must know that the proposed change effort has clearly defined parameters.

A dedication to honest, focused, and persuasive communication pays dividends to those spearheading a change effort. Eventually, most people in the organization will have at least a basic awareness that there are problems, and they will be prepared (in spite of lingering resistance) to accept the need for action.

Carrying out the transformation

After leaders have convinced their workforce of the need for change they must put the appropriate organizational architecture in place to help participants enact the new vision. Leaders must build coalitions with other key power-holders in the organization, who can then help to spread commitment and cooperation.

To expedite the change process, leaders driving a change effort need to empower their subordinates by sharing information fully and delegating responsibility. Leaders should keep surprises to a minimum, clearly delineate expectations, and maintain dialogue that is both ongoing and genuinely (rather than merely superficially) two-way. Furthermore, leaders need to communicate values by setting an example of clarity and consistency.

Employee participation and involvement are the key success factors of organizational commitment. People at all levels of the organization—not only those at the top—need to be involved in the change effort. And that participation should be rewarded: leaders can offer incentives, for example, to employees who support the change effort, signaling the benefits of change. Building the right competencies, practices, and creating the proper attitudes is crucial at this stage. Those who are willing to acquire these new competencies should be rewarded and serve as models to others.

Such small wins have a ripple effect, and leaders should therefore divide a big change effort into bite-size portions. Visible improvements—again, small wins—help convince people of the feasibility of the change effort. Figure 7.2 shows an overview of the whole corporate change process.

1. Creating a shared mindset	2. Changing behavior	3. Building competencies, practices, attitudes	4. Improving business performance
• a sense of urgency • external focus • collective ambition • commitment and motivation	• empowering leadership • customer-/process-driven • mutual sharing of information • cross-functional cooperation • internal and external benchmarking • aligning organizational architecture	Capabilities • marketing • technological • manufacturing • strategic • organizational • global • external linkages • emotional intelligence	• profitability • return on investment • market share • share price

Figure 7.2 The corporate transformation process

Staging a focal event

Once leaders have applied these techniques, most employees in the organization will probably have moved from contemplation of change to action. They will be committed to overcoming existing problems and working on how to do it, changing personal behavior, and making changes in the organization's structure, strategy, and culture. If leaders feel the need to expedite the change process, however, they can try to imitate the personal change process by staging a focal event. There are many ways of doing this. It could be an off-site gathering at which senior management announce plans for a new organization; a series of workshops; a seminar; or a meeting run by an outside consultant. Whatever the format, such a staged event should mandate and focus on strategic dialogue between top management (particularly the CEO and members of the executive committee) and their subordinates.

As a forum for feedback and critique, strategic dialogue offers the opportunity for more focused, organization-wide involvement. The resistance that people feel not only to initiating change themselves but to *being* changed is lessened by such involvement, because it gives participants a sense of control over their destiny. Since strategic dialogue is based on a direct feedback loop with senior management, it permits open and informed discussion of the challenges facing the company. Topics perceived as nondiscussable in the day-to-day work context can be put forward and addressed, thus diminishing the level of employee anxiety (especially among those who are willing to change but are afraid that they lack the necessary competence). Furthermore, strategic dialogue offers an opportunity to mourn the old way of doing things, to be nostalgic about the past, and to tackle a new beginning.

Such focal events provide the opportunity to address a number of issues systematically.

1. Even if most people seem to have bought in to the notion that the organization's present state is unsatisfactory, leaders should re-emphasize this crucial point during the strategic dialogue.
2. It is an opportunity to reiterate the need for company-wide commitment to a redefined corporate vision, mission, and new cultural values.
3. Leaders should work with focal-event participants to determine whether the appropriate organizational design, systems, and workforce are in place.
4. Given the need for change, leaders should address the question whether the company possesses the right mix of competencies. If it doesn't, are there adequate training and development programs in place to help employees acquire necessary competencies (and reinforce their belief in their own skills to change)? Do outsiders with specialized expertise need to be brought into the organization?
5. Should appraisal and reward systems be modified to encourage alignment of behavior with the new circumstances?
6. Are the right resources, including leadership, available to support the kind of change that is required? (See Table 7.1 for a summary of such an assessment process.)

As with personal change efforts, a public declaration of how people plan to contribute to the transformation process strengthens commitment to organizational change. However, a public declaration of intent is not enough. It has to be backed up with a way of measuring what has been announced. In other words, a follow-up procedure, perhaps in the form of a detailed personal action plan, has to be tied to such declarations.

One important benefit of a staged focal event is to drive the notion that 'we are the enemy' deep down into the organization—blaming others for current difficulties is unproductive. These sessions can offer the opportunity to explore the extent to which problems can be traced back to previously good practices that are now unaligned. Strategic dialogue should not be overwhelmingly negative, however. Focal-event workshops should facilitate a process of self-discovery of good and bad, allowing people the opportunity to reflect on what made the organization great, while emphasizing that what was good in the past may no longer

Table 7.1 Assessing the potential for organizational transformation

Criteria	Question
Barriers to change	Do people in the organization recognize the need to change?
Triggers of change	Are inside and outside forces pressuring the organization?
Degree of dissatisfaction	Is the organization as a whole dissatisfied with the present status quo?
Common vision culture and mission	Does the organization have shared values, goals, and expectations?
Structure and processes	Does the organization have the correct organizational design and process in place?
Competencies	Does the organization have the right mix of competencies: skills, attitudes, and knowledge?
Aligning behavior	Do performance appraisal and reward systems encourage the right behavior?
Capacity for change	Does the organization have the ability and resources to handle the kind of change that is required?
Leadership	Does the organization have the right quantity and quality of leadership?

be appropriate (given changing circumstances). Because the opportunity to reminisce and to mourn the past allows people to build on the old and create the new, strategic dialogue should permit expressions of nostalgia and grief; in doing so, it will encourage expression of excitement for the future. But this is a slow process: it takes considerable time for a new conception of the organization to be fully metabolized, and to go from superficial adoption of a new state of affairs to deep internalization.

Before attempting a staged focal event—given its potential impact on the change process—company executives must wrestle with the delicate question of leadership for change. This issue is particularly difficult if questions are raised about the CEO's capability to drive the change effort. If we look at organizations that have experienced successful, more dramatic change, we see that an outsider has generally been brought in to make the process happen. This is often a preferred option, since outsiders seem to be less bound than insiders to a particular way of doing things in a specific organization, and are thus freer to push the levers of change.

Changing the corporate mindset

Letting go of the old ways of doing things is not primarily a cognitive process; it is, first and foremost, a sequential emotional process. We have observed how corporate change, like personal change, often starts with a state of turmoil. With the anxiety level rising, sometimes to the point of panic (among those who fear for their jobs, for example), normal organizational processes generally come to a halt or become ritualistic. People fall back into familiar routines, going through motions they know well in order to deal with the proposed change. This early in the game, few people are ready to accept that a new way of doing things has become unavoidable.

As a reaction to the shock experienced by what is happening to and around them, people in the organization may regress into dependency, or adopt a fight or flight mode.

- Those in dependency mode may wish for (and imagine that they have) an omnipotent leader who will set things right. Their dependency may also manifest itself in passivity, equated with a lack of initiative.
- Fight behavior, on the other hand, may be characterized by displacement of anger—that is, blaming others for what is happening. People regressing to fight behavior often exhibit a great deal of irritability and bitterness. However, these emotions are often directed not toward the corporation itself (and the people and practices within it) but toward 'others'—customers, suppliers, the government, and competitors—who might be to blame. People resorting to fight behavior are not yet ready to see themselves in this difficult equation. Instead, they waste their energy on internal politics, engaging in turf fights rather than facing their real problems.
- Still others regress not to dependency or anger but to flight behavior. Some actually leave the organization at the first signs of stress, while others simply withdraw, stop participating in office activities, and redirect their focus toward other things.

These three modes of behavior cannot continue for long without incurring dangerous corporate consequences. In organizations that are fortunate—and whose change drivers have been astute and skilful—employees understand that there is no miracle waiting around the corner, that positive things happen to those who help themselves, that the steps needed to reverse the situation must be taken not by others but by themselves, and that fighting changes is of little use. As an increasing number of people in the organization share such thoughts, the corporate mindset begins to change. Resistance is worn down, and the first tentative explorations of the new reality take place, even as, during the period of adjustment, people mourn their losses.

In the next (and final) phase of organizational transformation, when adjustment is complete, people have come to accept the new way of doing things, recognizing its advantages, and are now collaborating. They have internalized new values and attitudes and have adopted a more positive attitude toward the future.

Astute leadership is essential in an organization that hopes effectively to regenerate itself. Leaders must recognize that it takes time to give up the old and embark on the new, that people facing organizational change need time to mourn the past. Effective leadership is a balancing act, especially during periods of change. Leadership that effectively fills the roles of envisioning, empowering, and energizing—and also takes on an architectural role in setting up appropriate structures and control systems—will go a long way toward restructuring the organization.

ORGANIZATIONAL TRANSFORMATION: A CASE ILLUSTRATION

On October 29, 1993, the chairman of the board of Bang & Olufsen (B&O) could for the first time after years of losses predict a profit of 126 million Danish kroner (DKK) for the financial year 1993–4. The company's share price had risen spectacularly, from DKK 325 in 1990–1 to DKK 1450 in 1994–5. These figures indicated a dramatic turnaround for a long-tottering company (Balazs and Kets de Vries, 1997).

B&O was the crown jewel of Danish industry, the exclusive producer of high-tech, high-fidelity audiovisual systems and other related products. Since its beginning, the company had been at the forefront of design innovation, a philosophy promoted by the two founders of the company. However, that original philosophy stressing product design—which had earned the company much acclaim—carried within it the seeds of failure. The holiness of the design function came to reign over everything else, particularly cost and customer considerations. Saying 'no' to a new product from the design department was taboo, an action that would not occur to anyone hoping to stay long in the organization. Unfortunately, while the company won one design prize after the other, financially it was anything but a winner. The balance sheet had tottered around the red line for 22 years, an unheard-of period of time. In the words of the then CEO, Anders Knutsen, 'Bang

& Olufsen was not interested in making money; it was interested only in winning prizes.'

In spite of dismal financial figures, not many at B&O seemed to be seriously worried. Most employees were used to the fact that the company was not making a profit, but they never had serious doubts about its survival. Employment security had always been an implicit part of their contract. If ever a doubt surfaced in anybody's mind about the company's future, top management's strong and confident statements reassured the worrier. As Knutsen put it, 'Every year when we had some problems, it was not our fault. It was the outer world that was so evil to poor Bang & Olufsen.'

Finally, when it became clear that the accounting period of 1990–1991 would bring a deficit of DKK 135.5 million, the company's dismal situation could not be ignored any longer. The supervisory board decided to pull the plug, replacing the CEO who for 10 years had been allowed to run the company at his own discretion, and made Anders Knutsen the new CEO. Knutsen had learned B&O from the ropes, starting out as a brand manager and working his way through different positions in production and product development, before finally ending up as technical director.

Knutsen became CEO on July 1, 1992, facing strong opposition both within and outside the company. When the former CEO left, both the supervisory board and the board of directors underwent reorganization at Knutsen's behest. Knutsen understood that he needed all the power he could get to change the company; thus one of his preconditions for taking on the role of CEO was that he would also become chairman of the supervisory board. Even with that precondition, there was opposition to his appointment. However, after rallying people inside and outside the company for a number of weeks, he managed to push it through: in September 1992, Knutsen was appointed chairman of the supervisory board and finally had the power to act.

External opposition to changing the organization came primarily from the banks with which B&O was affiliated. From the moment of Knutsen's appointment, the banks opposed his new ideas. Most never even gave him the benefit of the doubt, cancelling B&O's account or raising interest rates. These actions increased the crisis atmosphere that prevailed in the company.

Knutsen immediately demonstrated that he had what had been missing at B&O: leadership skills. He started by pronouncing a clear vision for the company, along with a mission statement that stated explicitly how the vision could be achieved. Then, together with the board of directors, he elaborated a plan for the rationalization and restructuring of the organization. He called it 'Break Point '93.'

The first step was an analysis of the company's cultural values, prepared by B&O's top executives, which centered on an intensive evaluation of the company's critical situation. In particular, the sacrosanct process of new-product acceptance was put under the microscope. Having overseen that analysis, and anticipating the difficulty of inculcating new values, the board of directors decided to turn to an organizational consultant, who presented a seminar centered on leadership, organizational culture, and corporate transformation. The seminar was intended to be a staged focal event; its implicit goal was to shake people up. Knutsen opened the seminar explosively, announcing that a considerable number of people in the factories had to be dismissed because of the poor order portfolio.

What followed was, as one B&O employee described it, 'an atmosphere of chaos and upheaval.' People were shocked and disoriented, uncertain how the future—theirs and the company's—would look. The shock therapy seemed to achieve the desired effect, however. Participants, trying to impose order onto the prevailing chaos, threw themselves wholeheartedly into the seminar activities. Despite the risks, they experienced for the first time the power to do something about their own company. They were asked to engage in a strategic dialogue with top management to help restructure and refocus the organization. Participating in the design for the future made for motivation, commitment, and a sense of ownership. Soon hope started to replace chaos. In addition, the seminar set the stage for a rewrite of the existing psychological contract in the organization. Job security was no longer the main pillar of the contract. Accountability and performance took its place.

The goal of Break Point '93 was radical: it included a complete rationalization and reorganization of every function in the company. Organizationally, the changes had major impact. The distance between top management and the shop floor was cut by reducing the overall number of executives and by slashing two management layers entirely; a total of 712 people were dismissed. As accountability was pushed deep down the lines, employees were expected to develop a sense of ownership and personal responsibility for the company.

To globalize the company, a new international sales and marketing head office was opened in Brussels. Product acceptance—the old Achilles' heel of the company—became much more selective. The most disturbing culture shock experienced during the transformation, this change in emphasis clearly signaled management's intent to change the company.

Over a two-year period, B&O moved from a deficit that seriously threatened the existence of the company to a surplus that exceeded all expectations. The first part of the change process had come to a successful end—and B&O has continued to be profitable.

PRIMARY FACTORS FACILITATING CHANGE

Having considered the psychodynamics of the change process, let me offer a few observations about the factors that facilitate change. Studies of successful personal change efforts indicate that there are two primary factors that influence the outcome:

1. the presence of some kind of social support system to ease the process of change;
2. the personality type of the individual involved.

Social support

People who experience a sense of isolation find it more difficult to change behavior patterns. Without the support of their environment, their reluctance to change is harder to overcome. Moreover, there is an established link between social support (a crucial buffering function against stress) and good physical health. Indeed, social support is often the single most important factor in helping an individual overcome barriers to change. People seem to sense this intuitively: those who decide to embark on a journey of transformation often seek out people who can give them the support they need, whether instrumental or emotional.

Instrumental support is task-directed, involving, for example, assigning another pair of hands to a job that needs to be done, obtaining specialized outside assistance for a challenging project, or providing authority along with responsibility—in short, providing whatever resources are needed to make the change effort a success. Emotional support, on the other hand, is about maintaining and bolstering a person's self-esteem. This support may be given by the spouse, other family members, friends, colleagues at work or other networks—in effect a network of people who offer reassurance, guidance, and an opportunity to share interests.

Sometimes, both forms of support come from the same source. People in the process of change often seek out individuals who have experienced a similar situation, partly to obtain practical help and advice, and partly to offset feelings of isolation. In addition, people who want to change are motivated by the success of others who have already completed the process.

Social support needs to be part of the corporate culture during a transformation process, and supplying it is a task that has to start at the top. The more effective leaders seem to have a considerable amount of emotional intelligence. They provide a sense of security for their followers and make sure their employees know that their concerns are being listened to.

Hardiness and locus of control

People with an internal locus of control feel that they are in charge of their own lives; they perceive their destiny as affected by their own decisions, not by outside factors. They recognize a strong relationship between their own actions and what happens around them. This secure belief in themselves makes them:

- less anxious;
- more active, striving, and achieving;
- more future- and long-term-oriented;
- more proactive and innovative (though less prone to engage in risky behavior).

They also possess a considerable amount of self-control. They tend to be more motivated and successful in life, both academically and professionally, than people with an external locus of control. Their strong belief in their own capabilities also makes them resistant to influence, coercion, and manipulation.

An internal locus of control enable individuals to take charge of, and carry through, major personal change with more ease and self-confidence. Their belief in their control of their own destiny prevents them from doubting the outcome of a self-initiated change process. Once they have realized the necessity for change, they go ahead rather than wait for some outside sign or agent to initiate it.

People with an external locus of control, on the other hand, often see change as a threat. Because they do not feel in control of the forces that affect their lives, they adopt a rather passive stance toward change. Being unable to take decisive steps toward a transformation of their own choosing, they have an outlook that makes them prone to depressive reactions.

The term 'hardy personality' has been coined to describe people characterized by an internal locus of control. There is more to hardiness, however, than just the feeling of being in control of the events of one's life. Hardy individuals feel a deep commitment to the activities in which they are engaged. Deeply curious and eager to initiate new experiences, they perceive change as a positive challenge to further development. Hardy individuals have strong commitment to self, an attitude of vigor toward the environment, and a sense of meaningfulness. In contrast, nonhardy people feel victimized by events, and have a tendency to look at change as something undesirable.

People who are characterized by a hardy personality possess affective, cognitive, and behavioral skills that make them better survivors in stressful situations. Hardy individuals' feeling of control over what is happening to them, and their lesser need for security, enable them to tolerate ambiguity better than others. Their thinking helps them to anticipate and internalize the changes they face. Consequently, they show greater job involvement than others and slip easily into the role of catalyst for change. Not surprisingly, research indicates that innovative, proactive companies are largely composed of employees with an internal locus of control. The same positive outlook makes hardy individuals more stress-resistant than others and less prone to helplessness, depression, and physical illness.

An individual's orientation—internal or external locus of control—and degree of hardiness is usually deeply ingrained and very difficult to influence. Companies subjected to a turbulent environment—those for whom change is the norm rather than the exception—would do well to select people with an internal locus of control.

CONCLUSION

In a constantly changing corporate world, organizations clearly need to be capable of adapting their behavior if they are to sustain a competitive advantage. An organization that is firmly stuck in past behavior patterns is doomed to failure. The paradox of success leading to failure by creating complacency and arrogance is the greatest challenge to organizational leaders. Given the environment in which we live, a secure grasp of the dynamics of change is a required competency of any leader.

Today's leaders face a difficult challenge: creating organizations in which a change orientation is a core value, in other words, to instill a regenerative culture in an organization. To prevent the turmoil that accompanies full-blown transformation processes, organizations need continuous, gradual change—which occurs naturally when both leaders and followers continually question whether their way of doing things is firmly embedded in reality.

The ultimate challenge is to create an organizational mindset in which people's exploratory dispositions are fully deployed, and where change is welcomed and desired. As we have seen, this is not an easy proposition. To prevent employees from settling down too firmly at their desks, leaders need to cultivate a culture of trust, a prevailing organizational attitude that encourages people to challenge established ways of doing things.

Organizations that foster an atmosphere of constructive conflict—in which people do not take the recommendations of their power holders for granted, where they question what their leaders have to say, and where strategic dialogue is the rule rather than the exception—will be in the best position to remain aligned with the environment, however much or often it changes. Organizations characterized by this sort of constructive dialogue will unearth missed opportunities, and inform top executives of the concerns of the employees. When such a mindset prevails, it serves as an early warning system of the need for change. This constant testing of the status quo enables organizational preventive maintenance and creates an atmosphere of continuous learning.

Making such an organizational culture a viable proposition takes sustained effort, since change runs counter to the built-in conservatism of human behavior. Even while old resistances are breaking down, new ones are emerging. However, the danger of rigidity is ever present. As John Kenneth Galbraith once remarked: 'Faced with the choice between changing one's mind and proving there is no need to, almost everybody gets busy with the proof.'

People who understand the dynamics of change and who realize the tremendous opportunities inherent in a proactive stance will be the winners in this world of discontinuities.

CHAPTER 8

THE DYNAMICS OF FAMILY
CONTROLLED FIRMS[1]

That business was built specifically for my family.
Anybody who wants to come in, there's an open place for him.
If the business is destroyed as a result of that, so be it.

—Sam Steinberg

While I am proud of a number of accomplishments, there are real costs to being unreasonable. Long hours. Too little time with family. A near incapacity for, as they say, stopping and smelling the roses.

—Eli Broad

I'll make him an offer he can't refuse.

—Marlon Brando, *The Godfather*

The child of a tiger is a tiger.

—Haitian proverb

INTRODUCTION

Family businesses account for the majority of jobs in most Western societies, in most other countries, even more. Given their importance to national economies, it is surprising that so little attention has been given to what affects this type of firm.

---

[1]Much of the material in this chapter is based on the article:
Kets de Vries, M. F. R. (1993) 'The Dynamics of Family Controlled Firms: The good and the bad news,' *Organizational Dynamics*, 21(3), pp. 59–70.

For the psychologically minded, family firms offer a tremendous variety of issues—as Tolstoy wrote in *Anna Karenina*, 'All happy families resemble one another, every unhappy family is unhappy in its own way.' In this chapter I consider two main issues relating to the management of family firms:

- What contributes to the problems these firms experience?
- Are there special dynamics characteristic of family firms?

CASE STUDY: THE STORY OF THE FAMILY FIRM

Once upon a time, there was a potter who made the most beautiful pottery in the world. Everyone who saw his pottery immediately fell in love with it and wanted to buy it. As a result the potter's shop flourished and became known far and wide. After some time, demand for his products became so great that the potter found it impossible to do all the work himself. He started a factory and hired people to help. As the years went by, he employed more and more workers. Eventually, the potter spent all day managing the factory. He no longer had time to make pottery. Sometimes he longed for the good old days when things seemed to be much simpler and he did everything himself. He didn't really like being so dependent on others and very few people could live up to his standards of excellence.

Fortunately, his children were now older and had begun to give him a hand. They became more and more helpful in managing the business. Although the potter was reluctant to let go, he began to realize that he really had no choice. His health and endurance were no longer what they were. But he wanted to keep the business in the family. He liked to see the family name on the building. For him, the business was a way of keeping the family together, and the very reason he had worked so hard was to create a better life for all of them.

When the potter died, he left the company to his two sons and only daughter. The pottery factory and the sales outlets continued to prosper under their guidance. More and more plants opened. The operation expanded across borders and diversified into related products such as glass, crystal, and silverware.

When the children's children became older, they were also brought into the business. Unfortunately, with so many family members around, things started to go downhill. The original family cohesiveness began to unravel. There were periods when those who could remember times past would think nostalgically of the good old days, when the old man was in control. Everything had seemed so much simpler then; everyone knew who was in charge.

The cousins and siblings began to argue about money, shares, power, and responsibilities: who got what and who made what. Envy reared its head. Eventually, what had started as mere bickering degenerated into bitter feuding. The two brothers and sister, their wives, husband, and children spent all their time and energy fighting. Employees were forced to choose one of the many factions with which to side. Soon the most capable employees began to leave. Product quality decreased, and customers stopped buying.

In the end, the strife led to bankruptcy for the company and the loss of the family members' personal fortune. Thus ended the potter's dream. The family had gone from rags to rags in only three generations.

The people in this fairy tale did not live happily ever after. This is in fact an all too common scenario for many family businesses since family businesses have a built-in Achilles' heel: the interaction of two systems (the family and the business) that are not necessarily compatible. Examples of destructive family feuds are not hard to find. One only has to think of how vendettas, shareholder fights, and lawsuits divided the Gucci family, one of Europe's great mercantile empires. Or there was the power struggle between the Steinberg sisters (the inheritors of the large Canadian shopping center emporium), a fight that eventually ripped the family firm apart. And in France there was the feud over money, power, and honor at Gallimard, one of the country's most prestigious publishing houses.

Although the statistics vary, it seems that only three out of ten family firms make it through the second generation, and only one in ten through the third. Analysts have estimated the average life-span of an entrepreneurial firm at only 24 years, the usual length of time the founder is associated with it.

So, why all this concern about family firms? Isn't all the 'real action' in publicly held corporations? On the contrary, I believe those who play down the importance of family firms are making an enormous mistake. According to some estimates, 80 % of all businesses in the world are family controlled, in the widest sense of the term—i.e. that the family has a significant say in the company's strategic direction and in the appointment of a new CEO (Kets de Vries, Carlock and Florent-Treacy, 2007a) .

Nor does the argument that these figures are misleading because they mainly apply to the mom-and-pop stores hold water. For example, in the US, more than one-third of the *Fortune 500* companies are family controlled.

THE GOOD AND BAD NEWS ABOUT FAMILY FIRMS

Advantages

One of the obvious advantages of working for a family firm is the sense of being in control of one's destiny. Running something in which one has a personal stake certainly creates a greater feeling of independence. The narcissistic pleasures derived from this should not be underestimated: there is something to be said for seeing one's name on the building, particularly if it is a well-known brand name. This can have other beneficial side effects. As the family member of one media conglomerate once said, 'The name I have has certainly helped me to get access to top executives of companies, persons who under other circumstances would have kept their doors shut.' Nor should we underestimate the possible financial benefits. There is always the possibility of becoming *really* successful. And these benefits represent only the tip of the iceberg.

The long-term perspective   In general, family firms tend to have a longer-term view of their business since they are not usually fly-by-night operations. Family owner-managers may have a different outlook vis-à-vis their employees, their customers, the community, and other important stakeholders, which can positively affect the quality of their product. The fact that the owners have their name on the building also makes them more conscious of their standing in the community and more jealous of their reputation.

In many instances, the company and its products affect the identity of family members. To be associated with defective or inferior products becomes a reflection on the self. Thus, the family will find it singularly unattractive to go for short-term financial gains if doing so will tarnish the company's standing. When a family has been publishing books for many generations, like the Bonnier family in Sweden, or been in the media business, like the Rothermere family, its members want to be proud of the product.

Moreover, compared with publicly held corporations, family firms are not the slaves of Wall Street, haunted by quarterly results. They are under less pressure; there is less public scrutiny, and they have greater independence of action. The fact that family firms do not have to divulge as much information as publicly held corporations can be a competitive advantage: it is not as easy for competitors to know what they are really up to. Those who have tried to get information about famous but more secretive family corporations, such as Mars (the confectionery manufacturer), Michelin (the tire maker), or C & A (the department store chain) will be well aware of the difficulties involved.

Also, privately held companies worry less about takeover threats. There is less need to create elaborate schemes with 'poison pills' and 'golden parachutes.' Executives can save their energy for other causes. Finally, family firms tend to be more resilient during hard times, because they are prepared to plow profits back into the business.

The family culture   This long-term outlook can be reinforced by greater certainty about what kind of leadership will prevail in the firm. With effective succession planning (a subject I discuss later in this chapter), everyone knows who is next in line. This can mean peace of mind and, consequently, less political behavior in the company.

The values family members express create a common purpose for employees and help to establish a sense of identification and commitment. In well-run family firms, the employees feel like part of the family. Access to senior management is easier. There is often less bureaucracy and thus quicker, more effective, decision-making.

The kind of corporate culture that permeates Herman Miller Inc., the furniture manufacturer, has become legendary. This company has repeatedly been listed as one of the best managed companies in America. The company was started in 1923 by D. J. De Pree, who was succeeded first by his son, Hugh, and then by Hugh's son, Max. At Herman Miller Inc. we find a group of people strongly committed to the beliefs and ideas of the senior family members, particularly Max De Pree. Employees share the family's outlook toward customer service, quality, and productivity. This is a covenant that works both ways. The family has a strong belief in the potential of people. This belief is backed up by a set of rights that determine the psychological contract between workers and management. Included in the 'ground rules' for working at Herman Miller Inc. are the right to be needed, the right to be involved, the right to understand, the right to affect one's own destiny, the right to be accountable, and the right to appeal.

This focus on rights goes beyond mere talk—it affects everyone's wallet. The company has a long-standing 'Scanlon Plan,' entitling workers to a share of the financial gains resulting from any suggestions they make for improving design, customer service, quality, and productivity. When Herman Miller Inc. went public, management established a stock option plan. Without exception, all regular employees who have worked in the firm for at least a year own stock. There are even 'silver parachutes' for all employees, in the case of an unfriendly takeover, not just golden parachutes for top management.

Herman Miller Inc. also exemplifies a family firm that is less bureau-cratic than an equivalent publicly held corporation. The family culture makes the firm much less impersonal. Encouraging employees to feel like part of the family facilitates access to senior management. Even the lowliest production worker has no difficulty knocking on Max De Pree's door. This kind of atmosphere expedites decision-making and leads to greater flexibility of procedure and action.

Knowing the business   Another important competitive advantage can be found in the extensive expertise family members have. After all, they have been in contact with the business from early childhood onward. Breakfasts, dinners, walks, family gatherings, and summer jobs will all have created opportunities to learn more about the business.

This kind of knowledge may give family members a head start, com-pared with executives entering the business later on. Early training like this helps to explain the sometimes puzzling appointments of very young family members to senior positions. Actually, such 'age inappropriate' appointments can have a beneficial effect, in that they may lead to a rejuvenation of an arteriosclerotic group of top executives.

The bad news

Obviously, it isn't only good news. On the debit side, the practical dif-ficulties that can dog family ownership spring immediately to mind. Tax code covering inheritance, for example, can create problems that threaten the continuation of the firm. Another obvious problem is that family corporations usually have greater difficulty obtaining access to capital markets, which can inhibit growth.

The organization of family firms frequently strikes the outsider as messy and confusing. Authority and responsibility may not be clearly defined; jobs may overlap; executives may hold a number of different jobs. The decision-making hierarchy may be completely ignored—existing only to be bypassed.

On interviewing people in family firms, however, one quickly dis-covers that many of the key problems are in fact psychological. They center on issues such as:

- the fit between senior executives' leadership style and the company's stage of development;
- the overflow of family conflicts into the business;

- coalition politics among the family members (detracting from the substance of the business);
- last, but certainly not least, the question of succession.

All these problems can turn into high drama. At times, life in a family firm veers between soap opera and the extremes of Greek tragedy.

The question of nepotism   Family logic often overrules business reason. In many instances family members are welcomed regardless of their ability to contribute anything useful to the business. Senior owner-managers often show a remarkable capacity for closing their eyes to the weaknesses of their beloved sons or daughters.

Working under a person who is clearly incompetent places non-family staff in a highly unattractive position. An imbalance between contribution and credit—the lack of a real meritocracy—can undermine one of the pillars of corporate culture: the need for trust. Lack of trust will influence the company climate, affecting job satisfaction, motivation, and performance.

This situation is particularly ironic if, as is often the case in many family firms, family members demand a high level of commitment from the non-relatives. Such demands are acceptable if management gives non-family members due credit for work well done. However, they are likely to be unacceptable if the existing incentive system is heavily biased toward noncontributing family members. In this case, it becomes difficult to attract capable managers—a development that may endanger the company's future.

Consider the example of a well-known global firm in the clothing business. The president of this company (encouraged by his wife) was blind to the incompetence of his only son. Having survived a severe coronary attack, he placed his son, who had flunked out of every school he had been sent to, in a senior position. The son's behavior soured the atmosphere. One of his worst habits was to lay the blame for whatever mistakes he had made (forgetting appointments, not following up on clients, allocating resources poorly) on others: nothing was ever his fault. Eventually, many of the more competent employees could take it no longer and left the company. When the son (against all advice) acquired a firm with outdated product lines and obsolete machinery, the company went into the red, and this finally opened the father-president's eyes. He realized what had really been going on and reasserted his control.

'Spoiled kid' syndrome   This story illustrates another aspect of the bad news about family firms—the 'spoiled kid.' In the typical scenario, the principal protagonist is the hard-working entrepreneur completely obsessed by his business. This kind of work behavior often leads to feelings of guilt in the entrepreneur, who then tries to deal with such feelings by bribing other family members—a kind of pay-off for not being available emotionally or otherwise. The pay-off might start with a big teddy bear when the children are young and then metamorphose into sports cars, jewelry, expensive vacations, or condominiums. Unfortunately, these gifts will never replace the attention that was missing during childhood. At the same time, for the giver, handing out material possessions becomes a way of making up for hardships that he himself experienced. He is giving to his children what he once longed for himself.

The Steinberg family feud, which captured headlines in many newspapers, provides a prime example of such behavior. The daughters of Sam Steinberg, who built up a shopping center empire, battled for control of the business. In their book *Steinberg: The Break-up of a Family Empire* (1990) journalists Ann Gibbon and Peter Hadekel concluded from interviews with the principal players that 'the girls were spoiled rotten,' having had clothes, cars, and condos in Florida lavished upon them. According to Gibbon and Hadekel: 'When it came to his daughters, his pockets were deep; there was nothing they couldn't have. They would never know the life Sam Steinberg had lived growing up in a crowded, unheated flat on The Main.'

Despite this apparent generosity, we could ask how much attention Sam Steinberg and his wife had paid to the more intangible needs of their daughters. They seem to have given little value to education, family values, work ethic, business training, and social responsibility. The notion that authority and responsibility should be awarded only in recognition of proven accomplishment did not apply to Steinberg's family members. A sense of entitlement may have been prevalent. And as his daughters wielded enormous power as the company's major shareholders, their poor understanding of the business and their dysfunctional behavior had catastrophic consequences. Moreover, the rivalry between the sisters, suppressed while their father was alive, made the situation far worse and led eventually to the company break-up.

The Wars of the Roses   A parent's emotional unavailability can have lasting repercussions on his or her children, who may start to fight for whatever quality time *is* available, however little, and who soon become expert judges in who has preference in the 'love equation.' These early feelings of envy and jealousy are not easily resolved and will likely remain troublesome throughout life.

In the process of growing up, siblings often separate and choose their own course in life. With time and geographical distance, residual childhood irritants and resentment are less likely to flare up. However, joining the family firm breaks this pattern. Parents may use emotional blackmail to induce their children to go into the business. Consequently, in one way or another, family members may be stuck with one another. They may feel trapped. And they may end up in a vicious circle of endlessly repeating conflicts—a continuation of the old emotional games of childhood.

Publicly held organizations may not be paragons of rational behavior, and family firms, given the greater likelihood of emotional drama, are most certainly not. Decisions in such firms are often made on an emotional basis only, rather than according to sound business sense.

A good example of numbing fraternal strife was the saga of the Horvitz brothers, heirs to one of America's largest fortunes: a $700 million newspaper, cable television, and real estate empire. After the father died, the fight over who would gain control of the business began in earnest, reaching a new crescendo when the mother, who had acted as peace-maker, died soon after. Accusations and counter-accusations flew. Fist fights were par for the course. Lawsuits led to years of legal wrangling. As a son of one of the three brothers said, 'Decisions were based on how the [brothers] felt when they were 12.'

Factional infighting can become extremely complex in family firms that have survived a number of generations and are run by large families. Obviously, maintaining a cohesive family unit becomes more difficult as the generations spread out. The danger is that too much time will be spent on conspiratorial activities and not enough attention paid to the substance of the business. When envy overpowers reason, the politics of succession may become a major pastime.

Parental relationships As well as the problem of the entrepreneurial father's emotional unavailability (these phenomena are more applicable to men than to women), there are also the effects of his often domineering behavior. It is not easy to live in the shadow of a captain of industry, and the eldest son often bears the brunt of entrepreneurial aggression. Children born later, or children of second marriages, tend to have a much easier time. The entrepreneur perceives them less as a threat to his power base and more as a symbol of his potency and vitality.

In his autobiography, *Father, Son & Co: My Life in IBM and Beyond* (1990) Thomas Watson, Jr, of IBM, recalls coming home from school in tears (he was not much of a student) saying that he *couldn't do it*—referring to the general expectation that he, as the oldest son, would take over the business from his father, Thomas Watson Sr. He had always found it difficult to live up to his father's expectations and was convinced that he was lacking in some way, feeling deep uncertainty about his ability to deliver.

Watson Jr recalled bouts of depression as a child, often accompanied by asthma attacks. His childhood experiences worsened when he noticed how everyone would bow and scrape and ingratiate themselves in his father's presence. He compared his father to a blanket, smothering everything. He recalled how he and his father had terrible fights, which frequently led to the brink of estrangement. Later on, as President of IBM, Watson Jr would perform a ritual on the anniversary of his father's death: he would take stock of what his company had accomplished and tell his wife that he had managed yet another year alone.

Many male entrepreneurs seem to have experienced a symbolic Oedipal victory in gaining the major portion of their mother's love and affection and in bypassing their fathers. However, they will not allow a similar triumph for their own sons. Instead, some entrepreneurs will go to great lengths to belittle their sons, continuously cutting them down to size. Consequently, some sons may give up, do poorly at school, and behave irresponsibly. They become the antithesis of their fathers, either temporarily or permanently. Of course, it should be stressed that these psychodynamic processes do not necessarily happen consciously. Nevertheless, whether conscious or unconscious, the experience is emotionally devastating.

The first Henry Ford and his son Edsel had a particularly destructive relationship, characterized by enormous ambivalence. Henry Ford was in the habit of building his son up at times, then going out of his way to humiliate him. One of Edsel's major frustrations came from his father's continuous rejection of his well-thought-out plans to improve products and conditions in the company. Instead, Henry Ford preferred to listen to people who were brutalizing the work environment. Edsel never found the nerve to stand up to his father, who preferred to portray his son as weak, incompetent, and 'too fond of cocktails and decadent East Side living.' The strain of this relationship let to medical problems for Edsel, and the stress probably contributed to his stomach ulcer and premature death. According to the biographer Robert Lacey, in his book *Ford: The Men and the Machine* (1986) when Edsel died, his wife, in a fit of anger, told her father-in-law that he had killed his own son.

The example of the Fords is not unique, although most father–son relationships do not come to this kind of tragic ending. In comparison, father–daughter, mother–daughter, and mother–son relationships seem to be less prone to conflict in a business context. However, given the current relative scarcity of case examples of female company presidents, it may be wise to suspend judgment about this for the time being.

Autocratic rule   As already mentioned, founders (I am referring to men, in particular) tend to have domineering personalities. After all, without their dominance and persistence the company would never have taken off. Their presence and their behavior give the company its particular flavor. In many such companies, a paternalistic attitude may prevail. But what started off as well-meaning may end up not only stifling but also, at times, perverted.

A good example of this is the house of Krupp, a 400-year-old dynasty that armed Germany during four major wars. For generations, members were guided by Alfred Krupp's *Generalregulativ*, the company constitution laid down in 1874. This document detailed the absolute obligations of the *Kruppianer* (Krupp employees), including a statement that the house of Krupp was entitled to receive from its workers full and undivided energy, punctuality, loyalty, and love of good order. On the other hand, a *Kruppianer* who ran up debt would be sacked; any man five minutes late would lose an hour's wages; troublemakers would be dismissed forever. But the *Kruppianer* were entitled to health services, an emergency relief fund, pension schemes, low-cost housing, nonprofit retail outlets, and homes for the aged. In terms of its social welfare policy, Krupp was undoubtedly ahead of its time. But this paternalistic attitude became a grotesque travesty during World War II, when the company willingly used almost 100 000 prisoners of war and concentration camp inmates as slave laborers.

The Krupp dynasty may be an extreme example of autocratic paternalistic rule. However, lesser examples are not hard to find. One can hypothesize that people willing to work under such conditions may possess many of the characteristics of the dependent personality. These companies will attract yes-men—hardly the kind of people to move it forward.

Such companies are often secretive, conservative, and traditional. Consequently, they can become too inward looking, ignoring developments in the environment. Naturally, such an attitude does not foster change and can seriously threaten the firm's survival.

Milking the business   When a number of family-member employees add little or no value, the company risks turning into a kind of welfare institution. It gives family members something to do without actually engaging them in any productive work. Most companies cannot afford to have too many of these people around. Apart from the financial strain, unproductive hangers-on can cause serious morale problems.

In one consumer products company, three of the five family-member employees drew large salaries, used company-chauffeured cars and planes, and lived in company-financed luxury apartments. However, the occasional hours they spent at the office did more harm than good. They spent most of their time at the hunting lodge or on the golf course, both of which were financed through company memberships. When the economy

Table 8.1 Advantages and disadvantages of family-controlled firms

Advantages	Disadvantages
Long-term orientation	Less access to capital markets may curtail growth
Greater independence of action • less (or no) pressure from stock market • less (or no) takeover risk	Confusing organization • messy structure • no clear division of tasks
Family culture as a source of pride • stability • strong identification/ commitment/ motivation • continuity in leadership	Nepotism • tolerance of inept family members as managers • inequitable reward systems • greater difficulties in attracting professional management
Greater resilience in hard times • willingness to plow back profits	'Spoiled kid' syndrome
Less bureaucratic and impersonal • greater flexibility • quicker decision-making	Internecine strife • family disputes overflow into business
Financial benefits • possibility of great success	Paternalistic/autocratic rule • resistance to change • secrecy • attraction of dependent personalities
Knowing the business • early training for family members	Financial strain • family members milking the business • disequilibrium between contribution and compensation
	Succession dramas

turned sour and the company went into the red, these individuals refused to accept the new reality—in spite of warnings by a company adviser. In due course, the company went bankrupt.

Table 8.1 summarizes a variety of advantages and disadvantages of family firms. In the next section, I look at one of the most laden issues in family businesses: succession.

THE SUCCESSION CONUNDRUM

Of the many problems associated with family firms, the most insidious center on the question of succession. And of all the roadblocks to succession planning, one of the most profound is the difficulty many people have in accepting their own mortality. It is not easy to confront the ultimate narcissistic injury: the disintegration of the body. Some presidents of family firms (particularly founder-owners) act as if death were something that happens to everyone except themselves. Talking about their death is taboo—raising the topic is viewed as a hostile act, and may even be interpreted as wishing someone dead. Although children, in moments of anger, may have wished their parents dead (which, in turn, may have resulted in strong feelings of guilt), as adults they may suppress or repress such thoughts altogether.

This conspiracy of silence can be augmented by the fear of abandonment. The children may wonder whether they will be able to cope without their parent around. If there are several children, they may worry about who is going to be *primus inter pares*. Some may be afraid—and often for good reasons—that there will be open conflict when the parents are no longer there to act as arbiters. All these issues may mean that they prefer to let matters slip rather than face succession problems head-on. Table 8.2 presents a summary of common barriers to succession planning.

The firm's symbolic value may also aggravate succession problems. For many founder-managers, the enterprise becomes part of their core identity. They depend on the company as a measure of their self-esteem and may be intensely anxious about whether their successors will respect their legacy or destroy what they built up so carefully. Shakespeare's tragedy *King Lear* dramatizes precisely this sort of crisis.

Choosing a successor from among one's children can be extremely difficult since it shatters the fiction that all the children are equal. Singling someone out may lead to discord. Many owner-managers, faced with

Table 8.2 Barriers to succession planning in family firms

Founder/Owner	Family
Death anxiety	Death as taboo • Discussion is a hostile act • Fear of loss/ abandonment
Company as symbol • Loss of identity • Concern about legacy	Fear of sibling rivalry
Dilemmas of choice • Fiction of equality	Change of spouse's position
Generational envy • Loss of power	

the necessity of making a choice, prefer to let the matter be, and procrastinate.

It is also very difficult for some people to let go of the power that comes with the job. They may have become addicted to all the tangible and intangible benefits attached to it. One example of this situation was Serge Dassault of Dassault Enterprises, the French airplane builder, who was 61 before he took over the chairmanship from his father. Another is Thomas Watson, Sr, of IBM, who only handed over control to his son when he was 82 years old. The late Armand Hammer of Occidental Petroleum was another prime example of someone who seemed to have experienced great difficulty in grooming a crown prince.

In the process of letting go, the operation of generational envy (i.e. the envy parents feel toward the emerging abilities of their children) should not be underestimated. Many owner-presidents display high artistry in finding reasons for crushing or humiliating their children. At the heart of this process—as I mentioned earlier in the context of Oedipal rivalry—is their concern about their waning physical powers. All of them seem familiar with Shakespeare's *King Lear,* and the destructive process of his succession and its aftermath.

In some instances, it is not only the CEOs who have problems in letting go, but also their spouses. The latter may have become accustomed to the perks and vicarious recognition that come with the job.

Facilitating forces

Fortunately, several powerful forces operate against these barriers, tax legislation being one example. To prevent an estate from being overburdened by high inheritance taxes—which may even endanger the continuation of the company—it is better to take some preventive steps and transfer ownership to the next generation in plenty of time.

Another effective (but hardly attractive) force is the aging process itself and the health problems that accompany it. A cynic could claim that nothing helps clear a stalemate about succession as effectively as a mild coronary attack. When one is lying in the hospital, it becomes more difficult to deny the possibility of death. In such situations, spouse, confidants, or board members can often give the extra push needed to help the founder overcome their reluctance to let go.

A more positive force is the founder's wish to see the business continue, to see his children continue the firm. In theory this seems obvious. To act on the desire, however, is a different matter, and it takes a certain amount of maturity and wisdom to make it happen. One needs to have acquired a sense of generativity—that is, instead of being envious of the younger generation, the founder needs the capacity to take vicarious pleasure from seeing young men or women do things on their own.

Making a choice

There are a considerable number of options available to a family firm when deciding on succession. Each has its complications, however. Should the rule of primogeniture be applied? What if the oldest child is not the most capable, or is not really interested in the business? If some form of nepotism is going to be inevitable in family firms, one should at least make the effort to pick the best family member available.

Will daughters be eligible? Choosing a daughter can make the situation messy as the sons-in-law may want to get in on the act. If both daughters and sons-in-law work in the firm, real problems arise in the case of divorce. And then there is the problem of names. A married daughter will probably have changed her name from the family one, which can disrupt the symbolic and emotional value many people attach to names and the company identity. (As a consequence of this daughters and sons-in-law often used to be unwelcome in family firms, although this situation has been changing.)

Some imaginative, but not always practical, solutions to dealing with the problem of succession include shared management or some form of management rotation. But with this strategy comes the threat of organizational paralysis. On the other hand, if it works well, the complementarity of individual skills can yield enormous benefits. However, to make this work, a lot of trust is necessary between the different family members.

There are also interim solutions, a typical one being to put a trusted employee in the saddle for a specific period of time. This person may be appointed as trustee of the family heirloom until a family member is groomed to take over. A more dramatic solution is to bring in professional management. At times, only a neutral non-family member can balance the interests of the different factions within the family unit.

Given the potential for family strife to spill over into the company, another quite popular and effective solution is to divide the business. One tactic puts each child in charge of a division or department. A more Draconian approach splits the business into separate companies and gives one to each family member. The added value is frequently much higher if this option is chosen. Moreover, it is often the ideal solution for keeping potentially quarrelsome family members apart. Other possibilities are selling the business, going public, or choosing liquidation.

Of course, the final issue is who should make the choice of successor. Should it be the outgoing president, a family council, the board of directors, or all the parties combined? Should the children be given the opportunity to choose among themselves? There is no perfect solution. However, because very powerful psychological processes can affect the outgoing president's judgment, it is important that he or she is not the sole decision-maker.

Managing for survival

A body such as a family council can play a crucial role in preventing a family company from becoming a casualty of the family drama. Such a council can define the rules of the game for the whole family and establish specific criteria for the selection of the company's future leadership.

Unfortunately, coalition politics, speed, and effective decision-making do not usually go together well. Although such councils are the right forum for discussing certain key issues, decisions will eventually have to be made. In business life more than in many other situations, speed is a competitive advantage. Also, unless there is one dominant family member (because of personality or seniority) or a dominant coalition with complementarity of interests, there is a danger that family councils will begin to resemble elective politics, leading to situations where compromise candidates, not leaders, gain the upper hand.

In an effective family council, the first task is therefore to decide what members want to accomplish. What is the overall family vision? Are they going for continuity of the family regime? Do they want to go public? Do they want to sell the business? Do they want to divide the business? Decisions have to be made about all these issues. The council can also articulate certain rules. For example, how should nonactive family members be dealt with? How can people get out and cash in their shares? Is there going to be some kind of shotgun clause as a way of getting a fair price in case of serious disagreements?

A carefully thought-through management development program can smooth succession planning. This kind of program takes account of two elements: what the company will require in the future, and what the members of the next generation expect for themselves.

In that context, the council can find answers to key questions. For example:

• How long should it take for a family member to assume a senior position?

- What experiences should he or she have before assuming that role?
- What will the compensation be like?
- Should future officers acquire some outside experience before committing themselves to the family firm? Doing so will be invaluable for self-esteem and prove to the individual and his associates that he is capable of making it on his own, not just because of family connections.

The family firm can also pick up a number of important lessons from practices in public companies. It is a *sine qua non* that outsiders should be welcomed and trusted, to prevent organizational myopia. Without the help of outsiders, the manpower supply soon becomes awfully slim. Consequently, the human resources management systems in the family firm should be compatible with those of public companies. For reasons of equity, and to avoid destructive envy, it is extremely important to design attractive incentive systems for non-family members.

Other standard company practices should be observed. Strategic planning should become a matter of course. Roles and responsibilities should be clearly defined. Having well-defined boundaries and clear division of labor will go a long way toward preventing conflict.

Family management should strive to build a corporate culture that is relatively open and minimally politicized. It should be a culture in which people are not afraid to speak their mind and where, through delegation, they have a certain amount of control over their life. True management professionalism can only occur when people have the feeling that non-family members are also eligible for senior management positions.

An independent-minded board of directors will also be needed to keep the company on course. Professional advisers will be equally important. They can take on the role of boundary guards, making sure the family dramas play on stages outside the company—maintaining the separation of business and personal life can be an uphill struggle in family firms.

As those who have experience with family firms know all too well when things go well, they can go very well—but the opposite is also true. For the coach, consultant, and organizational therapist, this is an area in which one certainly does not risk being bored.

PART 3

CHANGING PEOPLE AND ORGANIZATIONS

INTRODUCTION

I have talked about change in several of the earlier chapters in this book, but in these final chapters change becomes my main theme. In Part 2, we saw how enforced change affects individual and organizational psychodynamics; in the last part of the book, I take a closer look at the mechanisms we can use to facilitate both personal and corporate change.

Change means disruption, instability, contradiction, and paradox; yet it also means excitement, hope, reenergizing, and a future focus. Processing and dealing with these very different aspects presents a challenge for people working at all levels of an organization—it requires a high capacity for adaptability and tolerance of uncertainties, what I describe in Chapter 12 as 'organizational Zen.' Above all, it requires an organizational culture that prepares its people for dealing with change and provides the means to cope with a changing environment.

In Chapter 9, I discuss the significance of leadership coaching. In clinical leadership coaching I differentiate three kinds of intervention processes: individual (one-to-one) coaching; team coaching (particularly with natural working groups); and systemic (or organizational/cultural) coaching. I advocate the cultivation of a coaching-oriented culture and describe how individual, group, and organization-wide coaching initiatives can benefit the organization.

Leadership coaching is essentially about personal adaptation and transformation. I argue that personal change can be the trigger for setting broader, organizational change in motion. With the rise of networked organizations that have to operate in complex and ambiguous environments, something very different from the traditional hierarchical leadership model is needed. A coaching culture works at a deep level. Once organizational members have had a coaching experience they learn to practice coaching methods themselves—self-analysis, vicarious learning, and, most importantly, listening and reflective skills. When these methods are established and diffused throughout an organization—through peer interaction, group coaching and top-down, bottom-up communication—the effects on organizational culture and structure can be immensely powerful, demonstrated in a number of tangible ways: retention of staff, high performance, and increased returns. Great though the latter are, however, starting with the tangibles turns the process on its head. It is the larger, intangible, hard-to-define element that has to be got right first, and for that you need the right instruments.

In Chapter 10, I invite the reader to take up a privileged observatory position, be a fly on the wall in one of my top-flight executive coaching programs, and see how it's done. This chapter describes how the program works, from selection, through implementation, to participation and eventual outcomes. We follow the life case study of one particular participant to understand the group dynamics in terms of eliciting information, identifying and analyzing issues, and applying coaching techniques to outing and addressing them. As the chapter title suggests, change is always possible but the critical factor is individual willingness to change. Many participants come to my programs because they have reached a transitional point in their life. It may be something relatively benign—a feeling of sameness or boredom, of being stuck in a rut—or something less innocent—a health problem, marriage breakdown, or dismissal. Whatever the triggering event, they have realized that they have a problem to be dealt with, for the sake of their own health and happiness and that of those around them.

I have run these programs for many years, and they have provided me with a rich source of data for much of my research and program design. One recent study was prompted by the stock response I was given by participants over numerous iterations of the program when I asked them what they wanted out of life. They nearly all said, 'Success.' Fair enough—but what exactly did they mean by success? Further prompting produced a little more thought but most answers pretty much boiled down to 'Having a good job and making more money.' I used this feedback to inform a survey instrument to elicit more fine-tuned information and the results, as I recount in Chapter 11, were surprising. For a significant number of participants, the success they had been pursuing turned out to be a chimera. Their real concept of success lay elsewhere; much of their present discomfort was related to their unrealized feeling that they were in the wrong place, doing the wrong thing, in pursuit of the wrong goal.

In Chapter 12, I look at some ways in which the people responsible for development within organizations can make sure that they are doing exactly the opposite and putting the right people in the right places, pursuing the right goals. How can we reliably identify future stars in our organizations? And having identified them, how can we best develop them? Because I firmly believe, as a specialist in leaders and leadership development, that leaders are made, not born, and once we have identified potential, it is our responsibility to make sure it is nurtured and not squandered.

Most of us have no difficulty identifying the stars we already work with, the people on their way to the top. They have a certain quality that cannot be easily captured or defined, but is instantly recognizable. It has been described as gravitas, authority, personal power or self-assurance. High performers seem to feel good in their skin whatever the circumstances. Other people are attracted to them and like to work with them. They seem to have got hold of some magic formula that guarantees their success, whatever activity they undertake. For stars, no obstacle is too high, no difficulty too great. They have an uncanny ability to perform beyond expectations—and bring others along while they are doing so. Obviously, any organization would like as many of them as possible.

While I do not believe in a 'magic formula' for leadership stardom, I do believe that the stars who will shine in today's rapidly changing world share one distinguishing quality—a familiarity with ambiguity and uncertainty that helps them achieve a state of organizational Zen. I liken these future leaders, and their behavior, to embodied kōans. They will be the key to unlocking the contradictions and inconsistencies that characterize an environment of constant change.

The difficulty, however, is how to spot them. Nascent stars do not shine like those already in the ascendant and, to complicate matters, they share many characteristics with those I describe as 'pseudo-stars' and we have to learn to distinguish them. I begin by examining these characteristics as identification tools, then go on to define three main developmental methods that can be deployed in an organizational context, within a coaching culture, to help these high potentials.

I conclude this book by reprising many of the themes in the earlier chapters in an examination of what constitutes a healthy individual and, by extension, a healthy organization. If, as I stated in the introduction to Part 2, sick people create sick organizations, the obvious counter to that is that healthy people do the reverse. But it is not quite so straightforward as that. The right ingredients—culture, structure, strategy, and vision— need to be combined to create the kind of organization that will attract, retain, and develop healthy individuals. I call these places authentizotic organizations, places where members feel authentic, productive, and fully alive. My hope for the future of organizational life is that more leaders will take these lessons on board and that we will see growing lists of 'best places to work.' To quote Friedrich von Schiller:

'We speak with the lip, and we dream in the soul,
Of some better and fairer day;
And our days, the meanwhile, to that golden goal
Are gliding and sliding away.
Now the world becomes old, now again it is young,
But "The better" 's forever the word on the tongue.'

CHAPTER 9

LEADERSHIP COACHING FOR ORGANIZATIONAL TRANSFORMATION

It is a paradoxical but profoundly true and important principle of life that the most likely way to reach a goal is to be aiming not at that goal itself but at some more ambitious goal beyond it.

—Arnold Toynbee

A good coach will make his players see what they can be rather than what they are.

—Ara Parasheghian

You can motivate by fear, and you can motivate by reward. But both those methods are only temporary. The only lasting thing is self-motivation.

—Homer Rice

Probably my best quality as a coach is that I ask a lot of challenging questions and let the person come up with the answer.

—Phil Dixon

INTRODUCTION

Having gone through a period of relative stability, we live now in an age of permanent change—and the pace of this change is unrelenting. The traditional organization of the past has all but disappeared. Vertical structures—influenced by the power of the Internet—have been replaced by horizontal ones. In our knowledge society, we are moving from hierarchical to more network-oriented structures. Autocratic forms of leadership have been replaced by more authoritative-authentic kinds. People no longer have positions for life. The psychological contract between employer and employee has changed dramatically and the organization man or woman is a relic of the past. Organizational loyalty has gone down the drain since the advent of downsizing, rightsizing, and resizing. Organizations may offer opportunities but people have to take charge of their careers. Moreover, as we all live longer, protean, portfolio, or sequential careers are the rule rather than the exception. People are now expected to have several different careers in a lifetime.

In this climate of instability and confusion, retention of people—sometimes described as the war for talent—has become a real and serious problem. Retaining employees has been likened to the challenge of keeping frogs in a wheelbarrow: they can jump out at any time. Human talent is now the scarcest resource in organizations trying to survive in these highly competitive markets (Michaels, Handfield-Jones et al., 2001). But with change pressing from all sides, we need to find ways to keep the right frogs in the barrow while we steer the barrow in the right direction—and to persuade those frogs that they're better off not jumping. People have to learn to adapt to the new realities of a changing world or find other opportunities. What makes more sense: changing people? Or collecting a whole load of different frogs to put in the barrow? It may not be easy but organizations have to help their people to adapt to a changing environment.

To make employees more effective in dealing with continuous and discontinuous change, their learning trajectory in organizations has become more important than ever. They have to be kept up-to-date with the changes taking place around them. A new, but very different psychological contract needs to be established whereby continued learning stands central. To have people create a bond with the organizations they work in, a culture needs to be established that helps them deal with these new realities. Cultural parameters such as openness to change, creativity, learning, mutual respect, trust, and having a voice will play an important role in the retention of people. Inevitably, to make such an environment a reality implies the creation of a coaching-oriented culture. Personal adaptation and transformation lie at the heart of leadership coaching, as they can play a critical role in helping individuals, teams, and organizations deal with change, transforming change into an opportunity rather than an obstacle, making preparedness and willingness to change part of the employees' DNA.

BEING EFFECTIVE IN A WORLD OF PARADOXES

In the face of a dramatically changing, competitive marketplace, the biggest challenge organizations face today is to get the best out of their people; to have them work collectively toward common goals, thus achieving performance with purpose. Addressing new developments in the marketplace often requires a shifting strategy that may call for a dramatic organizational transformation. Organizations must move with speed to market products and services in these super-competitive exchanges. And as organizations need to implement change but are unsure how to bring these changes about, they are breaking down functional barriers and organizing themselves around value-creating, customer-oriented processes. Leading these new network-oriented organizations is quite different from giving direction in organizations characterized by traditional, functional, hierarchical leadership. It necessitates more imaginative organizational forms; it necessitates more imaginative leadership given the increasing complexity and ambiguity in the environment.

In organizations where there is a much greater degree of interdependency between the various functions, the pressures on executives and their employees to arrive at satisfactory solutions increase dramatically. Operating in those organizations requires leaders with collaborative, problem-solving, and influencing skills—executives with an astute understanding of how to analyze complex processes and grasp the intricacies of the company's value chain; who know how to deal with inefficiencies and recognize interdependencies with other stakeholders in the organization; and who are prepared to build positions that motivate and empower employees to perform at peak capacity (Kets de Vries, 2001; Kets de Vries, 2006a; Kets de Vries and Korotov, 2007; Kets de Vries, Guillen et al., 2010). It will take a lot of time, energy, and effort investing in people to create these high-performance organizations. Unfortunately, many organizations suffer from a lack of talented people to make this happen.

Although change historically triggers distress, trepidation, apprehensiveness, fear, anxiety, and other resistances, it also opens up new opportunities for growth and development. A changing environment sets the stage for creative opportunities. And this observation applies to both macro and micro changes. While macro changes can lead to organizational rejuvenation, changes on a more individual, micro level can be the starting points in helping people to reinvent themselves. And as a catalyst for change, leadership coaching can be extremely beneficial to set these processes into motion.

At a macro level, leadership coaching may help transform the organization's culture and patterns of decision-making. At a micro level it can contribute to greater satisfaction at work and at home; it may result in lower stress levels, less frustration, and increased self-esteem and satisfaction with life (Flaherty, 1999; Hudson, 1999; Hunt and Weintraub, 2002). This congruence between public and private life can help executives acquire a greater sense of authenticity when dealing with their constituency, contributing to the creation of better places to work. From this perspective, effective leadership coaching can be viewed as an ongoing partnership that helps clients produce fulfilling results in their personal and professional lives.

But what is leadership coaching? I define it (Kets de Vries, 2005a; Kets de Vries, Korotov and Florent-Treacy, 2007) as a one-on-one or group service to executives that is designed to create more effective and healthier organizations. When executives improve their performance by finding more creative ways in dealing with their work environment, a sort of contagion spreads the benefits throughout the organization— exposing senior executives to coaching disseminates a coaching culture within the workplace. In making this observation, it's important to understand what leadership coaching isn't—it isn't career counseling, consulting, mentoring, or training. Coaches do not necessarily provide answers. Essentially, they ask questions—and their skill lies in asking the right questions, helping people to think, and encouraging their clients to come up with their own ideas and answers.

It must also be emphasized that leadership coaching is not about identifying 'what's wrong.' Coaching is not about patching up dysfunctional executives; it is about how to make effective executives even better. Instead of zooming in on dysfunctionality, a more constructive approach is to focus on solutions and forward motion—assessing where executives are now and where they want to be, including the gaps that need to be addressed. The challenge for leadership coaches is to arrive at a systematic approach to bring about real change by providing structures for goal setting, standards of accountability, and a big-picture focus while giving honest feedback.

The challenge of talent management

Over the last ten years, organizations have removed management layers, built networks, increased spans of control, and increasingly relied on cross-functional and virtual teams for process improvement. However, working with highly diversified, virtual teams has created its own challenges. Although diversity has a positive effect on creativity, it comes at a price. Enabling collaboration in these complex constellations of people necessitates a serious emotional and cognitive investment up front to prevent the manifestation of paranoid thinking and other forms of dysfunctional behavior. If this kind of behavior raises its ugly head, regressive group processes may come to the fore, and the result will be toxic organizational cultures and neurotic organizations. Sadly enough, when these dysfunctional patterns prevail in an organization, they will eventually destroy it (Kets de Vries and Miller, 1984). Furthermore, it goes without saying that in organizations characterized by fear, anxiety, and distrust, it is highly unlikely that executives will perform at full capacity.

It cannot be articulated strongly enough to senior management that the cost of performing below capacity is considerable. And many senior executives have been listening. This explains why leadership coaching has become such a growth industry. Organizations with powerful leadership development practices—organizations that take talent management seriously—consistently produce more desirable long-term results. For these organizations, 'people are our greatest assets' is not merely an empty slogan but an expression of a serious commitment. Top management in these organizations uses leadership coaching as a tool to make their executives more effective. With their support, leadership coaching can help employees develop the qualities that have been proven to be associated with success; to make good people even better.

Leadership coaching is all about helping executives to identify and define their specific goals, then organize themselves to find ways to attain them. So coaching draws on clients' inner knowledge, resources, and ingenuity to help them to be more effective. Coaching creates impact by building executives' personal skills, finding better ways to communicate, and to sculpt leadership style, decision-making, and problem solving. Effective leadership coaches help executives develop cognitive agility, emotional capacities, motivation, skills, knowledge, and expertise. They assist executives in refining their goals and strategies, challenge and reassess their assumptions, and refine and improve their leadership style. Leadership coaches also encourage executives to be more effective at team management, constructive conflict resolution, creating commitments, and accountability for their people, contributing to better results (Palmer and Whybrow, 2007).

Moreover, leadership coaching becomes the key to unlocking executives' potential, improving their capacity to focus, learn, and innovate. Most important in this developmental process is helping executives tune in to their emotional intelligence, to be more self-aware of the impact they have on others, to have a better understanding of their strengths and weaknesses—and to work on their strengths. Leadership coaches help executives understand that career development has become an individual responsibility and lifelong learning a keen issue. People who do not continue to learn lose ground.

Leadership coaching should also be viewed as an iterative process in which innovation, adjustment, and correction are brought about by the outcomes produced. This is what makes coaching so alive, and what contributes to creativity and innovation in organizations. Leadership coaching is based on the concept that individuals learn most from the everyday application of their skills, by actually trying things out in practice. When leadership coaching is an effective element of an organization's leadership development portfolio, the visible business outcomes are long-term improvements, measured by profit or cost-containment, or both.

The organizational challenge

Continually changing external–internal performance requirements mean that any organization that wants to survive and thrive must learn how to grow and adapt to changes in the internal and external environment. In many instances, managing growth means shifting strategies that require broad and deep organizational changes. The difference between success and failure depends not only on helping executives adapt to change, but also on creating an environment that fosters creativity, innovation, and professional growth and development. Effective leadership coaching accelerates an organization's progress by providing it with a greater focus and awareness of various organizational strengths that will lead to better decision-making. A coaching culture within an organization creates a forum where individuals can discuss challenges, concerns, and appropriate actions. Leadership coaches can be especially effective in helping these individuals to create high performance teams.

Leadership coaching has changed the way many progressive organizations view professional and personal growth and development. In a dynamic and complex business environment, it makes sense to engage in strategic coaching during critical times of transition and growth. By aligning individual development with business outcomes, leadership coaching is an investment with future service potential—building the talent pool in the organization, and creating a mindset open to change (Crane and Nancy Patrick, 2002).

Overcoming resistances   Individuals and groups resist change when they perceive it as a threat to their power base (Press, 2005). Some individuals are also doubtful whether they will succeed in making the changes needed. But people are not necessarily afraid of change if they are offered the skills needed to deal with it. Successful change management implies new ways of looking at things. It requires innovative, transformational leadership development programs with a coaching component. Education should never end; the process of inquiry should never stop. And it is because of this permanent need for new learning that leadership coaching has become such a powerful force.

When an organization supports its executives through leadership coaching programs, both the individual and the organization will benefit. Coaching complements existing leadership development programs and can make an essential contribution to the success of any change initiative. Furthermore, leadership coaching that takes into consideration not only conscious but also out-of-awareness behavior facilitates increased self-awareness and an understanding of the kind of obstacles that people have to deal with in their journey through life. It helps people acquire a new lens through which to examine knotty personal and organizational problems. These inner journeys help provide answers to the existential conundrums we all face at times. Whether these dilemmas are conscious or unconscious, leadership coaching can help executives become more successful at managing their day-to-day responsibilities, meeting their goals, recognizing when they find themselves at crossroads, and, most importantly, creating a fulfilling life.

A Socratic method

Leadership coaching is more an art of discovery than a technology of delivery. Coaching, by its nature, has a Socratic quality—that is, it involves asking a series of questions about a central issue, and trying to find satisfactory answers through exchanges. The use of questions and conversation implies that a leadership coach begins from a position of humility and curiosity, not one of authority and knowledge. Leadership coaches are guides, not drill sergeants—catalysts in the client's journey of self-discovery. If this process of inquiry is to be effective, it is important for the coach to take the expertise of the client for granted. The inquiry model is built on a belief that real growth must come from within the other.

Leadership coaching through inquiry helps individuals understand what they are innately good at. It helps them build on their strengths (while realizing that overplayed strengths may turn into Achilles' heels), recognize their weaknesses, develop flexibility and change-readiness, create awareness of shortcomings, and build commitment to self-development and achievement. Coaching should be viewed as partnering with clients in a thought-provoking and creative way that inspires them to enhance their effectiveness as leaders in their personal and professional life. Furthermore, through leadership coaching, people will also have an opportunity to enhance the quality of their life. The coach's job is to provide support to manifest skills, resources, and creativity that the client has been only subliminally aware of. Applying this Socratic method, clients set better goals, take more effective action, make better decisions, run better teams, have a more holistic view of their organization, and use their natural gifts and talents more fully. Most importantly, the insights provided through leadership coaching may provide them with a more fulfilling and richer life.

Unfortunately, in far too many organizations, leaders waste a lot of time, energy, and frustration on common resource drains and organizational inefficiencies—high staff turnover, troublesome employees, low productivity, poor or mediocre customer service, failed change efforts, conflict between teams, turf fights, lack of cooperation among employees, job overload, role conflict, high stress, low morale, and other stress inducing factors (Kets de Vries and Miller, 1984). Coaches can help leaders to stay focused on what is essential to the success of the organization. They can push away the stuff that gets in the way. In such situations, coaching can be about facilitating change that will lead to successful results: facilitating movement from a current state to a more desirable future state. Effective coaching can contribute to executives' operating at optimal performance.

However, there are situations where a coaching intervention will be an uphill struggle. In organizations characterized by mistrust, fear, and a culture of blame; in companies with extremely short-term reward structures; and in organizations where people are viewed as disposable goods coaching efforts will yield poor returns. Neurotic organizations are not very fertile terrains to operate in. In some instances, it may be a challenge to try to change such an organization; in most cases it can be a recipe for failure.

Leadership coaching can also provide a sort of correctional safety belt for long-term developmental needs. Astute interventions made at the right time may prevent executives or new leaders derailing from their career. It may also help these people to more effective 'on-boarding'—taking on a new executive position with the least amount of difficulty. Although coaching will not necessarily eliminate failure, it may make time to success quicker. The reduction of development time, linked to organizational objectives, may contribute added value, if it prevents an organization taking the wrong course.

The holistic picture: culture and organization

To shift strategy effectively and become a high performance organization, however, companies need not only to pay attention to individual and team issues, but also take a broader perspective. As mentioned in Chapter 4, attention needs to be paid to an organization's corporate culture (Schein, 1985). Leadership coaches in organizations need to understand the impact they can have achieving breakthrough results by learning how to use aspects of the organizational culture to enhance creativity, productivity, and human motivation. A company culture that welcomes communication, rewards creativity, knows how to differentiate itself from its competitors, builds long-term client relationships, and fosters sound leadership practices conveys a unique experience to its various constituencies.

Understanding the role that culture plays in defining the opportunities available to an organization is like receiving the proverbial keys to the kingdom. Effective leadership coaches have an inside view that provides companies with the leverage to shift both organizational culture and behaviors so that they reflect an inclusive environment that respects a diversity of thought, personality, lifestyle, and ethnicity. Leadership coaches who are familiar with the vicissitudes of cultural change, and who conduct cultural audits through surveys, interviews, and/or focus group methods, will know how to establish a basis for cultural transformation. From the data they acquire, coaches can propose and conduct interventions to identify and articulate the salient elements of an organization's culture that can help develop and introduce positive, constructive behaviors.

A coaching organization creates an environment where the behaviors and practices needed for continuous learning, the exchange of both explicit and tacit knowledge, reciprocal coaching, and self-leadership development are actively encouraged and facilitated. A coaching culture contributes to a sense of mutual ownership, better networking, more effective leadership practices and higher commitment, creating better results across the organization.

But whether it is a new strategy, restructuring, a merger and/or acquisition, the change or transition will takes its toll. To effect real change, a multi-pronged approach will be needed—using a number of different change interventions simultaneously. The support of a leadership coach who knows how to operate at micro and macro levels, particularly one who is experienced in organizational change and transformation, can contribute dramatically to the success of a change and transition effort.

Being a role model

The behavior of an organization's leadership is crucial to the success of a coaching intervention. They are expected to create motivation by getting the best out of their people; they are expected to possess integrity. Setting an example and walking the talk are powerful symbolic gestures. The effectiveness of a coaching culture will depend on the degree to which the top executive team has internalized this kind of behavior. Trust is a very delicate flower. It takes time to nurture it, and it is quick to fade. A coaching culture starts at the top—senior executives should take every opportunity to demonstrate their commitment to it, and sanctions should be applied if the culture is transgressed.

When a coaching culture becomes part of the DNA of an organization, it means that an environment has been created where people have a healthy disrespect for the boss, where people know that they have a voice, and that their opinions count (Kets de Vries and Balazs, 1999). A leader's greatest contributions are the communication of ideas, acting as a role model, influencing those around them, and inspiring others to join in accomplishing a common goal. Nevertheless, it is a fact that, the further up the ladder a leader moves, the further he or she moves away from giving and receiving constructive feedback. The possibilities for miscommunication are plentiful.

Giving feedback to anyone is difficult for most people. If they are not careful, far too many leaders find themselves quite isolated from reality, with subordinates who are fearful of giving frank information—and fear is an antidote to innovation and creativity. Companies that are serious, however, about creating coaching cultures do not fall into this leadership trap. They keep their feet firmly on the ground. When it is managed well, a culture of frank feedback is a great asset in creating more effective leaders who can keep up with our fast-changing, transforming environment.

The ABC of coaching terminology

As I touched on earlier, I use 'leadership coaching' as a general term to describe a specific type of intervention that can be carried out strategically with individuals, teams, or the whole organization (Flaherty, 2005; Kets de Vries, 2005a; Orem, Binkert *et al.*, 2007). Its aim is to direct, instruct, or train a person or group of people toward a specific mutually determined goal. Given this element of mutuality, coaching can accelerate progress by providing focus and awareness. It is about helping the people who are being coached to reach fuller potential—a point at which they not only truly know themselves but also feel comfortable with who and what they are.

Leadership coaching can be an ongoing professional relationship that helps people produce extraordinary results in their lives, careers, and organizations. In a way, coaches act as a mirror; they help people work out what they want, what they are good at, what they are not so good at, and where and how they can improve. They provide their clients with a safe transitional space. Successful leadership coaches affect transformational change by providing their clients with a safe transitional space—a place where they can experiment with fresh perspectives and action plans (Winnicott, 1951)—giving them enough trust to be able to deal with 'undiscussables.' Confronting 'undiscussables' usually opens the way for new, highly productive discussions, and unblocks the decision-making process.

What's in a name?   Coaching in an organizational context goes by many names or aliases: business, corporate, executive, performance, life, workplace, and leadership coaching are usually all bracketed together. However, there are distinctions to be made. Competencies or performance coaching includes how-to techniques, skill development, and attaining stretch goals (Kilberg, 2000). On a somewhat higher plane, there is leadership/behavioral coaching, which is concerned with emotional intelligence or developing a more effective leadership style. Then there is career transition or life coaching, which focuses on personal growth and career development, and organizational change/strategic coaching, where the orientation is on introducing new change initiatives. The transition from one form of coaching to another is relatively fluid—and this is not even taking into consideration the (often subtle) differences between what is meant by coaching, counseling, mentoring, consulting, and psychotherapy.

Furthermore, organizations may employ internal or external coaches, or a combination of both. Internal coaches are regular employees of the organization, while external coaches are contracted to work with the organization. Although internal coaches will be more familiar with the ins-and-outs of the organization, the question of confidentiality is critical. For coaching to be most effective, there must be absolute trust between the parties involved. This means that the individuals who are being coached must feel certain that their exchanges with the coach will remain confidential and will not affect their employment or status within the organization. Given the culture of some organizations, will an internal coach be able to set and maintain 'Chinese walls'?

Coaching initiatives

There are literally hundreds of different types of coaching initiative and they fall into two main categories: small-scale, one-off interventions, and large-scale, longer-term interventions (coaching individuals, teams, or engaging in a systemic, overall organization intervention). Whatever change initiative is taken, in many programs, 360-degree feedback assessments are used as ice-breakers. These instruments can be the property of the organization that is being coached or instruments owned by a coaching organization. They may include assessments to measure multi-party feedback about a person's leadership style, an audit about the salient ingredients of a corporate culture, and various forms of personality assessment. For example, I have used extensively the Global Executive Leadership Inventory (Kets de Vries, 2004; Kets de Vries *et al.*, 2004) the Personality Audit (Kets de Vries, 2005b, 2005c; Kets de Vries *et al.*, 2006), the Leadership Archetype Questionnaire (2006c, 2006d), the Internal Theater Inventory (Kets de Vries, 2010c), and the Organizational Culture Audit (Kets de Vries, 2010a, 2010b). In the next section, I say more about the kinds of clinically based interventions I and many of my coaching colleagues undertake at the INSEAD Global Leadership Center (IGLC), the European Institute of Management and Technology (ESMT), and the Kets de Vries Institute (KDVI).

THE CLINICAL LEADERSHIP COACHING BRAND

The clinical leadership coaching brand is made up of three kinds of intervention processes. We distinguish between individual (one-to-one) coaching, team coaching (particularly with natural working groups), and systemic (or organizational/cultural) coaching. A distinguishing feature of the clinical coaching brand is that most of the coaching (but not all) takes place in a group setting, a deliberate strategy to exert more pressure for action on participants. It is our experience that many executives have a lot of dreams about what they want to do but when it comes to taking action, many of these dreams suddenly evaporate. When discussion takes place in groups (particularly groups that normally work together) there is a greater possibility that something will happen, as the other participants have a stake in the action plans of the person who is being discussed. (Peer coaching plays an essential role in getting action plans implemented.) This can lead to a public declaration of intent, plans of action, and the naming of people who will help accomplish them. To add pressure to the impetus to act, there are one or more follow-ups several months later when the person is asked to account for what has been accomplished. I sometimes say facetiously that my effectiveness is based on such factors as shame, guilt, and hope. I use shame and guilt to keep the participants on track, and keep hope in the background for a better future which includes personal growth and creativity.

The clinical paradigm

Much of our work in organizations is grounded in the clinical paradigm, meaning that we stay 'at the sick bed,' sticking close to the reality of the case and using concepts that have proved to have an impact. Although we have no specific ideological orientation, we apply ideas from psychoanalysis (in particular object relations theory), psychotherapy, developmental psychology, family systems theory, paradoxical intervention, appreciative inquiry, motivational interviewing, behavioral concepts, and cognition to understand the behavior of people in organizations (Kets de Vries, 2006a). Central to all this is a psychodynamic/systemic orientation. The clinical paradigm consists of a number of premises.

Rationality is an illusion Irrationality is grounded in rationality. 'Irrational' behavior is a common pattern in our lives, although in fact it will always have a 'rationale,' a meaning to it. Nothing that we do is random. Elements of psychic determinism are a fact of life. It is critical to understand this rationale in making sense of our own and other people's 'inner theater'—the core themes that affect our personality and leadership style.

What we see isn't necessarily what we get Much of what happens to us is beyond our conscious awareness. Most of our behavior is unconscious. To have a better understanding of unconscious patterns we need to explore our own and other people's inner desires, wishes, and fantasies; we need to pay attention to the repetitive themes and patterns in our lives, and the lives of others.

The past is the lens through which we can understand the present and shape the future All of us are the product of our past. Like it or not, there's a continuity between past and present. We are inclined to view the present through the microscope of past experiences. As the saying goes, 'The hand that rocks the cradle rules the world.' Our personality structure is due to the developmental outcome of our early environment, modified by our genetic endowment. To make sense of our behavior, we must explore our interpersonal 'history,' including our original attachment relationships.

The significance of transference and counter-transference relationships   Because of the heavy imprinting that takes place at earlier stages of life, we tend to repeat certain behavior patterns. To make sense of what makes us behave the way we do, we need to explore our interpersonal relationships. Adaptive and nonadaptive aspects of our operational mode will be affected by how our original attachment relationships—the relationships with our first caregivers—have evolved. As there will be repetitive themes in our lives and the lives of others, such themes will be re-activated in the relationships we have with the people we deal with in the present. To understand our and others' behavior we need to identify these recurrent themes and patterns. These problematic relationship patterns (which are technically described as transference and counter-transference reactions) provide a great opportunity to explore and work through difficult issues in the here-and-now. Exploring the relationships between past and present can be very illuminating, as it enables us to become liberated from stereotypical, ingrained behavior.

Nothing is more central to who we are than the way we express and regulate our emotions.

Intellectual insight is not the same as emotional insight, which touches us at a much deeper level. Emotions determine many of our actions and emotional intelligence plays a vital role in who we are, and what we do. In understanding ourselves and other people, we need to pay paramount attention to emotions.

We all have blind spots   There are many things we don't want to know about ourselves. We use defensive processes and resistances to avoid problematic aspects of experience. Many people derail due to blind spots in their personality. To explore these efforts at avoidance of distressing thoughts and feelings will give us another snapshot of our own personality and that of others. We need to realize that these resistances come to the fore due to conflicts within ourselves; we need to accept that inner dissonance is part of the human condition. We also need to recognize that most psychological difficulties were, at one point in time, adaptive solutions to the problem of living.

Our past determines our present   The goal of applying the clinical paradigm is to help people to revisit past experiences, expand their freedom of choice to explore new challenges in life, and to become more aware of their choices in the here-and-now. It is essential for healthy functioning that we do not remain strangers to ourselves. We need to free ourselves from the bonds of past experience to be able to explore new challenges in life.

Applying the clinical paradigm helps to tease out the central interpersonal role in which clients consciously and unconsciously cast themselves. It also helps us explore the complementary roles in which other people are positioned in an executive role constellation. It helps us identify self-defeating expectations and negative self-appraisal, as well as outdated perceptions of ourselves—behavior patterns that had a useful function at one point but are now counter-effective. Given the fact that organizational life is a people business, we pay great attention to people's relationships and interpersonal experiences. Furthermore, if possible, we scrutinize the here-and-now relationship between our clients and ourselves—the nature of the transference-counter-transference relationship can be a very important source of information. The attitude towards us, in the role of consultant/coach is a telltale sign. For example, if a client is hostile, suspicious, ingratiating, or feels rejected, these reactions can be taken as signs of more generalized behavior patterns that are worth exploring.

In our leadership coaching work (if the timing is right) we will also pay attention to defensive activities—attempts to avoid distressing thoughts or feelings. These provide a window into an individual's personality. We also zero in on recurring themes or patterns in a person's behavior, the telltale signs of the person's inner theater.

FORMS OF INTERVENTION

As mentioned earlier, in our interventions we like to operate at three different levels, individual, team, and organizational. Although we prefer to take a holistic approach, we do not always have the opportunity to do so, and concentrate our intervention at individual or team level.

Individual coaching

In our individual approaches to coaching, we don't make a clear distinction between the various elements of coaching I identified earlier. In our work, we are usually faced with a large degree of fluidity between all of them. In our coaching processes we facilitate the exploration of needs, motivations, desires, skills, and thought processes to assist the individual in making real, lasting change. To us, coaching is partnering with clients in a thought-provoking and creative process that inspires them to maximize their personal and professional potential. Individual coaching provides a place where the client's private self can be heard, honored, and challenged. This offers each client the opportunity to create the space for their vision, set clearly defined goals that support that vision, and see the results in both their personal and professional lives.

Individual coaching helps people to:

- become more effective and productive;
- learn to work smarter, not harder;
- find ways of communication with greater clarity;
- become more flexible, adaptable, and successful in dealing with change;
- respond more skillfully to organizational challenges and opportunities;
- become more effective in conflict resolution;
- recognize blind spots and defensive patterns;
- turn personal awareness into insight and insight into action;
- understand better the perceptions of other organizational participants;
- learn to be more assertive and self-confident;
- improve existing superior–subordinate relationships;
- learn to manage upward better;
- become more effective in giving and receiving feedback;
- learn to become a better (more active) listener;
- find greater enjoyment at work;
- find ways to decrease the levels of stress and tension in the organization;
- become more effective in time management;
- enhance the innovative potential of the people with whom they work;
- become better at finding creative solutions to knotty problems;
- become more effective in managing paradoxical situations;
- build stronger, more trusting relationships;
- show a more authentic leadership style;
- be successful in a new role;
- enhance the pace of development of promising new executives;
- make an effort to prevent executive derailment;
- work on the development of emotional intelligence;
- live life with more intensity, choice, and an increased ability to inspire others;
- establish stronger relationships with clients;
- be more deliberate in developing a career development plan, making an in-depth assessment of what is currently working and what is not;
- identify meaningful goals;
- develop new leadership capacities, especially coaching and other inter-personal and communication skills;

- gain a greater sense of ownership and responsibility for their behaviors and actions;
- help people in the creation of a legacy;
- acquire a better work–life balance.

Group coaching

Successful organizations are run by efficient teams. At organizations such as IGLC, ESMT, and KDVI, we have been in the vanguard of group coaching, particularly with natural working groups. Successful teams trust each other, commit to decisions and action plans, hold each other accountable, focus on collective team results, and understand how their team contributes to the success of the organization. These kinds of initiatives are designed to help teams within the organization achieve greater levels of collaboration and results, with a focus on key organizational challenges. The team coach has to facilitate open and simultaneous interaction between all of these parties, often against a background of overt or hidden conflict.

I have discovered that a group coaching intervention is also the ideal way to create virtual teams that really work. In our networked world, virtual teams are on the increase but if they are to operate effectively, challenging differences in culture, gender, age, and functional background have to be addressed by something more profound than tagging emails with emoticons. There will be many overt and covert issues to be dealt with and it goes without saying that a starting point is a greater understanding of the different backgrounds of team members. Effective teams are the cure for turf fights—in a team context, people are more inclined to see other stakeholders' points of view and be more willing to collaborate. Team interventions are a way toward creating boundaryless organizations.

Knowledge management is another issue in a team context and one that presents problems: it amounts to far more than merely setting up a database. While the process of data management is laudable, a major ingredient is missing: trust. People will only be willing to share information where there is trust and the various constituencies feel comfortable with each other. If there *is* that trust, participants will engage in constructive conflict resolution; they will make commitments, and they are more likely to be accountable. The usual result of this equation is better results for the company.

When leadership coaching is applied to teams, it creates a more egalitarian, high-trust interface that transcends traditional superior–subordinate relationships. The fundamental premise in team coaching is that all members of the team develop a true realization of what 'working for the same company' means. The capacity to build effective teams gives an organization an enormous competitive advantage. Furthermore, team coaching not only supports and enables the realization of a team's performance potential but also increases a team's capacity for self-sustained development. When a team operates at full capacity, everybody pulls their weight and is accountable for their contribution to team performance. Some of the 'undiscussables' come to the surface and can be discussed openly, in a manner where mutual responsibility is both implicit and explicit. Reaching this point takes a great deal of learning and behavior change on the part of the leader and the team members.

Team coaching is also strongly recommended for teams going through a significant change effort—including a new CEO. It is also ideal for new teams wanting a faster track to high performance to get off to a flying start. Highly successful teams engage in both individual and team coaching in order to address issues specific to an individual, and broader, more global issues related to the team. This may include team development with a specific focus on critical issues, vision, mission, goals, roles, corporate culture, team support, and leadership development.

The therapeutic dimension Group acceptance and support are essential therapeutic factors in team coaching. The group's perception that difficult issues can be resolved for the better instills a lot of hope (Kets de Vries, 2002). Letting go of pent-up emotions through self-disclosure can be cathartic, producing a feeling of 'cleansing,' renewal, or release from tension. Bringing unconscious matters to consciousness is a form of emotional relief. Making connections—perhaps between past experiences, unresolved issues, and present discomforts—can result in deep insights, the alleviation of symptoms, or even the permanent relief of a condition. A team exercise of this kind is a form of education. Personal transformation is enhanced by vicarious learning from the examples of others—an extremely powerful experience, not least because it helps people realize they are not alone in struggling with a specific problem. As suggestions for change are made, individuals may model their behavior on that of others. This process helps self-understanding and the acquisition of deep insights. Having a better understanding of the problem helps the working-through process of how to deal with complex issues—by oneself and with others.

Group coaching can help a team to:

* identify the characteristics of effective teams;
* align individual performance with team goals;
* clarify team goals, identify obstacles to change, explore options, and develop appropriate action plans;
* better understand the dynamics within the team;

- identify the role each member of the team plays;
- identify overt and covert conflict within the team;
- help the team deal better with conflict;
- help in 'assimilation coaching' introducing new members to a functioning team;
- have higher quality conversations;
- create a greater sense of trust and respect among members;
- fully develop the executive team into a more cohesive, trusting, collaborative, and high-performance unit;
- develop more effective leadership skills within the team;
- arrive at better team decision-making;
- take advantage of peer coaching in a team setting;
- align team norms with an accountability structure;
- assure that individual and team accountability structures are built into every task and project;
- help a team that's moving through a significant period of change and transition;
- deal with virtual and cross-functional team challenges;
- ensure that feedback, brainstorming, and challenging beliefs become accepted practices within the team;
- create self-organizing teams;
- increase the team's capacity to arrive at high performance;
- maximize and leverage the strengths of a team;
- understand the barriers to performance that hinder the team;
- clarify the team's objectives;
- create a better appreciation of the team's strengths and challenges;
- set the ground rules and logistics to improve processes, e.g. the frequency, location, and rules of team meetings;
- engage in regular process review meetings, assessing how successful team meetings have been.

Organizational coaching

The ultimate goal of a clinical coaching team is to make holistic interventions—to transform entire organizations through organizational (cultural) coaching. The objective of taking an organizational coaching approach is to create a culture where all members of the organization are able to engage in candid, respectful coaching conversations about how they can improve their working relationships and individual and collective work performance, unrestricted by hierarchical reporting relationships.

An organization's culture, as we saw in Chapter 4, comprises the collective (conscious and unconscious) attitudes, beliefs, values, and behaviors that define 'how things are done around here.' Leaders set the tone, pace, and expectations for the culture, providing role models of what is expected, desired, and/or tolerated in the organization. All participants learn to value and use feedback as a powerful learning tool to produce personal and professional development, high-trust working relationships, continually improving job performance, and ever-increasing customer satisfaction. Creating a culture where employees have a voice and can make a difference will ultimately improve the performance of the organization and its constituent parts. In our coaching work we have found that the most successful organizations are those with coaching skills embedded in their culture.

An organization with a true coaching culture not only offers formal, more prescribed coaching but also encourages people to use coaching behavior as a means of managing, influencing, and communicating with each other. These organizations integrate coaching modules into their leadership development and general way of doing things. A coaching culture promotes more open communication, is transparent, and builds trust and mutual respect. Introducing coaching competencies into an organization is a very powerful strategy if you are trying to create the kind of workplace that fosters learning and development. Not surprisingly, companies with a successful coaching culture report significantly reduced staff turnover, increased productivity, and greater job satisfaction. The model maximizes the resources of the organization, realigns relationships, and drives a focus on long-term strategy. These companies differentiate themselves by having a strong corporate identity and a committed workforce. All employees are aligned with the goals of the organization, and what is needed to get there. Creating a coaching culture helps leaders to think and plan more strategically, to manage risks more effectively, to create and communicate vision and mission more clearly.

The subtlest aspect of a coaching culture is the new way individuals perceive themselves and their world. They have a sense of connection. They feel part of a whole. They take responsibility. There is no 'us' and 'them.' With a sense of ownership in the organization, they are beyond the blame game and have the courage to speak their mind, knowing that they have the right to do so.

The role of the executive team   For a coaching culture to work, it has to be integrated with the business strategy. But that is not enough. The organization needs its powerholders to be champions of change. Few innovative initiatives succeed without the support of senior executives who are committed to the idea. If a coaching culture is to be successful, the first people to go through the coaching process should be the members of the executive committee. If they are satisfied with the outcome, coaching is more likely to cascade down through the organization and become part of the organization's fabric.

An example Let's look at an illustration of such an intervention. An energy company made a valiant effort to create a coaching culture after it almost failed because a 'macho' culture had infiltrated most of the organization, resulting in extremely risky moves. Rogue traders lost a significant amount of money and their losses were aggravated by a number of very poor acquisitions. Those events, combined with the dependency culture that had grown up due to extremely autocratic leadership, almost bankrupted the company. A number of the non-executive directors instigated the dismissal of most of the members of the executive committee, and brought in an outsider to stabilize the situation. The new CEO's main initiative was to implement a major culture change. He wanted a company where people were encouraged—and had the courage—to tell the truth, rather than a culture of 'killing the messenger' when there was bad news to be faced. Transparency, open communication, honesty, and having a voice were to be central to this new environment. Macho behavior was no longer acceptable and people who seemed wedded to that path were asked to leave. A series of workshops ('The Leader Within') demonstrated what a true coaching culture was all about. An important feature of the seminars was multi-party feedback, that is, not only feedback from people at work but also from friends and family members.

These workshops had a remarkable effect on the behavior of the executives. Some left or were asked to leave, but the majority appreciated the benefits of a more open, caring culture. But it was not only the employees who were affected: the ripple effect spread to performance figures. The culture change was accompanied by a remarkable financial turnaround. Another pleasing side effect was that, because of its enlightened coaching practices, the energy company changed from being the worst place to work in the specific country in which it operated, to the employer of choice.

This is a rather dramatic example of the effects of introducing practices like continuous learning, exchange of explicit and tacit knowledge, reciprocal coaching, and self-leadership in an organization. The 'new' organization was characterized by relationships of trust, collaboration, insightful guidance, and a focus on assisting people to maximize their potential. The CEO was extremely successful at unlocking the creative, emotional, and entrepreneurial power of his people. That potential had always been there, but because of the previous poor leadership it had gone underground.

Getting started A coaching culture can be created in different ways. Apart from timely team coaching, peer coaching is an invaluable element in establishing relationships across the organization to support communication, growth, learning, problem solving, productivity improvements, and enhanced working conditions.

Upward coaching is often more challenging to establish in many organizations. The success of this process is highly culture-dependent. The senior executive team may be enthusiastic about downward feedback, but far less happy about receiving upward feedback. In some national and organizational cultures, direct reports might not feel safe giving this kind of feedback, as it could be used against them. If this is the case, the nature of the relationship must transform dramatically if an open dialogue between executive and direct reports is desired.

The introduction of a coaching culture to any organization raises the same challenges as any other culture change program. It is not sufficient merely to announce it, provide information, and assume that the change will take place. Planning is essential to introduce any new initiative. It is important to examine all the costs and benefits and to anticipate, expect, and plan for resistance.

A coaching culture can help to:

- enable the creation of a transitional space where people can express themselves frankly;
- unleash creativity and innovation;
- cultivate and promote an environment that delivers increased motivation and performance;
- create meaningful organizational values;
- create a dynamic working environment that becomes a 'best place to work';
- make the organization an employer of choice;
- achieve new strategic objectives;
- assist organizations in developing a portfolio of leadership talent;
- learn how to manage in a networking culture;
- become better at clarifying interconnections;
- identify healthy and neurotic organizational constellations;
- create a system for overseeing, mentoring, and supporting coaches throughout the organization;
- provide ongoing coaching training;
- implement a succession planning system;
- create an organizational framework that supports a coaching culture, clarifies roles, and guides coaching;

- understand the interconnectedness that is at the heart of a coaching culture;
- help companies involved in mergers and acquisitions navigate a new culture, integrate new teams, and align divisions;
- create a true learning organization where learning is shared, reducing errors and cycle time.

A CONCEPTUAL MODEL

Figure 9.1 shows the various conceptual models used to facilitate the coaching process, initially used at the INSEAD Global Leadership Center in programs like the 'Challenge of Leadership' and 'Consulting and Coaching for Change.' These conceptual frameworks are used in all other change programs. They include psychodynamic conceptualizations, particularly ideas from short-term dynamic psychotherapy (Mann, 1973; Malan and Osimo, 1992). Theories of group dynamics also play an important role (Yalom, 1985). Motivational interviewing can be influential as

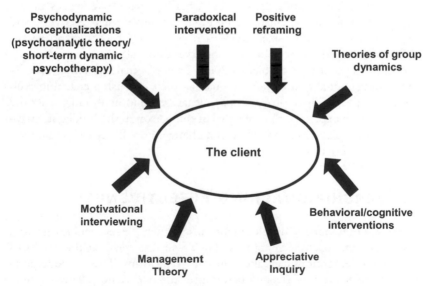

Conceptual Models Facilitating Change

Psychodynamic conceptualizations (psychoanalytic theory/ short-term dynamic psychotherapy)

Paradoxical intervention

Positive reframing

Theories of group dynamics

The client

Motivational interviewing

Management Theory

Appreciative Inquiry

Behavioral/cognitive interventions

Figure 9.1 Conceptual models facilitating change

it puts the burden on the coachee to argue for change (Miller and Rollnick, 2002). Furthermore, in situations where I encounter serious resistance, I have found ideas of paradoxical intervention (or strategic psychotherapy) helpful, a form of reverse psychology (Watzlawick, Weakland *et al.*, 1974). As always, appreciative inquiry (Cooperrider, Whitney *et al.*, 2008) and positive reframing are important to encourage an individual's sense of self-efficacy (Bandura, 1997). Because of the action component in our method of group coaching, behavioral/cognitive interventions are helpful when designing action recommendations. And, as in all forms of intervention, we must speak the language of the person we are dealing with in order to be understood. It is important that management terms are used to explain the steps that need to be taken.

Briefly, a graduate of the 'Consulting and Coaching for Change Program' or 'The Challenge of Leadership' is expected to move seamlessly from an individual to a systemic orientation to be able to lead change. They have to be familiar with various models of organizational change and the models or frameworks, explicit or implicit, within which the particular organization operates. In addition, any coaching program has to be tailored to the individual organization's unique systems needs. Generic solutions are no longer feasible or acceptable in the marketplace.

In creating a coaching culture in an organization, the leadership coach needs to create a safe transitional space in which executives will feel at ease while talking about themselves. Creating many safe spaces in the organization facilitates engagement in a journey of self-discovery and exploration, while other executives learn vicariously from the stories told, validating the experience. In these interventions, all the participants are not only engaged in a problem-solving exercise (making action recommendations) but also learn how to practice their leadership coaching skills with their peers. These processes of mutual exploration also implicate the participants in exploring the concerns of the person in the limelight, arriving at solutions and making behavioral change more likely (see Figure 9.2 for an overview of the process).

LEADERSHIP COACHING EFFECTIVENESS

Guardians of leadership development must regularly assess, and learn from, organizational coaching initiatives. They will discover that the results of coaching interventions can take many different forms. They include positive affective reactions (feeling better after the experience); new learning (the acquisition of new knowledge and skills); changes in on-the-job behavior; and organizational results (a positive effect on the overall pro-

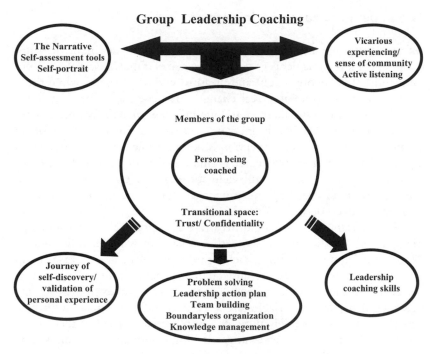

Figure 9.2 Group leadership coaching

ductivity of the organization). But unlike other aspects of leadership development, organizational leaders rarely evaluate the effectiveness or impact of coaching. Thus before proceeding with any large-scale coaching initiative, it is important to have a good understanding of the current state of affairs and what has to be accomplished.

The reason for expressing these words of caution is that it is quite common for leadership coaches to create sizeable practices under the auspices of key organizational leaders. Unfortunately, the growth of these practices is often well intentioned but may become detached from the organization's talent development strategy. It is therefore recommended that assessment is designed as an integral part of this strategy. In going through this assessment process, the assessors need to keep in mind that while individual coaching may produce positive results within short periods of time, its effectiveness as a leadership development strategy can only be determined over the long term. Regular reviews of the process should question whether coaching is truly making a difference to organizational strategy and performance improvement.

The benefits of coaching initiatives

Informed assessment begins and ends with a layered assessment. It is not enough to ask the recipients of coaching services if they are satisfied. Very frequently, they report delight and pleasure with the process while those around them fail to observe real change. However, this does not mean that coaching efforts should be abandoned if a few trials show only limited or meager results. Although an assessment of a particular coach or an isolated assessment of an intervention is not a reliable barometer of coaching effectiveness, a true 360-degree evaluation—involving suppliers, superiors, clients, and coaches—will yield more accurate information about the organization's coaching investment. In the summing up, it is long-term results that count.

Some coaching-consulting firms arrive at impressive return on investment (ROI) statistics but we have to use caution when establishing the expected ROI of a leadership coaching initiative. A qualitative assessment of coaching is problematic because so many factors can affect learning, performance, and results. Leadership coaching is a complex human activity in which many of the variables are very difficult to control. Controlled experiments are exceedingly difficult, complicated by the fact that we do not live in a static world. Leadership coaching is very different from selling widgets and calculating profits.

Caveat emptor

While there are coaching charlatans who hang out their shingle to make a buck, people largely choose to become coaches out of a desire to help people. Nevertheless, there should be an element of 'buyer beware.' Regardless of external certification, those who hire leadership coaches should perform due diligence, investigating and interviewing their coaching candidates to obtain a better understanding of their capabilities. Too often, there will be empty statements about the cost-effectiveness of coaching interventions. Frequently, closer investigation demonstrates the person's talent to perform number acrobatics—the figures showing remarkable returns on investments having very little base in reality.

BECOMING A REFLECTIVE PRACTITIONER

The challenge for leadership coaches is to make their clients more like reflective practitioners—people who do not just do things but also have the capacity to reflect and listen (Schon, 1983). As Epictetus said, 'We have two ears and one mouth so that we can listen twice as much as we speak.' In every conversation the coach and the person being coached need to ask themselves a series of questions, the most important of which are, 'How do I feel listening to this person?' 'What effect does this person have on me?'

Many people live under the illusion that they understand what is being said to them. This is not the same thing, however, as being sure that what they hear is what the speaker means. Many attempts at communication are nullified by our tendency to say too much. An old Chinese saying goes, 'To listen well is as powerful a means of influence as to talk well, and is as essential to all true conversation.'

In the previous book in this series,[1] I wrote at some length about 'listening with the third ear'—how coaches but also emotionally astrute executives should use their own unconscious as a receptive organ for the unconscious the client is transmitting. Briefly, we have to learn to look out for transferential and counter-transferential reactions. This confusion in time and place is common in interventions. People need to realize that behavior that may have been effective at one stage in their life has become obsolete, and avoid playing a role that is no longer appropriate (Kohut, 1971).

Leadership coaches and other change agents need to help their clients acquire the ability to listen to their own inner voice. Understanding-in-action is an essential quality that executives need to develop. If they do, they will have a clearer idea of themselves and be better at recognizing what is important to them. If the desire to reach somewhere is strong enough in people, their whole being, conscious and unconscious, will be at work, looking for and devising what it means to achieve that goal.

This is where effective leadership coaches can play an essential role. Based on the clinical paradigm, with its recognition of unconscious needs, the leadership group coaching intervention method I have developed over the years, takes us on a journey to understand what we are really about. Leadership coaching helps us to become aware not only of our conscious thoughts, but also of our unconscious prejudices, biases, and habits. As one recent participant of the 'Consulting and Coaching for Change Program' reported: 'This program [teaches] you things about yourself that will help you influence others by better understanding them first.'

[1]Kets de Vries, M. F. R. (2009) *Reflections on Leadership and Career Development*. Chichester: John Wiley & Sons Ltd, pp. 59–74.

CHAPTER 10

CAN LEADERS CHANGE? YES, BUT ONLY IF THEY WANT TO

Only the wisest and stupidest of men never change.

—Confucius

Look upon that last day always. Count no mortal happy till he has passed the final limit of his life secure from pain.

—Sophocles, *Oedipus the King*

We are all of us balloons dancing in a world of pins.

—Anthony Montague Browne, *Long Sunset*

The lion was completely convinced about his dominance of the animal kingdom. One day he wanted to check whether all the other animals knew he was the undisputed king of the jungle. He was so confident that he decided not to talk to the smaller creatures. Instead, he went straight to the bear. 'Who is the king of the jungle?' asked the lion. The bear replied, 'Of course, no one else but you, sir.' The lion gave a great roar of approval. He continued his journey and met the tiger. 'Who is the king of the jungle?' The tiger quickly responded, 'All of us know that you are the king.' The lion gave another roar of pleasure. Next on his list was the elephant. He caught up with the elephant at the edge of a river and asked him the same question, 'Who is the king of the jungle?' The elephant trumpeted, lifted his trunk, grabbed the lion, threw him in the air and smashed him into a tree. He fished him out of the tree and pounded him into the ground, lifted him up once more and dumped him into the river. Then he jumped on top of the lion, dragged him through the mud, and finally left him hanging in some bushes. The lion, dirty, beaten, bruised, and battered, struggled to get to his feet. He looked the elephant sadly in the eyes and said, 'Look, just because you don't know the answer, there's no reason for you to be so mean-spirited about it.'

Some leaders are like the lion. Reality testing isn't their forte. They are not good at making sense out of feedback. Instead, they create their own reality, wanting to see only what they like to see. They are not very open to change. What this tale illustrates is that change is neither a simple process, nor a comfortable one. The unlearning of habitual patterns can provoke a great deal of anxiety. Like the lion, many executives I have met are inclined to hold on to a specific logic, illogical as it may appear to others. They don't want to change. They prefer to stick to their current misery. Why so many executives cling so tenaciously to the status quo isn't easy to determine, but cling they do, heedless of the proverb that warns, 'All things change, and we change with them.'

In the case of senior executives, hanging on to dysfunctional behavior patterns can be particularly devastating. Given the power they wield, their behavior can have a dramatic downward spiraling effect in the organization, contributing to a toxic corporate culture, faulty decision-making, motivational problems, and high executive turnover (Kets de Vries and Miller, 1984; Morgan, 1986; Kets de Vries and Miller, 1988; Hamel and Prahalad, 1989; Pfeffer, 1998). Too many CEOs fail to realize that they are always on stage in their organizations. Their slightest move will be carefully observed, analyzed, and discussed. As one senior executive observed in one of my CEO workshops: 'Every day I come into the office I can make the lives of my ten thousand employees completely miserable. It doesn't take very much to do so. That's an awesome responsibility. I need to keep reminding myself daily of the role I play.'

Given the power that senior executives have to affect the lives of large numbers of people it is more important than ever—in this age of discontinuity—to help them make the right decisions. What can we do to help senior executives execute their roles in the most exemplary fashion? What can we do to make them more effective? How can we help them create healthy, sustainable organizations? And if changes in their behavior patterns are advisable, how should they go about it to become better at what they doing?

Leading is not easy and can be a daunting task. Many executives are bewildered by the responsibility that comes with the job and unclear what role they should play. They need a great deal of help to make it work and get the best out of their people—to create 'stretch.' To elicit this extra effort, they need to speak to the collective imagination of their employees, articulate the shared values that will create a group identity, and persuade them to buy into whatever dream they have for the future of their organization (Kets de Vries, 2001).

People who realize the responsibility that comes with their position lead companies that keep on doing well. They are guided by individuals who know what it means to be a leader—individuals who put the interests of the organization before their self-interests, people who are truly committed to make their organizations great places to work and who see things in perspective (Collins and Porras, 1994; Pfeffer, 1995; Greenleaf and Spears, 1998; Kets de Vries and Balazs, 1999; Collins, 2001; Kets de Vries, 2001). For the long-term health of organizations, we need leaders who are unafraid to face reality as it is, not as they would like it to be—people who are comparatively well adjusted.

WHY RIDE A DEAD HORSE?

I have encountered many senior executives who hang on to dysfunctional behavior patterns, ignoring any constructive suggestions they receive about trying to do things differently. They keep on doing the same things over and over again despite the dismal consequences. I can only assume that what drives them is the perverse hope that the outcome will be somehow different. They are obviously not familiar with the old Sioux Indian saying: 'When you discover you are riding a dead horse, the best strategy is to dismount.' These people hang on to the unrealistic fantasy that they can resuscitate the horse.

Even people who claim to believe in the value of change may do so half-heartedly. What they mean is that they want *others* to change. There is a Calvin and Hobbes cartoon that sums this up perfectly. Calvin says, 'I thrive on change.' Hobbes is astounded by this statement. 'You threw a fit this morning because your mom put less jelly on your toast than yesterday!' he counters. 'I thrive on making other people change,' says Calvin.

Sometimes it is less a matter of resisting change than of being baffled by it. Many people have the will but not the skill to change. They need help to navigate the process. Generally, it is my experience that people don't resist change itself—what they resist is being changed.

How, then, can corporate leaders run their organizations proactively? What can they do to deal with continuous and discontinuous change?

What do they need to do to make their organizations great places to work, to create healthy organizations? What can they do to get the best out of their people? Because it's important to remember that when organizations go bad, the rot generally starts at the top (Kets de Vries and Miller, 1988)—or, as one wit put it, 'the bottleneck is usually in the neck'. If senior executives are unwilling to position themselves more vulnerably, if they aren't prepared to reassess their actions, how can they expect their people to act differently?

Greater self-awareness is a first step in becoming more effective as a leader. To become more capable we have to start taking a hard look at ourselves. If we want to reinvent or renew ourselves, we have to look at what happens inside us and explore our inner theater. As Socrates famously said, 'The unexplored life is not worth living.' A willingness to engage in self-exploration—being ready for personal change—is a *sine qua non* for people in responsible executive positions.

Falling off the fast track

As I have seen all too often, those whom the gods destroy, they first call promising. Many senior executives fail because they become too full of themselves. They become caught up in the web of narcissism. Their self-centered behavior encourages their people to tell them what they want to hear. Hubris follows and eventually, their self-delusions will contribute to their fall.

Of course, narcissism is not the *only* reason why leaders fail (Zaleznik, 1966; McCall and Lombardo, 1978; Kouzes and Posner, 1995; Pfeffer, 1998; Collins, 2001; Kets de Vries, 2001, 2006a). When I look at the derailment of senior executives one obvious observation that keeps recurring is lack of vision. Like it or not, vision is vitally important. The ability to think outside the box and be a rule breaker often makes all the difference between being a great executive and being a mediocre one. As the expression goes, if you have no idea where you are going, you may end up somewhere else. Having a helicopter view—possessing the ability to think strategically, distinguish the wood from the trees, and look into the future—is a plus for effectiveness as a leader (Jaques, 1989).

Can out-of-the-box thinking be learned? It's unlikely. Usually, by the time we are grown up, the die is cast for most of us. This may sound pessimistic, but psychologists tell us that little can be done to acquire greater efficacy in disentangling complex cognitive situations (Heatherton and Weinberger, 1994; Hogan, Johnson *et al.*, 1997). We have to learn to live with the cognitive assets we already have. Realizing, however, that we aren't good at 'reducing environmental noise' will be helpful. This kind of self-realization will encourage us to enlist the help of others who can counterbalance our own competences. It can lead to an executive role constellation where other executives can play a complementary role and fill the gap (Kets de Vries, 2006b).

But there are other factors that contribute to career derailment. Vision without execution is just a hallucination. Some leaders stumble because they aren't very good at following through. They lose interest in the nitty-gritty of management. They don't make their people accountable. They let things slip with disastrous consequences. Micro–management and conflict avoidance are other frequent traps in the executive career trajectory. I could go on.

After observing hundreds of CEOs, I have noticed, however, that a major factor contributing to derailment can be summarized as a lack of emotional intelligence (Salovey and Mayer, 1990; Goleman, 1995; Goleman, 1998; LeDoux, 1998; Gardner ,1999; Matthews, Zeidner et al., 2002). We can definitely do something about this deficiency at later stages in life. As we know, IQ is relatively set by the time we are grown up, but emotional intelligence (EQ) is more malleable. By EQ, I mean understanding and managing our emotions, recognizing emotions in others, and handling relationships. In exemplary leadership, self-awareness and empathy are critical factors that differentiate highly effective executives from mediocre ones. Closely associated with these essential aspects of EQ (and leadership effectiveness) are the ability to reframe thorny situations in a more positive way, having the courage to hang in when things get tough, the ability to function effectively in teams, and the talent to build them.

What can senior executives do to develop these competences? What can they do to change? How can they modify dysfunctional behavior patterns? How can they get out of their rut? To clarify this process we need to take a closer look at what makes people act the way they do. What kind of inner theater drives our behavior and actions? In this chapter, I try to find answers to these questions.

The triangle of mental life

To simplify what are in effect very complex processes we can look at human behavior as being made up of a triangle of forces: cognition, emotion, and behavior. This force field will determine the kind of script acted out in our inner theater. This script is written in response to the motivational need systems on which choice is grounded (Freud, 1933;

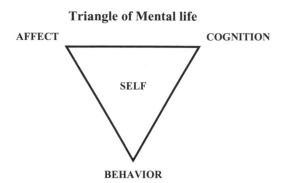

Figure 10.1   The triangle of mental life

Sullivan, 1953; Bowlby, 1969; Emde, 1981; Lichtenberg, Lackmann *et al.*, 1992). Need systems become operational in infancy and continue throughout our life (though they are altered by age, learning, and maturation). At the risk of oversimplification, the most basic need systems are made up of our physiological requirements, such as food, drink, elimination, sleep, and breathing; next comes our need for sensual enjoyment and (later) sexual excitement; finally, there are our adverse responses (like antagonism, withdrawal and aggression) to certain situations. But in addition to these, there are two further systems that impact the workplace directly and powerfully: the need for attachment/affiliation, and the need for exploration/assertion. Just as an engine is fueled by gasoline, cognitive and emotional patterns that develop out of these need systems fuel our behavior and actions. These motivational need systems are the triangle of mental life (see Figure 10.1).

Taking this basic triangle as point of departure, it becomes clear that for any change effort to be successful, executives have to be swayed both cognitively and emotionally; in other words, both the head and the heart have to be affected to change behavior. Although intellectually, we need to see the advantages that a change effort will bring, cognition alone isn't enough; we also need to be touched emotionally. The three sides of this triangle of mental life are closely interwoven.

Beating your head against a brick wall

In my early work as an educator, psychotherapist and consultant, I used to engage in lengthy (almost) harangues explaining to executives the error of their ways when they made faulty decisions and their organizations malfunctioned. I would go to great lengths to argue why and what they had to change. I used every kind of logic explaining why they couldn't continue to do things the way they had been doing. Although intellectually, I may have been quite correct, my interventions didn't make an iota of difference. Most executives agreed with what I had to say, but merrily kept on doing the same thing anyway. Eventually I realized that beating my head against the wall was unproductive. I needed to find a different angle. I was using a filibuster of logic when logic alone was not good enough. I had to reach these people in a different way.

In one of my workshops,[1] a particular executive received a considerable amount of feedback from the other participants and faculty about his tendency to remain emotionally aloof in difficult situations, using distancing as a defensive mechanism. When stressed, he would just withdraw and not react. Cognitively he must have been quite aware of the problem. But knowing the problem in his head was clearly not enough. He had to experience whatever was going on in his 'stomach.' It was obvious that additional 'ammunition' was needed to make him change his ways interpersonally. What could be done to get a 'hook' into him? What could I do that would make a real difference? As part of a 360-degree feedback exercise, I decided to gather information about him from people important and emotionally close to him. During the second week of the workshop I presented him with a large amount of feedback not only from the people at the office but also from close friends, his wife, children, and other family members. This time I could see that the feedback began to stick. What really shook him was a very emotional statement from his 19-year-old daughter. With very unusual tears in his eyes, he shared a note from his daughter expressing her sadness about his inapproachability. She wrote about her long frustrated wish to be closer to him—to have a real relationship with him. She referred to all the efforts she had made in the past to do so. This note proved to be a turning point. From that moment on the other participants noticed a change in his behavior. He became emotionally involved in the discussions that took place at the seminar. He finally *heard* the insights provided by the other participants. The other presentations began to touch him emotionally. Most importantly, however, he began to experiment with other ways of behaving when in a stressful situation. That is not to say that there were no lapses. But what kept him on course were the comments made by the other participants reminding him of the feedback from his daughter any time he fell back into his old behavior patterns. The other participants

---

[1] All case examples have been disguised.

functioned as a 'learning community' to reinforce desired behavior. Gradually, over the course of half a year, his new, more expressive behavior became like second nature to him.

This incident helped me to look at personal change processes in a different manner. It illustrated the power that various constituencies can have in furthering the change effort. By drawing in people whose opinions were valued from home and the office (not forgetting the push provided by the newly established learning community of peers), all parties acquired a stake in the change effort, reinforcing experimentation in approaching situations in different ways.

WHEREVER I SIT IS THE HEAD OF THE TABLE

To help senior executives change I have been struggling for many years trying to find a format that would foster the change process. I tried to deal with the question of how to help senior executives to become more effective, at work and at home. How could I help get them out of the rut? What could be done to help them reinvent themselves?

Developmental psychologists have estimated that at the age of thirty, two-thirds to three-fifths of an individual's personality is formed (McCrae and Costa, 1990). The realization that people have greater plasticity early in life doesn't rule out their ability to change at a later life stage. To jumpstart a change effort, however, certain conditions need to be met. Specific steps have to be taken to help people who are at the summit of their career trajectory to reinvent themselves. This question is especially timely, as many CEOs I have met seem to be stuck in some kind of mental prison. They don't know how to do things differently. Learning has largely stopped, playfulness has left, and pleasure is gone. I discovered long ago that mental health is having a choice but many leaders find making new choices very difficult. They need help to get out of their self-inflicted prison. They are not the sort, however, to look for change through lengthy therapeutic procedures. They are looking for more time-efficient methods to reinvent themselves.

As a psychoanalyst, psychotherapist, and leadership coach (as well as a management educator and consultant) I am steeped in traditional methods of creating personality change. More traditional psychoanalytic thinking dictates that the main route to insight and lasting change occurs through a lengthy treatment procedure involving anywhere from two to five sessions a week. Needless to say, this prospect is not very attractive to senior executives who have neither the time nor the patience to engage in such a monumental undertaking. Many senior executives tend to be quite self-centered and have a very short attention span. My challenge became to work successfully with a group of people all of whom think they are the center of the universe. I needed to find a procedure to get their attention fast, early in the first week, otherwise they would not hang around.

The task became to develop a method of intervention that would accelerate and condense the more traditional therapeutic process while remaining true to basic clinical principles. I had to find a less traditional way to overcome resistance to change and to confront problems that were often out-of-awareness—preconscious and unconscious problems. I had to mobilize unconscious mental processes to achieve therapeutic results. In addition, the challenge would also be to create changes in behavior patterns that wouldn't turn out to be 'flights into health'—transient 'highs'—as is so often the case with the miraculous 'cures' offered by too many psychological snake oil salesmen. What conceptualizations and settings could I use to jumpstart the change process?

One theoretical approach that offered considerable promise in accelerating the process of change was experiments done in short-term dynamic psychotherapy (Freud, 1893–5; Balint, Ornstein et al., 1972; Winnicott, 1972; Mann, 1973; Malan, 1976; Sifneos, 1979; Mann and Goldman, 1982; Horowitz, Marmar et al., 1984; Strupp and Binder, 1984; Gustavson, 1986; Crits-Christoph and Barber, 1991; Malan and Osimo, 1992; Davonloo, 1994; Molnos, 1995; Groves, 1996; McCullough Vaillant, 1997; Luborsky and Crits-Cristoph, 1998; Davenloo, 2000; Rawson, 2002). This therapeutic approach offered a different avenue to help people acquire a speedier insight into the life events and ongoing experiences that contributed to their problems. Therapists using this technique discovered that focused interventions of a more direct nature combined with a solid dose of empathy and psychological support frequently resulted in remarkable improvement of their patients' mental state. Clarification of defensive reactions—analyzing a problem closely and bringing it into sharper focus—also appeared to contribute to behavior change. The presenting problem was made more explicit so that patients acquired greater awareness of the psychological forces that affected their behavior.

After experimenting with short-term dynamic psychotherapy in one-to-one encounters with executives (with a modest dose of success), I realized that more was needed to create lasting change in their behavior patterns. Simple one-to-one coaching had only limited results (Balint, 1957). I needed to increase participants' *discomfort* zone. I discovered that if I could create a situation of high intensity and total involvement by establishing a learning community—where each member had a stake in creating a corrective emotional experience for others—the change process might be accelerated (Alexander and French, 1946). Research also suggested that I needed to create some kind of 'transitional space' for participants—a space in which, protected from the reality of the outside world, they could experiment safely with new forms of interacting (Winnicott, 1951; Bion, 1962; Winnicott, 1971).

After a great deal of trial and error, I conceived an intense learning community by combining some of the methods used in short-term dynamic psychotherapy with the interventions derived from group dynamics, adding concepts taken from organizational and leadership theory (Freud, 1921; Foulkes, 1975; Scheidlinger, 1982; Rosenbaum, 1983; Yalom, 1985; Kaplan and Sadock, 1993; Harwood and Pines, 1998; Scott Rutan and Stone, 2001). Using the most effective principles of the first two, I was able to set the stage for a more intensified change effort. The result was a program (that I have mentioned before) created for a highly select number of CEOs and senior executives run over a period of one year in four modules. (This program became the model for many of the other programs I have designed.) So how does it work and what makes it so different? Let me take you behind the scenes of 'The Challenge of Leadership: Creating Reflective Leaders' and give you a snapshot of what happens within the safe learning space I create for the participants.

THE CEO 'RECYCLING' SEMINAR

Once a year, 'The Challenge of Leadership' gives 20 very senior executives (most of them CEOs) the opportunity to participate. These executives apply to the program for a variety of reasons. They may be faced with seemingly insoluble dilemmas, negative feelings about themselves, or perceptions of the world and others that tend to make fulfillment seem impossible. Typically, these dilemmas are not clearly articulated in the applicants' mind when they apply to the program. To be accepted each potential participant has to complete a complex application form. The information provided helps me to make a first assessment about the suitability of the candidate for the program. In addition, each future participant—wherever they are located—is interviewed by me face-to-face or over the phone to see if they have what it takes to go through this kind of workshop, where the 'life' case study will be the main source of interpretive material. In my interview I look for traces of psychological mindedness, the capacity to be open and responsive, and a serious interest in understanding themselves better. The workshop consists of three five-day periods with breaks of approximately seven weeks in between. The expectation is that during each week the participants learn more about themselves, agree a 'contract' on what to work on while back on the job and at home during the time they are away from the workshop, and return to the workshop to deepen their understanding. 'Home work' assignments are monitored by peer participants. Mutual coaching is part of the program design.

I run this particular seminar with a very close colleague who is a clinical anthropologist, psychoanalyst, and novelist. Having a second person in the workshop allows for a fuller and more complete view of what happens in the group and protects both faculty members from blind spots. In addition, having two faculty members in the workshop at all times gives each of us the opportunity to move in and out of active and passive observational modes. The interchange between the two workshop leaders also provides a model for the participants of ways of relating to each other and handling conflict. Furthermore, seeing two people at work provides the participants with a richer way of understanding complex human phenomena.

Although the basic material of the workshop is the 'life' case study, the first week is somewhat structured. Part of the time is spent on a number of interactive lectures on high-performance organizations, organizational culture, leadership (exemplary and dysfunctional), the career life cycle, cross-cultural management, and organizational stress. However, the central model of psychological activity and organization is the personal case history. At some point, each participant of the workshop volunteers to sit in the 'hot seat.' This experience is extremely important. As participants narrate their life story, experiences and actions become organized. The presentation becomes a process of self-discovery, and also helps others to understand their own problems, in their public or private life.

During the second week some time is devoted to processing a number of feedback instruments. A key part of this activity is the *Global Executive Leadership Inventory*, a 360-degree feedback instrument I developed, which consists of 12 dimensions contributing to leadership effectiveness (Kets de Vries, Vrignaud *et al.*, 2004; Kets de Vries, 2004). In addition, the *Personality Audit* contains feedback gathered from spouse/partner or significant other(s) (Kets de Vries, 2005b, 2005c; Kets de Vries *et al.* 2006). Additional information is collected from other family members and good friends. This information provides the basis for a more refined action plan in the interval between the second and third periods. The main focus of the third week is the consolidation of the acquired insights, the internalization of change, and future action plans. This process is fostered, using yet another instrument: *The Leadership Archetype Questionnaire* (Kets de Vries, 2006c, 2006d). A fourth module is scheduled six months later, as a way of finding out if the many good intentions have become internalized.

Apart from the plenary sessions, participants spend a considerable amount of time in small groups in and outside the classroom. These interactions are extremely valuable as these encounters serve to consolidate newly acquired behavior patterns. Eventually, the 20 people form an intense learning community where each participant gives the others constructive feedback whenever they fall back into behavior patterns that they are trying to unlearn. Peer coaching is an essential part of the process. It can be said that by the third week many of the participants know each other better than many of their family members do. At this point the interchange in the plenary session has become extremely free-flowing, with much less intervention needed by the faculty. The group has turned into a self-analyzing community. Compared to the first week, the members of the group demonstrate a remarkable level of EQ, given the quality of their interventions. In many instances there will be a follow-up session a year later (some group follow-ups have occurred year after year), which offers the faculty an opportunity to assess the degree to which certain behavior patterns have become truly internalized.

A FLY ON THE WALL

The pre-program cocktail party has the artificial quality common to similar occasions. There is the usual nervous laughter, the noise of glasses. People mill around, making an effort to meet others, trying to initiate conversation. Quite a few of the people present seem ill at ease. There is a certain charge in the air. What to talk about? How to relate to each other? The topics range from recent political events, to travel, to cross-cultural anecdotes. Is this just another random encounter of a group of executives? Not really. In spite of appearances, the cocktail party is carefully choreographed. There is a purpose behind the ritual. It is an awkward but necessary step to get the leadership workshop on its way.

Participants have come here from all over the globe. Now, they are trying to feel their way around. Specialists in group behavior would say that this way of acting is part of the 'being polite' group phase. The members of the group struggle with questions of inclusion and exclusion. The participants are trying to find out about the other members. Who has been selected into the program? What are the other participants like? What countries do they come from? Their behavior demonstrates excitement mixed with a certain degree of anxiety. A spectator from Mars, however, would be amused to see this gathering where so many captains of industry look like fish out of water. For once, they aren't in control; for once, they don't really know what to expect. For once, they aren't masters of the universe: someone else is pulling the strings. There is nobody to push around. Instead, they are anxiously putting out feelers. They introduce themselves to each other. They engage in small talk. Some feel awkward and don't quite know how to position themselves. Consequently, some of them talk too much, their way of coping with an uncomfortable situation. Others try to numb their anxiety by drinking too much. At a subliminal level, however, they are aware that, in contrast to the role they play in the office, it will be harder to keep their mask on. They are caught up in a totally unknown situation with its specific fantasies and defensive reactions. Many thoughts race through their mind. Why didn't I stay at the office? Why did I leave familiar ground? There must be a better way to spend my time. What am I going to get out of all this? Isn't this all a waste of time? What am I doing here? What am I doing to myself?

Although, over the years, word-of-mouth has been the most powerful driver for applications to the program, for a number of executives, the process started when their VP human resources or another colleague gave them the brochure about the program. It sounded quite interesting. The design aroused their curiosity and stimulated their fantasy. Some saw the workshop as an opportunity to do something different—to take a break from the routine of office life and do something for themselves. It looked as though the program might provide answers to some of the questions they had been asking themselves. Lately, life had lost much of its novelty. Work didn't feel the same any more. The original sense of excitement was gone and work had become too much of a routine. They were stuck in a rut and were doing nothing new. What had happened to their original sense of discovery? Their creativity? When was the last time they experienced that feeling of total involvement? They were no longer losing themselves in their activities. Instead, all they seemed to be doing was more of the same. The original rush of having reached the top of the pyramid had faded away.

Completing the complex admission form was a total drag. The form asked too many personal questions and it was a real pain having to respond to them all. Such forms were OK for students, but at their level? Some of the questions still puzzled them—they weren't the sort of questions they usually got from journalists or investment analysts. Who wants to write about the things they aren't good at? How do you respond when asked about the risky things you've done in your life? Whatever irritation they had, the type of questions asked on the admissions form indicated that this was not going to be a traditional executive program. But then, they didn't really want another traditional executive program. They had tried them all—been there, done that.

Then there was the telephone interview. Out of the blue, there was this person—apparently the workshop leader—at the other end of the line asking bizarre questions. Why should he give you a place in the program? What would you contribute? What complaints does your spouse make about you? What kinds of thing make you angry? Why does he want to know about your wild fantasies? What has all this got to do with becoming more effective as a leader? Strangely enough, when asked—at the end of the interview—if they still wanted a place in the program, they had all said yes. Of course, without their realizing it, the workshop had already begun.

A short introduction followed the cocktail party, describing the daily workshop schedule, followed by a tour of the campus, and dinner. That took care of the initial formalities. There was a last chance for polite dinner conversation. But by this time they knew that was the calm before the storm.

The next day the seminar started in earnest. At the opening session anxiety seemed high; people appeared apprehensive, and looked expectantly at the workshop leader, who gave a short lecture on emotional intelligence and irrational behavior in organizations. Subsequently, he reiterated the basic premise of the workshop—the 'life' case study. Case presentations would be the main learning tool. Each life case study would present a unique situation that would contribute to the learning process. He explained that there could be 'no interpretation without association': participants would get as much out of the workshop as they put into it. The workshop leader made it clear that he had spoken to all participants, that all had accepted the ground rules to work on a number of significant problems—professional or private—that needed resolution.

From then on the workshop was on its way. How the various participants would handle the emerging anxiety would depend on their personality structure, their historic defense mechanisms, and the specific dynamics that evolved within the group. The immediate behavioral data that would emerge in the group would be used as data to explore conscious and unconscious material, and defensive operations. And with that, the first life case study began.

TAKING THE ROAD LESS TRAVELED

What can executives expect when they go on this journey of self-discovery? What is the process all about? How do people change? What obstacles do people have to overcome to 'own their own life'?

Challenge 1: Preparing for the journey

A major precondition for change is the willingness to do so. You have to be motivated. Certain conditions have to be met, however, before you can take this kind of journey. Only comparatively healthy people have the psychological strength to participate in this type of intensive seminar. Not everyone has a personality make-up suited to participation. So what are these conditions?

Selection criteria   If you decide 'to own your own life,' you have to ask yourself, what is your *level of motivation*? Are you prepared to take a hard look at yourself? Are you willing to do the work? Or are you merely looking for a quick fix—a magic pill that will take care of all your problems? Do you have the capacity to be *open and responsive*? Are you willing or able to open up to others? This brings us to the ability to establish relationships. Do you have the ability and willingness to engage in meaningful *emotional interaction*? Having the capacity to talk about very personal thoughts and feelings makes the change process a lot easier. Experience tells us that people who have a history of give-and-take with a number of significant people in their lives are more likely to change. The way you *manage emotions* is another significant factor in receptivity to change. Can you tolerate the anxiety that comes with putting yourself in a more vulnerable position? How do you experience your emotional life? Is it passionate or flat? When other people talk about the ups-and-downs of their life, do their accounts move you? Do you cry in the movies? *Psychological mindedness* is a further important factor. Are you curious about your inner life? Would you *like to learn* more about why you behave the way you do? Can you look beneath the surface and grasp the emotional meaning of maladaptive behavior? Can you verbalize your thoughts, feelings, fantasies, and inner personal life? Do you have the *capacity for introspection*? Do you have the ability to recognize how contemporary psychological processes are integrated and related to past experiences? Understanding the *connection between past and present* is an important variable in the change equation. Your *responses to the observations of others* are also highly relevant. Are you receptive to others' interpretations? Do you become defensive? Do you understand what other people are trying to tell you? Finally, the *flexibility* and appropriateness of your reactions to certain stressful interventions is another indicator of receptivity to change.

Let's step back inside the workshop and look at how this preparedness works in dealing with a life case study within the program context.

One CEO started her presentation, making a number of the other executives highly uncomfortable by declaring that she was an unwanted child—a latecomer, an unexpected arrival after her parents already had four daughters. Her fellow participants' discomfort was understandable: the workshop had only just started and they expected to hear about knotty business problems. The CEO recounted that throughout her childhood her mother made her disappointment about her unexpected arrival quite clear. If they had planned another child, they would have liked it to be a boy. The executive expressed her sadness about her mother's comments and explained how her mother's attitude had been the story of her life— the theme of being unwanted had always haunted her. She also talked about her father, who wasn't very present. He worked long hours as a specialist at a local hospital. Even when he was around, he remained quite distant; it was extremely difficult to get his attention. When she had a fight with her mother about whatever behavior the latter found inap- propriate (and there were many such incidents), he always took her mother's side. She could rarely count on his support and always felt excluded. She described how she had fought for her father's attention and that the youngest of her sisters had to bear the brunt of her competitive- ness. She told a funny story about the way she succeeded in shifting the blame for a dent in the family car to this sister. She mentioned, as an aside, that she had always been very good at shifting responsibility, so that others took the blame.

This CEO realized that a major theme in her life was proving that she counted for something. To get her parents' attention she had excelled in school. She also had been good at sports. But she emphasized that she wasn't just a teacher's pet. There was another side to her. She had an unobtrusive rebellious streak that took the form of promiscuity from her teenage years.

After graduation, to impress her father, she had chosen to study engi- neering. Computers had been her specialty and after obtaining her engineering degree she decided to find a job in the industry. This was also the time of her first, failed marriage and the birth of her daughter. After an uphill struggle (as a woman, she faced quite a few set-backs in her engineering career) she had become the CEO of a very successful software company. The price she had paid for her success were two failed marriages, a difficult relationship with her only daughter, and a long list of stress symptoms. When commenting on her leadership style, she noted that she had a temper. Half jokingly, she said, 'Speak when you are angry, and you'll deliver the best speech you'll ever regret.' She felt that people in her company either loved or hated her. Because she set extremely high standards for herself, she could be a very harsh taskmaster to others. As a result she had lost a number of very capable executives. The latest depar- ture (a high potential woman) had annoyed her non-executive chairman who strongly suggested that she needed to work on her leadership style. She had heard his comment but let it lie. What had really motivated her to think about her life was the discovery of a lump in her breast, which fortunately proved to be benign. As a close family member had died of breast cancer, this discovery had given her a real scare. Her application to the program had been a response to all these things converging on her at the same time.

Her frankness about her life so very early in the program loosened up the group that, as always, consisted mostly of men. Many were moved by the intensity with which she described her experiences. Because of the strength of her presentation, she made it easy for others to visualize what she had gone through. Many of the themes she touched upon echoed themes in their own lives. For many, it awakened a host of dormant memories.

From this executive's story it became quite clear that here was a woman who was highly motivated to do something about her present situation. She realized that her personal life was a mess. She also recognized that she had to work on her leadership style. She was aware that going on as before was not an attractive option. When presenting her problems she frequently had tears in her eyes. From the little I had seen of her, emotional interaction was not a problem. In spite of her being a harsh taskmaster at the office, she related well to most people. Neither was psychological mindedness an issue. She was very interested in understanding herself better. My questioning made it clear that she was able to make connections between her present behavior and her past experiences. She seemed to be ready to take the leap, and try to change some of her behavior patterns.

Catalysts for change If the human tendency is to resist change, how does the process of change ever get underway? Why does a person's resistance start to weaken? As I discussed in Chapter 8, and as we can see in the life case of the female CEO in our workshop, getting the process of change into motion requires a strong inducement in the form of pain or distress—discomfort that outweighs the pleasure of 'secondary gains' (psychological benefits such as sympathy and attention) that hanging on to the present situation offers. The trigger may be family tensions, health problems, negative social sanctions, an accident, feelings of isolation leading to a sense of helplessness and insecurity, problem behavior at work, distressing incidents happening to someone close, or basic daily hassles and frustrations. The female CEO in our example certainly had the motivation to do something about her life. She recognized that she would end up as a very lonely person if she continued on her merry way.

Surveys of people who have undergone major internal change confirm that they experience a high level of unpleasant emotion in the period prior to change, generally precipitated by a stressor like one of those listed above. This negative emotion, which brings to awareness the serious negative consequences to be expected if dysfunctional behavior patterns continue, makes the status quo increasingly difficult to maintain.

When we realize that our bad days are turning into a bad year—in other words, that occasional discontent has become a steady pattern of unhappiness—it becomes harder to deny that something needs to be done. From this point on, every new disturbance is recognized as part of the general pattern of dissatisfaction. Many people experience a moment when they are finally able to interpret what's happening to them. They see clearly that neither the passage of time nor minor changes in behavior will improve the situation—indeed, things are likely to become even worse if nothing is done.

Even the insight that drastic measures are required doesn't automatically compel us to take action. However, it does set into motion a mental process where we start to consider alternatives. We all have a conscious and unconscious wish to redress our grievances. This can turn into one of the engines of change. Having made the transition from denial to admitting that all is not well, we are able to undertake a reappraisal process. Initially every alternative to the troubling situation appears more frightening than the status quo. Gradually, however, a preferable alternative begins to emerge. Although there are hurdles in the way, a goal is in sight.

Accepting the need for change is a necessary first step, but on its own it is no guarantee of action. People need a push, in the form of some kind of crisis. In Chapter 7, where I discuss the process of organizational change, I describe this as a 'focal event' (see page 155). As I showed earlier, although we think of a crisis as something acute and obvious, the focal event that triggers change is often relatively minor, the proverbial last straw that enables a discontented person to take that long-delayed first step, and is only retrospectively interpreted as a milestone. In the case of our female CEO, she had quite a few things to worry about. Not only the problems at work that became a catalyst, but also her cancer scare and her problems with her daughter. These three problems served as a wake-up call for her to reevaluate her lifestyle. When her chairman joined the fray she became ready to do something about her life.

Challenge 2: Identifying the problem

In order to change it is necessary to describe what you *want* to change and establish the *focal problem*. Without a clear agenda and explicit goals it is difficult to assess progress. Fortunately, when listening to someone's history we often detect a thin red line that begins in the past and continues over time. The challenge is to identify this thin red line and clarify what it's all about. That means carefully listening to the story and engaging in a process of sense making.

More often than not the stories we tell about ourselves have to do with seemingly insoluble dilemmas, a negative self-concept, or a misguided perception of the world and of others that contributes to unhappiness and lack of fulfillment, and can contribute to problems at work. Ordinarily, however, these dilemmas are not clearly conceptualized in our mind. They are often preconscious and only vaguely experienced. What we feel more keenly are various combinations of helplessness and hopelessness. At this point the challenge is to arrive at greater specificity. Within the context of our workshop, agreement needs to be reached by the person in the 'hot' seat and the 'audience' about what specific dilemma or dilemmas need working on. This forms the basis for a 'contract' between the individual and the rest of the group.

Major themes Looking back at the hundreds of CEOs and other senior executives who have passed through my change workshop, a number of themes emerge. One theme can be summarized as *loss*, whether past, present, or impending. Loss is one of the most difficult things to deal with (Bowlby, 1969; Parkes, 1972; Bowlby, 1969, 1973; Marris, 1974; Dietrich and Shabad, 1993). Regardless of the form it takes, its consequences may linger for months or even years in the form of depressive reactions as people grieve about what might have been, or the poor hand of cards they were dealt (Solomon, 2001). The most dramatic example of loss is the loss of some important figure in our life through separation, divorce, or death. This kind of loss can have enormous repercussions. Another form of loss is the loss of our personal health and well-being through illness. A physical handicap has a dramatic life-changing effect.

Within the world of work, there is the loss of a job, and with it the loss of the community to which we belonged. Career setbacks, such as a demotion or retirement, can be experienced as loss. A frequent issue here is an imbalance between career expectations and actual achievement. People reach a point when they have to face the probability that their original dream of career success will not be fulfilled. They will not become the chairman of the company, or a member of the board. How will they cope with the encroaching disappointment? The challenge is to break out of this depressive cycle, to reframe the situation and arrive at a more hopeful outlook to life. People need to discover that there are alternatives and new beginnings. They need to be encouraged to look for new opportunities.

Another area of difficulty that can be a catalyst for enrolling in the program is an intensification of an *interpersonal conflict*. This kind of conflict can occur in intimate relationships within the family or with friends, or in disputes between work colleagues. In one example, an executive described how stressed he was by an ongoing battle with one of the non-executive members of his board. He enlisted the help of the group to find a constructive solution to the impasse. Another senior executive running a family business was looking for insights to stop a long-lasting feud with one of his brothers that affected the future direction of the company. A CEO caught up in a merger process was looking for ways to solve an organizational culture (and cross-cultural) incompatibility problem.

Quite a number of seminar participants suffered from boredom, a condition that can have dire consequences not only for their own mental health (i.e. suffering from depressive symptoms) but also for the health of their organization. One participant explained that he had engaged in a disastrous acquisition spree as a way of warding off his boredom. He got away with playing the serial acquirer until the financials caught up with him and he was asked to resign. One of the reasons he had enrolled in the seminar was to find ways to renew himself without becoming destructive to his organization.

Within more personal relationships, disputes frequently develop when people have differing expectations about their interaction and relationship. These can be marital disputes, arguments between parents and children, or disputes between the extended family and friendship network. Often the core of these problems is a lack of interpersonal competencies. Some executives have trouble initiating relationships because they lack the skills needed for sustaining interpersonal relationships (Sullivan, 1953). Some can start a relationship but cannot maintain it if it requires commitment, intimacy, fidelity, and loyalty.

At times, the thin red line that determines the specific problem area is more *symptomatic* and more easily identifiable. This may include a range of potentially troublesome symptoms, including habit disorders, sexual dysfunction, promiscuity, and numerous phobias. A substantial number of executives suffer from alcohol or drug problems. Others are phobic about public speaking or social situations, suffer from fear of flying, or are insomniac. The origin of these symptoms varies but many are triggered by long-forgotten frightening experiences. Whatever the origin, these symptoms can become so severe that they interfere with everyday functioning and become a significant source of distress.

Another issue that emerges regularly is *developmental imbalance*, meaning that certain expectations about life remain unfulfilled (Erikson, 1963; Vaillant, 1977; Levinson, 1978; Sheehy, 1995; Sheehy, 1998; Stassen

Berger, 1998). A good example of a developmental imbalance is when people realize that everybody else of their age has a stable partner but this state seems to have passed them by. The loneliness of this realization is often worsened by the desire to have children. People who fail to cope adequately with these transitions can develop depressive reactions. The workshop may help them discover a way of coping through establishing new connections and exploring new relationships.

For example, one executive during one of the leadership workshops referred repeatedly to his terrific relationship with his girlfriend and went to great lengths to explain what a good time they had together. Questioning revealed that the relationship had been going on for more than seven years and that the girlfriend was becoming increasingly exasperated by his lack of commitment. The other participants learned that a previous girlfriend had eventually given up on him. During discussion, the problems he experienced with commitment became increasingly clear. His parents' marriage had ended in a painful divorce, a factor that seemed to play a role in his reluctance to take the next step with his girlfriend. At the same time he talked about his pleasure in playing with his brother's children— how he had become their favorite uncle. His lack of commitment also spilled over into his life at the office. He was a great procrastinator who had to be pushed for closure on decisions. This pattern of behavior had also delayed his career progression. Not surprisingly, the other participants pointed out to him the unfairness of the situation, which created the tipping point for his finally committing himself and getting married.

Life balance is inevitably a recurring theme in most presentations (Sheehy, 1995; Sheehy, 1998; Hochschild and Machung, 2003). As life passes and children grow up many people increasingly feel that they are leading a mortgaged life. Finding time for the family becomes an uphill struggle. They feel they have no quality time with their children and miss the important moments in their life, even becoming estranged from them. At the same time they are prisoners of their own ambitions. They like the fast track but feel guilty about what this implies for the family. They look for ways to rearrange their priorities and strike a better balance. They are desperate for advice. One CEO told me that the turning point for him to give real attention to life balance was when he found himself alone with his seven-year-old daughter and discovered that he had nothing to say to her. He felt very uncomfortable. She had become like a stranger to him. That was his wake-up call.

Last but not least, many of the executives in the leadership workshop raise questions about *meaning* (Frankl, 1962; Frankl, 1967; Kets de Vries, 2002, 2009a). For some, the search for meaning may have been a theme all through their career. For others, it is more recent, and related to their

Figure 10.2 The triangle of conflict

age. After having been very successful in their career, they have a strong urge to give something back. But how can they do this? Can it be achieved within the context of work? Or do they have to look outside for this kind of gratification? How can they have the biggest impact? What is most suitable given their personality make-up?

The triangle of conflict To understand the reasons behind the emergence of a focal problem or central theme in an individual's life we need to look at the 'triangle of conflict' (Figure 10.2) that is part and parcel of the human condition (Freud, 1933; Menninger, 1958; Malan and Osimo, 1992). Individuals experience conflicts arising from unacceptable feelings or impulses that create anxiety and lead to defensive reactions. Ironically, these defensive processes stir only a vague awareness of what they are defending themselves against, as the exact nature of the unacceptable thoughts and wishes may not always reach consciousness. Nevertheless, they evoke anxiety. Defensive behavior is a means of avoiding the awareness or experience of unpleasant thoughts or feelings. One simple indication of defensive behavior is when someone quickly changes the subject when a certain issue is raised. Our task as a psychological detective is to find out what people are defending themselves against. What are the underlying fantasies that drive people's actions?

The challenge for workshop participants is to identify the central issue. *Clarification* by the workshop leaders and members of the group will lead to greater specificity (Greenson, 1967; Balint, Ornstein *et al.*, 1972; Kets de Vries and Miller, 1984). For example, in the case of our female CEO the other participants asked about her interaction with other women. They also prompted her to say something about her daughter. Clarification brings the problem into sharper focus. The female CEO was asked if she tended to have problems managing women. Did she have different demands from women than from men? Clarification has a supportive effect in that it shows the person in the hot seat that the others understand what is going on. It helps to sort out cause-and-effect relationships and to make a connection between past and current patterns, setting the stage for various interpretations. It truly *confronts* the person in the hot seat with conflictual issue.

The associations made by members of the group following a presentation create the groundwork for a thoughtful, detailed reappraisal of goals and for experimentation with new alternatives to the status quo. Ideas and plans become clearer and more defined. The destination of this sometimes painful inner journey is increased self-knowledge and a new beginning. Greater awareness of a central life theme reduces ambiguity and leads to greater peace of mind.

Furthermore, the process of clarification—the way the group reaches out to the person in the 'hot' seat and grasps so much in such a short space of time—gives that person a feeling of being truly supported. Support, validation, and the provision of safe and encouraging relationships with members of the group become crucial while this inner journey takes place.

Empathy expressed by others makes a real difference when confronting someone with major issues (Rogers, 1951; Rogers, 1961; Kohut, 1971; Kohut and Wolf, 1978). More than the workshop leader, the role of the group is critical. People in the 'hot seat' see that the other members of the group are not frightened, depressed, or even disgusted by what they learn. They are accepting, offering to remain to help, and optimistic about the future. Because of this group attitude, the person at the center of the life case study feels deep gratitude and trust.

Returning to our female CEO, and relating her account to the triangle of conflict, one underlying issue was her anger toward her mother. At times, she said, she felt like she 'could kill her.' Of course, expressing that thought as a very small child would be a conflict-ridden proposition, given her real dependence on her mother. The thought alone caused an enormous amount of anxiety. She would repress these angry thoughts and take them out of conscious awareness. She was also angry with her father for not standing up for her. However, she would deny that she was angry by pretending that everything was all right. To defend against her anxiety about her anger at mother (not necessarily a conscious process) she used not only repression but also displacement, redirecting her angry feelings toward people who were less 'dangerous' than her mother: her sisters, girl friends, and, later, her husbands and colleagues. She also suffered from conversion symptoms (psychic conflicts transformed into somatic symptoms) in the form of migraine headaches.

Challenge 3: Using 'false connections'

The interpretive process is complicated by another triangle, the triangle of relationships, which points out is that there are two kinds of relationship in every situation. First, there is the 'real' relationship between the individual and others. This real relationship becomes the background or context for another: the transference relationship (Freud, 1905; Greenson, 1967; Etchegoyen, 1991). I have written extensively about transference elsewhere in this series.[2] Briefly, transference signals confusion—of people, time, and space. No relationship is a new relationship; all our current relationships are colored by those we had with our earliest caretakers. As we relive those earlier, primary relationships again and again, we act toward people in the present as if they were people from the past. Like it or not, these past relationships have become organizing themes in our personality structure. Maladapted attitudes, thoughts, and emotional responses that emerge are directly related to interpersonal processes prevalent in our earliest experiences.

During the course of the workshop, intolerable feelings that were originally experienced toward family members in the distant past are repeated in relation to people in the person's current life, and directed to the other participants and the workshop leader. This relationship triangle (Figure 10.3) provides a conceptual structure for assessing these transferential patterns of response (Malan, 1963; Luborsky, Crits-Christoph *et al.*, 1988; Malan and Osimo, 1992; McCullough Vaillant, 1997). Anyone

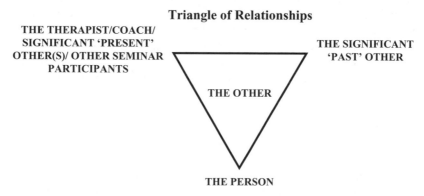

Figure 10.3   The triangle of relationships

[2]Kets de Vries, M. F. R. (2009c) *Reflections on Leadership and Career Development.* Chichester: John Wiley & Sons Ltd, pp. 64–8.

hoping to make sense of interpersonal encounters needs to understand these transferential processes.

Linking the Past with the present   Returning once more to our female CEO, the other workshop participants pointed out similarities between her relationship with her mother and her relationship with female executives at the office, a comparison that made sense to her. Her irrational outbursts of anger at seemingly innocuous comments, and her assumption that 'men are weak,' were perceived as transferential reactions relating to her feelings about her resentful mother and unsupportive father. Both themes were familiar to her fellow participants. When she snapped at one of the female executives in the workshop for no apparent reason, this point became even more explicit. When others confronted her with the connection, she realized the dysfunctional behavior pattern in which she was stuck. The survival behavior she had adopted when small was no longer functional in her adult life.

Let's take another example to illustrate how transference works. A CEO in another leadership workshop described his father as autocratic and always wanting to have his own way. The executive discovered that the best way of dealing with his father was not to confront him (which only led to violent arguments) but to comply. This executive described how irritated he would be at himself when he let people have their way against his better judgment. At times, he felt, people just walked over him. Without understanding why (transferential reactions occur at an unconscious level), he would find himself angry for not having stood up to them and be unable to explain his own behavior. This executive's personal case presentation focused on the problems he had with the chairman of his board, who just rolled over him. Helping this man understand the extent to which his past behavior influenced his present behavior, as well as its origin, was the first step in making him see that he had a choice: he could either stay on automatic pilot and do more of the same, or stop the process and say, 'There must be a better way of handling this situation.'

Challenge 4: Creating a 'holding environment'

Change is so difficult that, even with the best of intentions, we can rarely manage it single-handedly, so the next step in the change process is involving other people in what we would like to change. Making a public commitment about the changes we like to see is crucial because it doubles momentum: it involves both the person making the announcement and the group, which becomes a kind of 'holding environment,' a transitional space providing containment for each participant's emotional experiences. By taking a public stance,[3] people give themselves an ultimatum: go through with it or lose face. In the case of the female CEO, her public commitment in the workshop centered on finding better ways of dealing with her temper. Success would be indicated by better relationships with people at work, improving her contact with her daughter, and the ability to establish a new, meaningful relationship with a significant other.

Restructuring the inner theater

From a conceptual point of view, the three triangles (behavior, conflict, and relationships) clarify the dynamics of the change process. In applying the insights derived from these three triangles pressure is exerted upon the individual to work on a number of different fronts. These fronts are *defense*, *affect*, and *self-perception* restructuring (Wachtel, 1982; McCullough Vaillant, 1997).

The first challenge in defense restructuring is to identify patterns of defensive behavior, work out why they emerge, and give them up. To illustrate, it didn't take long to identify our female CEO's use of specific defenses. She had a tendency to deny responsibility for some of her actions; she would forget the more unpleasant things she had to do; she would redirect angry feelings toward others; and she had conversion symptoms (incapacitating migraine headaches) when under stress.

As her case illustrates, many defensive reactions, now maladaptive, may have been quite adaptive in the situation when they were first learned. Denial of responsibility and forgetfulness were successful survival mechanisms in her family. Migraine headaches were her way of getting some attention from her father, the doctor. Her behavior demonstrates that there is a natural human tendency to achieve gratification by means learned in the past. Unfortunately, these solutions stop working after a while and problems emerge instead, occasionally with catastrophic results in the longer term. To change, however, the person first has to recognize this defensive behavior, understand its origin, and build a better coping mechanism.

After the identification of specific defensive reactions, the next step is to get rid of them. But what happens if we give up our defenses? How will we deal with the vicissitudes of life?

After our female CEO described an incident when she publicly humiliated someone and failed to take responsibility for the consequences, participants asked: 'Did it work?' 'Does not thinking about this issue make

---

[3]See Chapter 7 for a more detailed examination of public commitment to change.

you feel better?' 'Do you believe you were effective in not apologizing for this incident?' 'Couldn't you have handled the situation in a different way?' If someone believes strongly that not thinking about a conflicted issue makes her feel better than thinking about it, it is hard to change that behavior pattern. Using denial as a defense can be very adaptive. In the case of our CEO, however, and the prominent position she had in the company, this strategy no longer worked very well.

The second aspect of reconstructing our inner theater concerns how we experience and express emotions. In emotional restructuring, we have to explore verbal, nonverbal, physiological, and action tendencies in fantasy. Emotional reactions can be both in and outside of awareness; they can be labeled or remain unknown. All these variations on a theme necessitate our being extremely observant. We have continually to ask ourselves: What kind of emotion do certain situations evoke? Do certain types of emotional reaction lead to conflict? How do we feel physically when expressing a certain emotion? Are there other ways of expressing emotions? Is it possible to role-play certain difficult emotional situations?

We might ask our CEO whether she believes her anger has the desired results. She could reply: 'That's the way I am. I can't act differently.' A more constructive response would be for her to reflect on the repercussions of her anger on the morale of the other people in the company. This discussion could make her realize that it is acceptable to express anger but that it needs to be channeled in the proper way. Outbursts of rage (particularly in public) merely frighten people. Greater awareness of the effect of her emotional outbursts on others is the beginning of a change process.

A third area of change is restructuring perceptions about the self—self-esteem and self-image. Over time we develop habitual patterns or theories about how we expect others to respond to us. This process of organizing experiences into patterns of expectation starts in infancy. These patterns will determine future self-confirming interactions with others. The child who is treated with empathic respect and understanding is likely to grow up into an adult who likes herself, enjoys human interaction, and has no difficulties in establishing supportive relationships. In contrast, it is very likely that the mistreated or misunderstood child will develop a dysfunctional understanding of relationships and frequently behave in a manner that invites further abuse or misunderstanding. The way we construct reality tends to create the reality that we confront. Having a negative sense of how others perceive us and how we view others can lead to serious interpersonal problems. To stop this dysfunctional perception of ourselves we have to trace the origins of this feeling and rebuild our perception of ourselves and of others (Winnicott, 1951; Kohut, 1971; Winnicott, 1975; Kohut, 1977; Kohut and Wolf, 1978; Basch, 1988; Basch, 1995). However, it is not easy to do this alone. We need the help of others.

In the case of the female CEO, fellow participants pointed out that she was engaged in a self-fulfilling prophecy in her relationships with men. Because she perceived herself as dislikable (as she was an unwanted child) she created situations that made people dislike her. Her two failed marriages were proof. While married, she would pick fights with her husbands—testing their attachment to her—until they left. By acting in the way she did, she proved her theory of feeling unloved. The challenge in her case was to change her perception of being unlovable. Recognizing this pattern in her behavior was another step in the direction of change. The next step was to trust and accept other people's view that she could be likable.

Techniques of intervention   To create a holding environment where people feel relatively at ease to talk about their feelings, anxieties, and other concerns, I use various supportive techniques, such as positive reframing, encouragement, and anticipation or rehearsal of dealing with difficult situations (Watzlawick, Weakland *et al.*, 1974; Winnicott, 1975; Weeks and L'Abate, 1982; Seltzery, 1986). Reframing is a cognitive technique used to assist someone in diffusing or sidestepping painful situations, enhancing self-esteem. Encouragement includes reassurance, praise, and empathic comments that are part and parcel of daily life in making people feel better. Typical empathic comments are: 'That must have been very hard for you,' 'I guess you must have been quite scared,' 'It sounds like you handled that situation quite well.' Anticipation allows the person to move through new situations hypothetically, helped by role-play. Rehearsal permits people to work out more appropriate ways of engaging in future events, expanding their adaptive repertoire. I also find it important that the client should argue for change, not the other way around. Many of the concepts from motivational interviewing have proven very effective (Miller and Rollnick, 2002).

All these therapeutic interventions were used with the female CEO to help her deal with her defensive structure, her emotions, and her perception of herself. It was particularly interesting to see how she would deal with a hypothetical messy situation following her experience in the hot seat. One of the CEOs in the workshop presented a dilemma he was facing with one of his subordinates. He asked her how she would deal with the situation. Instead of lashing out at the person responsible for the screw-up (which would have been her habitual way of doing things), the CEO stated that she would go to his office and work with him to find a way out of a difficult situation. She explained that she had discovered a way to control her hair trigger temperament by asking the person to whom her anger was directed lots of questions. She said she was getting better at recognizing the warning sign that her anger was about break loose—a tense feeling in her chest. When that happened, she knew she had to get a grip on herself.

Assessing the situation   Questions that we need to ask ourselves repeatedly when we are engaged in a change effort are:

- What habitual defenses do I use to deal with stressful situations? Are there certain recognizable patterns? What can or should be changed about these defenses?
- What kind of emotion do I use? How can I express these emotions more effectively?
- How do I perceive myself? Do I feel secure about who I am? What do I think others think about me? Do I see myself in a one-down position? Am I capable of honest self-appraisal?

These questions are difficult and we need help to obtain the answers, including investigative and affirmative behavior from others. Change requires us to relinquish defenses, express emotions honestly, and perceive ourselves and others in ways that accord with reality. We need others to help us deal with the loss that accompanies every change effort and to recognize patterns of interaction that continuously reinforce maladaptive attitudes and feelings. The sooner this recognition takes place, the greater the potential for change. It cannot be stressed enough that therapeutic learning is experiential learning. People change as they work through emotionally painful and ingrained interpersonal scenarios and as the interaction with the group gives rise to outcomes different from those expected, anticipated, feared, or hoped for.

Challenge 5: Actively working on the problem

Far-reaching personality changes can be achieved through active pursuit of an identified theme. While confrontation and clarification are directed toward more conscious material brought up by the person, interpretation is aimed at clarifying hidden connections. The timing of interpretative interventions is important. Interpretation will not be heard, let alone effective, when people are in the middle of an emotional crisis.

Critical to this process is that the people in the hot seat perceive the group as a safe place to experiment and that the members of the group and the seminar leader have their best interests at heart. If the climate becomes too confrontational some people may become too anxious to 'play' and learn. When participants gain confidence in the beneficial effects of collaborative examination of dysfunctional behavior patterns, they will be better able to confront emotions and fantasies associated with these patterns. The result is progressively more freedom to modify conflict-ridden attitudes and behavior in the direction of more adaptive and flexible responses to changing circumstances. Confidence is needed to experiment with new ways of doing things.

The group as projective screen Although interpretations by the seminar leader can have an impact, peer interpretations are particularly important. Leaders often have less resistance to learning about themselves from peers than they have from people in a position of authority. Consequently, one of the challenges for the seminar leader is to resist the urge to make an interpretation and wait for the group to arrive at solutions.

The group provides 'transitional space,' which I have already mentioned briefly in Chapter 9. This space has its beginnings in the illusory transitional world of childhood—a play area created by parents and children between reality and fantasy to help in resolving the developmental tasks of childhood (Winnicott, 1971). Transitional space is the incubator of creative thought. It is the place processes like symbolization, make-believe, illusion, daydreaming, playfulness, curiosity, imagination, and wonder all begin. The challenge in the workshop is to recreate this illusory space so that participants are encouraged to express themselves in ways that are out of the ordinary.

The transitional space provided by the group offers great opportunities to facilitate the working-through process, to develop the participants' capacity to examine themselves, to understand conflicts and areas of vulnerability, to examine their own behavior, and to develop more varied and flexible defensive systems that protect them from emerging anxiety (Scott Rutan and Stone, 2001). Self-understanding is facilitated, as the person who is the center of attention has the opportunity to re-experience problematic relationships in the here–and–now of the group and so to gain more meaningful insight that can lead to greater freedom of action. The group setting provides an opportunity where executives try to experiment with greater intimacy with others, try different forms of behavior, and pick up the broken thread of their own creative potential. Members of the group give feedback about behavior and character on a continuous basis at every occasion.

Therapeutic processes within the group In the transitional space provided by the group, each presenter does something to the other participants (and vice versa), evoking subtle unconscious reactions known as 'countertransference reactions.' These countertransference reactions then shape the observations of each member (Heimann, 1950; Racker, 1968; Etchegoyen, 1991). The emotional responses of the group members to any given presentation reveal members' sensitivities and offer evidence of the presenter's attempts (both conscious and unconscious) to evoke certain reactions in others.

The spectrum of countertransference reactions ranges from subtle to dramatic. For example, participants may experience vague feelings of anxiety, sleepiness, boredom, futility, helplessness, or disdain. They may have more blatant responses—feeling angry, intimidated, sexually aroused, or discover they have stopped listening. At the further extreme, people may act out, blowing up at a fellow member, leaving the room in a huff, or being paralyzed by the fear of losing control and causing harm. Over time, participants become increasingly proficient at translating these subtle (and not so subtle) signals into imagery that has meaning, and they learn to notice not only what is expressed verbally and nonverbally, but also what is avoided.

For example, in the case of the female CEO, every time the harsher side of her personality came to the fore, she was reminded of it happening. A comment about her behavior would be made in the plenary session, within the smaller groups, and during social occasions. Every act inside the seminar and outside in the social setting became a new learning opportunity. Each encounter with another participant offered another occasion to gain a new understanding, attempt new behavior, and work through chronic personality problems. In contrast to one-to-one situations, the group setting provides a breadth of experience in the here-and-now. People have ample opportunities to live out many manifestations of their current problems, connecting in-group insights with real world experiences and historical data.

By using the group as a projective screen, an extremely complex interpersonal encounter is created in which past and present experiences intertwine. People are trying to unravel past life situations, current life situations, and transferential patterns. They are bringing to awareness hidden feelings and wishes, defensive reactions, and causes of anxiety. In the process, they have to integrate *what was, what is*, and *what will be* in their mind and emotions. *What was* consists of memories, mostly connected to important people in our life, and attached to these memories are feelings. As we recall memories, self-knowledge increases because memory is closely tied to knowledge. By facing up to the past we acquire some mastery of the present and free ourselves to shape the future.

Change requires conscious and unconscious conceptual processing. Achieving change requires many repetitions in the effort to recognize new realities and practice new ways of thinking and acting. Experiments in new behavior need to be tried and assessed. This is a period of increased creativity leading to a resumption of psychological growth and it takes time. Pathological behavior patterns may disappear, to reappear in another form, and disappear again.

Challenge 6: Consolidating the change

At this point the critical task for workshop participants involves maintaining acquired gains. They have to restructure their inner theater, an inner transformation that takes place only once a new way of looking at things has been internalized. Internalization is a gradual process during which external interactions between the individual and others are taken in and replaced by internal representations of these interactions. The challenge is to hold on to the acquired insights through this internalization process when the group is no longer there to keep individual members on target. This new way of looking at things has become part of the person's internal psychic structure. The retelling of one's own story and listening to the stories of others—recognizing similarities—contribute to this process of internalization (Pine, 1985).

After this process of internalization has taken place, do people feel changed? It is hard to tell. When I talk to people at a follow-up session a year after the program they may say: 'I'm basically the same.' But they may add something like: 'I do feel stronger about what I can and can't do. I have more confidence in my abilities. Previously, in the office, I always felt a bit like an impostor. It was like I was acting in a role. That's quite different now. I enjoy what I am doing. I guess something must have happened. My wife tells me so. I play much more with my children. Also I have a more positive outlook to life. I am no longer so opinionated. I find it easier to open up to others. But have I changed? I really don't know.'

Most people are able to hold on to the gains they have made, although with some erosion over time. Interestingly enough, with greater clarity about the issues they need to deal with, a significant number of the participants make the decision to see a coach, counselor, or therapist on a regular basis to keep them on target. They have begun to enjoy having sparring partners who do not tiptoe around them.

Generally, the principal indicator of a positive outcome is a better quality of life. Quality of life can be assessed in terms of increased self-esteem, reduction in anxiety, fewer stress symptoms, and an increase in adaptive functioning. It is also indicated by the individual's ability to play. Automatic defense mechanisms will have been replaced by the awareness of choice. Also, better feelings about who we are allow a broader vision of our relationships with others and facilitate different and better ways of responding.

MAKING THE BEST OF A POOR HAND OF CARDS

The aim of most forms of personal growth and development is self-direction and autonomy. Paradoxically, total autonomy leads to chaos, while total control leads to suffocation. Wisdom implies realizing that we cannot have it both ways. Our challenge becomes feeling free in a gentle harness, meaning that we are willing to subordinate our impulsive strivings to controls from the outside that evolve into self-control. From the start our challenge is to create a wider area of choice. That is what mental health is all about.

The journey taken in the workshop is to educate for optimal personal freedom while taking into account the demands of reality and society. Our challenge is to recognize our impulses and actions and to own our own lives.

In the leadership workshop, participants learn that to develop a strong sense of what they are all about, to achieve growth and maturation, they first have to be able to trust the people who will guide them on their inner journey. Trust fuels self-disclosure and learning. Helped by the others, during the telling of the life case study, participants gain a better perspective on their past, present, future, wishes, and desires. They also discover newer patterns of behavior more suited to present-day reality, gaining greater control over their actions so that new situations can be approached more flexibly. They make an effort to overcome self-defeating patterns of behaviors and thoughts. A new, internalized dialogue will evolve that makes them more resistant to internal and external stressors. They acquire a more flexible, self-directive, and mature way of dealing with others. The result is progressively more freedom to modify conflict-ual attitudes and behavior in the direction of more adaptive and flexible responses to changing circumstances; the creation of realistic opportunities for satisfying interpersonal needs. The workshop helps participants realize that they have choices, so rather than respond to a new relationship in the old manner they can stop, think, and choose other ways of responding.

One of the lessons I have learned from listening to senior executives is that all outward success has to be matched by inward success. To succeed in whatever we are trying to do, we need faith and confidence in our own powers. We have to realize that living a full life—reinventing oneself—is not just the luck of having been dealt a good hand of cards. On the contrary, it is our ability to make the best of a poor hand. And the recipe (if there is such a thing) for living life to the full is to laugh more often, play, appreciate beautiful things, have deep friendships, take pleasure in our family, and enjoy whatever we are doing. It is the journey—that is, life—that counts, not the destination. How we cope with the inevitable obstacles we will encounter will determine the richness of our journey. And as we discover, when we take this journey of self-exploration, most of the obstacles are homemade, usually by ourselves. If we want, we can change them. We can learn from experience.

CHAPTER 11

THE MANY COLORS OF SUCCESS: WHAT DO EXECUTIVES WANT OUT OF LIFE?

No one can cheat you out of ultimate success but yourself.

—Ralph Waldo Emerson

Money may be the husk of many things, but not the kernel. It brings you food, but not appetite; medicine, but not health; acquaintances, but not friends; servants, but not faithfulness; days of joy, but not peace or happiness.

—Henrik Ibsen

We never know, believe me, when we have succeeded best.

—Miguel de Unamuno

Eighty percent of success is showing up.

—Woody Allen

Getting leaders together in an environment—a safe space—that emphasizes trust, cooperation, and constructive feedback leads to some lively discussions, not least when I ask them what they want out of life. The instant response is, 'To be successful.' When I press them about what success actually means to them, the variety of replies demonstrates that success is a metaphor for many things, made up of different combinations of patterns, values, and ideas. The most common answer to my question is, 'Having a good job and making money.' But further probing produces richer responses. When I get leaders to really talk, I discover that there are no known algorithms to determine success; it is not quantifiable. To complicate matters, success has a downside of which some are all too painfully aware.

For this research project, 160 senior executives were interviewed in a semi-structured way, both individually and in a group context. Some of the questions I asked were:

- What do you want out of life?
- What does success actually mean to you?
- Do you have an idea where this desire to be successful comes from?
- List what you perceive as important to feeling successful in order of priority.
- What do you need to do in order to be successful?
- Do you feel that you have to pay a price in order to be successful?
- What would you be willing to give up to pursue your definition of success?
- How far are you prepared to go to acquire wealth?
- Would you be ready to do things you hate in order to make tons of money?
- Would you be prepared to sacrifice your health and/or your principles in order to be successful?
- Do you need an audience to recognize your success?
- Who would that audience be?
- What would you do in life if you couldn't fail?

Many of the respondents were participating in one of two programs, spread out over a year, given at INSEAD: *The Challenge of Leadership: Creating Reflective Leaders* for top executives (described in Chapter 10), or the *Consulting and Coaching for Change* program designed for consultants, HR professionals, and executives. As I have described before both of these two programs contain a strong dose of dynamic psychotherapy, giving participants an in-depth understanding of psychological processes, and helping them to be better prepared to deal with complex human situations in organizations.

The benefit of such programs to leaders lies in the words carved over two thousand years ago in the Temple to Apollo at Delphi—'Know thyself.' If we can understand what motivates and drives us, we can find ways not only to improve our own performance, but also to improve the performance of our organizations. To do this, we have to look at various definitions of success and then relate them back to our own felt experience. We have to understand how our feelings of success are validated, both internally and externally. We also have to understand the scripts that play out in our inner theater and determine how we perceive and experience success. Once armed with this information, we can apply techniques to ensure that the success we seek is indeed our true north, and bring others along for the ride.

DEFINING SUCCESS

Success touches us all, from the lowliest worker to the most elevated executive. For most of us, it is a highly emotional experience. It gives us highs, but it can also bring us lows. And for many of us, our definition of success is what gives us a bearing on life; it points to where we should be heading. Our perception of success influences the way we measure our days and desires.

So what is success? Let's look at two very different and very successful people: the Russian oligarch billionaire, Roman Abramovich and the Nobel Prize winning human rights and environmental activist, Professor Wangari Muta Maathai. Abramowich is one of the wealthiest people in the world, but his success is not only financial; he is also successful in politics and sport. He is a member of the Duma; was (albeit reluctantly) the governor of Chukotka, the most northeasterly region of Russia, from 2000–8; and owns Chelsea football club, one of the top teams in the UK.

In 2004, Professor Maathai became the first African woman to receive the Nobel Peace Prize, for 'her contribution to sustainable development, democracy and peace.' She founded the Green Belt Movement, a grass-roots environmental nongovernmental organization, which has planted over 40 million trees across Kenya to prevent soil erosion. She is known affectionately as the 'Tree Woman' and 'The Tree Mother of Africa.' Professor Maathai has also become increasingly active on women's issues. Her unique forms of action have helped to draw attention to political oppression, nationally and internationally. She has inspired many in the fight for democratic rights and encouraged women to better their situation.

While we think of both Abramowich and Maathai as successful, one is all about money, the other all about meaning. Their very different achievements suggest the difficulty of defining success. In this context, just think of an athlete, a homemaker, a surgeon, or an actor. One person's idea of success will mean very little to someone else.

What complicates the success equation further is that what we perceive as success at one stage of our life may no longer be relevant at another. Success is a very fluid concept. But whatever its meaning, success makes the world go round. It helps give life a purpose. And a sense of purpose is important to all of us. Hasn't it been said that the purpose of life is a life of purpose?

Many of the 160 executives I interviewed said that they wanted their lives to be extraordinary rather than merely ordinary. But closer inspection revealed that 'extraordinary' meant being successful, and did not get us any nearer to a definition of success. So I asked them to list what they felt was important to their feelings of being successful, in order of priority. The major indicators of success that emerged from this exercise were, in order of the frequency with which they were mentioned: family, wealth, work/career, recognition/fame, power, winning/overcoming challenges, friendships, and meaning. Most respondents mentioned more than one theme.

Family

The most frequently cited marker of success was family, despite the fact that many of the respondents could be described as workaholics. Success was described as having a good relationship with the family, rather than wealth, possessions, or career, notwithstanding how others perceived their success. To these respondents, happiness was not something that could be bought with money.

'Success is being a good dad to my two kids, and seeing them becoming responsible adults,' said the COO of a technology company. 'Also, I want to give them the things I didn't have when I was a child.' This idea was cited on numerous occasions: many of the executives I interviewed described growing up in dysfunctional families and being determined that their own children would have a different environment. They wanted their children to be happy.

But not every person who grows up in a dysfunctional household becomes a successful executive. The importance of family to these respondents was informed by their values and beliefs, which determined how they treated the people closest to them, and by the choices they had made in the light of their own experience. Where success was defined as having contributed to the creation of a close-knit family, we can see that those who did not grow up in such a family made conscious decisions to do things differently.

'My own professional ambitions have to take a back seat,' the COO said. 'To me, the highest priority is to remain connected to the family.'

Wealth

Acquiring wealth was the second most popular indicator of success. To a large number of respondents, financial security was a priority—and had very much determined (and was determining) the life trajectory they were on. This definition of success translated as the pursuit of money, securing finances, and having minimal debt. One CEO in the sports wear business commented, 'Money was short when I was growing up. My parents were very preoccupied with their lack of money. By the time I was seven years old, I had decided that I didn't want to be in the same situation as them.'

It is not surprising that success means financial security to those who grew up with little, but achieving their goal could be a hollow victory, as the CEO pointed out. 'It will take me several lifetimes to spend all the money I've made. But ironically, instead of having greater peace of mind, I am more driven than ever. I don't compare myself to my parents now, but to other wealthy people, and I want to have more than them. Money has become my way of keeping score. It's a blessing but also a prison sentence.'

As this statement indicates, many of the executives who equated success with money also felt ambivalent about its pursuit, because this type of success often came at a price. I asked how far the respondents were prepared to go to acquire wealth. What would they be willing to give up in order to pursue what they defined as success? Would they be prepared to do things they hated to make tons of money? Would they be willing to sacrifice their health? Or their principles? Many seemed to be quite ready to do several of these things; quite a few respondents had divorced, had problems with their children, or had lifestyle-related health issues.

Obviously, it hadn't dawned on some of these executives that how they spent their time might be more important than the time they spent making money. After all, money mistakes can be corrected, but time, once past, is gone forever. And while they may have thought they possessed wealth, it might actually have been the other way around: wealth may have possessed them. They didn't realize that a position of wealth might well represent another form of poverty.

A tragic irony of life is that we so often achieve financial independence after the chief reason for which we sought it has gone. Upon reflection, some respondents commented that making money their primary objective may have been the greatest mistake of their lives. Money could buy them everything—except the chance to do it again.

Work/career

For a considerable number of respondents, real success equated to finding work they loved. For these people, pursuing a satisfying career provided them with a considerable amount of gratification. One entrepreneur said she didn't want to wake up every morning not wanting to go to work; she wanted to wake up every morning with a smile on her face, and added, 'I believe in the adage that if you do work that you love and the work fulfills you, the rest will come.' Another respondent quoted Voltaire: 'Work banishes those three great evils: boredom, vice, and poverty.'

By contrast, a number of respondents viewed work as a necessary evil. These executives didn't recognize the enjoyment factor in work. Although enjoyment is a subjective concept, it's not difficult to understand that executives who judge themselves to be happy in their work are likely to be more productive and perform better than those who admit to being unhappy (unless they happen to have a masochistic disposition).

Many of the respondents were also strong believers in hard work. They felt that the only way they could get anywhere in life was to work hard at it. As one observed, 'Hard work makes a difference, no matter what you do—whether you're a painter, an actor, a physician, or a businessman. There is no way around it… Life is like riding a bike. It is impossible to maintain your balance while standing still.' For these people, the fact of having made an effort, and remained true to certain ideals, justified the struggle itself. A leading banker pointed out, 'When you see a man at the top of a mountain, he didn't fall there.' Although it is quite possible to work without results, it is unlikely one will achieve results without work.

Recognition/fame

The influence of recognition or fame as a success indicator should not be underestimated. The respondents who cited recognition as important were motivated by the acceptance, approval, and appreciation of their achievements by others. Positive feedback was extremely important to them.

To some people with a narcissistic disposition, fame and recognition boil down to the desire to be more than just a faceless member of the community; they want to be visible, and to be noticed. At its extreme, this tendency leads celebrities to do crazy things because fame, or perhaps notoriety, heightens their perception of self-worth. The more people react, the more such behavior is reinforced, leading to the phenomenon of fame that is only very loosely linked to achievement, if at all. In the long run, logic tells us that fame through achievement is best: after all, who is the more significant role model, Paris Hilton or Mother Teresa?

Why do some people have a desperate urge to be recognized, to be famous? The obvious and most usual answer is lack of emotional support and recognition when growing up. Just as some of those respondents driven by the need to acquire wealth came from poor backgrounds, those who cited fame as their motivation were trying to compensate for an earlier deficit.

Not all respondents understood this. One stated rather naively, 'If you're famous, you're free. If you're famous, you don't have to work very hard. If you're famous, you can buy anything you want. If you're famous, nobody can tell you what to do. If you're famous, you will have interesting friends and go to interesting parties!'

For most, however, a little thought revealed that fame is largely about 'getting there,' and is illusory: on arrival, you may find out that there's no 'there' there. Or the fame disappears almost as soon as it is won. This was expressed by the CFO of a successful restaurant chain who said, 'Finally, I have come to realize that fame is a very elusive thing—here today, gone tomorrow. But, in spite of knowing that, I tell myself that it is better to be a has-been than a never-was.'

It was evident to some that they continued to be driven by the need for recognition and fame, despite acknowledging its ephemeral nature. 'Fame is a beast that just gets hungrier; it needs to be continuously fed,' one respondent told me. Another pointed out that, 'Getting what I want from others only feels good for a moment. It's tiring to always be trying to get from others what I need to be able to give to myself.' 'Recognition and fame doesn't make for tranquility,' said the first, 'but it does make for loneliness.'

Power

As a success indicator, power was not just about having it, but also about feeling that it was still growing. The theme of righting earlier wrongs was strong in this group, with many having previously known situations where they were quite powerless. For many of the respondents I listened to, power also symbolized freedom, independence, and liberty. The confidence that came with possessing power made them feel better in themselves. Power helped build self-worth and a sense of self-efficacy.

In spite of their fascination with power, there were those who recognized its corrupting influence. They were quite aware of power's darker side. They also commented on the danger of people using power arbitrarily.

The executives who identified power as an important factor felt that it could be a great positive force, if used selectively and for constructive ends. They talked about the need to combine power with responsibility. As one executive said, 'Power can be used for good or bad. My challenge is to use the power I possess wisely, so the way I use power must always be accompanied by moral choice.' However, he went on to point out, 'If you're in a position to make things happen, if you have the power to do so, it gives you tremendous opportunities.'

According to these executives, effectiveness in an organizational setting will always require the recognition, acquisition, and use of power. They made it quite clear that although absolute power corrupts absolutely, so too does absolute weakness. It makes people dependent. Power used in a positive way can enhance organizational commitment and teamwork, and raise morale. The perception was that, if those in leadership positions did not exercise power, people in organizations would be more likely to ignore the need to cooperate, participate, engage in, or be subjected to other influences. They added that without power, new ideas might be generated but would not be implemented. Hence having the power of decision gave these executives the opportunity to get things done.

Unfortunately, some people may have a lot of power but fail to harness it in the right way, and accomplish little. Some respondents noted ruefully that power can contribute to inner rot; it can become toxic. Furthermore, they acknowledged that power, however it has evolved, is not usually given up without a struggle. All too often, those who have been intoxicated with power, and have derived any kind of benefit from it, have great difficulty abandoning it. The greater the power gained, the greater the appetite for it. Although many people love power, those who desire it most are seldom the fittest to have it.

I put one last question to them: Isn't true freedom having power over ourselves? Perhaps the ultimate purpose of getting power is to be able to give it away.

Winning/overcoming challenges

When the Russian oligarch, Roman Abramowich, was asked why he wanted to buy an English football club, he replied: 'The goal is to win.

It's not about making money. I have many much less risky ways of making money than this. I don't want to throw my money away, but it's really about having fun—and that means success and trophies.' Perhaps this need to challenge oneself helps explain why so many executives become obsessed by golf.

Challenges make us discover new things about ourselves that we might never have known otherwise. The respondents described this as a need to find ways to stretch themselves. 'I have to compete at the highest level to feel good about myself,' said an investment banker. 'To feel truly alive, I need to get out of my comfort zone. For me, to compete is to exist.'

The desire to compete is a very basic need within us all. Society and the environment in which we live contribute to competitive intensity—and indeed, in some ways, competition can be extremely beneficial and contribute to excellence. Someone with competitive spirit is always raring to go, to experiment, to take initiative, and to take on new challenges. But problems arise because one win is almost never enough. 'I love to compete,' said a senior government official. 'I love to win. I have always competed with everyone, and everything, I can't really help myself. But even if I win, it is never good enough. I have to enter the next race. When you reach the top, you have to keep on climbing.'

An overemphasis on continually winning can have negative repercussions in the business world, when the pursuit of short-term goals can be detrimental to long-term benefits. Leaders obsessed with winning may be managing for economic decline.

Another problem with this view of success emerged when a number of respondents mentioned that the desire to win was as much about the reactions of others as it was about pushing oneself to the limit. 'Being able to beat others and making them envious,' was how the CEO of a large accountancy firm put it. They seemed to agree with the writer Gore Vidal, who claimed, 'Whenever a friend succeeds, a little something in me dies.'

Such an attitude indicates a stark view of life; a world where there are only winners and losers, and losers may well harbor grudges. The visibility and power associated with winning imply that this type of success comes with ample reasons to watch one's back; the need to compete can turn into a toxic pursuit and become quite destructive.

Our discussion led to a deeper insight when the government official reflected, 'Maybe it's because I have something to prove. Maybe it's because I don't feel good enough in my skin. Maybe it's because there is something missing inside me.'

Friendships

'Friendships are very important to me,' said the CEO of a telecommunications company. 'Having good friends signifies how successful I am in life. It means I have treated others well.' She went on to explain the importance of friendships in the context of self-expression, saying, 'If you are not happy and confident with who you are, you will find it very difficult to form true friendships.'

Those who viewed success as the ability to make good friends and keep deep friendships throughout their lives believed that without friendships, they would never be able to achieve their ultimate goals and dreams. In that respect, friendships could be viewed as a means to an end.

Some commented on what they did to make their friendships last. One talked about the need to be a 'giver' rather than a 'taker,' sharing in her friends' successes and empathizing when things didn't go so well. Most of them emphasized the importance of continuing to do things together to have new shared experiences—an important factor in maintaining the durability of friendships.

Meaning

Success tended to be linked with meaning among the older respondents, who had begun to ask themselves whether they would be leaving this world better than they had found it. Had they done enough meaningful things in their life? Their interpretation of success had the wider connotation of success as a human being, rather than as an organizational leader, and was evidenced by their differentiation from others through their ability to engage in altruistic behavior.

One CEO had engaged in a variety of apparently altruistic activities, including helping to set up a school in Tanzania, but he recognized that his actions might sometimes be viewed ambivalently. 'I know that even when I appear to act altruistically, there might be other reasons for my behavior,' he pointed out. 'It might be viewed as a way of earning future favors, or of boosting my reputation. Whatever the reasons may be, the most important one to me is the feeling that comes from acting unselfishly.' This executive's attitude encapsulates reciprocal altruism, a natural pattern of social interaction where one person provides a benefit to another. This type of human behavior allows the expectation of future reciprocity, a situation where altruistic and egotistical needs combine.

The classic exercise of writing our own obituary often throws up thoughts about how we define success and meaning in our lives. I have often asked executives if they wanted to be 'the richest person in the graveyard,' which reflected neatly how some of the older respondents were viewing success. Since the typical measures of success—awards, money, promotions, responsibility, accolades—mean nothing once we are gone, they had come to think that their success might best be measured by how many people's lives they had touched—and, they hoped, made better. 'If, after you are gone, people remember you for the good you have done, or if you have made the world better in some way, then I'd argue that you have been successful in a meaningful way,' said one senior executive.

For this group of respondents it was important to build value into the lives of the people coming after them—younger colleagues at work, children at home, or both. My conversations with this group made it clear that these people actualized their values. Through their helpful acts they ratified the kind of people they were, or wanted to be, and the kind of world they wanted to live in. They also satisfied a fundamental human interest in shaping the world in the light of their values as a way of affirming their identity. As the old saying goes, 'People work for money but they die for a cause.'

WHAT LIES BENEATH

If we cannot define a universal notion of success for the individual, can we describe its nature, and get closer to an understanding of where our feelings of success come from? It seems from my discussions that there are several routes to feeling successful, including envisioning a plan, and the interplay between internal and external validating factors. Ultimately, our perceptions of success come from our inner script, the internalization of everything we have learnt from our very earliest days onward.

One unusual life trajectory, and a remarkable success story, is that of Arnold Schwarzenegger, the Austrian-American bodybuilder, actor, businessman, and politician, and currently the Governor of California. He began body building at an early age, was awarded the title of Mr Universe at age 22, and went on to win the Mr Olympia contest a total of seven times. In addition, Schwarzenegger gained worldwide fame as a Hollywood action film icon, noted for his lead role in such films as *Conan the Barbarian* and *The Terminator*. He has also had a highly successful business career, engaging in enterprises such as bricklaying, mail order, real estate, restaurants, and other ventures. Schwarzenegger became one of the highest paid actors in the film business. All his life, he has been a prolific goal setter, writing down his objectives at the start of each year on index cards. In 2003, he was elected Governor of California, and re-elected in 2006.

Schwarzenegger's childhood reminiscences are interesting to better understand the person behind the public image. To the best of our knowledge, he had a good relationship with his mother but a poor one with his father. The latter, a police officer, seems to have been very authoritarian, and favored the older of his two sons. He also believed in 'spare the rod and spoil the child'—his child-rearing practices bordered on abuse. Schwarzenegger Sr wanted his son to become a soccer player but Junior opted instead for bodybuilding.

The kind of dynamics existing in his nuclear family may have induced in Schwarzenegger the will to excel. His comments to the press reveal his huge determination not to be broken by his father, and enormous need to prove himself. One of his main drivers was to be in control. In 2004, in an interview in the *Daily Mail,* he remembered his childhood: 'My hair was pulled. I was hit with belts. So was the kid next door. It was just the way it was. Many of the children I've seen were broken by their parents, which was the German-Austrian mentality. They didn't want to create an individual. It was all about conforming. I was one who did not conform, and whose will could not be broken. Therefore, I became a rebel. Every time I got hit, and every time someone said, "You can't do this," I said, "This is not going to be for much longer, because I'm going to move out of here. I want to be rich. I want to be somebody."'

Schwarzenegger wanted to be a winner. He felt that he was destined for great things. From early onwards, he had a dream to move to America and he saw bodybuilding as his ticket to escape from his home environment. Sport became his way to channel his competitive spirit, and nothing was allowed to interfere with it. Of his success in numerous ventures, he has said: 'I consider myself an expert in looking into a particular idea or goal and then going after it without anything else in mind … We all have great inner power. The power is self-faith. There's really an attitude to winning. You have to see yourself winning before you win. And you have to be hungry. You have to want to conquer.' Schwarzenegger met his wife, journalist Maria Shriver, at a charity tennis tournament. Hers is a political family (her father is the politician Sargent Shriver and her mother Eunice a sister of John, Robert, and Ted Kennedy) and under their influence Schwarzenegger became interested in entering public service. And according to him, doing so brought new meaning to his life.

Plan to succeed

As Schwarzenegger's example shows, planning is a very important part of the success equation. The etymological origins of the word success are the Latin *successus*, meaning an advance, succession, or happy outcome, and *succedere*, 'to come after.' Success alludes to winning, overcoming something, or a record of achievements. Success is therefore the completion of something intended, something planned.

So making plans and following them through spells success. But by the same reckoning, making plans and not following them through constitutes failure. The assumption is that without a plan, or an attempt to achieve a target, goal, objective, or desire, we cannot know whether we have actually succeeded. This thinking, however, begs the question of whether success is solely the end result of an action or the accumulation of a series of actions. Is it still possible to be successful if we don't achieve what we desired, planned, or attempted? Although we may feel successful when we reach a target, goal, or objective, can we feel successful on our way there? Is reaching a planned outcome the only criterion for success?

Clearly, the answers to these questions depend on our idea of what success means. If we consider success as only an end result, we will not be satisfied until we achieve whatever targets, goals, and objectives we have set for ourselves. This formula, as many of my respondents have discovered to their dismay, can reveal that the closer we get to the top, the more we discover that there is no 'top.' Perhaps success should be measured by our ability to obtain satisfaction from the steps we take on the way? From this perspective, reaching an ultimate goal is less important. Success is then a continuing series of accomplishments.

Who is watching—and applauding?

Whatever we plan—and achieve—will feel hollow unless it is validated in some way. Success isn't success until it is measured or otherwise recognized. Schwarzenegger had his particular way of dealing with his inner demons. Each of us has our own way. From my discussions, it became clear that many of the executives in this study needed an audience in order to feel they were successful. However, their answers to the question, 'Who is your audience?' demonstrated that some felt that the 'audience' was really themselves—it was internal validation they sought—whereas others needed validation from an external audience to confirm their achievements. Many needed both.

An orchestra conductor once told me, 'I do not find success in the applause of the audience; it lies rather in the personal satisfaction of accomplishments. I know when I have done an excellent job directing. Although it is nice to be appreciated, I don't really need others to tell me so.' The writer Oscar Wilde went one step further. When asked how his new play had been received, he replied, 'The play was a great success but the audience a total failure.' Clearly, the individuals in these two examples seem have no need of external validation. They value and rely on their own judgment about whether or not they have succeeded, and that is sufficient for them.

Another famous figure from the world of the arts, the actress Sarah Bernhardt, revealed the pressures in seeking external validation—'Once the curtain is raised, the actor ceases to belong to himself. He belongs to his character, to his author, to his public. He must do the impossible to identify himself with the first, not to betray the second, and not to disappoint the third.' While we perhaps shouldn't view external validation as always 'doing the impossible,' needing outsiders, especially strangers, to validate one's feelings of being successful produces a tenuous psychological equilibrium.

We can relate this back to the different criteria for success described by our executives. Those who prioritized family and meaning were seeking internal validation, whereas those who prioritized money, winning, etc., tended to be more focused on the external validation that came with the trappings of their chosen type of success—the recognition, the large house, the expensive car, and the yacht.

When we feel positive about ourselves—when we possess a solid sense of self-esteem—we do not need much external validation for success. It is not really the events taking place in our lives that disturb our psychological equilibrium; what matters is how we perceive and interpret them. A source of despair for one person may be a source of joy to another. It is good to be praised for something we have done, but if we don't feel in our guts that we deserve it, the praise just doesn't go far enough. The question is not whether something looks good to the outside world but whether it feels good inside.

High dependency on others suggests the lack of a solid sense of self-esteem, and a high degree of insecurity. People with this need will require a continual stream of reassurance, support, and approval from external sources in order to feel successful.

For most of us, the experience of success is actually determined by both internal and external factors. We will only reach our goals with the help of others, and we can only enjoy the fruits of our success with the help of others, whether active or passive. If we accept the idea of an intrinsic/extrinsic duality in the success equation, the widest definition of success is achieving our personal goals. The key word here is 'personal.' Most respondents agreed that a successful life is lived through understanding and pursuing our own path in life, not chasing the dreams of others. In particular, we don't want to be sent on a 'mission impossible' by our parents, trying to achieve what they failed to achieve for themselves.

The idea of contrasting intrinsic and extrinsic success implies that we measure ourselves against ourselves and nobody else. In the case of intrinsic success, the real contest in our internal world will be between what we have done and what we believe we are capable of doing. Intrinsic success indicators are our assessment of whether we have displayed authenticity, sincerity, truth, and goodness in reaching our goals. In contrast, the objects of extrinsic success, such as wealth, fame, and outward appearances, can seem extremely facile.

IT *IS* ALL ABOUT YOU

No one is born successful, but our perception of what constitutes success starts early in life, when we start to write our inner script. In the very early years, our principal caretakers are also our scriptwriters, influencing how our fantasies and daydreams of success are internalized.

There is an African tale about a grandfather and grandson, sitting by the fire at night, contemplating the meaning of life. The grandfather said quietly, 'We all have a war going on inside us between the hyena and the eagle. Each one of them is a formidable warrior, eager to combat the other. The hyena brings anger, hatred, revenge, spite, vindictiveness, sadness, and despair, emotions that may destroy our soul. The eagle brings hope, joy, faith, generosity, optimism, growth, resilience, laughter, and love, which allows our soul to soar to ever greater heights.' The grandson reflected on the story for a few moments, and then asked, 'Grandfather, which one of the animals will be victorious?' The grandfather looked deep into the boy's eyes and said, 'The one we feed.'

The inner script we all develop while growing up might include a positive, 'can-do' attitude to life, or it might be negative, full of limiting beliefs about ourselves, our abilities, and the joys we are entitled to. Negative scripts can create mental tapes in our head that play continuously, telling us that we do not deserve success, that we are incapable of it, cannot achieve it, or cannot sustain it. If we listen, we are feeding the hyena.

Whether the hyena or the eagle predominates in our personality will very much depend on the kind of support we receive from our parents, grandparents, siblings, peers, teachers, and friends. Children who receive 'good enough' care while growing up will acquire an inner sense of security, a sense of self-efficacy, and the capacity for self-improvement. Children who receive inadequate care, due to over-stimulation, under-stimulation, or inconsistent parenting, may become psychologically damaged and less able to create a successful life. Often they will have been told that they are worthless, that they will amount to nothing. Nonetheless, some will have had enough positive experiences to enable them to over-come the negative aspects of their upbringing, despite what they have been told about themselves. To these people, one of the greatest pleasures in life will always be found in doing what others have told them they cannot do. They will have a greater drive for success than most. Their urge to overcome, to master their inner insecurity, and to control their own destiny, is enormous. These people are prepared to take respon-sibility for their lives; they do not blame others for the poor hand of cards they have been dealt but, on the contrary, play cleverly with what they have. They feed the eagle.

There are others, however, who lack the will to prove their 'tor-mentors' wrong and seem to build their own psychic prison, with *leitmotifs* such as self-destruction, self-indulgence, and self-pity. Either they give up before they have started, or they develop a debilitating sense of entitlement. These are the people for whom success seems elusive.

Unfortunately, quite a few of my respondents seemed to be feeding the hyena, and were very confused about the meaning of success. For them, failure to succeed had become a self-fulfilling prophecy. They made half-hearted attempts to pursue their dreams, but whatever they did, they were cursed by their negativity and self-doubt, setting themselves up to fail before they had even tried.

So what distinguishes those who feed the eagle from those who feed the hyena?

Focus

As Arnold Schwarzenegger's story demonstrates, the key to success for many people is making their dreams come true, so the first essential step is to decide what those dreams are, and what they really want. The real tragedy in life is not failing to reach our goals; it is having no goals to reach. Sometimes, given the power of unconscious processes, it will take time before we are able to articulate these dreams.

The very successful executives I have interviewed generally have a considerable amount of fantasy and imagination. They think ahead and create a mental picture of what they want to achieve, filling in the details as they go along. They have focus.

Persistence

Successful people also have constancy of purpose in pursuing their dreams. They don't wait for success to come along; they actively pursue it. As one entrepreneur told me, 'Desire is the key to motivation, but it is determination and commitment to pursuing your goal that brings success.'

All the successful people I have met have been extremely persistent. They never took no for an answer; they never gave up; they had the ability to hang on after others had let go. Persistence is crucial because success in any area requires a lot of practice. It is not just talent that contributes to success; it is also the desire to hone this talent, to persevere. Recent research on overachievers has demonstrated that any outward success is the result of 10,000 hours of application (Gladwell, 2009).[1] From my observation, successful people not only take hard work for granted, but, more often than not, they also succeed through failure. Failure is a great teacher in telling us how to do things better. When asked why he continued to try to make a light bulb after failing hundreds of times, Thomas Edison replied, 'I have not failed to make a light bulb, I have succeeded in finding hundreds of ways not to make a light bulb and, therefore, do not need to try them again.' He added, 'Many of life's failures are people who did not realize how close they were to success when they gave up.' Victory belongs to the most persistent.

Success and failure are very closely linked, and we learn more wisdom from failure than from success. We may be disappointed if we fail, but we will be worse off if we don't try. As I listened to people's success stories, it was noticeable how often success was associated with the ability to go from failure to failure without loss of enthusiasm. In many instances, success seemed to be largely a matter of holding on after others had let go. 'I don't think I'd be the success I am now if I hadn't been fired earlier in my career,' said a senior management consultant. 'There have to be some disasters along the way, or you may lose touch with reality.'

Excellence is the brother of persistence. Successful people often do ordinary things extraordinarily well. They abhor mediocrity; they want to be the best in whatever they do. Richard Branson once told me he wanted 'to be proud of what we are doing.' 'I tell my people that we don't need to be the biggest in the industry we are in as long as we are the best. I want our company to be known for its quality products and services. Wherever I go I make an effort to get that message across. I have been extremely persistent in doing so.'

Self-mastery

Benjamin Franklin once said, 'There are three things extremely hard: steel, a diamond, and to know oneself.' Without self-knowledge, or an understanding of the working and functioning of our inner world, we will be slaves to forces beyond our control. Real success begins with the mastery of our thoughts. Although we cannot always control what happens to us, we can control our attitude toward what happens to us, and be in a position of self-mastery. Winners are people who think they can—or who succeed in overcoming feelings that they can't.

Many successful people have been troubled by lack of self-confidence and self-doubt, despite their demonstrable successes, financial or otherwise. However, they have been prepared to confront the problem and make an effort at self-mastery. 'Everything I've ever done was out of fear of being a nothing in life,' the CEO of a company in the travel industry told me. 'Success is very much a state of mind—if you want to succeed, you have to start thinking of yourself as a success.'

Often, the major cause of human failure is lack of faith in what we can do. People can become remarkable when they start to think that they can do things. Barack Obama tapped into this strength on the presidential campaign trail, telling American citizens that change was possible, however bad things seemed—'Yes, we can' left no room for doubters.

THE PRICE OF SUCCESS

Ironically, success has made failures of many people. Let's look at a case example of the high price one person paid for success.

> Bill Keenan,[1] the CEO of a Fortune 500 company, was known for his 'can-do' attitude, and a compulsive worker who rarely took time out for a vacation. Bill craved success because he had a great fear of failure. He didn't want to be like his father, whose career had stalled at a mid-management level in a small firm. The clear message Bill received from his mother when growing up was not to become like his father. Being a middle manager was not good enough. Success meant becoming the head of a large corporation. It seemed at times to Bill that his mother had tasked him with a mission impossible.

[1] Name disguised.

After a successful education, Bill was hired as a trainee at a large multinational corporation. He was rapidly regarded as a rising star, and in his early thirties was put in charge of one of his company's major divisions. In a very short time, he increased the market share of his division from $50 million to $1 billion. Eventually, he became the frontrunner to succeed the outgoing CEO.

But despite his outward success, Bill felt extremely stressed. He was putting himself under immense pressure to maintain the appearance that everything was fine, and when he was selected for the top job, his stress level grew exponentially. To make things worse, once he was in the new position, he experienced a sense of let down—was this all there was to life? This feeling of emptiness was an additional strain on him. Bill began to have sleeping problems and nightmares. He experienced a great deal of anxiety about being good enough. In addition, he was prone to dwelling obsessively about how to deal with the emptiness he felt inside. Was the answer to enter another 'race'? Was there another level of success he could pursue? After all, there were always more prestigious jobs in the market. But would that imply even more pressure—and stress?

As well as these feelings of emptiness, Bill lived in fear of losing what he had achieved. At times, he would ask himself increasingly whether he really deserved to be CEO. Did he have what it took to handle the job? Would he be able to maintain the respect of others? He also knew that other people envied him. There were plenty who would like to take what he had achieved away from him.

What looked like success from a distance did not feel good to Bill once he had achieved it and, as time passed, the strain took its toll on him. He felt increasingly empty, and drained. Progressively, he felt that he was living on the edge, liable to fall into the abyss at any moment.

The only thing that helped Bill to maintain his psychological equilibrium were occasional outings with his three kids. Doing things with them helped him to relax. But that solace was dramatically removed when Bill's wife announced she was leaving him and wanted a divorce. Although this did not come as a complete surprise, Bill realized that he had been too self-involved to hear her repeated complaints. She had finally had enough after too many years of being ignored, pointing out that money had been no substitute for his lack of attention. What really hurt was that she was moving to another part of the country and taking the children with her.

Soon after that bad news, Bill collapsed in his office with heart palpitations. Doctors' orders were to take time off. Bill persuaded the members of his board that he had a reoccurring back injury and needed two months' medical leave, but this didn't help. Almost as soon as he got back on the job two months later, his depression returned. Antidepressants didn't have much effect and Bill's general practitioner advised him to see a psychotherapist. Initially reluctant, Bill was forced to acknowledge that he had no choice.

Bill found the opportunity to talk to someone about his fears and anxieties extremely helpful. The sessions with the psychotherapist made him realize how much his identity and self-esteem had been built on a continuous string of perceived successes. He also understood his persistent unconscious need to show his mother that he was successful. He had been colluding with her mission impossible—to better his father—and it drove him incessantly.

Bill realized that he needed to learn what was important to him, not to others. Encouraged by his therapist, he decided to take my senior executive seminar. Mixing with a group of other CEOs in an environment that emphasized trust, cooperation, and constructive feedback helped Bill to understand that he was not alone in his misery. There were many others trying to deal with similar issues. What also helped was the realization that no success or failure is necessarily final. Vicarious learning, listening to the stories of his fellow participants, became a very powerful experience, putting Bill on the road to recovery. The interchanges with his colleagues and the faculty clarified his needs, rather than the needs of others. Participating in these courageous conversations increased his self-confidence that he was good enough.

There is certainly a downside to success, as Bill's story demonstrates. Whatever goal has been achieved, for some people it never seems satisfactory, and they straight away set new ones. 'There is no point at which you can say, "Well, I've done it. I can relax,"' (said a senior consultant). 'On the contrary, the toughest thing about success is that you've got to keep on doing it. It's like being on an endless treadmill. As soon as you reach one goal you have to set off for another.' George Bernard Shaw maintained that he dreaded success: 'To have succeeded is to have finished one's business on earth, like the male spider, who is killed by the female the moment he has succeeded in courtship. I like a state of continual becoming, with a goal in front and not behind.'

Interestingly, another consequence of success can be the sense of failure that comes when we perceive that we have actually achieved our goals: what I refer to as the Faust syndrome.

The Faust syndrome

According to the poet Joachim Du Bellay, 'Happy the man who, like Ulysses, has made a fine voyage, or has won the Golden Fleece, and then returns, experienced and knowledgeable, to spend the rest of his life among his family!' However, Homer's *Odyssey* doesn't tell us very much about what happened after Ulysses' return. As I explored in the concluding chapter of Volume 2 of this series, was he happy sitting on his throne idling his days away? Was his wanderlust satisfied? I don't think so, given his previous track record. Sitting on the throne, his adventures behind him, may have made him disillusioned and depressed and prey to the Faust syndrome.

The Faust syndrome refers to what Nietzsche described as the 'melancholia of everything completed.' It suggests a state where we feel we have achieved everything possible and that there is nothing more to aim for. This state evokes melancholic feelings that, if they are not dealt with, may contribute to irresponsible action as we try to ward off the encroaching depression. Successful executives are especially vulnerable to this syndrome as a combination of forces impinges on them, both from within and without.

SUCCESS LESSONS

Understanding our own success indicators can help us both personally and in our work. By examining the many facets of success, we become more certain about what makes us feel successful. By analyzing our inner scripts and seeing how they affect our feelings of success, we can decide whether the direction we are heading is really our true north, or if we have let someone else choose the road for us. And once we know ourselves, we can start to understand what drives others to succeed, and harness that energy in beneficial ways.

My respondents had had surprises on their roads to success. In many instances, success didn't materialize in the way they originally expected. As this discussion suggests, people found success in their jobs, material things, relationships, and/or self-value or self-worth. Some people felt successful when they made money and others felt successful when they helped the less fortunate. In general, however, the respondents seemed to be most motivated when they were working toward personally significant, challenging, but attainable goals. Most of them discovered, as time went on, that success is a moving target.

Ultimately, real success for many of these executives has more to do with what they have done for others than in material gain for themselves. Many of them, in seeking happiness for others, found success for themselves, a deep sense of contentment and satisfaction that came with seeing that they had made a difference for good in the world. These strong feelings of wellbeing may signify that the success of any life can only be measured by its impact on the lives of others. There is a strong argument for the idea that we are not really successful until we do something for someone who cannot reciprocate.

My final question in the interview process was to ask the executives what they would do in life if they couldn't fail. This prompted a great deal of thought and a wide variety of responses. Many talked about regrets—the other careers they would have chosen if they had not felt constrained by family and society. Many fantasized about what they would have done and uncovered some interesting ideas—some of which, they realized, they could still make come true. Although no one can go back and make a brand new start, it is possible to start in the present and make a brand new ending. Of course, you can always follow Orson Welles' advice: 'If you want a happy ending, that depends, of course, on where you stop your story.'

CHAPTER 12

COACHING TO STARDOM: HOW TO IDENTIFY AND DEVELOP TOP PERFORMERS

To succeed in life you need two things: ignorance and confidence.
—Mark Twain

Try not to become a man of success, but rather to become a man of value. He is considered successful in our day who gets more out of life than he puts in. But a man of value will give more than he receives.
—Albert Einstein

I want to stay as close to the edge as I can without going over. Out on the edge you see all kinds of things you can't see from the center.
—Kurt Vonnegut

kōan *n.* a paradoxical anecdote or riddle without a solution, used in Zen Buddhism to demonstrate the inadequacy of logical reasoning and provoke enlightenment.
—Oxford English Dictionary

THE ZEN OF STARDOM

I have always liked kōans—those baffling, challenging, frequently infuriating, thought-provoking, learning tools that in the Zen tradition are the way to enlightenment—perhaps because, in my role as a psychoanalyst, I see parallels between the master–student relationship of Zen Buddhist learning and the process of psychoanalytic intervention. Zen masters use kōans to guide their students toward enlightenment. For example, one of the most famous kōans is 'What is the sound of one hand clapping?' The response is obvious. And I use material my clients present to me in a similar way, although I probably direct my clients more overtly. In an intervention, almost anything can be used as a kōan—taking the essential meaning of that term, a puzzle or riddle that contains the key to a deeper reality. In Zen teaching, kōans are used to open minds to other alternatives than habitual responses to day-to-day reality.

Let's take an example. A client told me about her problems working with a particular colleague. 'Just being in the same room as her makes me mad. As soon as she opens her mouth I feel myself seething. Although I'm not the only one who thinks she's a pain in the ass, I know that my reaction is out of proportion. I feel so mad when I'm around her.'

I started with a straightforward leading question: 'What does this situation remind you of?' She revealed that her colleague was 'lazy' but 'gets away with it,' while her own performance ('I never miss deadlines, I haven't taken a day's vacation in nearly three years') went unacknowledged. 'Maybe I'm envious of her,' she said.

I then asked, 'Does this remind you of anything else? What role has anger played in your life?' These questions created an insight. It made her realize that her disproportionate anger at her lazy colleague echoed the anger and hurt she felt as a child because of her parents' apparent favoritism toward her charming but somewhat feckless sister. In this case, I was using the client's acknowledged feelings of anger and envy as a sort of kōan. Once she could decode her disproportionate anger and follow it to its source, she gained insight into the deeper cause of her current distress.

Some traditional kōans are off-puttingly obtuse. It can often help to retell the story by updating the context. Here's a thought-provoking classic dilemma presented by a kōan, given a new scenario. The executive chairman of a company was notorious for being excessively protective of his territory. Trespassing on his turf was a perilous business. Senior executives did so at their own risk; over time, a number of them had tried it, and been fired. However, the chairman had a playful-cum-sadistic side. Trespassers into his territory would either be fired on the spot (without severance pay) or receive a more generous severance package (with benefits)—depending on the kind of statement they chose to make. If they lied in response to his questioning, they would be fired on the spot; if their statement was true, they would be eligible for dismissal with benefits. The most recent victim faced with this choice thought for a while, and then said, 'I am going to be fired on the spot.'

Faced with one kōan-like riddle, this crafty executive threw down another like a gauntlet. How would the chairman deal with the predicament the executive's answer presented? If he fired the executive on the spot, his own rule would be broken. But it would also be broken if the executive walked away with benefits. Given the way his damned-if-I-do, damned-if-I-don't position had rebounded on him, perhaps the most sensible thing the chairman could do would be to hang on to someone who could handle a dilemma with such dexterity. Here was clearly a star in the making.

Over the years I have observed that organizational stars are often a study in paradox. They display many contradictory behavior patterns; without consciously realizing it, they are true masters of the kōan, as their deportment is always more complex and nuanced than perceived at first glance. But their paradoxical behavior is what makes them so successful. The way of the kōan is the royal road to deep understanding of what they are all about.

However, it's not so easy to spot nascent stars, not least because we can't always be sure what we're looking for. Some may impress us as 'golden larvae,' but never turn into butterflies. Others do. But what makes the ones that turn into butterflies so special? What makes them so successful? What are the mysterious forces that turn them into top performers? And are these qualities identifiable? Or are we wasting our time looking for them? Is it luck or their connections that get them where they are? Or are they just the right people, in the right place, at the right time?

Through the clinical lens I use in studying thousands of highly successful executives, I can see that stardom is not merely a matter of luck; it's a question of choice, and beyond that of cause and effect. Although chance can be a factor, it is not a sufficient explanation. Being successful is not like playing the lottery. For stars, the old saying 'The harder I work, the luckier I get' contains more than a grain of truth. Luck is a combination of preparation and opportunity. The stories I am told by top performers suggest that their 'luck' can be helped and advanced as the consequence of their particular *modus operandi*, because they take more chances and more initiatives. They usually put in a considerable amount of hard work and preparation before they become 'lucky.' Thousands and thousands of hours of practice help them to attain stardom. As the eminent scientist Louis Pasteur maintained, 'Chance favors the prepared mind.' Top performers are ready to grab any opportunity that comes their way. Or as one star confided to me, 'It took me 20 years of hard work to become an overnight success.' We have to wake up our luck.

Neither is stardom merely a question of having the right connections. It can be very helpful, but many very well connected people turn out to be highly unsuccessful. What these stories show is that success is not something to take for granted or to wait for; it is something to be achieved through effort. Most stars achieve stardom because they know how to make it happen.

I suggest that what differentiates stars is their kōan-literate operational mode. They are walking contradictions; they have a knack for dealing with paradoxes; they know how to reconcile opposites. Stars have a talent for managing conflicting but necessary ideas or goals. They have the creative ability to manage short-term and long-term orientation, action and reflection, extroversion and introversion, optimism and realism, control and freedom, holistic and atomistic thinking, hard and soft skills. In addition, they are great at visioning, possess a solid dose of emotional intelligence, take calculated risks, are accountable for their actions, have great tenacity, high energy, and make a heroic (although often unsuccessful) effort to attain some form of work–life balance.

Stars seek out the unfamiliar—they are curious, imaginative, insightful, have a wide span of interests, and are open to new experiences. They like to play with new ideas; they find familiarity and routine boring; they have a great tolerance of ambiguity. And they are prepared to take a detour from the tried-and-tested just because it is different. What's more, their behavior is contagious; others follow their example. Given this mindset, stars are more inclined to give people who work for them the opportunity to experiment, rather than move to premature closure. They are willing to give others the benefit of the doubt, and multiple chances. Above all, they are creative, they want freedom to explore, and the authority to examine and re-test what they find. Stars can make decisions quickly, but can also be extremely cautious. They are rebellious and conservative, playful and responsible, reflective and proactive. They like to be sociable but also need to be alone; they are highly imaginative but maintain a solid sense of reality. And they know how to handle divergent and convergent thinking.

Convergent thinking involves solving well-defined, rational problems that have one correct answer. Divergent thinking is not geared to solutions. It means getting out of the comfort zone, leaving comfortable daily routines, and looking for novelty. Both styles of thought are used in problem solving, and each complements the other. The imagination that accompanies divergent thinking is balanced by the selective critique of convergent thinking. Stars have the ability to switch effortlessly from one mode to the other. (See Text Box 12.1 for a description of an unusual business leader.)

Text Box 12.1

Mahatma Gandhi once said, 'The best way to find yourself is to lose yourself in the service of others.' This may be the leitmotiv of the life of Narayana Murthy, known not just for building the biggest IT empire in India but also for his simplicity. The Infosys chief mentor and chairman puts other business leaders to shame with his refreshing view of what leadership is all about. He is a giant of a role model for most leaders—a person of many paradoxes. Although he may not like to hear it, he very much fits the definition of a star.

Here we have a business leader who knows that people will work for money but die for a cause; who knows how to separate need from greed, not wanting to be the richest person in the graveyard; someone who—in spite or may be because of his simplicity—has been voted one of the Asian heroes who has brought about revolutionary changes in Asia in the last 60 years by *Time* magazine. (The list also includes Mahatma Gandhi, the Dalai Lama, and Mother Teresa.)

Murthy founded Infosys with six other software professionals, and served as the founder CEO of the company for 21 years. Under his leadership, Infosys became the first company in India to find its place in the American stock exchange. But Murthy is everything but another IT nerd. He is a man of many colors. His leadership style has a kōan-like quality. He is an introvert, but can be very passionate if he believes in something. He is a thoughtful risk-taker. He is a man of reflection, but also of action. Holistic and atomistic thinking are not strange to him. Divergent and convergent thinking come naturally. He radiates positivity and realism. As a business leader he is committed to compassionate, not exploitative capitalism. Due to his leadership, Infosys holds specific values such as hard work, ethical practices, and living up to commitments in high regard.

To create trust in leadership (something that is not obvious in contemporary society), Murthy has been an advocate of simple living, human decency, respect, and fairness. He has always been strongly committed to bring into being something worthy, exemplary, and honorable. He always wanted Infosys to be a place where people of different genders, nationalities, races, and religious beliefs work together in an environment of intense competition but utmost harmony, courtesy, and dignity, adding more and more value to its customers day after day. Murthy also has an unusual attitude to wealth creation. He has distributed the company's profits among the employees through a stock-option program, and adopted the best corporate governance practices. He strongly believes that unless Infosys has a mechanism to make its employees its principal shareholders, it would be difficult for the company to grow. His ultimate aim has always been to make Infosys India's most respected company—to provide meaningful work, not just create wealth.

Murthy's overriding goal has been to create a worthy dream for all; to create meaning. He is currently one of the wealthiest people in India, yet he does not own a private jet or yacht. He still lives in the same house he was living in when Infosys was founded. His wife maintains, 'Murthy and I are very comfortable with our life style and we don't see the need to change it.' Both have also said that most of their wealth is not theirs; most of it will go to worthy causes.

Murthy is a strong believer in the 'earning, learning, and returning' equation. He is very concerned for the greater common good. To him ethical behavior is essential—having faith in the ultimate victory of ethical over unethical actions and truth over untruth. Thanks to his efforts, these cultural factors are very much part of the DNA at Infosys. According to Murthy, performance leads to recognition, recognition brings respect, respect enhances power, and humility and grace in one's moment of power enhance the dignity of an organization.

Social responsibility is also very important to Murthy. In 1996, Infosys created the Infosys Foundation, run by his wife, which is focused on supporting and encouraging underprivileged sections of society. To Murthy, the real power of money is the power to give it away. Unsurprisingly, Murthy has been the recipient of an extraordinary number of awards and honors, including over 26 honorary doctorates from universities across the world. He has been an exceptional agent for change with his contribution to the information world we live in today.

To get a flavor of Murthy's philosophy of management, here is the text of an e-mail he sent to the Infosys staff on May 31, 2008.

> It's half past 8 in the office but the lights are still on … PCs still running, coffee machines still buzzing … And who's at work? Some male species of the human race … Look closer … again all or most of them are bachelors … And why are they sitting late? Working hard? Any guesses? Let's ask one of them … Here's what he says … 'What's there to do

after going home … Here we get to surf, phone, food, coffee that is why I am working late … Importantly no bossssssss!' This is the scene in most research centers and software companies and other off-shore offices. Now what are the consequences … 'Working' late hours soon becomes part of the company culture. With bosses more than eager to provide support to those 'working' late … They aren't helping things … Very soon, the boss starts expecting all employees to put in extra working hours. So, my dear bachelors let me tell you, life changes when you get married and start having a family … the office is no longer a priority, family is … and that's when the problem starts … because you start having commitments at home too. For your boss, the earlier 'hardworking' guy suddenly seems to become an 'early leaver' even if you leave an hour after regular time … after doing the same amount of work. People leaving on time after doing their tasks for the day are labeled as work-shirkers … So what's the moral of the story? Very clear, LEAVE ON TIME! Never put in extra time 'unless really needed.' Don't stay late unnecessarily and spoil your company work culture which will in turn cause inconvenience to you and your colleagues. There are hundred other things to do in the evening. Learn music … Learn a foreign language … Try a sport … Most importantly, get a girl friend or a boy friend, take him/her around town … Take a tip from the Smirnoff ad: 'Life's calling, where are you?' PEOPLE WHO REGULARLY SIT LATE IN THE OFFICE DON'T KNOW TO MANAGE THEIR TIME. SIMPLE!

Murthy is truly a man of paradoxes, who knows that example moves the world more than doctrine (Agrawal and Ket de vries, 2006; Murthy, 2009a, 2009b).

IDENTIFYING STAR QUALITY

The good news for anyone aspiring to stardom, or those out stargazing, is that top performers can be made. They are not born. Without discounting nature altogether, nurture has a significant influence. The developmental actions of top performers weigh heavily in their personal progress. This doesn't mean that becoming a star implies embarking on a developmental process late in life. When we are young our personality is very malleable and early experiences carry much weight. But if the right foundation is in place, later developmental activities go a long way toward creating stars. Many of their psychological factors and behavioral characteristics can be learned.

Our starting point is working out what makes stars different. What are the factors that make them high performers? Knowing these will help us design better developmental learning journeys and make us more effective in selecting, attracting, and retaining future stars.

I have been studying top performers for the past 30 years. In particular, the year-long CEO seminar that I run at INSEAD (described in Chapter 10) offers me holistic, in-depth psychological portraits of top performers, provides me with a wealth of data, and gives me the opportunity to observe stars in an intimate setting. In acquiring this information I have also been helped by data about them derived from a battery of 360-degree feedback instruments (including feedback from collaborators at work as well as family—including children—and friends) giving me a wealth of information about the seminar participants' personality and behavioral patterns.

This kind of knowledge is important, because one twenty-first-century challenge is identifying and developing top performers who will not only succeed today, but will create and lead the world-class organizations of tomorrow. Although many leaders know 'intuitively' a number of defining characteristics that differentiate stars, they often assume that stardom is somehow innate. My observations may help tease out some of our common myths about stars and will help us accept their kōan-like qualities, not all of which come naturally. While there will always be some people with stronger talents than others, I believe it is possible to develop anyone and make everyone better.

I should add as a caveat that I am not suggesting that leaders should install a kind of a Procrustean bed for potential stars to fit. Successful executives come in many different shapes and sizes. Although highly successful people have many qualities in common, context matters. Just as there is no baby without a mother, there is no star without a constellation. Stardom depends very much on the highly complex interface between stars, the kinds of people they work with, and in what context (such as the national and organizational culture, the nature of the industry, the life cycle of the organization, the state of the economy). However, I'd like to give it a go, and identify some of the kōan-like qualities that distinguish stars from other people, by looking at concepts of narcissism, extroversion, self-management, intelligence, risk-taking, tenacity, and reflection.

Narcissism

As I have noted in the two previous volumes in this series, narcissism has been getting a bad press.[1] But is it always a bad thing? I don't think so.

[1] Kets de Vries, M. F. R. (2009b) *Reflections on Leadership and Character*. Chichester: John Wiley and Sons Ltd. Kets de Vries, M. F. R. (2009c) *Reflections or Leadership and Career Development*. Chichester: John Wiley and Sons Ltd.

We all need a modicum of narcissism to function. A much more important differentiator is the amount and intensity of our narcissistic predisposition. How much is too little and how much too much? As with most things in life, it is all a question of degree.

Narcissism is just one spectrum of the human condition, with healthy behavior at one end and dysfunctional behavior at the other. Toward the positive end, narcissists are outgoing and secure, the kinds of people who function well under pressure. Their sense of self-worth and self-esteem helps them to know their limits, their advantages, their faults, and when to assert themselves. Healthy narcissists maintain a clear distinction between what they are, and what they dream of becoming.

In contrast, unhealthy narcissists have little or no self-generated sense of their own worth or self-esteem. Why they turn out this way has much to do with the nature of the feedback they receive while growing up. If this feedback is not good enough, it can have serious repercussions. They may become starved of narcissistic supplies. Without an audience to cheer them on, these people feel dead inside, hence their predatory habits, their incessant pursuit of narcissistic gratification.

So while a certain amount of self-absorption is common among highly motivated individuals, the Greek myth of Narcissus shows us that a love affair with oneself is at best suspect, and at worst, will lead to a tragic fate. The clinical diagnosis of narcissism elaborates this point, describing narcissists as extremely self-centered, with an exaggerated sense of self-importance, an exhibitionistic need for attention and admiration, feelings of entitlement, a tendency to exploit interpersonal relationships, and lacking empathy for others.

Constructive and reactive narcissism As I have described before, developing a narcissistic disposition has a complex history. In many of my other writings I have made a distinction between constructive (healthy) and reactive (unhealthy) narcissism. Healthy narcissism develops in the growing child as the result of parenting that creates a well-calibrated equilibrium between receptivity for others, and self-directed attention. As adults, constructive narcissists have the ability to distinguish fantasy from reality, accept boundaries, and to empathize with others.

In contrast, reactive forms of narcissism have a very different source and may have a very different outcome. Unlike constructive narcissists, reactive narcissists received confusing and inconsistent messages from their parents. When children (and adults for that matter) are told that everything they do is wonderful, we shouldn't be surprised that they feel wonderful too. But these self-deceptive messages merely contribute to a state of confusion and self-delusion. In the same vein, when children are protected from failure and the consequences of their actions, they may come to regard themselves as infallible, with similar negative consequences for reality-testing.

Again, if the parents never give their child encouragement (or do so very inconsistently), their style of child rearing may contribute to a reactive narcissistic disposition. The child's feelings of uncertainty and insecurity can lead to a constant desperation to be noticed or recognized. Their feelings of entitlement may become so intense and all-pervasive that they turn into very demanding, egotistical, and aggressive people.

Just to complicate things further, there is a group of reactive narcissists who don't turn out this way. They succeed in overcoming the faulty mirroring they were exposed to when growing up. In an effort to find a more constructive way of dealing with the hurts of childhood, these originally reactive narcissists are able to dampen their narcissistic needs, reducing them to more realistic proportions. They are able to master their feelings of envy, jealousy, rage, and vindictiveness, and move toward reparation.

Narcissism as a driver It is sometimes difficult to distinguish between healthy self-esteem and narcissistic dysfunctionality. I have found that a substantial number of stars are constructive narcissists (or reactive narcissists who have learned to modify their behavior). With their positive sense of self-esteem, they feel good in their skin, self-confident, and capable. They have a proper sense of boundaries and a proportionate and realistic appraisal of their own achievements.

So a modest amount of narcissism fuels the motivational engine of top performers: it makes them feel they can overcome any obstacle, and meet any challenges. And in spite of their successes, stars also know how to keep their ego in check; they retain a sense of humility. They are life-long learners, aware that they don't know what they don't know. When they receive feedback, they take note and act on it.

On the negative side, excessive narcissism may lead people to dominate simply to feed their ego. Reactive narcissists tend to indulge in make-believe, daydreaming, and delusions of grandeur, constantly in search of glory and applause. In the process, they may lose their sense of reality. Their maladaptive and rigid behavior can cause significant distress, and functional impairment, and is exacerbated by their sense of entitlement. They are under the illusion that rules are for others, not for them. As they only hear what they want to hear, they are unable to handle negative feedback or criticism constructively. They surround themselves with yeasayers. Unsurprisingly, most of their relationships are exploitative—their selfishness rules out reciprocity.

Reactive narcissists can turn into self-centered predators, concerned only with satisfying their narcissistic cravings. They are driven, relentless, tireless, and can be ruthless. Team play is anathema to them. Impulsiveness, narcissistic rage, character assassination, and defenses like projection are some of the overt ways in which they express themselves. And because they can be quite intimidating, they get what they want—at least temporarily.

Pseudo-stars The tell-tale sign of pseudo-stars is their incessant need for recognition. Pseudo-stars always need an audience to applaud, affirm, approve, admire, adore, fear, or even detest them. Unfortunately, this kind of mindset makes them incapable of working effectively with others, or of engaging in the kind of team behavior required in complex contemporary organizations. The way pseudo-stars fool others is through excellent short-term results. The proof of real stardom is in the long-term, however. In the case of stardom, we always need to ask: What do true stars leave behind? How well do their successors do? An important signifier is that pseudo-stars do not develop others. Their mentoring, coaching, and succession planning are ineffective. And their self-absorption may create a toxic organizational culture, which inevitably translates into stress symptoms, high employee turnover, absenteeism, and other complications that affect the bottom line. The best and the brightest will not stay in the organizations where they are in charge.

Human behavior can be compared to a seesaw: humility can lose ground to arrogance and pride, selflessness to selfishness, generosity to greed. Leadership style, like leadership in general, is more easily described than defined, leaving us at risk of piling adjective on adjective. When leadership becomes toxic, and the dark side of narcissism comes to the fore, some stars can, and do, damage the organizations they work in. Their narcissistic disposition (whether constructive or reactive)—originally a key factor in their effectiveness—becomes a serious handicap. Their originally laudable obsession with success turns sour. They intimidate others with their intensity and push people too hard. Paradoxically, in their incessant striving for perfection, they harvest imperfection.

To all appearances, stars come across as secure, self-confident, and self-assured. But is what we see what we get? The reality can be quite different.

Insecure overachievers and neurotic impostors Many stars can be labeled 'insecure overachievers,' or 'neurotic impostors,' who, despite appearances, do not have a glorious self-image. Although they are unlikely to rate at the unhealthy extreme on the narcissism scale, they are not at the other end, either. Many feel like impostors, despite their success. Some even believe they are fakes, and that they do not deserve their success. With each milestone passed, they tell themselves, 'I was lucky, I fooled everyone this time, but will my luck hold?' 'When will the others discover that I'm not up to the job?' 'When will they realize I am a fake?'

This peculiar way of thinking is due to their perfectionism, a passion that is rarely fully developed but at the same time is never wholly lacking. While perfection can be a great motivator, the desire for perfection, like narcissism, is ambiguous; it is all a matter of degree. In its mild form perfectionism contributes to great accomplishments. People do ordinary things extraordinarily well. Neurotic impostors (as discussed in Chapter 5 of Vol.1)[2], however, are seldom merely benign in their striving for perfection. While their pursuit of excellence can be exhilarating, striving for absolute perfection can be extremely demoralizing. These 'absolute' perfectionists set excessively high, unrealistic goals for themselves, and then experience self-defeating thoughts and behavior when they cannot reach them. Although to the outside world they look like stars, what happens in their internal world is another matter altogether. They are a study in contrasts. They are constantly driven by the belief that they are not good enough, and could do so much better if only they worked harder. These people incessantly challenge themselves and push the limits of their experience and skills, reasoning that the greater the handicap, the greater the triumph.

This tendency can mean that work becomes neurotic impostors' sole preoccupation, sometimes to the point of self-abuse. They seem unable to quit—incessant work is their way of warding off feelings of low self-esteem. In cases like this, family, social, and leisure time becomes indistinguishable from work and work–life balance is a meaningless concept. And not only do they drive themselves crazy, they do the same to others. They never seem to be satisfied whatever their subordinates, colleagues, or superiors are doing. No one ever seems to be able to reach the esoteric heights they aspire to.

Often, the only way such people get a guilt-free break is when they get sick. But encouraging these people to take breaks rather than working themselves to death can be an uphill struggle—their self-worth is derived too much from doing rather than simply being. Fortunately, as time goes by, there are a few of these neurotic impostors who learn to accept and enjoy their successes and to be less harsh on themselves. Some never reach this stage of development, however.

[2] Kets de Vries, M. F. R. (2009b) *Reflections or Leadership and Character*. Chichester: John Wiley & Sons Ltd.

True stars don't subscribe to this kind of compulsive work behavior. They pursue harmony between their public and private life. They go to great lengths to maintain a work–life balance. Equally importantly, they realize the importance of setting an example for the people who work for or with them. They are well aware of the effect workaholic behavior can have on the work environment. Stars don't want their people to burn out.

Pseudo-extroverts   Perhaps surprisingly, many stars are not flamboyant extroverts. On the contrary, test results have demonstrated that top performers tend toward introversion (Kets de Vries, 2005b, 2005c; Kets de Vries, *et al.*, 2006).However, they have learned—again, a paradox—to become of a sort of pseudo-extrovert. They have recognized the importance of reaching out to people and building social networks. After all, social skills are useful, and can be learned like any other skill set, although not as easily as extroverts.

Real stars feel just as comfortable staying at home with a book as going to a social event and introducing themselves to people they have never met. They know how to balance their introvert and extrovert sides. In addition—to lay to rest the myth that most stars have an ebullient personality—some have a mildly depressive side that they use to their advantage. Depression, like narcissism, shouldn't be regarded as entirely negative. It can help foster our reflective abilities, a great asset in decision-making.

High energy   Stars' positive mental attitude makes them very stimulating and enthusiastic. They know how to galvanize people with ideas and actions. They get where they are not by sitting on their hands, but by working long and hard to do better than the rest of the pack. They react to new challenges flexibly and effectively. Stars often believe (and can make others believe) that they can undertake anything, whatever effort it takes. Stars also encourage others to reach for the impossible. And by attempting the apparently impossible, they may actually attain it.

Self-management

Stars realize that to accomplish great things, they need to go beyond traditional boundaries; they need to dream. They need to find the answers to tomorrow's questions. Their dreams make them architects of their own destiny, and help them to face their fears of the future. Stars know that arriving at one goal is the starting point of another. When facing complex themes, they know the usefulness of thinking with the end goal in mind. Long-term goals stop them being frustrated by short-term failures. But stars also visualize how they can actualize, or make things happen. They know that dreams can be contagious. They also believe that success is a journey, not a destination.

A question of control   Top performers like to control their own destiny—if they don't control their life, others will. They don't want to be at the mercy of events or the victim of circumstances; they believe they have a choice. For obvious reasons, they don't like to be micro-managed, nor do they like micro-managing themselves.

Once again, stars juggle various contradictions and paradoxes. They recognize that control is a matter of balance and needs to be carefully calibrated. Too much control stifles people's creative potential; too little control may end up in chaos. Stars, however, seem to be able to move seamlessly between freedom and control.

A systemic view   As I have suggested, stars are both visualizers and actualizers. But although theirs is a holistic view, they also take care of the parts. While they recognize the relevance of detail, they also know its limitations. So not only do stars move effortlessly between freedom and control, they also move seamlessly between holistic and atomistic themes—seeing the big picture, and filling out the details. Whatever they want to achieve, they align their results with the overall objectives of the bigger picture.

Accountability   Stars feel responsible for their decisions and for the outcome of their actions, positive or negative. They buy into the old-fashioned idea that they are the owners of their own behavior. They don't blame others; they don't make personal excuses; they don't pretend help-lessness. Accountability is part of their DNA.

Furthermore, accountability means more than merely doing a job. It includes an obligation to make things better, to pursue excellence, and to do things in ways that will further the goals of the organization, not merely their own. This includes a strong belief in the organization's social respon-sibility. At the same time, they also acknowledge others' accountability. They know that people who psychologically 'own' a problem are much more likely to solve it than people who merely acknowledge that a problem exists.

Intelligence

Intelligence definitely counts. It helps people to solve problems and make decisions. But IQ is really a measure of cognitive abilities, and although it is important, it is not everything—in fact, IQ may merely indicate people's potential. What they do with this potential is another matter. We've all met some very dumb geniuses and some very smart fools. Many people with an extraordinarily high IQ have radically underachieved, in terms of their intellectual potential. In my observations of highly successful executives, I have learned that motivation always beats talent. IQ is useful to a certain extent, but beyond that, we need other skills.

Unfortunately, traditional intelligence tests are not the best predictors of performance. After a certain point, IQ does not seem to be correlated with superior performance in real-life situations. There are many other factors needed to be a star, not least situational. The appearance of intelligence may be dependent on an audience. In the context of organizational life, audiences like to see hard evidence that their leaders convey ideas in an intelligent manner.

IQ versus EQ   What we need are additional forms of intelligence, and there are several that play an important role in the success equation. For example, many intellectually gifted people lack interpersonal skills. Although they may have a great IQ, their emotional intelligence—in particular, their interpersonal intelligence—seems rather limited.

Interpersonal intelligence is especially relevant to working in organizations, where the assessment of others' emotions, motivations, desires, and intentions is a continuous challenge. Stars, with their talent for emotional sense-making, are very effective at interacting with others, understanding them, and interpreting their behavior. Real stars have empathy, compassion, assertiveness, and a knack for expressing their needs and wants. Their ability to empathize, to put themselves in others' places, makes them highly effective in situations of conflict.

But although stars are attuned to their emotions, they are not swayed by them. Here is another example of their talent for managing paradoxes—their ability to combine logic and emotionality. Stars are very astute at reading others, and subsequently critically analyzing their feelings, thoughts, and the experience itself. By taking their time to reflect on the information provided, stars arrive at more thoughtful decisions.

Networking   Social networking skills are an aspect of emotional intelligence. Close observation shows that stars have more extensive communication networks than most, both within and outside their own organization. Through these networks they create social capital, access to information, support, and knowledge crucial to their long-term effectiveness.

Stars are also great advocates of team work. The era of the heroic leader (on whom everyone depends) is long past. Today, running highly complex, highly diverse, matrix-like organizations requires team power. Stars are effective team members and leaders. They recognize and reward others' contributions. They work collaboratively with others, build positive relationships, create connections, motivate people to work together, and build boundaryless organizations.

Stars also enjoy mentoring and coaching people. One of their strengths is developing the skills and talents of others. To do so, they are generous with their time. They can implement 'stretch,' directing and challenging the very best in the people they lead. Nobody ever achieves success by simply doing what is required of them; it is the amount and excellence of what is done over and above what is required that determines the greatness of ultimate distinction.

Reflection

A reflective mindset helps top performers recognize the assumptions, beliefs, and values that underlie their decision-making processes as they tackle problems, anticipate outcomes, and justify their actions. Reflection will help them remain open to changing their perspectives, and to using their information about the competitive landscape to create winning business propositions.

Reflection and action   Stars not only need the capacity for reflection, but also for action. They know how to juggle these two conflicting orientations. They know that there will always be a number of unknowns in dealing with challenges, and that there are no perfect solutions: attention to detail will only get them so far. They recognize the point at which information gathering produces diminishing returns. They know when the time has come to 'call' it.

Stars are well aware that action is the foundation of success—and they also know that success will not come to them; they have to go to it. They are always prepared to develop new opportunities. They take personal responsibility for making things happen and are very result-oriented.

Tenacity

We have all met people with only modest talents who achieve outstanding success because they don't know when to quit. Tenacity, persistence, perseverance, and determination will almost always beat raw talent. Real success comes to those who persevere whatever the obstacles in their way. Many stars can be regarded as ordinary people with extraordinary determination. As the old saying goes, in the battle between the stream and the rock, the stream always wins.

It is easy to be successful when things are comfortable. The measure of success becomes significant only when things are really difficult. Even the most enthusiastic of ideas will not succeed without the determination to convert that idea into reality. As Winston Churchill once said: 'Never give in! Never give in! Never, never, never, never—in nothing great or small, large or petty.' Stars have this level of determination, and we can only imagine the kind of success top performers will have if they manage to inspire a group to follow their lead.

We all experience anxiety from time to time. It is a typical reaction to our realization that we have to do something, or that something is going to happen for which we are unprepared. But stars are courageous, tenacious and determined: they can act and move forward even in the presence of their own fears. Stars rarely take 'no' for an answer. The words 'impossible,' 'never,' or 'too difficult,' only spur them on to finding ways to overcome such negatives.

Furthermore, stars are not easily swayed by crowd behavior. They know that there will always be somebody telling them that they are wrong, creating doubt whether they are going in the right direction. But when it comes down to it, they have the courage to stick to their decision, and not to give in. Stars pursue their goals when they believe what they are doing is right, but they will listen to others. They are stubborn, within reason.

Optimism

The writer Robert Louis Stevenson advised, 'Keep your fears to yourself, but share your courage with others.' Stars are masters at positive reframing, seeing obstacles as exciting challenges and opportunities. They are very talented at translating others' negative attitudes into positives. Reframing and restructuring the way people look at difficult situations makes most feel better, and more confident. And by seeing the best in every situation, stars disseminate a positive attitude to those around them.

Setbacks, negative feedback, and new obstacles can be discouraging, but they are an inevitable part of life and it is a significant asset to be able to reframe such difficult situations. Stars can do exactly that, building the self-esteem of others, giving positive indications of their ability to succeed. This positive attitude notwithstanding, they have very little patience with negative thoughts and gossip. The nature of our thinking drives our perceptions and has an effect on the actions we take. Far too many people become stuck in vicious circles of negative preconceived ideas or perceptions, missing out on great opportunities. Top performers—through their efforts at positive reframing—stress the qualities and skills that their people have and that will enable them to succeed. But at the same time they retain a realistic outlook to the challenges they encounter, addressing emerging concerns honestly. Positive reframing is fine, but not at the expense of reality. Once again, stars demonstrate how they manage paradox—in this case positivity and negativity.

Risk-taking

There is a lot of negativity associated with the word 'risk'—it implies danger, loss, damage, or misfortune. As a result, many of us are afraid to take risks because we are scared of loss. But attempting to remove risk from our lives is a futile activity. We need to remind ourselves that although risk-taking may be feared, it also has its positive aspects. Taking risks means new experiences, encounters with new people, new places, new learning—it means adventure. Many of us need adventure if we are to succeed in knowing and finding ourselves. In fact, we probably risk much more in failing to take risks.

Stars rise naturally above the crowd by taking risks. However, they know that the only risks worth taking are calculated ones. They like to take the kind of risk that has been given thoughtful consideration and for which the potential costs and benefits have been weighted and considered. Stars take chances only after careful estimation of the probable outcomes.

Stars play the odds intelligently but keep sight of the consequences. Taking the counsel of others (but keeping their own counsel), they carefully consider whether the upside to a decision outweighs the downside, preparing escape routes should things go wrong. They study others who have taken similar risks and examine how they succeeded or failed.

As a rule, stars are more willing than others to go out on a limb and, if they fail, have the capacity to bounce back and start over. Listening to their stories, it is clear that those who pursued their dreams and failed lived a much more fulfilling life than those who put their dreams on a shelf for fear of failure.

DEVELOPMENTAL ISSUES

So the stars I have identified—these embodied kōans—are either innately or developmentally comfortable with ambiguities. They are not fazed by conflict, contradiction, or inconsistency. Their talent for empathy and positive framing enables them to turn difficult situations into creative opportunities. Their worlds are not polarized by oppositional factions or ideas; they like fluidity in their environment, and actively respond to diversity. Unsurprisingly, quite a few of them have culturally diverse backgrounds, perhaps parents of different nationalities, the experience of living in a number of different countries, or of working in many different areas. 'They belong to multiple worlds and carry those worlds with them; they are defined by ambivalence and complexity; they are leading the world in important new ways.' (Giridharadas, 2010) Kim Smith, CEO of the venture philanthropy firm NewSchools Venture Fund, describes the kind of hybrid leaders she looks for in her organization: 'We joke on our team that we know we've the right candidate when we hire because they're so excited that we think their resume looks great because everybody else thinks that they look schizophrenic.' (Smith, 2003)

Supporting nascent stars

But having identified potential stars, how can we make the most of them? My experience is that to develop stars, the most effective strategy is to engage in self-assessment, action learning, and shadowing. The best approach is to use all three types of intervention. Let me say something about each of them.

Creating self-awareness   In my experience, the journey to stardom begins inwardly. Self-awareness is one of the most important factors in building self-esteem and confidence. Self-awareness helps us understand what drives us, what turns us off, what makes us happy, and what we are passionate about. It helps us clarify what we need to do to improve as a person.

As these stars in the making grow in self-awareness, they will understand better why they feel what they feel and behave as they behave. They will acquire a more realistic sense of their capabilities. They will realize when they are not using their full potential. They will gain awareness of how they are caught up in their own internal dramas and beliefs, allowing out-of-awareness thought processes to determine their feelings and actions. With greater self-awareness, they will be able to expand their imagination, creativity, intuition, will, and purpose.

Unfortunately, the road to self-awareness is not always easy. As Leo Tolstoy once wrote, 'Everyone thinks of changing the world, but no one thinks of changing himself.' The road of ignorance can be far more attractive. Frequently, defensive processes take over when embarking on inner journeys. So how can these stars in the making be made aware of developmental areas? How can we confront them with their blind spots? As I have suggested a number of times, an ideal method is the use of 360-degree, multi-source feedback, a method of systematically collecting and rating perceptions of an executive's performance from different vantage points including private life.

I have found that multi-party feedback—especially in a team setting— is unsurpassed as a means of setting developmental processes in motion. Group interventions (supported by one-to-one coaching) can facilitate the exploration of people's strengths and weaknesses and help create personal development action plans signed off by multiple stakeholders. For a behind-the-scenes view of a group coaching intervention, see Chapter 10.

Action learning Action learning is a process of bringing together a group of people with different levels of skills and experience to analyze an actual work problem and develop an action plan, using their jobs as the basis for learning. This is a reversal of the traditional model of learning, which takes people off the job for courses and external instruction, etc. Action learning is learning by doing, or learning on the job. Through this kind of learning process, executives learn more about their own and others' way of solving problems, with a group dimension added.

Action learning is a great way for high performers to practice working with important real-world problems as a basis for learning. What makes the impact of this learning even greater is that it is anything but an academic exercise and is not without risk. Typically, top management will identify real, relevant, and critical organizational concerns and sponsor a selected team to work on them. This is an ideal opportunity for management to observe how well their selected executives perform and assess the quality of their output. As for the future stars, they are taken out of their comfort zone and given the chance to work and learn collaboratively with other high potentials.

Many organizations solicit the help of a coach to support action learning, building time into the process for team members to reflect on the total learning experience. Guidance from a coach can be accompanied by peer coaching—many of the participants' meetings will take the form of individual members taking turns to present updates on their work, and then being questioned on it by their peers. In this way, participants in the learning process act as consultants and mentors to each other.

Apprenticeship/shadowing   Most of us learn by example, and learn most from our earliest job experiences. Our bosses at this period in our life are those we will remember best. While it is obviously more attractive to learn from good bosses than bad, many future stars have also learned from the bad ones. These less than happy experiences may teach them how not to approach leadership—what things they should avoid doing to others. Some organizations make a great effort to manage this kind of apprenticeship process by giving high potentials deep insight in how to handle various aspects of the business under the guidance of a senior executive.

Shadowing is closely related to the apprenticeship system but here a person observes an executive in action with the aim of learning something about how that role is performed. The time frame, however, will be much shorter than an apprenticeship. Shadowing is exactly that—following and watching an executive for developmental purposes. It can provide an excellent opportunity for potential stars to increase their knowledge and understanding of a particular career field by allowing them to observe, at first hand, someone working in that field or a related area. By observing experienced executives tackling their day-to-day duties, these stars in the making can 'look and learn,' asking questions as they go along and bringing their professional studies to life. The executive shadowed can also stimulate the learning process by regularly taking time out to explain his or her decisions.

THE ZEN OF ORGANIZATIONAL LIFE

Many of the psychological and behavioral characteristics I have described here can be developed and used by anyone wanting to become a top performer and interested in maximizing their potential for long-term success. Most of us will find that we already possess at least some of these behavior patterns, but may need to develop others. High on the list will be our capacity for managing uncertainty, contradiction, and ambiguity—all features of an environment characterized by constant change. We need to develop a form of organizational Zen.

Over the years, I have listened to the narratives of many stars and I have learned that the only true failure is not having attempted a developmental journey. The only way of discovering the limits of the possible is to venture a little way past them into the impossible. Excellence is not an event—it needs to become a mindset. It is doing common things in uncommon ways. It is the desire always to do things better. To be successful, we must break out of our comfort zone and learn to become comfortable with the unfamiliar and the unknown—like the executive in my final, contemporized kōan.

One day, a CEO was holding a champagne reception in the board room, a beautiful space with large windows that opened onto equally beautiful gardens, with woods and valleys beyond. The room was thronging with noisy, happy people. The CEO noticed one of her younger executives outside and stepped up to the window. 'Hey,' she called, 'why don't you get in here?' 'Thank you,' replied the executive, 'but I don't actually see myself as outside. Why come in?'

CONCLUSION: CREATING AUTHENTIZOTIC ORGANIZATIONS

No man is worth his salt who is not ready at all times to risk his well-being, to risk his body, to risk his life, in a great cause.
—Theodore Roosevelt

Well-being is attained little by little, and is no little thing itself.
—Zeno

Happiness is nothing more than good health and a bad memory.
—Albert Schweitzer

Happiness is no laughing matter.
—Richard Whately

As we move further into the second millennium, many disquieting themes in the world of work are being revealed. One is stress in the work place. Statistics on illness, under-performance, and absenteeism tell a dramatic tale of dysfunctionality. In many organizations the balance between working and private life has been completely lost. Horror stories abound of how dysfunctional leadership, work overload, conflicting job demands, poor communication, lack of opportunities for career advancement, inequities in performance evaluations and pay, restrictions on behavior, and excessive travel lead to depressive reactions, alcoholism, drug abuse, and sleep disorders.

Yet work does not need to be stressful. On the contrary, it can be an anchor of psychological well-being, a way of establishing identity and maintaining self-esteem. Sigmund Freud considered that mental health depended on *'lieben und arbeiten'* (love and work). We invest the organizations to which we belong with a considerable amount of psychological meaning. Accomplishing something tangible through work can give us a dose of stability in a highly unstable world. Organization means putting things and concerns in order and by extension, organizations are ideal environments for helping us to cope with the stresses and strains of our daily life.

Throughout this book, I have emphasized the importance of individual psychological well-being for organizational functioning. A major item that should be on everybody's agenda is creating healthy places to work—places where people feel good in their skin, places that contribute to, and reinforce, adaptive functioning. In concluding this book—and this series—I would like to raise some questions about well-functioning individuals, the motivational need systems that drive people, and the conditions that make for healthy organizations.

THE BEST COMPANIES TO WORK FOR

Every year, since 1983, *Fortune Magazine* has published a 'most admired American companies' list. Since 1997—in keeping with the zeitgeist—a 'most admired' global list has been added. To compile these lists, the editors of *Fortune* poll something like 11 000 people: senior executives, external directors, and investment analysts. The criteria for being placed include factors like quality of management, quality of products and services, innovation, long-term investment value, wise use of corporate assets, financial soundness, and responsibility to the community and the environment. To be placed high on the list of most admired companies is one thing; however, the real question is whether these organizations are also the healthiest places to work for.

Fortune has attempted to answer this question by publishing a 'best company to work for' list, drawing on a database of more than 1000 companies. In an article entitled 'The 100 Best Companies to Work for in America' (Levering and Moskowitz, 1998) the authors looked at the practices that make certain organizations so special—companies such as Southwest Airlines, W. L. Gore, Microsoft, Merck, Hewlett-Packard, Corning, and Harley-Davidson. Corporate characteristics such as inspirational leadership, excellent facilities (perks), and a sense of purpose are seemingly essential for gaining a prominent position on this list. According to the information supplied, employees in these organizations have great trust in management, pride in their work and company, and a sense of camaraderie. The companies themselves subscribe to practices such as stock option plans, profit sharing systems, no layoff policies, nonhierarchical structures, information sharing systems, flexible hours, and casual dress codes. They also hold a considerable number of events that help to create a sense of community (for example, Friday evening beer bashes, parties to celebrate company milestones, company picnics, and so on). The provision of innovative imaginative family perks adds to this positive picture, including state-of-the-art fitness centers, leisure facilities, on-site clinics, on-site childcare, great cafeterias with great food, and generous health insurance policies. These organizations are usually very family-friendly. The companies high on this list go to great lengths to create humane corporate cultures that have a positive effect on mental health.

The interesting question for architects of potentially exemplary organizations is how to deconstruct the humane philosophy that informs these values, behaviors, and practices. What steps do companies need to take to contribute to the well-being of their people? What are the psychological dimensions that make companies great places to work? How can we tap the human potential present in each organization?

THE CONTAINMENT ROLE OF ORGANIZATIONS

In the context of providing a stabilizing influence, organizations have always been important navigation points in a sea of change. The last two decades, however, have not been the best of times for many corporate employees. The companies featured on the 'best to work for' hit parade are more the exception than the rule. Life in organizations has never been more turbulent than it is today.

In the past, being associated with a company was an effective way of affirming one's role in the world. It involved making a commitment that helped integrate the experiences of the employee from a phenomenological point of view. Belonging to an organization became a way of coping with economic and social upheaval; it was a fixed point in turbulent times. As we saw in Chapter 6, in this era of business re-engineering and excessive preoccupation with shareholder value, the psychological contract between employee and organization has been broken. Increasingly, employees have become independent agents, less attached to the organization, and organizational identification and loyalty have become far less important. Very few people nowadays join an organization and expect to spend the rest of their working life within it.

However, there is a more profound effect of breaking the psychological contract. Organizations used (consciously or unconsciously) to serve as a 'holding environment' for their participants by containing anxiety through the agency of senior management. Nowadays companies seem less prepared to take on this function. The loss of the psychological contract has weakened the identification process and made the work situation more stressful. And this development does not augur well for the mental health of employees. It has contributed to an increasing sense of meaninglessness about the time spent in organizations. These concerns, again, lead to the question of what organizational leadership can do to make their companies healthier places to work.

THE 'HEALTHY' INDIVIDUAL

As an old Arab proverb goes, 'He who has health has hope, and he who has hope has everything.' One way of answering the question of what makes an organization a great place to work is to begin by trying to understand what makes a well-functioning individual. Under what conditions does a person feel most alive? Answering this question is easier said than done, however. Definitions of a 'healthy' individual vary according to the person making the observations (Kernberg, 1980; McCullough Vaillant, 1997).

Of course, health and illness should be viewed as dimensions on a continuum. In general, when psychotherapists, psychiatrists, psychoanalysts, and coaches are asked to respond to this question, they say that a healthy person is someone operating at full capacity, and that their role consists of helping people do this. They encourage their patients to gain insights into their goals and motivations; they help them understand better their strengths and weaknesses, and prevent them from engaging in self-destructive activities. The emphasis is on widening individuals' areas of choice, enabling them to choose more freely, instead of being led by forces that are outside of their awareness and control.

Although this answer has considerable merit, it needs some elaboration. From my experience in working with large numbers of executives, I have concluded that the healthier among them share a particular set of characteristics.

First of all, in the context of personality make-up, healthier people have a stable sense of identity and a great capacity for reality testing. In addition, when dealing with the outside world, they have recourse to mature defense mechanisms. They take responsibility for their actions rather than blaming others for setbacks. They are resourceful and have a strong sense of self-efficacy. They trust their own ability to control the events that affect their lives.

Second, healthy individuals have an accurate perception of their body image and body functioning. They do not suffer from cognitive distortions that lead them to engage in self-destructive activities. They experience the full range of emotions, live intensively, and are passionate about what they do. Their sexuality is fulfilling; they know how to manage anxiety; they do not easily lose control; and they are not given to impulsive acts.

A third theme is intimacy and reciprocity. Healthy people establish and cultivate relationships, know how to use help and advice, and maintain a support network. They have a sense of being a part of a larger group and obtain a great sense of satisfaction about the social context in which they live. They feel connected.

Healthy individuals also know how to deal with issues of dependency and separation. When growing up, they went through the process of individuation in a constructive manner, without suffering developmental arrest. They accept that interdependency is a fact of life. They do not exhibit clinging behavior; they do not stay detached. They establish mature relationships. Their strong sense of identity gives them the strength to deal with the setbacks and disappointments that are an inevitable part of the trajectory of life. They know how to handle depression and have a great capacity to work through loss.

Fourth, people on the healthy end of the spectrum are comfortable with ambivalence; they do not interpret people and phenomena in categorical terms (good or bad, black or white); they have the ability to assess people and events in a balanced manner. Scapegoating others is not their forte. They are creative and playful and prepared not to conform. Above all, they maintain a positive outlook toward the world. Whatever the circumstances, they reframe experiences in a positive way; they are able to construct a positive view of the future and retain a great sense of hope of what is to come. Finally, healthy individuals have the capacity for self-observation and self-analysis and are willing to spend time on self-reflection.

OUR SEARCH FOR MEANING

For very fundamental reasons, healthy people need healthy environments. The influence of our various motivational needs systems determines our outlook on the world, creating a subjective reality that acts as our guide throughout life. To attain a balance between our inner and outer reality, our experiences of meaning need to relate to activities that reverberate with our basic motivational needs. This 'match' between subjective and social world is what creates our sense of authenticity and constancy. Establishing and maintaining this congruence needs to be borne in mind when designing organizations.

In the search for continuity in a world of discontinuity, finding meaning through this congruence between inner and outer reality is a way of challenging the pressures of day-to-day life. When this match happens, we experience a feeling of doing something special and meaningful. The convergence affirms our sense of authenticity; it gives us a sense of accomplishment and personal competence; and it motivates us to transcend our usual activities.

Work has a hugely important place in our search for meaning. It gives us a sense of significance and orientation. Meaningful work is a way to transcend our personal concerns; it creates a sense of continuity. Leaving a legacy through our work is an affirmation of our sense of self and identity, a significant form of narcissistic gratification. Given these basic human motivational needs, organizational leadership—more than ever in times of discontinuity—has the responsibility to institute collective systems of meaning. This means creating the conditions in which work is done in ways that make sense to members of the organization, so that there is congruence between personal and collective objectives. When this congruence is established in the world of work it contributes to both individual and organizational health.

THE SEARCH FOR CONGRUENCE

If we take a closer look at the companies featured in *Fortune's* list of 'best companies to work for,' we can see that a major factor of their success is that they have achieved this congruence. They attain profit with purpose. If the reason for a company's existence is merely profit, it will not be very profitable in the long run. As an ultimate objective on its own, the pursuit of profit alone is not very satisfying.

We are stuck in a paradox: companies that exist *only* to produce a profit will not last long. And companies that don't pay attention to profits will not be able to fulfill their long-term obligations. So how do they do it? How have they managed to integrate our search for meaning within organizational life?

Overwhelmingly, these organizations are steeped in values that are translated into specific forms of behavior: trust, fun, empowerment, respect for the individual, social responsibility, teamwork, entrepreneurship/ innovation, competitiveness, result orientation, customer orientation, responsibility and accountability, continuous learning, and change orientation. Although these values and practices go a long way to explain the success of many of these vibrant organizations, the question remains whether they are enough to explain their exceptional performance. How exactly do they make life within these organizations more meaningful?

Leaders who want to get the best out of their people—who want to create an ambiance in which people feel inspired and give their best—need to find ways to satisfy the motivational need systems of healthy individuals I outlined earlier in this chapter. They need to *create a vision* of the organization's fundamental purpose and culture—its values and beliefs. A vivid description of the organization's future—when imbued with sufficient meaning—will have a connecting value and contribute to group identity.

However, this is not good enough. Organizational leadership also needs to create a greater *sense of self-determination* among employees. Organizational health depends on employees feeling they have control over their lives. Employees should feel that they own their own lives, not look on themselves as mere pawns in a larger scheme of things. They need to have a voice.

Another important criterion is a *sense of impact*. Organizational members need to be convinced that their actions can make a difference to their organization. This means drawing on our own capabilities. Empowerment is the process of increasing the capacity of individuals to make choices and to transform those choices into desired actions and outcomes.

Organizational leadership also has to create the right conditions for a *sense of competence*, so that organizational participants have a feeling of personal growth and development. *Developing a sense of competence* with regard to our skills and abilities is an important aspect of identity formation. For this, continuous learning is essential. When the exploratory motivational need system is blocked, frustration will increase, and creative action will dissipate.

THE AUTHENTIZOTIC ORGANIZATION

These four conditions are necessary conditions for creating a 'best place to work'—but they are not sufficient. The best companies also have a set of meta-values that closely echo our motivational needs systems. I sometimes identify these as love, fun, and meaning. In other words, these firms create a *sense of belonging* (a feeling of community that comes from being part of the organization, addressing basic attachment and affiliation needs); a *sense of enjoyment*, and a *sense of meaning*.

Because attachment and affiliation are such powerful underlying motives in our search for meaning, the first important meta-value contributing to the creation of healthy organizations may well be love, implying a *sense of belonging* and sense of community within the organization. This sense of community can be enhanced in various ways, through the organizational architecture or specific practices (Kets de Vries and Florent, 1999).

A sense of community, and preparedness to help others, helps to create a cohesive culture and goal-directedness. It also contributes to the emergence of 'distributed leadership,' where leadership is not concentrated at the top, but is spread throughout the organization. In these organizations, senior executives obtain vicarious pleasure through coaching their younger executives and take pride in their accomplishments. A sense of generativity contributes to feelings of continuity: this happens when we can see efforts continued through the work of our successors.

Having fun is another important ingredient. Fun strengthens mental health. In too many companies, however, this *sense of enjoyment* is completely ignored. Instead, the organizational experience becomes extremely weighty, crushing out imagination and innovation. Funless organizations are peopled by zombies and sleepwalkers (Kets de Vries, 2000), while exemplary organizations take their people on an exciting journey. Having fun gratifies another essential motivational need for exploration and assertion.

If our basic motivational need systems and search for meaning are contextualized so that they are associated less with our own personal needs and more with improving the quality of life, helping people, or contributing to society, the impact can be extremely powerful. We like working in organizations that recognize the importance of providing a *sense of meaning*. Organizations where people can put their imagination and creativity to work stimulate a sense of 'flow'—a feeling of total involvement and concentration in whatever they are doing (Csikszentmihalyi, 1990).

I have coined a term to describe these more enlightened organizations: I refer to them as *authentizotic*. This term is derived from two Greek words: *authenteekos* and *zoteekos*. The first conveys the idea that the organization is *authentic*. In its broadest sense, the word *authentic* describes something that conforms to fact and is therefore worthy of trust and reliance. As a workplace label, *authenticity* implies that the organization has a compelling connective quality for its employees in its vision, mission, culture, and structure. The organization's leadership has communicated clearly and convincingly not only the *how* but also the *why,* revealing meaning in each person's task. These are the kinds of organizations where people find a sense of flow; where they feel complete and alive.

The term *zoteekos* means 'vital to life.' In the organizational context, it describes how people are invigorated by their work. People in vital organizations experience a sense of balance and completeness. These organizations meet the human need for exploration, which is closely associated with cognition and learning. The *zoteekos* element of authentizotic organizations allows self-assertion in the workplace and produces a sense of effectiveness and competency, autonomy, initiative, creativity, entrepreneurship, and industry. These are the organizations we need to hope for.

In my view, the biggest challenge of organizational leadership today is to create corporations with these authentizotic qualities. Working in these organizations provides an antidote to stress, a healthier existence, and contributes to a more fulfilling life. These organizations help their employees maintain an effective balance between personal and organizational life. Above all, these are organizations where we continue to learn— where we learn from experience.

There is a famous Sufi story about the legendary figure Nasrudin. Once upon a time, an eager student visited him and asked, 'Oh, great sage, I must ask you a very important question, the answer to which we all desire. What is the secret to attaining happiness?' Nasrudin thought for a time, and then responded, 'The secret of happiness is to make the right decisions.' 'Oh!' said the student, 'But how do we know to make the right decisions?' 'From experience,' answered Nasrudin. 'Yes, but how do we get that experience?' asked the student. 'By making the wrong decisions,' said Nasrudin.

An old proverb tells us that a smart man learns from his experience, but a wise man learns from the experiences of others. We live much of our lives without thinking about significant emotional experiences. We busily go about our daily activities without thinking about their meaning, surrounded as we are by a mass of undigested experiences. We need to digest and transform these experiences. We need to deal with them in a creative manner.

One way of doing so is to create theories and abstractions as a means of writing and talking to each other about our work. Many of my experiences in making organizations better places to work have been frustrating and painful, but also hopeful. My wish is that this book, and the previous volumes in this series, will help the reader to learn from some of my painful and hopeful experiences, contribute to a deeper understanding of ourselves, and of others, and help to create better places to work.

REFERENCES

Agrawal, A. and Kets de Vries, M. F. R. (2006) 'The Moral Compass: Value Based Leadership at Infosys,' *INSEAD Case Study*, 04/2007-5391.

Alexander, F. and French, T. M. (1946) *Psychoanalytic Therapy*. New York: Ronald Press.

American Psychiatric Association (2000) *Diagnostic and Statistical Manual of the Mental Disorders, DSM-IV-TR* (4th edn). Washington, DC: American Psychiatric Association.

Appelbaum, S. H., Simpson, R., and Shapiro, B. T. (1987) 'The Tough Test of Downsizing,' *Organizational Dynamics* 16(2), pp. 68–79.

Asch, S. (1956) 'Studies of independence and conformity: A minority of one against a unanimous majority,' *Psychological Monographs*, 70(9).

Bahuchet, S. (1991) 'Les Pygmées d'aujourd'hui en Afrique centrale,' *Journal des Africanistes* 61(1), pp. 5–35.

Bailey, R. C. (1989) 'The Efe: Archers of the African Rain Forest,' *National Geographic*, November, pp. 664–6.

Balazs, K. and Kets de Vries, M. F. R. (1997) 'Bang & Olufsen: A company in transition,' INSEAD case study.

Balint, M. (1957) *The Doctor, his Patient and the Illness*. New York: International Universities Press.

Balint, M. (1965) *Primary Love and Psychoanalytic Technique*. London: Liversight Publishing Corporation.

Balint, M., Ornstein, P. H., and Balint, E. (1972) *Focal Psychotherapy*. London: Tavistock.

Bandura, A. (1997) *Self-Efficacy: The Exercise of Control*. New York: Freeman.

Barron, J. W., Eagle, M. N. and Wolitsky, D. (1992) *The Interface of Psychoanalysis and Psychology*. Washington, DC: American Psychological Association.

Basch, M. F. (1988) *Understanding Psychotherapy*. New York: Basic Books.

Basch, M. F. (1995) *Doing Brief Psychotherapy*. New York: Basic Books.

Bennett, A. (1991) 'Management: Downsizing Does Not Necessarily Bring an Upswing in Corporate Profitability,' *Wall Street Journal*, June 6, p. B-1.

Bion, W. R. (1959) *Experiences in Groups*. London: Tavistock.

Bion, W. R. (1962) *Learning from Experience*. London: Heinemann.

Bonnard, A. (1954) 'The metapsychology of the Russian trials confessions,' *International Journal of Psychoanalysis*, 35, pp. 208–213.

Bowlby, J. (1969) *Attachment*. New York: Basic Books.

Bowlby, J. (1973) *Separation*. New York: Basic Books.

Breuer, J. and Freud, S. (1893–5) 'Studies on Hysteria' in *The Standard Edition of the Complete Psychological Works of Sigmund Freud*, vol. 2. London: The Hogarth Press and the Institute of Psychoanalysis.

Brockner, J. (1988) 'The Effect of Work Layoffs on Survivors: Research, Theory, and Practice,' in Staw, B. M. and Cummings, L. L. (eds), *Research in Organizational Behavior*, vol. 10, Greenwich, CT: JAI Press.

Brockner, J. (1992) 'Managing the Effects of Layoffs on Survivors,' *California Management Review*, 34(2), pp. 9–28.

Brockner, J., Davy, J., and Carter C. (1985) 'Layoffs, Self-Esteem, and Survivor Guilt: Motivational, Affective, and Attitudinal Consequences,' *Organizational Behavior and Human Decision Processes*, 36, pp. 229–44.

Brockner, J., Gorver, S., Reed, T., DeWitt, R., and O'Malley, M. (1987) '"Survivors" Reactions to Layoffs: We Get By with a Little Help from Our Friends,' *Administrative Science Quarterly*, 32, pp. 526–41.

Cameron, K. S. (1994) 'Strategies for Successful Organizational Downsizing,' *Human Resource Management*, 33(2), pp. 189–211.

Cameron, K. S., Freeman, S. J., and Mishra, A. K. (1991) 'Best Practices in White-Collar Downsizing: Managing Contradictions,' *Academy of Management Executive*, 5(3), pp. 57–73.

Cameron, K. S., Freeman, S. J., and Mishra, A. K. (1993) 'Organizational Downsizing and Redesign,' in Huber, G. P. and Glick, W. H. (eds), *Organizational Change and Redesign*. Oxford: Oxford University Press.

Cameron, K. S., Kim, M. U., and Whetten, D. A. (1987) 'Organizational Effects of Decline and Turbulence,' *Administrative Science Quarterly*, 32, pp. 222–40.

Cascio, W. F. (1993) 'Downsizing: What Do We Know? What Have We Learned?' *Academy of Management Executive*, 7(1), pp. 95–104.

Christakis, N. A. and Fowler, J. H. (2009) *Connected: The Surprising Power of Our Social Networks and How They Shape Our Lives*. Boston: Little, Brown & Company.

Collins, J. C. (2001) *Good to Great*. New York: HarperCollins.

Collins, J. C. and Porras, J. I. (1994) *Built to Last*. New York: HarperBusiness.

Cooperrider, D. L., Whitney, D. and Stavros, J. M. (2008) *Appreciative Inquiry Handbook: For Leaders of Change*. Brunswick, Ohio: Crown Custom Publishers.

Cordes, C. L. and Dougherty, T. W. (1993) 'A Review and an Integration of Research on Job Burnout,' *Academy of Management Review*, 18(4), pp. 621–56.

Cox, J. S. and Theoharis, A. G. (1988) *The Boss: J. Edgar Hoover and the Great American Inquisition*. Philadelphia: Temple University Press.

Crane, T. J. and Patrick, L. N. (2002) *The Heart of Coaching: Using Transformational Coaching to Create a High-Performance Coaching Culture*. San Diego: FTA Press.

Crits-Christoph, P. and Barber, J. P. (1991) *Handbook of Short-Term Dynamic Psychotherapy*. New York: Basic Books.

Csikszentmihalyi, M. (1990) *Flow: The Psychology of Optimal Experience*. New York: Harper and Row.

Custer, G. (1994) 'Downsizing's Fallout May Be Widespread,' *APA Monitor*, October, 49–50.

Czander, W. M. (1993) *The Psychodynamics of Work and Organizations*. New York: Guilford Press.

Davanloo, H. (1994) *Basic Principles and Techniques in Short-Term Dynamic Psychotherapy*. London: Jason Aronson.

Davanloo, H. (2000) *Intensive Short-Term Dynamic Psychotherapy*. New York: John Wiley & Sons, Inc.

DeBoard, R. (1978) *The Psychoanalysis of Organizations*. London: Routledge.

Denison, D. R. (1990) *Corporate Culture and Organizational Effectiveness*. New York: John Wiley & Sons, Inc.

Deutsch, H. (1938) 'Folie à Deux,' *Psychoanalytic Quarterly*, 7, pp. 307–318.

Dewhurst, K. and Todd, J. (1956) 'The Psychosis of Association, Folie à Deux,' *Journal of Nervous and Mental Diseases*, 123, p. 451.

Dietrich, D. R. and Shabad, P. (1993) *Problem of Loss and Mourning: Psychoanalytic Perspectives*. New York: International Universities Press.

Duffy, K. (1984) *Children of the Forest*. New York: Dodd, Mead.

Dunlap, A. and Andelman, B. (1997) *Mean Business*. New York: Fireside.

Emde, R. N. (1981) 'Changing Models of Infancy and the Nature of Early Development: Remodelling the Foundation,' *Journal of the American Psychoanalytical Association*, 29: 179–219.

Erikson, E. (1963) *Childhood and Society*, 2nd edn. New York: Norton.

Etchegoyen, R. H. (1991) *The Fundamentals of Psychoanalytic Technique*. London: Karnac Books.

Fairbairn, W. R. D. (1952) *An Object-Relations Theory of Personality*. New York: Basic Books.

Fenichel, O. (1945) *The Psychoanalytic Theory of Neurosis*. New York: W. W. Norton.

Festinger, L. (1954) 'A Theory of Social Comparison Processes,' *Human Relations*, 7, p. 117.

Flaherty, J. (2005) *Coaching: Evoking Excellence in Others*. Boston: Butterworth Heinemann.

Fliess, R. (1953) 'Countertransference and Counteridentification,' *Journal of the American Psychoanalytic Association*, 1, pp. 268–284.

Foulkes, S. H. (1975) *Group Analytic Psychotherapy: Methods and Principles*. London: Gordon & Breach.

Frankl, V. (1962) *Man's Search for Meaning: An Introduction to Logotherapy*. Boston: Beacon Press.

Frankl, V. E. (1967) *Psychotherapy and Existentialism: Selected Papers on Logotherapy*. New York: Washington Square Press.

Freedman, A. M., Kaplan, H. I., and Sadock, B. J. (1975) *Comprehensive Textbook of Psychiatry*, vols 1 and 2. Baltimore: Williams and Wilkins.

Freeman, S. J. and Cameron, K. S. (1993) 'Organizational Downsizing: A Convergence and Reorientation Framework,' *Organization Science* 4(1), pp. 10–28.

Freud, A. (1946) *The Ego and the Mechanisms of Defense*. Madison, CT: International Universities Press.

Freud, S. (1893–95) 'Katharina'. *Standard Edition of the Complete Psychological Works of Sigmund Freud*, vol. 2, pp. 125–34. London: Hogarth Press.

Freud, S. (1905) 'Fragment of an Analysis of a Case of Hysteria.' *The Standard Edition of the Complete Psychological Works of Sigmund Freud*, vol. 7. London: Hogarth Press and The Institute of Psychoanalysis.

Freud, S. (1921) 'Group Psychology and the Analysis of the Ego'. *The Standard Edition of the Complete Psychological Works of Sigmund Freud*, vol. 7. London: Hogarth Press and the Institute of Psychoanalysis.

Freud, S. (1933) 'New Introductory Lectures.' *The Standard Edition of the Complete Psychological Works of Sigmund Freud*, vol. 22. London: Hogarth Press and the Institute of Psychoanalysis.

Fries, M. E. and Woolf, P. J. (1953) 'Some hypotheses on the role of congenital activity types in personality development,' *Psychoanalytic Study of the Child*, 8, pp. 48–62.

Gabriel, Y. (1999) *Organizations in Depth*. London: Sage.

Gardner, H. (1999) *Intelligence Reframed*. New York: Basic Books.

Gibbon, A. and Hadekel, P. (1990) *Steinberg: The Break-up of a Family Empire*. Toronto: Macmillan.

Giridharadas, A. (2010) 'New leaders find strength in diversity,' *International Herald Tribune*, May 7.

Gladwell, M. (2009) *Outliers*. London: Penguin.

Goleman, D. (1995) *Emotional Intelligence*. London: Bloomsbury.

Goleman, D. (1998) *Working With Emotional Intelligence*. New York: Bantam Books.

Gralnick, A. (1942) 'Folie à deux—the psychosis of association: Review of 103 cases and entire English literature with case presentations.' Part 1, *The Psychiatric Quarterly*, 16, pp. 230–263.

Greenhalgh, L. and Jick, T. (1989) 'Survivor Sense Making and Reactions to Organizational Decline: Effects of Individual Differences,' *Management Communication Quarterly*, 2(3), pp. 305–28.

Greenhalgh L. and Rosenblatt, Z. (1984) 'Job Insecurity: Toward Conceptual Clarity.' *Academy of Management Review*, 9(3), pp. 438–48.

Greenleaf, R. K. and Spears, L. C. (1998) *Power of Servant Leadership*. San Francisco: Berrett-Koehler.

Greenson, R. R. (1967) *The Technique and Practice of Psychoanalysis*. New York: International Universities Press.

Groves, J. E. (1996) *Essential Papers on Short-Term Dynamic Therapy*. New York: New York University Press.

Guntrip, H. (1969) *Schizoid Phenomena, Object Relations, and the Self*. New York: International Universities Press.

Gustavson, J. P. (1986) *The Complex Secret of Brief Psychotherapy*. New York: Norton.

Hallet, J.-P. (1973) *Pygmy Kitabu*. New York: Random House.

Hamel, G. and Prahalad, C. K. (1989) 'Strategic Intent,' *Harvard Business Review*, May–June, pp. 63–76.

Handy, C. (1993) *Understanding Organizations*, 4th edn. New York: Oxford University Press.

Harrison, R. and Stokes, H. (1992) *Diagnosing Organizational Culture*. San Francisco: Pfeiffer.

Hartman, H. and Stengel, E. (1931) 'Studien zur psychologies des induzierten Irreseins,' *Jahrbuch für Psychiatrie und Neurolidie*, 48, p. 164.

Harwood, I. N. H. and Pines, M. (1998) *Self Experiences in Groups: Intersubjective and Self Psychological Pathways to Human Understanding*. London: Kingsley.

Heatherton, T. and Weinberger, J. L. (1994) *Can Personality Change?* Washington, DC: American Psychological Association.

Heimann, P. (1950) 'On Countertransference.' *International Journal of Psychoanalysis*, 31, pp. 81–84.

Henkoff, R. (1994) 'Cost Cutting: How to Do It Right,' *Fortune*, 121(8), pp. 40–49.

Hewlett, B. S. (1991) *Intimate Fathers: The Nature and Context of Aka Pygmy Paternal Infant Care*. Ann Arbor: University of Michigan Press.

Hochschild, A. R. and Machung, A. (2003) *Second Shift*. New York: Penguin.

Hogan, R. T., Johnson, J. A., and Briggs, R. (1997) *Handbook of Personality Psychology*. New York: Morgan Kaufman.

Horowitz, M. J., Marmar, C., Krupnick, J., Wilner, N., Kaltreider, N., and Wallerstein, R. (1984) *Personality Styles and Brief Psychotherapy*. New York: Basic Books.

Hudson, F. M. (1999) *The Handbook of Coaching: A Comprehensive Resource Guide for Managers, Executives, Consultants, and Human Resource Professionals*. San Francisco: Jossey-Bass.

Hunt, J. M. and Weintraub, J. R. (2002) *The Coaching Manager*. London: Sage Publications.

Jacobson, E. (1964) *The Self and the Object World*. New York: International Universities Press.

Jacobson, E. (1971) *Depression*. New York: International Universities Press.

Janis, I. L. (1958) *Psychological Stress*. New York: John Wiley & Sons, Inc.

Janis, I. L. (1972) *Victims of Groupthink*. Boston: Houghton-Mifflin.

Jaques, E. (1951) *The Changing Culture of a Factory*. London: Tavistock.

Jaques, E. (1970) *Work, Creativity, and Social Justice*. New York: International Universities Press.

Jaques, E. (1974) 'Social Systems as Defense Against Persecutory and Depressive Anxiety.' In Gibbard, G. S., Hartmann, J. J., and Mann, R. D. *Analysis of Groups*. San Francisco: Jossey-Bass.

Jaques, E. (1989) *Requisite Organization*. London: Gower Publishing.

Jung, C. G. (1920) *Psychological Types, or the Psychology of Individuation*. New York: Harcourt, Brace, Jovanovich.

Kaplan, H. I. and Sadock, B. J. (1993) *Comprehensive Group Psychotherapy*. Baltimore: Williams and Wilkins.

Keeley, M. (1980) 'Organizational analogy: a comparison of organismic and social contract models,' *Administrative Science Quarterly*, 25, pp. 337–62.

Kelman, H. (1961) 'Processes of opinion change,' *Public Opinion Quarterly*, 16, p. 230.

Kernberg, O. (1975) *Borderline Conditions and Pathological Narcissism*. New York: Aronson.

Kernberg, O. (1980) *Internal World and External Reality*. New York: Aronson.

Kets de Vries, M.F.R. (1978) '*Folie à deux*: Acting out your superior's fantasies', *Human Relations*, 31(10), pp. 905–24.

Kets de Vries, M. F. R. (1979) 'Managers can Drive their Subordinates Mad,' *Harvard Business Review*, July–August, pp. 125–34.

Kets de Vries, M. F. R. (1980) *Organizational Paradoxes: Clinical Approaches to Management*. London: Routledge.

Kets de Vries, M. F. R. (1984) *The Irrational Executive: Psychoanalytic Explorations in Management*. New York: International Universities Press.

Kets de Vries, M. F. R. (1991) *Organizations on the Couch*. San Francisco: Jossey-Bass.

Kets de Vries, M. F. R. (1993) 'Doing a Maxwell: Or Why Not to Identify with the Aggressor,' *European Management Journal*, 11(2), pp. 169–74.

Kets de Vries, M. F. R. (1994) 'The Leadership Mystique,' *Academy of Management Executive*, 8(3), pp. 73–92.

Kets de Vries, M. F. R. (2000a) 'The Clinical Paradigm: Manfred Kets de Vries' Reflections on Organizational Theory: Interview by Erik van de Loo,' *Academy of Management Executive* 18(1), pp. 2–21.

Kets de Vries, M. F. R. (2000b) *Struggling with the Demon: Essays in Individual and Organizational Irrationality*. Madison, Connecticut: Psychosocial Press.

Kets de Vries, M. F. R. (2001) *The Leadership Mystique*. London: Financial Times/ Prentice Hall.

Kets de Vries, M. F. R. (2002) 'Can CEOs change? Yes, but only if they want to.' *INSEAD Working Papers Series*, Fontainebleau, France.

Kets de Vries, M. F. R. (2002) *The Happiness Equation*. London: Random House.

Kets de Vries, M. F. R. (2003) 'Lessons on Leadership by Terror: Finding Shaka Zulu in the Attic.' *INSEAD Working Paper Series*, Fontainebleau, France.

Kets de Vries, M. F. R. (2004) *The Global Executive Leadership Inventory: Facilitator's Guide*. San Francisco: Pfeiffer.

Kets de Vries, M. F. R. (2005a) 'Leadership Group Coaching in Action: The Zen of Creating High Performance Teams,' *Academy of Management Executive*, 19(1), pp. 61–76.

Kets de Vries, M. F. R. (2005b) *The Personality Audit: Facilitator's Guide*. Fontainebleau: INSEAD.

Kets de Vries, M. F. R. (2005c) *The Personality Audit: Participant's Guide*. Fontainebleau: INSEAD.

Kets de Vries, M. F. R. (2006a) *The Leader on the Couch*, Chichester: John Wiley & Sons Ltd.

Kets de Vries, M. F. R. (2006b) 'The Eight Roles Executives Play,' *Organizational Dynamics*, 36(1), pp. 28–44.

Kets de Vries, M. F. R. (2006c) *Leadership Archetype Questionnaire Facilitator's Guide.* Fontainebleau: INSEAD.

Kets de Vries, M. F. R. (2006d) *Leadership Archetype Questionnaire Participant's Guide.* Fontainebleau: INSEAD.

Kets de Vries, M. F. R. (2009a) *Sex, Money, Happiness and Death: The Quest for Authenticity.* Houndsmills: Palgrave/MacMillan.

Kets de Vries, M. F. R. (2009b) *Reflections on Leadership and Character.* Chichester: John Wiley & Sons Ltd.

Kets de Vries, M. F. R. (2009c) *Reflections on Leadership and Career Development.* Chichester: Wiley.

Kets de Vries, M. F. R. (2010a) *Organizational Culture Audit: Facilitator's Guide.* Fontainebleau: INSEAD.

Kets de Vries, M. F. R. (2010b) *Organizational Culture Audit: Participant's Guide.* Fontainebleau: INSEAD.

Kets de Vries, M. F. R. (2010c) *Internal Theatre Inventory Facilitator's Guide.* Fontainebleau: INSEAD.

Kets de Vries, M.F.R., and Balazs, K. (1997) 'The Downside of Downsizing,' *Human Relations*, 50(1), 11–50.

Kets de Vries, M. F. R. and Balazs, K. (1998) 'Beyond the quick fix: The psychodynamics of organisational transformation and change,' *European Management Journal*, 16(8), pp. 611–22.

Kets de Vries, M. F. R. and Balazs, K. (1999a) 'Creating the "Authentizotic" Organization: Corporate Transformation and its Vicissitudes—A Rejoinder,' *Administration Society*, 31(2), pp. 275–94.

Kets de Vries, M. F. R., Balazs, K. (1999b) 'Transforming the Mind-set of the Organization: A Clinical Perspective,' *Administration & Society*, 30(6), 640–75..

Kets de Vries, M. F. R. and Carlock, R.with Florent-Treacy, E. (2007a) *Family Business on the Couch: A Psychological Perspective, Chichester:*, John Wiley & Sons Ltd.

Kets de Vries, M. F. R. and Florent, E. (1999) *The New Global Leaders, Percy Barnevik, Richard Branson, and David Simon and the Making of the International Corporation.* San Francisco: Jossey-Bass.

Kets de Vries, M. F. R., Florent-Treacy, E. and Korotov, K. (eds) (2007) *Coach and Couch: The Psychology of Making Better Leaders*, Houndsmills: Palgrave/Macmillan.

Kets de Vries, M. F. R., Guillen, L., Korotov, K. and Florent-Treacy, E. (eds) (2010) *The Coaching Kaleidoscope: Insights from the Inside*, Houndsmills: Palgrave/Macmillan.

Kets de Vries, M. F. R. and Korotov, K. (2007) 'Creating Transformational Executive Education Programs,' *Academy of Management Learning and Education*, 6(3), pp. 375–87.

Kets de Vries, M. F. R. and Miller, D. (1984a) *The Neurotic Organization: Diagnosing and Changing Counterproductive Styles of Management.* San Francisco: Jossey-Bass.

Kets de Vries, M. F. R. and Miller, D. (1984b) 'Neurotic style and organizational pathology', *Strategic Management Journal* 5, pp. 35–55.

Kets de Vries, M. F. R. and Miller, D. (1984c) 'Unstable at the top,' *Psychology Today,* October 1984.

Kets de Vries, M. F. R. and Miller, D. (1986) 'Personality, culture and organization,' *Academy of Management Review* II(2), pp. 266–79.

Kets de Vries, M. F. R. and Miller, D. (1987) 'Interpreting Organizational Texts,' *Journal of Management Studies,* 24(3), pp. 233–347.

Kets de Vries, M. F. R. and Miller, D. (1988) *Unstable at the Top.* New York: New American Library.

Kets de Vries, M. F. R., Vrignaud, P. and Florent-Treacy, E. (2004) 'The Global Leadership Life Inventory: Development and Psychometric Properties of a 360-Degree Feedback Instrument,' *Journal of Management Studies,* 15(3), pp. 475–92.

Kets de Vries, M. F. R., Vrignaud, P., Engellau, E., and Florent-Treacy, E. (2006) 'The Development of the Personality Audit: A Psychodynamic Multiple Feedback Assessment Instrument,' *International Journal of Human Resource Management,* 17(5), pp. 898–917.

Kilberg, R. R. (2000) *Executive Coaching.* Washington, DC: American Psychological Association.

Klein, M. (1948) *Contributions to Psychoanalysis 1921–45.* London: Hogarth Press.

Kohut, H. (1971) *The Analysis of the Self.* New York: International Universities Press.

Kohut, H. (1977) *The Restoration of the Self.* New York: International Universities Press.

Kohut, H. and Wolf, E. S. (1978) 'The Disorders of the Self and their Treatment: an Outline,' *International Journal of Psychoanalysis,* 59, pp. 413–26.

Kotter, J. P. and Heskett, J. L. (1992) *Corporate Culture and Performance.* New York: The Free Press.

Kouzes, J. M. and Posner, B. Z. (1995) *The Leadership Challenge.* San Francisco: Jossey-Bass.

Lacey, R. (1986) *Ford: The Men and the Machine.* New York: Little, Brown.

Lalli, F. (1992) 'Learn from My Mistakes,' *Money,* February, p. 5.

Lang, H. B. (1936) 'Simultaneous psychoses occurring in business partners,' *The Psychiatric Quarterly,* 10, p. 611.

LaPlanche, J. P. and Pontalis, J. B. (1973) *The Language of Psychoanalysis.* London: Hogarth Press.

Lasswell, H. (1960) *Psychopathology and Politics.* New York: Viking Press.

Leana, C. and Feldman, D. (1988) 'Individual, Responses to Job Loss: Perceptions, Reactions, and Coping Behaviors,' *Journal of Management* 14(3), pp. 375–90.

Leana, C. and Feldman, D. C. (1990) 'Individual Responses to Job Loss: Empirical Findings from Two Field Studies,' *Human Relations*, 43(11), pp. 1155–81.

LeDoux, J. (1998) *The Emotional Brain*. London: Weidenfeld & Nicolson.

Lefcourt, H. M. (1976) *Locus of Control*. New York: John Wiley & Sons, Inc.

Levering, R. and Moskowitz, M. (1998) 'The 100 Best Companies to Work for in America,' *Fortune*, January 12, pp. 26–35.

Levinson, H. (1962) *Men, Management, and Mental Health*. Cambridge, MA: Harvard University Press.

Levinson, H. (1972) *Organizational Diagnosis*. Cambridge: Harvard University Press.

Levinson, H. (1978) 'The Abrasive Personality,' *Harvard Business Review*, May–June, pp. 86–94.

Levinson, H. (2002) *Organizational Assessment*. Washington, DC: American Psychological Association.

Lewin, K. (1947) 'Frontiers in group dynamics: Concept, method, and reality in social science,' *Human Relations*, 1, p. 5.

Lichtenberg, J. D., Lackmann, F. M., and Forshage, J. L. (1992) *Self and Motivational Systems: Toward a Theory of Psychoanalytic Technique*. New York: Analytic Press.

Lindner, R. (1956) *The Fifty-Minute Hour*. New York: Bantam Books.

Luborsky, L. and Crits-Christoph, P. (1998) *Understanding Transference: The Core Conflictual Relationship Theme Method*. Washington DC: American Psychological Organization.

Luborsky, L., Crits-Christoph, P., Mintz, J., and Auerbach, A. (1988) *Who Will Benefit from Psychotherapy?* New York: Basic Books.

Maccoby, M. (1976) *The Gamesman*. New York: Simon and Schuster.

Malan, D. and Osimo, F. (1992) *Psychodynamics, Training, and Outcome in Brief Psychotherapy*. Oxford: Butterworth Heinemann.

Malan, D. H. (1963) *A Study of Brief Psychotherapy*. New York: Plenum.

Malan, D. H. (1976) *The Frontier of Brief Psychotherapy*. New York: Plenum.

Mann, J. (1973) *Time-Limited Psychotherapy*. Cambridge: Harvard University Press.

Mann, J. and Goldman, R. (1982) *A Casebook in Time-Limited Psychotherapy*. New York: McGraw-Hill.

Mann, T. (1936) 'The Blood of the Walsungs.' In *Stories of Three Decades*. New York: Knopf.

Marris, P. (1974) *Loss and Change*. London: Routledge & Kegan Paul.

Matthews, G., Zeidner, M., and Roberts, R. D. (2002) *Emotional Intelligence: Science and Myth*. Boston: MIT Press.

McCall, M. W. J. and Lombardo, M. M. (1978) *Leadership: Where Else Can We Go?* Durham, NC: Duke University Press.

McClelland, D. (1961) *The Achieving Society*. New York: Irvington.

McClelland, D. (1975) *Power: The Inner Experience*. New York: Halstead.

McCrae, R. R. and Costa, P. T. (1990) *Personality in Adulthood*. New York: Guilford Press.

McCullough Vaillant, L. (1997) *Changing Character*. New York: Basic Books.

McNeil, J. N., Verwoerdt, A., and Peak, D. (1972) 'Folie à deux in the aged: Review and case report of role reversal,' *Journal of the American Geriatrics Society*, 20(7), pp.316–23.

Menninger, C. (1958) *Theory of Psychoanalytic Technique*. New York: Harper.

Menzies, I. E. (1960) 'A Case Study of the Functioning of Social Systems as a Defense against Anxiety: A Report on a Study of the Nursing System in a General Hospital,' *Human Relations*, 13, pp. 95–121.

Merton, R. K. (1968) 'Bureaucratic structure and personality,' in Merton, R. K. (ed.) *Social Theory and Social Structure*. New York: Free Press, pp. 249–59.

Michaels, E., Handfield-Jones, H., and Axelrod, B. (2001) *The War for Talent*. Boston: McKinsey & Co.

Milgram, S. (1963) 'Behavioral study of obedience,' *Journal of Abnormal and Social Psychology*, 67, pp. 371–78.

Milgram, S. (1965) 'Some conditions of obedience and disobedience to authority,' *Human Relations*, 18, pp. 57–76.

Miller, D. (1976) 'Strategy Making in Context: Ten Empirical Archetypes.' Doctoral dissertation, McGill University, Montreal.

Miller, D. and Friesen, P. H. (1978) 'Archetypes of strategy formulation.' *Management Science*, 24, pp. 921–33.

Miller, D. and Friesen, P. H. (1984) *Organizations: A Quantum View*. Englewood Cliffs, NJ: Prentice-Hall.

Miller, W. R. and Rollnick, S. (2002) *Motivational Interviewing*. New York: Guilford Press.

Millon, T. (1981) *Disorders of Personality: DSM III, Axis II*. New York: John Wiley & Sons, Inc.

Molnos, A. (1995) *A Question of Time: Essentials of Brief Psychotherapy*. London: Karnac Books.

Mone, M. (1994) 'Relationships Between Self-Concepts, Aspirations, Emotional Responses, and Intent to Leave a Downsizing Organization,' *Human Resource Management*, 33(2), pp. 281–8.

Morgan, G. (1986) *Images of Organization*. London: Sage.

Murray, H. A. (1938) *Explorations in Personality*. New York: Oxford University Press.

Murthy, N. (2009a). *A Better India, A Better World*. New Delhi: Penguin Books.

Murthy, N. (2009b) Mail sent by Narayan Murthy to all Infosys staff, www.maharashtraspider.com/businessresources/2321, November 22.

Navran, F. (1994) 'Surviving a Downsizing,' *Executive Excellence* 11(7), pp. 12–13.

Nicholi, A. M. (1978) *The Harvard Guide to Modern Psychiatry*. Cambridge: Belknap.

Nietzsche, F. (1989) *Beyond Good and Evil*. New York: Knopf.

Noer, D. M. (1993) *Healing the Wounds: Overcoming the Trauma of Layoffs and Revitalizing Downsized Organizations*. San Francisco: Jossey-Bass.

O'Neill, E. (1972) 'Where the Cross is Made,' in *Seven Plays of the Sea*. New York: Vintage Books.

Ogden, T. H. (1982) *Projective Identification and Psychotherapeutic Technique*. New York: Aronson.

Orem, S., Binkert, J., and Clancy, A. L. (2007) *Appreciative Coaching: A Positive Process for Change*. San Francisco: Jossey-Bass.

Palmer, S. and Whybrow, A. (2007) *Handbook of Coaching Psychology, A Guide for Practitioners*. London: Routledge.

Parkes, C. M. (1972) *Bereavement: Studies of Grief in Adult Life*. New York: International Universities Press.

Pascale, R. T. and Athos, A. G. (1981) *The Art of Japanese Management: Applications for American Executives*. New York: Simon & Schuster.

Payne, R. and Pugh, D. S. (1976) 'Organization Structure and Climate,' in Dunnette, M. D. (ed.) *Handbook of Industrial and Organizational Psychology*. Chicago: Rand McNally.

Pearlstein, S. (1994) 'Corporate Cutbacks Yet to Pay Off,' *Washington Post*, January 4, p. B-6.

Pfeffer, J. (1995) 'Producing Sustainable Competitive Advantage Through the Effective Management of People,' *Academy of Management Executive*, 9(1): 55–72.

Pfeffer, J. (1998) *The Human Equation: Building Profits by Putting People First*. Boston: Harvard Business School Press.

Phares, J. E. (1976) *Locus of Control in Personality*. Morristown: General Learning Press.

Pine, E. (1985) *Developmental Theory and Clinical Process*. New Haven, Connecticut: Yale University Press.

Polatin, P. (1975) 'Psychotic disorders: Paranoid states,' in Freedman, A. M., Kaplan, H. I., and B. J. Sadock (eds), *Comprehensive Textbook of Psychiatry*, vol. 1, 2nd edn. Baltimore: Williams and Wilkins.

Popper, K. (2002) *The Logic of Scientific Discovery*. London: Routledge Classics.

Press, H. B. S. (2005) *Managing Change to Reduce Resistance*. Boston: Harvard Business School Press.

Pulver, S. E. and Brunt, M. Y. (1961) 'Deflection of hostility in folie à deux,' *Archives of General Psychiatry*, 5(3), pp 257–65.

Racker, H. (1968) *Transference and Countertransference*. New York: International Universities Press.

Rawson, P. (2002) *Short-Term Psychodynamic Psychotherapy: An Analysis of the Key Principles*. London: Karnac.

Rioux, B. (1963) 'A review of folie à deux, the psychosis of association,' *The Psychiatric Quarterly*, 37, pp. 405–428.

Rodgers, W. (1969) *Think: A Biography of the Watsons and IBM*. New York: Stein and Day.

Rogers, C. R. (1951) *Client-centered Therapy*. Boston: Houghton-Mifflin.

Rogers, C. R. (1961) *On Becoming a Person*. Boston: Houghton-Mifflin.

Rokeach, M. (1960) *The Open and Closed Mind*. New York: Basic Books.

Rosenbaum, M. (1983) *Handbook of Short-Term Therapy Groups*. New York: McGraw-Hill.

Salovey, P. and Mayer, J. (1990) 'Emotional Intelligence,' *Imagination, Cognition, and Personality*, 9, pp. 185–211.

Scheidlinger, S. (1982) *Focus on Group Psychotherapy: Clinical Essays*. New York: International Universities Press.

Schein, E. H. (1961) *Coercive Persuasion*. New York: Norton.

Schein, E. (1985) *Organizational Culture and Leadership*. San Francisco: Jossey-Bass.

Schon, D. A. (1983) *The Reflective Practitioner: How Professionals Think in Action*. New York: Basic Books.

Schott, J.L. (1975) *No Left Turns: The FBI in Peace and War*. New York: Praeger.

Scott Rutan, J. and Stone, W. N. (2001) *Psychodynamic Group Psychotherapy*. New York: The Guilford Press.

Seltzery, L. F. (1986) *Paradoxical Strategies in Psychotherapy: A Comprehensive Overview and Guidebook*. New York: John Wiley & Sons, Inc.

Shapiro, D. (1965) *Neurotic Styles*. New York: Basic Books.

Sheehy, G. (1995) *New Passages*. New York: Ballantine Books.

Sheehy, G. (1998) *Understanding Men's Passages: Discovering the New Map of Men's Lives*. New York: Random House.

Sifneos, P. E. (1979) *Short-Term Dynamic Psychotherapy*. Cambridge: Harvard University Press.

Siy, A. (1993) *The Efe: People of the Rain Forest*. New York: Dillon Press, p. 16.

Smith, K. (2003) 'Video Lecture, Stanford University,' *Video Lectures*. November 19.

Smith, L. (1994) 'Burned-Out Bosses,' *Fortune*, 130(2), pp. 100–105.

Solomon, A. (2001) *The Noonday Demon: An Atlas of Depression*. New York: Simon & Schuster.

Speer, A. (1971) *Inside the Third Reich*. New York: Avon Books.

Stassen Berger, K. (1998) *The Developing Person through the Life Span*. New York: Worth Publishers.

Strupp, H. H. and Binder, J. L. (1984) *Psychotherapy in a New Key: A Guide to Time-Limited Dynamic Psychotherapy*. New York: Basic Books.

Sullivan, H. S. (1953) *The Interpersonal Theory of Psychiatry*. New York: Norton.

Thornburg, L. (1992) 'Practical Ways to Cope with Suicide,' *HR Magazine*, 37(5), pp. 62–6.

Tosi, H. (1970) 'A Reexamination of Personality as a Determinant of the Effects of Participation,' *Personnel Psychology*, 23, pp. 111–37.

Turnbull, C. M. (1961) *The Forest People: A Study of the Pygmies of the Congo*. New York: Simon & Schuster.

Turnbull, C. M. (1965) *Wayward Servants: The Two Worlds of the African Pygmies*. London: Eyre & Spottiswoode.

Vaillant, G. E. (1977) *Adaptation to Life*. Boston: Little Brown.

Volcan, V. (1988) *The Need to have Enemies and Allies*. New York: Aronson.

Vroom, V. H. (1960) *Some Personality Determinants of the Effects of Participation*. Englewood Cliffs: Prentice-Hall.

Wachtel, P. (1982) *Resistance: Psychodynamic and Behavioral Approaches*. New York: Plenum Press.

Watson, T. J. (1990) *Father, Son & Co: My Life at IBM and Beyond*. New York: Bantam Books.

Watzlawick, P., Weakland, J. and Fisch, R. (1974) *Change: Principles of Problem Formation and Problem Resolution*. New York: Norton.

Weeks, G. R. and L'Abate, L. (1982) *Paradoxical Psychotherapy: Theory and Practice with Individuals, Couples, and Families*. New York: Brunner/Mazel.

Westen, D. (1998) 'The Scientific Legacy of Sigmund Freud: Toward a Psychodynamically Informed Psychological Science,' *Psychological Bulletin*, 124(3), pp. 333–71.

White, R. W. (1972) *The Enterprise of Living*. New York: Holt, Rinehart, and Winston.

Winnicott, D. W. (1951) 'Transitional Objects and Transitional Phenomena,' in *Collected Papers: Through Pediatrics to Psycho-analysis*. London: Tavistock.

Winnicott, D. W. (1971) *Playing and Reality*. New York: Basic Books.

Winnicott, D. W. (1972) 'Basis for Self in Body,' *International Journal of Child Psychotherapy*, 1, pp. 7–16.

Winnicott, D. W. (1975) *Through Pediatrics to Psycho-Analysis*. New York: Basic Books.

Yalom, I. D. (1985) *The Theory and Practice of Group Psychotherapy*. New York: Basic Books.

Zaleznik, A. (1966) *Human Dilemmas of Leadership*. New York: HarperCollins.

INDEX